Realtime, Conflict-Free
Machine Shorthand for Expanding Careers

StenEd ®

10 STEPS TO REALTIME WRITING

Based on the Realtime, Conflict-Free StenEd Theory

Beverly Loeblein Ritter

Stenotype Educational Products, Inc.
P.O. Box 959, Melrose, Florida 32666
Phone: 352/475-3332 • Fax: 352/475-2152

ISBN 0-938643-34-7
StenEd #151

CONTENTS

CONTENTS

INTRODUCTION

It's fast becoming a realtime world. Realtime writing is becoming the norm, rather than the exception, for all stenotype careers—stenocaptioning, reporting, stenoscription. The realtime writer not only puts our profession at the forefront of the Information/Communication Age, but gives the individual realtime writer enormous advantages.

Most reporters—experienced and novice—realize that the future of reporting is realtime and are anxious to update their writing to be an important part of this future.

WHAT IS REALTIME?

Realtime Translation means that, as you write, your outlines are immediately translated by the computer and, generally, displayed on a computer screen. (There may be a slight delay of a second or so, but it's still considered realtime.) Often the translation can be displayed on multiple screens.

In a trial situation, this means that the judge, attorneys, and witness(es) can see an immediate translation of the proceeding. In a school or seminar-type situation, the translation can appear on a large screen for many to see. In some instances, an instantaneous printout is also made.

Current technology allows this instantaneous translation to occur, and, of course, some software programs are more sophisticated than others. However, it is up to you, the writer, to update your writing style so that words translate correctly. If you have conflicts in your writing style, you are going to have conflicts in your translation. If you have lots of shadows or omissions in your writing, the computer will not recognize the correct word to be translated. The translation will occur in a realtime fashion, but the translation will not be correct.

Realtime technology is meaningless without realtime writers.

WHY REALTIME?

Becoming a realtime writer will benefit you and your profession by:

- Creating job security for yourself and the profession;
- Exposing the technology of court reporting and related skills to as many people as possible;
- Providing your clients with an immediate data base;
- Assisting the hearing impaired; and
- Becoming a better, more confident reporter. (Watching the translation scroll by on the screen makes you more aware of what you are stroking. This instant feedback will make you a better, cleaner writer.)

Reporters who utilize realtime, conflict-free writing skills and technology to produce faster, more accurate transcripts, coupled with the resultant computer data base, are fast becoming the leaders—some would even say the saviors—of our profession. Realtime stenocaptioners are becoming more numerous and more sought after for the hearing-impaired community and beyond. Text entry fields, such as medical transcription, are opening up for realtime stenotranscriptionists because of the speed advantage and, even more important, the accuracy and efficiency of computer translation.

WHAT ARE THE USES OF REALTIME?

- Computer Integrated Courtrooms (CIC);
- TV captioning;
- Assisting the hearing impaired (in court, deposition, and classroom situations);
- Text entry (medical and other transcription services);
- Interpreters; and
- General education settings. (The added dimension of seeing, as well as hearing, the words of lectures and of educational TV is gaining new interest.)

As the technology and the sophistication of stenotypists mature, new uses are sure to be introduced.

HOW DO YOU WRITE FOR REALTIME?

The important elements for realtime writing can be summarized as following the three C's.

1. **Clean**
2. **Consistent**
3. **Conflict Free**

Clean: Clean writing is the production of notes in which words are clearly defined and in which shadowing and omitting letters are eliminated to the greatest degree possible. Such clarity calls for well-defined (not necessarily long) outlines for words. The reduction of shadows and other keying errors is important because the computer is not nearly as able as a human to "read through" keying errors.

Consistent: Consistency is an important element in realtime writing. Consistency also makes the writing of new words easier in that old principles can usually be applied to other words fitting the pattern. This makes it easier to alleviate those moments of indecision and "How do I write that?" thoughts.

Conflict Free: The writer should learn to write in such a way that conflicts never arise. Keeping conflicting outlines out of one's writing is particularly important when one of the words or phrases represented by an outline is a commonly occurring one. **Writers should never use the same outline for more than one English word or phrase.**

HOW DO I START?

One of the hardest things about becoming a realtime writer is knowing where to begin. This text has divided realtime writing skills into ten steps. The ten steps have been prioritized so that you work first on those areas which will result in the greatest improvement in your translation. Once you have mastered one technique/conflict, you move to the next.

All major conflict areas are covered in this text. Hints are also given to make your writing cleaner and more consistent. You are not expected to change your entire way of writing. It is recommended that you read through the entire text, starting with the Overview on page 1. Later principles build on material already covered, so beginning at the beginning is the most efficient way to proceed. There will be those of you, however, who will just want to refer to certain portions of the text. If you feel you are already quite knowledgable about realtime writing and don't need the structured approach, that's fine. StenEd principles and outlines are referenced throughout. They are highly recommended for the most efficient use of this text, but they are not mandatory.

 Introduction

OVERVIEW

10 STEPS TO REALTIME WRITING

This text is designed for both

- **Reporters and advanced students who did not learn StenEd theory *and***
- **Advanced StenEd students who did.**

NON-StenEd WRITERS

Those of you who did not learn the realtime, conflict-free StenEd theory will find a wealth of writing hints and principles that will ease your transition to realtime writing.

<u>**One of the hardest things about becoming a realtime writer is knowing where to begin.**</u> This text has divided realtime writing skills into ten steps. These ten steps have been prioritized so that you work first on those areas which will result in the greatest reduction of conflicts and, consequently, the greatest improvement in your translations. Once you have mastered one technique/conflict, move to the next.

Many principles are interrelated. These steps have been ordered so that later principles build on material covered earlier.

Obviously, every reporter does not have every conflict. Certain steps will be of more interest and importance to you than others. It would be helpful to read through each step, however, to get a better understanding of the total structure of the StenEd theory. You're sure to pick up some useful hints along the way. This text is fully indexed for easy location of a particular conflict or family of words.

StenEd WRITERS

Those of you who did learn StenEd should already be realtime writers. However, this text will serve as a excellent review of your conflict-free theory principles–a finishing course before graduation, so to speak. And, if any of you have adopted non-StenEd outlines and principles that have inadvertently introduced some conflicts into your writing, this text can help you return to writing a purer form of StenEd.

It is recommended that StenEd writers pace through this text step by step, reviewing the instructional material and writing the dictation exercises. As you do so, you will be reviewing the principles and techniques you learned as a beginning theory student that have made StenEd such an effective realtime theory.

The writing exercises, of course, are much more difficult than they were when you were a beginning student, thus they are excellent practice for the real world. It is suggested that you take these exercises using a realtime translation system, if possible, so you can benefit from the immediate feedback that realtime offers.

GENERAL WRITING PRINCIPLES

Before we begin, a few general writing principles are appropriate.

1. Definitively outline the sounds in the words. Unaccented syllables can often be omitted. Do not omit accented syllables.

2. When the sound is the same but the spelling is different in a conflict set, take advantage of the spelling to show what the word is.

3. Do not use the same outline for more than one word or phrase regardless of how frequent or infrequent a particular word may be.

4. Use only briefs and phrases that do not conflict with another word or phrase.

5. Use only briefs and phrases that you can easily remember.

6. Avoid word boundary problems by distinguishing between words and high frequency word parts. For example, differentiate between the word "a" and the prefix "a-," between the word "miss" and the prefix "mis-," between the word "less" and the suffix "-less," etc. This is essential for accurate realtime writing.

All of these principles will be reinforced as you go through the *10 Steps to Realtime Writing*.

DIFFERENT STROKES FOR DIFFERENT FOLKS

It is extremely difficult to present consistent conflict solutions to experienced reporters who have varying non-StenEd writing styles. What solves a conflict for one writer may cause a conflict for someone else.

Traditionally, in many non-StenEd schools, even students who learn the same theory often write quite differently. There are three main reasons for this: 1) students are allowed to create their own outlines and/or briefs without being overly concerned with conflicts; 2) students do not have realtime CAT practice, while in school, using a comprehensive, conflict-free CAT dictionary; and 3) individuals create their own dictionaries from scratch, with little or no guidance on how to avoid entering conflicting entries.

StenEd reporters, too, have some variations in their writing; that is, all StenEd writers do not necessarily write every word exactly the same way. (There are many conflict-free optional outlines allowed in StenEd.) However, because StenEd writers are not taught conflicting outlines and because most have practice using CAT with the comprehensive, conflict-free StenEd CAT translation dictionary early in their training, they learn the importance of never introducing a conflict into their writing. (Of course StenEd graduates can personalize their copy of the StenEd CAT dictionary as much as desired, but since they have been schooled in a conflict-free atmosphere, it is less likely that they will add conflicting entries to their dictionary.)

The techniques and outlines contained in this text are based on the StenEd theory. Because StenEd is conflict-free based on the "entire" StenEd theory, some outlines presented may conflict with your current writing if you were not taught StenEd as a student. Some of you will want to make major changes in your writing, incorporating most or all of the StenEd theory. Others may want to pick and choose, getting ideas from this text while retaining much of your original theory.

Thus, if the StenEd solution conflicts with something else you write, you can either decide to use the StenEd outline for all words/phrases involved or you may make up your own solution. As a minimum, this text will identify the problem areas for you.

Please don't try to change everything at once. That would be unnecessary and confusing. The best way to become a realtime writer while still maintaining your reporting schedule is to work on one type of conflict at a time. This might sound like it would take forever, but if you work on the conflicts with the highest frequency first, you will achieve the most results with the least changes.

Some of you will be tempted to skip around to different sections of this text. However, the most efficient way to become a realtime writer based on StenEd principles is to start with Step 1 and proceed step by step. Many of the principles are interrelated and later steps build on material covered in previous steps.

The suggested approach for using *"10 Steps to Realtime Writing"* is to first read through the instructional material included with each step to understand the total concept. Following the instructional material, action steps and recommendations for dictionary maintenance are given. Once you have determined your "action," you will probably want to reread appropriate sections of the instructional material.

Practice exercises are given for each step. Of course you will also be practicing your changes "on the job." But many of you have requested practice material that specifically deals with a particular conflict. You may choose to take only the practice material related to any changes you are making, or you may decide to take them all "just for fun."

Most practice exercises are also available on professionally recorded audio tapes. The Exercise ID, Tape Number and Side, and Words Recorded Per Minute are given at the beginning of each exercise. This material has not been counted. The intent of these tapes is to give "audio" practice to help resolve your conflicts, not practice for the merit test. Speed is important, of course, but we're concerned with accuracy at this point.

If you are not sure whether you have any conflicts or mistranslations for a certain category, take the practice exercise using CAT (realtime, if possible). Your translation should tell you what areas you should work on.

SOME HOUSEKEEPING MATTERS

THOSE WIDE KEYS

A special note about the stenotype machine itself is appropriate here. Most of you will find that a wide asterisk key (and possibly the wide -DZ key) will help you in your quest to eliminate your conflicts. There will be some of you who have never used the asterisk key as part of an outline. (You've only used it, by itself, for error correction.) Don't be afraid of it. Decide now that the asterisk is "just another key" on the stenotype keyboard. You will need it to be a realtime writer.

CONVENTIONS USED IN GIVING OUTLINES

<u>Hyphens</u> have been used in outlines to show the location of the consonants.

W-	with	(initial consonant)
WAEBG/-PB	weaken	(final consonant)
T-PL	testimony	(initial & final consonant)

<u>Hyphens</u> have been used to denote prefixes and suffixes.

in-	indifferent	(prefix)
-less	careless	(suffix)

<u>Slashes</u> have been used to denote stroke separation.

WAOEBG/TKAEU	weekday	(sample two-stroke word)
/-D	-ed	(the inflected ending)

The <u>grammatical class</u> has been given in those cases where the pronunciation of a word depends on how the word is used grammatically.

n	noun	au	auxiliary	j	adjective
v	verb			a	adverb

Occasionally <u>other</u> abbreviations are given to identify the type of word/outline/stroke being covered.

(c)	any consonant	(v)	any vowel

<u>Optional outlines</u> are enclosed in brackets [ ] after the original outline. (For additional StenEd outlines, refer to StenEd's *Realtime Professional Dictionary.*

and	APBD [SKP-]
it's	EUT/AOES [T*S]

All words have been given in <u>raw steno</u>. This is so there is no confusion as to what letters should be stroked. For example, to a StenEd-trained writer, -V automatically means to hit *F. To writers who don't distinguish between final -F and final -V, it could mean to hit -F without the asterisk.

save	SA*EUF	safe	SAEUF

Good luck! Tackle your conflicts one at a time. By following the guidelines in this text, you will begin to have better translations almost immediately. And remember that trying to change too much too fast will be counterproductive. It took years to establish your current writing style. You can't change it overnight. So, don't rush, take it a step (or partial step) at a time, and you will succeed.

We applaud you for "daring to change." You will be helping yourself and your profession continue to be an indispensable and valued leader of the information/communications age.

If you want additional information on the realtime, conflict-free StenEd theory, we recommend the following StenEd texts:

- *Volume I: Realtime Theory*   (the text used in schools to teach beginning students the realtime, conflict-free StenEd theory)
- *Professional Dictionary*   (an alphabetized listing of English and realtime StenEd outline[s] for over 30,000 words)
- *Legal Dictionary*   (an alphabetized listing of English and realtime StenEd outline[s] for over 18,000 legal words and phrases)
- *Medical Dictionary*   (realtime StenEd outlines for all medical terms in *Dorland's, Stedman's, Taber's,* and the *PDR*)
- *Medical Terminology*   (an academic text covering medical terminology and anatomy & physiology; includes realtime StenEd outlines for medical terms covered)
- *Advanced Literary Dictation*   (reviews conflict resolution while giving "difficult" literary practice)

STEP 1

THE ALPHABET

Most stenotype theories use the same alphabet; that is, TK- = d-, so the word "dog" would be written TKOG regardless of what theory you write. However, some precomputer theories do not distinguish between words with initial s- and initial z- or between words with final -f and final -v.

CONSONANTS & SHORT VOWELS

The StenEd representations for the consonants and short vowels used when writing words follow.

<table>
<tr><td colspan="3">Initial Side</td><td colspan="3">Final Side</td></tr>
<tr><td>a</td><td>=</td><td>A</td><td></td><td></td><td></td></tr>
<tr><td>b-</td><td>=</td><td>PW-</td><td>-b</td><td>=</td><td>-B</td></tr>
<tr><td>c-</td><td>=</td><td>K- (for k sound)</td><td></td><td></td><td></td></tr>
<tr><td></td><td>=</td><td>S- (for s sound)</td><td></td><td></td><td></td></tr>
<tr><td></td><td>=</td><td>KR- (if conflict)</td><td></td><td></td><td></td></tr>
<tr><td>d-</td><td>=</td><td>TK-</td><td>-d</td><td>=</td><td>-D</td></tr>
<tr><td></td><td></td><td></td><td>e</td><td>=</td><td>E</td></tr>
<tr><td>f-</td><td>=</td><td>TP-</td><td>-f</td><td>=</td><td>-F</td></tr>
<tr><td>g-</td><td>=</td><td>TKPW-</td><td>-g</td><td>=</td><td>-G</td></tr>
<tr><td>h-</td><td>=</td><td>H-</td><td></td><td></td><td></td></tr>
<tr><td></td><td></td><td></td><td>i</td><td>=</td><td>EU</td></tr>
<tr><td>j-</td><td>=</td><td>SKWR-</td><td>-j</td><td>=</td><td>-PBLG</td></tr>
<tr><td>k-</td><td>=</td><td>K-</td><td>-k</td><td>=</td><td>-BG</td></tr>
<tr><td>l-</td><td>=</td><td>HR-</td><td>-l</td><td>=</td><td>-L</td></tr>
<tr><td>m-</td><td>=</td><td>PH-</td><td>-m</td><td>=</td><td>-PL</td></tr>
<tr><td>n-</td><td>=</td><td>TPH-</td><td>-n</td><td>=</td><td>-PB</td></tr>
<tr><td>o</td><td>=</td><td>O</td><td></td><td></td><td></td></tr>
<tr><td>p-</td><td>=</td><td>P-</td><td>-p</td><td>=</td><td>-P</td></tr>
<tr><td>q-</td><td>=</td><td>KW-</td><td></td><td></td><td></td></tr>
<tr><td>r-</td><td>=</td><td>R-</td><td>-r</td><td>=</td><td>-R</td></tr>
<tr><td>s-</td><td>=</td><td>S-</td><td>-s</td><td>=</td><td>-S</td></tr>
<tr><td>t-</td><td>=</td><td>T-</td><td>-t</td><td>=</td><td>-T</td></tr>
<tr><td></td><td></td><td></td><td>u</td><td>=</td><td>U</td></tr>
<tr><td>v-</td><td>=</td><td>SR-</td><td>-v</td><td>=</td><td>*F</td></tr>
<tr><td>w-</td><td>=</td><td>W-</td><td></td><td></td><td></td></tr>
<tr><td>x-</td><td>=</td><td>KP-</td><td>-x</td><td>=</td><td>-BGS</td></tr>
<tr><td>y-</td><td>=</td><td>KWR-</td><td></td><td></td><td></td></tr>
<tr><td>z-</td><td>=</td><td>S*</td><td>-z</td><td>=</td><td>-Z</td></tr>
</table>

Three of the above representations may be different from what you were taught and, thus, need further discussion.

z- = S* Do not use S- for both s- and z-; e.g., zip = S*EUP, sip = SEUP. Some theories use STK- for z-. You may use STK- unless you also use it for another representation; e.g., don't use STK- for both z- and dis- or you will have conflicts such as STKOEPB = zone and disown.

-v = *F Do not use -F for both -F and -V; save = SA*EUF, safe = SAEUF.

c-	=	K-	When sounded; e.g., cat = KAT
		S-	When sounded; e.g., civil = S*EUFL
		KR-	To avoid a conflict; e.g., cell = KREL, sell = SEL. This use will be discussed more in *Step 4: Soundalikes—Consonant Variations*. There are only a few of these words in the English language.

ACTION STEP

If you do not distinguish between initial s- and initial z-, continue using S- for s- and begin using either S* or STK- for z-. If you do not distinguish between final f- and final v-, continue using -F for -f and begin using *F for -v. (See pages 8 and 9 for practice exercises.)

Don't worry about KR- to solve cell/sell type conflicts yet. That will be covered in more detail in *Step 4: Soundalikes*. If there are other consonants that differ from what you use, you may want to change them if they cause conflicts. You can do that now or when the type of word that conflicts is covered later in this text.

LONG VOWELS

Almost all stenotype theories now teach long vowels. In addition, most reporters who did not originally learn long vowels have now incorporated them into their writing style. Hundreds of short, single-stroke words will cause conflicts unless you distinguish between long and short vowels.

Most stenotype theories use the same letter representations for long vowels. Following are the StenEd representations.

Long Vowel			Long Vowel Example			Short Vowel Example		
AEU	for	long A	pain	=	PAEUPB	pan	=	PAPB
AOE	for	long E	feel	=	TPAOEL	fell	=	TPEL
AOEU	for	long I	file	=	TPAOEUL	fill	=	TPEUL
OE	for	long O	coat	=	KOET	cot	=	KOT
AOU	for	long U	fuel	=	TPAOUL	full	=	TPUL

ACTION STEP

If you don't write long vowels, you will need to incorporate them. Work on one vowel at a time until distinguishing between long and short becomes automatic.

If you don't use the long vowel form(s) shown above, it is recommended that you adopt it (them). Some writers use AE rather than AOE for long e or AE rather than AI for long a. To best prepare yourself for solving soundalike conflicts (covered in Step 4), it is recommended that you write long vowels as shown above.

Using AE for long e causes an additional problem for reporters who use the inversion principle for words ending in -y. Using AE for long e and an inverted -y results in conflicts such as HAEP = heap and happy, TKAED = deed and daddy. Similar conflicts would result in using AE for long a and an inverted -y. StenEd does not use the inverted -y. (Words ending in -y are covered in *Step 6: Suffixes & Word Endings*.)

Note: Some high frequency words with a long vowel sound use a brief instead of the long vowel representation. This is to avoid conflicts. High frequency words are covered in Step 2.

DIPHTHONGS

Most stenotype theories use the same letter representations for diphthongs. In the past, some theories taught OEU for long i. It is recommended that long i be written AOEU and OEU be reserved for the diphthong oi/oy.

		Diphthong		Example			Example	
AU	for	au, aw	cause	=	KAUZ	saw	=	SAU
OU	for	ou, ow	loud	=	HROUD	now	=	TPHOU
OEU	for	oi, oy	toil	=	TOEUL	toy	=	TOEU
AO	for	oo (all sounds)	book	=	PWAOBG	soon	=	SAOPB

ACTION STEP

If you don't write diphthongs as listed above, it is recommended that you incorporate them into your writing style. Work on one diphthong at a time until the sound and stroke become automatic.

SUMMARY
CONSONANTS & SHORT VOWELS
LONG VOWELS
DIPHTHONGS

The amount of time you spend on this step will vary with your current writing style. Many of you will only have a change or two to make at this time.

However, even if you are changing a lot of your vowels and consonants at this stage and don't feel that you're making much progress in eliminating your conflicts, keep in mind that making any changes necessary in Step 1 will make future steps flow more smoothly. Future steps build on concepts previously covered. If you choose not to make some of these changes, you can either alter the outline suggestions given in some future steps or decide to change any troublesome consonant or vowel representations at a later date.

Regardless of how many vowels or consonants you have to change, don't try to do too much at one time. Changing anything in your writing style is difficult. It's as though your fingers have been laboriously and remarkably trained to "think" for themselves. As an example, generally when one writer asks another "How do you write that?" the fingers answer before the mouth does. Having to "intellectualize" too much will slow you down. Tackling one or two changes at a time is all that is recommended.

DICTIONARY MAINTENANCE

You will want to update your dictionary as you change your writing style. Some writers prefer to make the change(s) in their dictionary before mastering the change(s) in their writing, reasoning that the translation will reward them when they remember to write the new outline and punish them when they forget. This "positive" reinforcement has proven effective for many.

Except in extreme circumstances, it is not recommended that you change too much in your translation dictionary at one time. If you are going to start writing *F for -v and AOE for long e, just do one at a time. Search for all words to be updated (e.g., words with a final or medial -v that will require the *F) and replace your old outline with the new. (How you search and replace items in your dictionary will vary according to your CAT system.)

STEP 1—EXERCISES

Following are word and paragraph exercises reinforcing the material covered in Step 1. These exercises are also available on audio cassette.

Practice the exercises that cover the technique(s) you are adopting. **Concentrate on the actual words which represent any changes you are making in your writing style. Write other words the same as you normally would, even if they currently represent a conflict.** (They will be covered in a later step.)

We have included exercises for the types of words/principles most likely to cause conflicts in many of the theories that have been taught in the past 20 years. If any change you are making is not represented, it is suggested you make up your own word list for practice.

CONSONANTS & SHORT VOWELS

S* (or STK-) for Z-
Word List—Ex. RT-1 (Tape 1/A @ 60 wpm) & RT-1 (Tape 1/A @ 90 wpm)
Narrative—Ex. RT-2 (Tape 1/A @ 125 wpm) & RT-2 (Tape 1/A @ 180 wpm)

zag	zap	zeal	zinger	zinc	zipper	zit
sag	sap	seal	singer	sink	sipper	sit
zagged	zaps	zing	zinging	zip	zipping	zits
sagged	saps	sing	singing	sip	sipping	sits

    As she <u>zipped</u> into the <u>zoo</u> parking lot, she noticed the <u>zinnias</u> were just beginning to bloom. The blimp overhead, looking like an old-time <u>zeppelin</u>, was <u>zigzagging</u> across the sky over the <u>zoo</u> advertising the day's events. There was a <u>zany</u>, happy atmosphere in the air. A <u>zebra</u> had recently given birth, and it seemed a <u>zillion</u> people were in line to see the gangly little creature.

    She never tired of her job at the <u>zoo</u>. She had majored in <u>zoology</u> in college. When the <u>zoological</u> park offered her a job as a <u>zoologist</u>, she <u>zealously</u> accepted. She had a real <u>zest</u> for life at the <u>zoo</u> and never tired of the animals' <u>zany</u> antics.

*F for -V(E)
Word List—Ex. RT-3 (Tape 1/A @ 60 wpm) & RT-3 (Tape 1/A @ 90 wpm)
Narrative—Ex. RT-4 (Tape 1/A @ 125 wpm) & RT-4 (Tape 1/A @ 180 wpm)

believe	leave	plaintive	proves	save	serve	
belief	leaf	plaintiff	proofs	safe	serf	active
						act if
believes	live	prove	relieve	saves	strive	act I have
beliefs	life	proof	relief	safes	strife	

 Step 1: The Alphabet

During the last <u>five</u> years, the nation's rural areas have been growing faster than its urban areas. More and more people are finding the <u>nerve</u> to <u>leave</u> the <u>strife</u> of the large city and to try the rural or small-town <u>life</u>.

The crime, pollution, overcrowded schools, and high cost of <u>living</u> found in many urban areas are <u>driving</u> people away—are causing people to <u>move</u> in search of a more <u>attractive</u> <u>life</u>style. Many people have left <u>lucrative</u> <u>executive</u> positions in search of a <u>safer</u>, saner <u>life</u>.

The majority of these migrants have been relatively pleased with <u>themselves</u> and their new <u>lives</u>. They <u>believe</u> that they have made the right decision and are <u>relieved</u> that they have left many problems behind them.

The big question, of course, is whether the problems of the big cities will <u>move</u> to the small towns. Most migrants are optimistic. Awareness and <u>cooperative</u> effort, along with careful zoning, they feel, will keep the sins of the city from invading the more rural areas of the nation. What is even less clear, <u>however</u>, is what <u>rehabilitative</u> measures will be needed to <u>save</u> the current urban areas if their most <u>productive</u> and <u>creative</u> people seek a <u>life</u> outside the big city.

S* (or STK-) for Z- and *F for -V(E)
Ex. RT-5 (Tape 1/A @ 125 wpm) & RT-5 (Tape 1/A @ 180 wpm)

1. She chose to <u>sit</u> on the sidelines hoping no one would notice the big <u>zit</u> on the end of her nose.
2. I was <u>sitting</u> there <u>sipping</u> my iced tea when I noticed the skaters <u>zipping</u> by.
3. This area is <u>zoned</u> commercial.
   He had almost been <u>disowned</u> because of his preposterous acts.
4. Bonnie handed Clyde <u>half</u> of the money from the bank robbery.
   It was necessary to <u>halve</u> the banana so we could each eat <u>half</u>.
5. They had a little <u>tiff</u> about whether it was <u>safe</u> to put all their <u>savings</u> in the <u>safe</u>.
6. The <u>plaintiff</u> was sure that justice would prevail.
   We heard a <u>plaintive</u> cry coming from the woods.

LONG VOWELS

AI for LONG A
Word List—Ex. RT-6 (Tape 1/A @ 60 wpm) & RT-6 (Tape 1/A @ 90 wpm)
Narrative—Ex. RT-7 (Tape 1/A @ 125 wpm) & RT-7 (Tape 1/A @ 180 wpm)

am	bat	dam	glad	mad	pan	rap	snack
aim	bait	dame	glade	made	pain	rape	snake
at	cam	fad	hat	mat	par	rat	spat
ate	came	fade	hate	mate	par	rate	spate
back	cap	far	lack	nap	plan	sat	stack
bake	cape	fair	lake	nape	plain	sate	stake
bad	car	fat	lad	pad	quack	scat	tap
bade	care	fate	laid	paid	quake	skate	tape
bar	chaff	gap	lass	pal	rack	slat	van
bare	chafe	gape	lace	pail	rake	slate	vain

The lad slid the boat out onto the lake. Day was just breaking above the distant glade. He raked his cap back and wiped his face. He tugged at the motor's cord. The motor spat and then came to life. "I'll have to repair that cam," he thought to himself.

Slowly the boat gained speed and raced toward the center of the lake. Once at the right place, he reached down to take his rod from the rack on the boat. He then pulled a worm from the bait box and baited his hook. Hearing a noise, he looked back to see a snake planing through the water.

He sat back on the mat and, wasting no time, tossed his line into the lake. Soon he felt the tug that meant a fish on the line. He knew right away it was a big bass. With a spate of activity, he pulled the fat fish into the boat and laid it in the sack he kept at the base of the boat. Soon he caught eight more fish of varying weights.

That night he was very glad as he sated himself eating some baked fish and planning to go out to the cape the next day.

AOE for LONG E
Word List—Ex. RT-8 (Tape 1/A @ 60 wpm) & RT-8 (Tape 1/A @ 90 wpm)
Narrative—Ex. RT-9 (Tape 1/A @ 125 wpm) & RT-9 (Tape 1/A @ 180 wpm)

bed	bred	dead	fest	led	pep	sped	ten
bead	breed	deed	feast	lead	peep	speed	teen
best	check	den	glen	less	pet	stead	sweat
beast	cheek	dean	glean	lease	peat	steed	sweet
bet	chess	fed	head	lest	sell	stem	wed
beet	cheese	feed	heed	least	seal	steam	weed
bled	clever	fell	ken	met	set	step	whet
bleed	cleaver	feel	keen	meet	seat	steep	wheat

A long path lined by sedge grass leads to the old castle. The castle was the scene of many sieges and battles during medieval times. Here it was that a mean and evil tyrant met his death and that shrieking hordes were beaten back.

Atop each turret waves the red and green banners of the regal family. Inside the ancient keep can still be seen the crest and seal of the family and the deer's head which hangs above the steep steps.

The banquet hall was a huge room where meals were given. At least three hundred people could be seated at the long table which would be set with every sort of meat, vegetable, bread, and sweet dessert. Above the table there is a plaque which reads: "Here were held the greatest feasts in the realm."

There is a steep stairway which led to the deep dungeon where prisoners were sealed in cells and fed only water and bread made from moldy wheat — hardly feed for animals and not something to whet the appetite.

As one leaves the castle, walking across the creaking drawbridge, he can almost hear and feel the spirits of the men who fell in battle in and near the ancient citadel.

Note: Soundalikes (e.g., plane/plain, scene/seen) will be covered in Step 4. For now, write them as you normally would. Just concentrate on the long vowel sound for these exercises.

   Step 1: The Alphabet

AOI for LONG I

Word List—Ex. RT-10 (Tape 1/A @ 60 wpm) & RT-10 (Tape 1/A @ 90 wpm)
Narrative—Ex. RT-11 (Tape 1/A @ 125 wpm) & RT-11 (Tape 1/A @ 180 wpm)

bill	fir	hid	lit	pill	rip	slim	till
bile	fire	hide	light	pile	ripe	slime	tile
bit	fill	hit	mill	pin	shin	spin	tip
bite	file	height	mile	pine	shine	spine	type
dill	fin	ill	mitt	prim	sin	spit	trip
dial	fine	isle	mite	prime	sign	spite	tripe
dim	fit	kit	nil	rid	sir	still	tinny
dime	fight	kite	Nile	ride	sire	style	tiny
din	gill	lick	pick	rim	slid	strip	win
dine	guile	like	pike	rhyme	slide	stripe	wine

A <u>slim</u> <u>sliver</u> of <u>light</u> <u>slipped</u> through the <u>pine</u> trees and <u>lit</u> up the <u>dim</u> swamp. A <u>little</u> <u>white</u> rabbit ran past to <u>hide</u> itself from the fox <u>eyeing</u> it. A <u>bit</u> farther into the woods, some <u>mice</u> were hopping across the <u>slime</u>.

Off in the distance, a <u>tiny</u> <u>bird</u> was <u>dining</u> on a <u>ripe</u> berry <u>while</u> below him scampered a <u>lithe</u> squirrel. From <u>time</u> to <u>time</u>, the <u>quiet</u> was broken by the <u>din</u> of a noisy <u>wild</u> boar tramping through the <u>thick</u> undergrowth.

All at once there was a sudden <u>stillness</u>. Out of the <u>mist</u> rose a <u>thin</u> <u>line</u> of smoke. It <u>climbed</u> slowly above the <u>tips</u> of the <u>fir</u> trees and carried <u>high</u> in the air. Soon it was followed by a <u>fine</u> red <u>line</u> which moved across the floor of the forest glowing with a <u>fine</u> heat. It was the worst <u>type</u> of danger: a <u>fire</u>.

With a rush, the animals began to <u>flit</u> and run across the forest in frantic <u>flight</u> before the flames. Each animal rushed to stay <u>alive</u> as the <u>fire</u> <u>ripped</u> across the land. Some animals <u>hid</u> in burrows below the ground. Others took to the <u>sky</u>. Many just ran, <u>trying</u> to <u>dive</u> and leap ahead of the <u>living</u> flame, each <u>excitedly</u> seeking an <u>exit</u> from the <u>widening</u> <u>line</u> of <u>fire</u>.

OE for LONG O

Word List—Ex. RT-12 (Tape 1/A @ 60 wpm) & RT-12 (Tape 1/A @ 90 wpm)
Narrative—Ex. RT-13 (Tape 1/A @ 125 wpm) & RT-13 (Tape 1/A @ 180 wpm)

block	cod	crock	got	mop	pock	rot	sop
bloke	code	croak	goat	mope	poke	rote	soap
blot	con	dot	hop	nod	pop	slop	stock
bloat	cone	dote	hope	node	pope	slope	stoke
clock	cop	gloss	lob	odd	rob	smock	toss
cloak	cope	glows	lobe	ode	robe	smoke	toes
cock	cot	god	mod	on	rod	sock	tot
coke	coat	goad	mode	own	rode	soak	tote

Atop a high peak, where only mountain goats would seem to be at home, is found an ancient temple. Here, in days of old, priests, in robes and with bodies coated with oil from head to toe, would toss incense on the glowing altar fire and pray to the gods for success with the crops the people sowed.

It was a huge job to build the temple. Great stones had to be cut from the rock and toted slowly up the steep slope on a narrow road to the site. As the stones got to their destination, beasts, under the threat of being goaded by whips and rods, hauled hods of mortar to hold the stones in place.

Within the temple is a huge low chamber where the holy codes are stored in great tomes. In the temple core, supported on great poles, are glossy mosaics showing the road to heaven. Off in the rear are the rooms which lodge the priests.

There is one other room which is known to only a few. This is the treasure room which is stocked with gold and precious ores. Bold men tried to rob it but were always caught and slowly killed by the priests by soaking them in great pots of oil over a well-stoked fire.

AOU for LONG U
Word List—Ex. RT-14 (Tape 1/A @ 60 wpm) & RT-14 (Tape 1/A @ 90 wpm)
Narrative—Ex. RT-15 (Tape 1/A @ 125 wpm) & RT-15 (Tape 1/A @ 180 wpm)

butt	cur	dud	fuddle	fuzz	muss	sup
butte	cure	dude	feudal	fuse	muse	soup
cub	cut	dully	fug	jut	mutt	tub
cube	cute	duly	fugue	jute	mute	tube
crud	duck	dun	full	mull	nubble	
crude	duke	dune	fuel	mule	nubile	

The old road cut through the butte was once an important route to the old gold town. Down this rude, rutted road came cubes and bars of pure gold to use for coins and jewels.

The gold is gone now, and the road is only a mute reminder of the days when the miners would pay in gold dust for a bowl of soup and a few crackers.

Every June there is a brief renewal of life when the nearby dude ranch resumes its busy season. Then groups of tourists set out down the road on sure-footed mules to view the ruins of the old town. The enthusiastic tourists are amused by all they view, be it a cute bear cub or some desert bug crawling toward the dunes.

When they reach the gold town, they eagerly rush through the old buildings, buzzing excitedly around the chutes from the old mill and running through the huge old warehouse where skins were cured to make sacks for gold. They can see the crude flues of the smelter and the huts the miners lived in.

At night, the tourists sup around the campfire and hear gruesome tales of ghosts shut up in the denuded mines.

 StenEd®

AOE for LONG E
AE for INVERSIONS

AE is a <u>non-StenEd principle</u> shown here because of potential conflicts in traditional theories. *Step 6: Suffixes* covers words ending in -y. For now, it is recommended that you begin using AOE for long e if you currently use AE, whether or not you use the inversion principle. (Note: in *Step 5: Soundalikes*, you will learn how to distinguish between homophones with the long e sound; e.g., meet and meat.)

airy	cranny	daily	gassy	lacy	natty	vary
ear	careen	deal	geese	lease	neat	veer
alley	crazy	fairy	gravy	lady	Sally	wavy
eel	crease	fear	grieve	lead	seal	weave
canny	daddy	Gary	happy	marry	valley	
keen	deed	gear	heap	mere	veal	

DIPHTHONGS

Word List 1—Ex. RT-16 (Tape 1/A @ 60 wpm) & RT-16 (Tape 1/A @ 75 wpm)
Word List 2—Ex. RT-17 (Tape 1/A @ 60 wpm) & RT-17 (Tape 1/A @ 90 wpm)
Narrative—Ex. RT-18 (Tape 1/B @ 125 wpm) & RT-18 (Tape 1/B @ 180 wpm)

<u>AU for AW & AU</u>	<u>OI for OI & OY</u>	<u>OU for OW & OU</u>	<u>AO for OO</u>
awe	boil	cloud	bloom
brawl	boy	clout	book
brawn	broil	couch	boom
caught	choice	cow	boot
claw	coil	crowd	broom
crawl	coin	doubt	cook
dawn	coy	foul	doom
drawl	foil	grouch	fool
drawn	groin	house	foot
fawn	hoist	loud	gloom
fraught	join	louse	hook
jaw	joint	mound	loom
law	joist	mouse	loose
lawn	joy	now	moon
paw	loin	ought	moot
pawn	loyal	plow	noose
prawn	noise	pounce	pool
raw	ploy	proud	room
saw	point	round	root
scrawl	royal	shout	shook
shawl	soil	sound	smooch
sprawl	spoil	spout	soon
straw	toil	stout	soot
taught	toy	towel	took
yawn	voice	trout	zoom

OI for OI & OY
AOI for LONG I

boil	devoid	loin	noise	poise	soy	Troy
bile	divide	line	nice	pies	sigh	try
boy	foil	loiter	ploy	Roy	toil	voice
buy	file	lighter	ply	rye	tile	vice
choir	Freud	loyal	point	royal	toy	
quire	fried	lisle	pint	rile	tie	

I remember when I was a little <u>boy</u> I used to love to go to the store for my mother. She would give me a list of things to <u>buy</u>, and I would hurry off to the store. I always had great fun.

Usually, she sent me to the supermarket. I <u>enjoyed</u> going down the <u>aisles</u> looking for the things on the list. I <u>liked</u> to pretend I was an explorer looking for new <u>kinds</u> of things. The aluminum <u>foil</u> would be some newly <u>coined</u> money, a pork <u>loin</u> would be some strange work of art, the <u>rye</u> bread would be a rare jewel, and a <u>pint</u> of salad <u>oil</u> <u>might</u> be some valuable chemical.

I would stalk the <u>aisles</u>, careful not to <u>loiter</u> in one place for fear of being caught by unfriendly natives who <u>might</u> <u>boil</u> me in <u>oil</u>. I remember that <u>Roy</u>, the clerk, would play along with me at <u>times</u>. When I was in <u>line</u>, he would pretend to be the <u>royal</u> customs agent marveling at my exotic "<u>finds</u>."

On some occasions, my mother would send me to other stores. I was thrilled the first <u>time</u> she let me go to the men's store to pick out a <u>tie</u> for my father's birthday.

She also sent me to the hardware store. To a little <u>boy</u>, it was a fascinating place filled with things <u>like</u> <u>files</u> and <u>plywood</u> and <u>tile</u>. Even if I was just there to get some <u>lighter</u> fluid or some <u>alloy</u> nails, I would always take a few minutes to look around.

The most fun of all was when my mother would send me to the <u>toy</u> store. If I had been good, my mother would give me some money and let me go and <u>buy</u> a <u>toy</u>. I would always ask <u>Lloyd</u>, who worked in the store, what they had that was new. He would always <u>point</u> with <u>pride</u> to the latest <u>toy</u>. I won't say he <u>lied</u>, but he did exaggerate <u>sometimes</u> about how wonderful the <u>toys</u> were. It was sort of a <u>ploy</u> of his to sell me something. Usually, though, I would just look around and <u>buy</u> something else. I think it used to <u>rile</u> him a little bit that I ignored the sales pitch, but to me it was just a game.

As I remember all those trips to the store, I have to <u>smile</u> a bit. I guess a lot of <u>boys</u> would consider such errands to be <u>toil</u>, but to me they were always great fun. I think it is because I always found a way to make them a game. In fact, it seems that the <u>time</u> always seemed to <u>fly</u> by when I was at the store. It seems that the shopping was done almost as soon as it was begun. I always wished that I could <u>find</u> an excuse to stay longer. There was always something fascinating to see or do. In a way, I miss the <u>boyhood</u> fun I had at that <u>time</u>.

 Step 1: The Alphabet

STEP 2
HIGH FREQUENCY WORDS

The 100 most frequently used words in the English language account for up to 47% of spoken English. Therefore, you can easily see the advantage of resolving any of these conflicts in your writing style. Following are these words ranked by frequency.

HIGH FREQUENCY WORDS RANKED

1. the	34. were	67. time
2. of	35. her	68. these
3. and	36. all	69. two
4. to	37. she	70. may
5. a	38. there	71. then
6. in	39. would	72. do
7. that	40. we	73. first
8. is	41. their	74. any
9. was	42. him	75. my
10. he	43. been	76. now
11. for	44. has	77. such
12. it	45. when	78. like
13. with	46. who	79. our
14. as	47. will	80. over
15. his	48. more	81. man
16. on	49. no	82. me
17. be	50. if	83. even
18. at	51. out	84. most
19. by	52. so	85. made
20. I	53. said	86. after
21. this	54. what	87. also
22. had	55. up	88. did
23. not	56. its	89. many
24. are	57. about	90. before
25. but	58. into	91. must
26. from	59. than	92. through
27. or	60. them	93. back
28. have	61. can	94. year
29. an	62. only	95. where
30. they	63. other	96. much
31. which	64. new	97. your
32. one	65. some	98. way
33. you	66. could	99. well
		100. down

If you are on CAT, you should have no trouble picking out the high frequency words that create conflicts for you. If you are not on CAT, the list of potential conflicts on pages 16 and 17 should help you identify your conflicts. Work on one conflict at a time, preferably using StenEd's recommended outline. (If you use the StenEd outline, you are less likely to create a potential conflict with a principle covered later in this text. However, you may choose your own outline, if preferred.)

These 100 high frequency words are alphabetized below for easy reference. Suggested outlines are included. Also listed are suggested outlines for other fairly high frequency words that often cause conflicts. Note: Some of these high frequency words do not use long vowels (e.g., WE = we, WAOE = wee). Others are assigned a brief (e.g., THA = that, THAT = that the).

HIGH FREQUENCY WORDS ALPHABETIZED

a	A	her	HER	so	SO
about	ABT	him	HEUPL	some	SOPL
after	AF	his	HEUZ	such	SUFP
all	AUL	I	EU	than	THAPB
also	ALS	if	TP-	that	THA
always	AULS	in	TPH-	the	T-
am	APL	into	SPWAO	their	THAEUR
an	APB	is	S-	them	THEPL
and	APBD [SKP-]	it	EUT	then	THEPB
another	AOT	its	EUTS	there	THR-
any	TPHEU	just	SKWR*US	these	THAOEZ
are	R-	justice	SKWRUS/TEUS	they	THAEU
around	ARPBD	knew	TPHAOU	thing	THEUPBG
as	AZ	know	TPHOE	think	THEU
ask	SK-	known	TPHOEPB	this	TH-
at	AT	like	HRAOEUBG	threw	THRAOU
back	PWABG	little	HREUT/-L	through	THRU
be	PW-	made	PHAED	time	TAOEUPL
became	PWAEUPL	make	PHAEUBG	to	TO
because	PWAUZ	man	PHAPB	too	TAO
been	PW-PB	many	PH-	two	TWO
before	PW-FR	may	PHAEU	under	URPBD
but	PWU	me	PHE	up	UP
buy	PWAOEU	men	PHEPB	upon	POPB
by	PWEU	more	PH-R	us	US
can	K-	most	PHO*ES	use (N)	KWRAOUS
come	KOPL	much	PHUFP	use (V)	KWRAOUZ
could	KOULD	must	PH*US	very	SR-R
day	TKAEU	my	PHEU	was	WUZ
did	TKEUD	new	TPHU	we	WE
do	TKO	no	TPHO	well	WEL
does	TKUZ	none	TPHUPB	were	W-R
down	TKOUPB	not	TPHOT	what	WHA
each	AOEFP	now	TPHOU	when	WHEPB
enough	TPHUF	of	OF	where	WR-
even	EFPB [*EFPB]	off	AUF	whether	WHR-
ever	-FR [*FR]	often	AUFPB	which	KH-
every	EFR [*EFR]	on	OPB	who	WHO
eye	KWRAOEU	one	WUPB	whom	WHOPL
few	TPU	only	OPBL	whose	WHOZ
first	TP*EURS	or	OR	will	HR-
for	TP-R	other	O*ER	with	W-
from	TPR-	our	OUR	within	W-PB
go	TKPWO	out	OUT	woman	WOPL
gone	TKPWOPB	over	OEFR [O*EFR]	women	WEUPL
good	TKPWAOD	people	PAOEPL	would	WOULD
had	HAD	said	SAEUD	year	KWRAOER
has	HAZ	see	SAOE	yes	KWRE
have	SR-	she	SHE	you	KWROU
he	HE	should	SHOULD	your	KWROUR

  Step 2: High Frequency Words

POTENTIAL CONFLICTS WITH HIGH FREQUENCY WORDS

The potential conflicts listed on pages 18-19 have been culled from theories (other than StenEd) taught during the last 20 years. You certainly won't have all of them, but you may have a few.

The words are presented in potential conflict groups. The key word in each group has the highest frequency. The number to the left of the key word shows the frequency rank. If a word has already been covered, there will be a "see #" beside the word. If the word has no common potential conflicts, the word will stand alone.

In addition to words which may conflict with the key word, some groups include prefixes and/or suffixes that often cause word boundary conflicts. These are included at this point to make the list more comprehensive. With a few exceptions, don't worry about changing prefixes or suffixes in your writing style now. This will be covered in Steps 5 and 6.

StenEd outlines are listed for all words, prefixes, and suffixes listed. Outlines in brackets (e.g., they are = THAI/R- [THER]) are optional StenEd outlines. Prefixes are represented with a hyphen following (e.g., be-); suffixes are represented with a hyphen preceding (e.g., -ed).

ACTION STEP
Start reading from the top of the list on page 18 to find the first conflict element in your writing style. This is the first conflict you should work on in Step 2.

We suggest you work on the conflict(s) you have that have the highest frequency first. And by working on just one conflict at a time, you will minimize any confusion of "how am I going to write this?" while actually on the job.

Practice exercises have been given for the more common and frustrating conflict groups. However, because of their frequency, these 100 words occur often in your daily taking. Most of your practice will be "on the job."

Note: Because of their frequency, many of these words use a short form (e.g., this = TH-, not THIS) or drop the long vowel (e.g., I = I, not AOI). In addition, StenEd uses the initial side of the keyboard for briefs (e.g., T- = the, S- = is). The final side of the keyboard is reserved for endings (e.g., /-S = -(e)s, /-D = -ed). Inflected endings are covered in Step 3.

DICTIONARY MAINTENANCE
Many writers using CAT have found that changing their personal CAT dictionary to reflect the way they *want* to write reinforces their changes. For example, if you used to write the word "is" as /-S and you want to start writing it S-/ and reserve the /-S for inflected endings (see Step 3), enter S- for "is" in your dictionary. Enter /-S as a suffix (delete space s).

That way you are rewarded each time you write the way you want to and are reminded, in the proofing stage, each time you forget your new outline. Only do this with a couple of words at a time. As you well know, it is not easy to change, but this reinforcement gives you a "pat on the back" when you remember your new outline.

POTENTIAL HIGH FREQUENCY WORD CONFLICTS
(Those Words Ranked 1 through 50)

Following are potential conflicts for the fifty most frequently occurring words in the English language. Starting with "the," which is ranked #1, go through the list to identify your first conflict. Suggested StenEd outlines have been given.

(1)	the	T-	(16)	on	OPB	(33)	you	KWROU	
	it	EUT					ewe	KWRAOU	
	at	AT	(17)	be	PW-		yew	KWRAO*U	
	they	THAEU		bee	PWAOE				
				be-	PWE	(34)	were	(see #13)	
(2)	of	OF		been	PW-PB				
	if	TP-		about	ABT	(35)	her	HER	
	have	SR-					here	HAOER	
	very	SR-R	(18)	at	(see #1)		hear	HAER	
	off	AUF							
			(19)	by	PWEU	(36)	all	AUL	
(3)	and	APBD [SKP-]		buy	PWAOEU		awl	A*UL	
	a	A		bye	PWAO*EU		awe	AU	
	an	APB		bi-	PW*EU		al-	AL	
							-al	/(c)AL	
(4)	to	TO	(20)	I	EU		Al	A*L	
	too	TAO		eye	KWRAOEU				
	two	TWO		aye	AO*EU	(37)	she	SHE	
				i-	AOEU				
(5)	a	A		-y	/(c)EU	(38)	there	THR-	
	a-	AEU					their	THAEUR	
			(21)	this	TH-		they are	THAEU/R- [THER]	
(6)	in	TPH-					they're	THAEU/AO*ER	
	inn	*EUPB	(22)	had	HAD			[THA*EUR]	
	in-	EUPB		did	TKEUD				
				-ed	/-D	(39)	would	WOULD	
(7)	that	THA					wood	WAOD	
	that the	THAT	(23)	not	TPHOT				
				knot	TPHO*T	(40)	we	WE	
(8)	is	S-					wee	WAOE	
	as	AZ	(24)	are	R-				
	as-	AS				(41)	their	(see #38)	
	ass	ASZ	(25)	but	PWU				
	his	HEUZ		butt	PWUT	(42)	him	HEUPL	
	hiss	HEUSZ					am	APL	
	-s	/-S	(26)	from	TPR-		many	PH-	
							hymn	H*EUPL	
(9)	was	WUZ	(27)	or	OR				
(10)	he	HE		oar	AOR	(43)	been	(see #17)	
				ore	OER				
(11)	for	TP-R		or-	O*R	(44)	has	HAZ	
	for-	TPOR		-or	/(c)OR	(45)	when	WHEPB	
	four	TPOUR		other	O*ER	(46)	who	WHO	
	fore-	TPOER				(47)	will	HR-	
	fore	TPOER/SP-S	(28)	have	(see #2)	(48)	more	PH-R	
			(29)	an	(see #3)				
(12)	it	(see #1)	(30)	they	(see #1)	(49)	no	TPHO	
							know	TPHOE	
(13)	with	W-	(31)	which	KH-				
	were	W-R		witch	WEUFP	(50)	if	(see #2)	
(14)	as	(see #8)	(32)	one	WUPB				
(15)	his	(see #8)		won	WOPB				

 Step 2: High Frequency Words

POTENTIAL HIGH FREQUENCY WORD CONFLICTS
(Those Words Ranked 51 through 100)

Following are potential conflicts for the rest of the 100 most frequently occurring words in the English language. Starting with "so," which is ranked #52 (#51 has no potential word conflict), go through the list to identify your first conflict. Suggested StenEd outlines have been given.

(51)	out	OUT	(67)	time	TAOEUPL	(86)	after	AF	
				thyme	TAO*EUPL		after-	AFR	
(52)	so	SO							
	sew	SOE	(68)	these	THAOEZ	(87)	also	ALS	
	sow (v)	SO*E	(69)	too	(see #4)		always	AULS	
	sow (n)	SOU					wills	HR-S	
			(70)	may	PHAEU				
(53)	said	SAEUD		May	PHA*EU	(88)	did	(see #22)	
	sed	SED		Mae	PHAE	(89)	many	(see #42)	
						(90)	before	PW-FR	
(54)	what	WHA	(71)	then	(see #59)				
	what the	WHAT				(91)	must	PH*US	
	watt	WAT	(72)	do	TKO		muss	PHUSZ	
				due	TKAOU				
(55)	up	UP		dew	TKAO*U	(92)	through	THRU	
							threw	THRAOU	
(56)	its	EUTS	(73)	first	TP*EURS				
	itself	*EUTS		firs	TPEUR/-S	(93)	back	PWABG	
	it's	EUT/AOES							
		[T*S]	(74)	any	TPHEU	(94)	year	KWRAOER	
	it is	EUT/S- [T-S]	(75)	my	PHEU				
			(76)	now	TPHOU	(95)	where	WR-	
(57)	about	(see #17)	(77)	such	SUFP		ware	WAEUR	
(58)	into	SPWAO	(78)	like	HRAOEUBG		wear	WAER	
(59)	than	THAPB	(79)	our	OUR	(96)	much	PHUFP	
	then	THEPB		hour	HOUR				
						(97)	your	KWROUR	
(60)	them	THEPL	(80)	over	OEFR [O*EFR]		you're	KWROU/AO*ER	
				offer	AUFR			[KWRO*UR]	
(61)	can	K-		over-	O*FR		you are	KWROU/R- [UR]	
(62)	only	OPBL		-over	OFR				
(63)	other	(see #27)				(98)	way	WAEU	
			(81)	man	PHAPB		weigh	WAEUG	
(64)	new	TPHU	(82)	me	PHE		whey	WHAEU	
	knew	TPHAOU	(83)	even	EFPB [*EFPB]				
						(99)	well	WEL	
(65)	some	SOPL	(84)	most	PHO*ES		we will	WE/HR-	
	sum	SUPL		mows	PHOE/-S		we'll	WE/AOEL [WAO*EL]	
	-some	SPH-		moss	PHOSZ				
						(100)	down	TKOUPB	
(66)	could	KOULD	(85)	made	PHAED		do you know	TKO/KWROU/TPHOE	
	co-	KO						[TKAO*UPB]	
	cow	KOU		maid	PHAEUD		dune	TKAOUPB	
	company	KOFRP/TPH*EU							
		[KPAEPB]							

SUMMARY

The amount of time you spend on this step will vary with your current writing style. Any high frequency conflicts you resolve should make a very noticeable change in your translation. Similarly, you will begin to spend less time during the edit phase weeding out these frustrating high frequency conflicts.

STEP 2—EXERCISES

Following are sentence and paragraph exercises reinforcing the most frequent conflicts in Step 2. These exercises are also available on audio cassette.

The sentence exercise contains potential conflicts for the 100 most frequently occurring words in the English language, starting with #1, the. No one will have all these conflicts. You can practice resolving just the conflicts in your writing style, or you can take all the sentences for review and awareness. Some prefix/suffix word boundary-type conflicts are also included. You can practice them now or when they occur later in this text.

The narrative exercises cover the most common conflicts contained in theories that do not teach realtime writing. Because of the frequency of these words, you will also get a lot of practice on the job. If you're adventurous, make up some of your own practice sentences using your most common and time-consuming conflicts. It doesn't matter if they're somewhat silly, as long as they help you eliminate your conflicts and, thus, get better translations.

When adopting a new outline, whether from textual exercises or on the job, **concentrate on the actual words which represent any changes you are making in your writing style. Write other words the same as you normally would, even if they currently represent a conflict.** (They will be covered in a later step.)

HIGH FREQUENCY WORDS
Ex. RT-19 (Tape 1/B @ 120 wpm) & RT-19 (Tape 1/B @ 175 wpm)

In the audios for this lesson, the potential conflicts are dictated first, then the practice sentences. In those cases where the potential conflicts are soundalikes, just listen to the introductory words, don't write them since you don't know which word is intended out of context. Do write all sentences.

1. **the/it/at/they**
   They told the man to look at it more carefully.

2. **of/if/have/very/off**
   If she can have Christmas week off, she will be among a small group of very happy people.

3. **and/a/an**
   All I had for lunch was a pear and an apple.

4. **to/too/two**
   Two months is too long to stay away from work.

5. **a/a-**
   He waited a long time for the right woman to come along.

6. **in/inn/in-**
   He left his bicycle in the yard of the old inn.
   She was indifferent about them living in different states.

7. **that/that the**
   That is the same book that the other teacher recommended.

8. **is/as/as-/ass/his/hiss/-s**
   His pet snake is hissing too loudly.
   As expected, this hard-working ass is one of the farmer's greatest assets.

11. **for/for-/four/fore-/fore**
   It was necessary for the four golfers to yell "fore" when the ball nearly hit another player.
   She was forgiven for giving the four new puppies extra snacks.

13. with/were
They <u>were</u> <u>with</u> me all day.

17. be/bee/be-/been/about
The <u>bee</u> grew to <u>be</u> a nuisance as it buzzed around my head.
It has <u>been</u> <u>about</u> four months since I <u>began</u> this project.

19. by/buy/bye/bi-
The girl could not pass <u>by</u> a shop without stopping to <u>buy</u> something.
They waved good-<u>bye</u> as they left the <u>biannual</u> office party.

20. I/eye/aye/i-/-y
"<u>Aye</u>, <u>I</u> sure did hit him in the <u>eye</u>," exclaimed the boxer.
The <u>noisy</u>, <u>irate</u> driver insisted that the crash had been caused by the <u>icy</u> road conditions.

22. had/did/-ed
<u>Did</u> you know he <u>had</u> hurt his head when he <u>pried</u> open the window?

23. not/knot
Ben was <u>not</u> able to tie the <u>knot</u> for his Boy Scout badge.
All his labors were for <u>naught</u>.

25. but/butt
I asked him to properly dispose of his cigarette <u>butt</u>, <u>but</u> he refused.

27. or/oar/ore/or-/-or/other
It was quite an <u>ordeal</u> when we lost the <u>other</u> <u>oar</u> and could not move the boat.
Either gold <u>or</u> silver <u>ore</u> was required to pay the ransom.
It's a <u>minor</u> point whether it's mine <u>or</u> yours.

31. which/witch
<u>Which</u> <u>witch</u> is the ugliest?

32. one/won
<u>One</u> of the twins <u>won</u> a blue ribbon in the contest.

33. you/ewe/yew
Do <u>you</u> really believe the word "<u>ewe</u>" would ever come up in a court case?
Did <u>you</u> know the cancer treatment drug taxol is made from the <u>yew</u> tree?

35. her/here/hear
Did you <u>hear</u> that <u>her</u> brother is <u>here</u>?

36. all/awl/al-/-al/Al
<u>Al</u> wanted to change the <u>normal</u> location so <u>all</u> of us would be able to attend.
<u>Al</u> used the <u>awl</u> to <u>alter</u> the appearance of the wood.

38. there/their/they are/they're
<u>They are</u> her cousins, and she is going to stay at <u>their</u> house until <u>they're</u> tired of having her <u>there</u>.

39. would/wood
<u>Would</u> the strongest boy be elected to chop the <u>wood</u>?

42. him/am/many/hymn
They convinced <u>him</u> to sing his favorite <u>hymn</u> for the gathering.
I <u>am</u> sure <u>many</u> of them will help <u>him</u>.

49. no/know
I <u>know</u> of <u>no</u> family that is moving in the near future.

52. so/sew/sow
I'll <u>sew</u> the clothing tomorrow <u>so</u> I'll have time to <u>sow</u> the fields and take care of the <u>sow</u> today.

53. said/sed
The doctor <u>said</u> the <u>sed</u> rate was below normal.

54. what/what the/watt
<u>What</u> do you care <u>what</u> <u>watt</u> that bulb is?
Do you remember <u>what the</u> lawyer said?

56. its/itself/it's/it is
<u>It's</u> almost certain <u>its</u> paw will heal by next week.
<u>It is</u> not unusual for the cat to stare at <u>itself</u> in the mirror.

59. than/then
First he wants a week's free trial. <u>Then</u> he'll decide whether this new system is better <u>than</u> his old one.

64. new/knew
They <u>knew</u> the <u>new</u> boy had gone into the haunted house.

65. some/sum/-some
Some of the boys were unable to figure out the sum of the numbers on the blackboard.
Hand some snacks to those handsome guys over there.

66. could/co-/cow/company
Could you tell me how long ago she became co-owner of the company?
They knew the cow could coexist peacefully with the other animals.

67. time/thyme
This time don't add so much thyme to the stew.

70. may/May/Mae
She said she may be able to finish the project by May 15.
Is her name spelled Mae or May?

72. do/due/dew
It was all we could do to make the payment when it was due.
The early morning dew soaked the grass and flowers.
Don't undo all the good that's been done.
He seemed to have an undue concern for insignificant events.

73. first/firs
The first time the logger went into the forest, he couldn't tell the firs from the hardwoods.

79. hour/our
The hour for our Latin exam arrived, and we were very nervous.

80. over/offer/over-/-over
Let me think over your offer, and I'll get back with you.
I was overcome with joy when they asked me to come over for some leftovers.

84. most/mows/moss
He mows the lawn most Sunday mornings.
They left most of the moss that was on the live oak trees.

85. made/maid
The maid made all the beds in the house and picked the clothes up off the floor.

86. after/after-
After math class, we will better appreciate the aftermath of not doing our homework.

87. also/always/wills
They always make sure their wills are up to date.
I always like to finish work before midnight, also.

91. must/muss
He must be careful or he'll muss his hair.

92. through/threw
He threw the ball through the hoop.
She did a very thorough job of analyzing the situation.

95. where/ware/wear
She did not know where to wear her new dress.
The ware the silversmith created in his shop was very valuable.

97. your/you're/you are
You're the first one to hand in your test paper.
You are mistaken if you think your opinion is the only one that counts.

98. way/weigh/whey
Is this the way you're supposed to weigh produce?
Unless Little Miss Muffet is called to the stand, I doubt that the word "whey" will ever occur in a transcript.

99. well/we will/we'll
We will do well to write these words differently.
Well, when do you think we'll hear about it?

100. down/do you know/dune
Do you know how long ago they went down to the dune?
He's down in the dumps because he expects them to dun him for payment of his long overdue bill.

   Step 2: High Frequency Words

THE   (T-)
IT   (EUT)

Ex. RT-20 (Tape 1/B @ 125 wpm) & RT-20 (Tape 1/B @ 180 wpm)

They have just started the new building. It is considered one of the feats of the century. The building, when completed, will rise 73 stories, and it will be topped by the largest broadcasting antenna ever. The architect has given the building several unique features which give it a different look.

For one, the glass used is of a new type. It is highly resistant to damage from the wind. It also helps to prevent the interior from being subjected to the glare and the heat of the sun. It turns darker as the sun's rays grow hotter, and it has special optical properties to filter out the glare.

Another special feature is the glass and plastic elevator which goes up the exterior of the building to serve the rooftop lounge. It is designed to give the riders a feeling of floating in space. It is also designed to carry 100 passengers to the top in only three minutes.

The interior of the building contains 12 elevators which are almost as fast as the outside one. They are designed to be the safest ever put in any of the city's buildings.

When the ground was broken for the building last week, the mayor said that it was a historic day for the city. The building will represent the first stage of the renewal of the center city, and it will serve as the centerpiece for the new complex of office buildings to be erected around it.

Already the pilings are being driven into the soil, and the first steel girders are being erected. The construction superintendent says that it won't be long before the framework will begin to take shape.

In the special meeting for the press last night, the mayor gave the following additional information. The building should be open in 18 months. It will contain 300 offices and 42 shops on the first floor. When finished, it should provide space for 2,000 workers, and the building will require a maintenance crew of 40. The air conditioning system will be large enough to cool the homes in one square mile of the city.

The building will also have underground parking for 3,000 cars on eight levels. It will also be connected to the new subway system expected to be completed in the next few years. The goal is to make it easy for the populace to get to and from the new office and shopping area.

The building has already been praised by the people as the most important new thing to happen in the city in the last decade. It is felt that the building will serve to bring new life to the city and to reverse the trend to decay.

"It is important," the mayor told us, "that the people of the nation see the city as a dynamic force, and it is our hope that the erection of this building will serve to renew the faith of the nation in the ability of the city to reverse the collapse of city life and the problems associated with it."

THE (T-)
THEY (THAEU)
Ex. RT-21 (Tape 1/B @ 125 wpm) & RT-21 (Tape 1/B @ 180 wpm)

The treatment of the elderly has been the subject of much talk in recent years. People have come to the realization that old people are not being given a fair deal by society. Older people have to live on fixed incomes. They find that their pensions or Social Security are just not adequate. They have been forced to live in second class housing, and they often must subsist on inadequate diets because they cannot afford to buy the food they need.

The aged have also been neglected. They have often been sent off to live in homes and institutions by their families. In many of those places, they have been mistreated or ignored. They have received inadequate medical care, and they have often just been left to die.

It seems that many people have the attitude that, when people have stopped working, they are only burdens to society and that they are no longer the responsibility of anyone. Many people complain that they pay taxes to help support old people who are of no use to the nation. They seem to forget that they will soon be old, too.

It is always sad to see the aged sitting alone in the park with nothing to do, ignored by the people around them. They are the innocent victims of the attitude that a person is socially dead at 65.

Happily, though, many Americans now realize that the elderly can still contribute much to the society. New programs have been created which can make use of the wisdom and the experience of the older citizens both to help the nation and to give the older people a sense of productivity. Old people are now serving as foster grandparents to children and as consultants to businesses. They are serving as babysitters in child care centers. They are teaching people some of the skills that they have learned. They are beginning to get a chance to show the nation that they have something to offer.

Happily, too, there is more being done to improve the care of the aged. A more humane approach is replacing the older one. Efforts are being made to see that the aged have housing they can afford and that they have adequate food and medical care. Charitable and governmental agencies seem to be making a real effort to see that the elderly have the care and the comfort that they have earned over the years.

The important thing is that the efforts to help and involve the aged not be slowed down or ended. The new trend must not be reversed. The plight of the aged is not yet over. They still often must struggle to survive, and they still face the coldness and neglect of many people.

The effort to help the elderly and to educate the younger people about the problems of the aged must continue. The time has come when people must see that the aged have the opportunity to live the remainder of their lives happily.

 StenEd® **Step 2: High Frequency Words**

OF (OF)
IF (TP-)
HAVE (SR-)
VERY (SR-R)
Ex. RT-22 (Tape 1/B @ 125 wpm) & RT-22 (Tape 1/B @ 180 wpm)

Very few people have seen as much of the world as the Dawsons. Mr. and Mrs. Dawson have run a very successful travel agency for many years. As part of this job, they have visited many of the world's cities and towns. They have always felt an obligation to check out places to visit to be sure of providing the very best of tours and accommodations. If they have found anything wrong, they have quickly taken care of it or removed the tour from their list of recommendations.

They have been to every city of Europe and the Americas at least once. They have amassed a very thorough list of the best hotels and restaurants. If anything new comes to their attention, they make a careful check of it.

The very first thing they have always tried to find out about a place is if it has something of interest to people. This has led them to a consideration of more than just London and Paris. They have discovered delightful little towns full of beautiful old churches or quaint villages perched at the very top of low peaks. These are the places that very few tourists are ever aware of but which very often have more to offer than the big cities. If there is something worth seeing anywhere, the Dawsons probably have information about it.

One of their most recent discoveries was a beautiful temple in Peru which is very old. As if that were not enough, they have discovered that the walls of the temple are covered with some of the most beautiful carvings yet seen. If enough people show interest, the Dawsons have plans to arrange a tour of the temple later in the year.

If these interests of theirs in the more exotic places have convinced you that they have neglected the traditional tours, you are mistaken. They have always been very careful with the kinds of tours most people take. They have earned a reputation for preparing packages which have enabled people to really enjoy their trips. The tour of England they have recently arranged was delightful and at a very modest price. If you would like to see Paris, the Dawsons have arranged a very attractive tour of that city.

I have almost neglected to mention the very important factor of service which the Dawsons have always stressed. If any traveler is ever dissatisfied with the tour, the Dawsons have always been glad to make it up in some way. This is a very rare attitude for the travel business. I have never heard of any other travel bureaus which have this policy.

If you are in the mood to travel, I have only one suggestion. See the Dawsons. Let them give you the benefit of their very great experience. They have, I am very sure, a tour which will fit your needs and budget. And, if you are at all adventurous, ask them to tell you about some of the exotic tours they have designed.

A   (A)
AN   (APB)
AND (APBD [SKP-])
Ex. RT-23 (Tape 2/A @ 125 wpm) & RT-23 (Tape 2/A @ 180 wpm)

A lion is an interesting and unusual beast. The "king of the beasts" is really a lazy and lethargic beast. A male lion is also a perfect "male chauvinist pig."

A male lion is usually surrounded by several females and their cubs. It is the female who must do all the hunting and caring for the young. While a female is out hunting, a male will spend his time sleeping and scratching. When the female has caught an antelope or some other beast, the male will come and eat his fill and the female cannot eat a bit until he is finished.

Lions eat a great deal at once and may not have to eat a meal for a few days afterward. Between meals, the entire family sprawls and sleeps in a shady spot. The rule is, of course, that a male gets the shadiest and softest spots.

The domination of the male starts early. A male cub will quickly assert himself over his sisters, and they will have to be careful and not anger him. By the time a male is grown, he is just as lazy and domineering as his father.

It is always interesting to observe a female sleeping and snoring under a tree. All a male has to do is walk over and give a single roar and the female will get up and leave the spot to him.

An interesting fact about lions is that a male can remain remarkably fit despite a life of indolence. This is because a male lion has an elaborate set of stretching exercises which keep his muscles strong. Supposedly, isometrics were discovered by a man watching a lion stretching and pacing in a zoo.

On a rare occasion, a male may be forced to help a female in the hunt. Even then, he limits his job to serving as a decoy while the female still has to catch and kill the prey.

The basic laziness and nonaggressive behavior of a male is a prime reason why most circus lions are males. A male lion is just naturally more docile and less likely to injure and maim a trainer. As long as he is well fed, a lion will generally not be a danger to man. This is not as true for a female since she must be more aggressive in a wild environment and does not take to a caged existence as well as a male.

An old circus lion tamer said he once had a lioness in an act he did. He said she was the only cat who had given him an ounce of trouble. He had a couple of scars and a nasty puncture mark to show for her stay. He said that a lioness is just meaner than an old grizzly bear. This may be an exaggeration, but it is not without a basis in fact.

A lion and a lioness can present quite a contrast in temperament and behavior. The next time you go to a zoo, watch the male and female. The male will be in a shady spot, and the female will be relegated to a less pleasant and comfortable spot.

    Step 2: High Frequency Words

TO (TO)
TOO (TAO)
TWO (TWO)

Ex. RT-24 (Tape 2/A @ 125 wpm) & RT-24 (Tape 2/A @ 180 wpm)

America has gotten a reputation as the nation where people want to own two of everything. There are many families with two cars, two televisions, and two phones. Now everyone wants to own two homes, too. The trend is growing to have a regular home and a vacation home, too.

This has led to a boom in recreational land. People are rushing to buy acreage in the mountains or by the shore. Unfortunately, this has led to various abuses, too. Unscrupulous real estate agents have sold land to people which is too marshy for houses to be built. They have sold land to trusting people which had no provisions for water or sanitation. There was even a case where land belonging to the government was "sold" to unsuspecting people.

Too often, people have listened to the vague promises about future clubhouses and swimming pools to be built nearby. Of course, the contracts fail to include any mention of them, and they never seem to be built. Unfortunately, it is too late to ask questions after the contract is signed.

There are two pieces of advice to be given to the prospective buyer of recreation land to avoid any later heartache.

First, do not rush to buy a piece of land simply because the sales agent says you can't afford to wait or intimates that the price is due to go up tomorrow. An honest salesperson will be willing to give you a chance to consider the purchase.

Go to see the land. Then go home to talk it over. Then come back two or three days later to look again. Do not allow the agent to use high pressure tactics to force you to sign. Take the time to check the agent and the land carefully. Be sure to find out from other people if they are happy with their land.

Secondly, before you sign a contract, take it to a lawyer. Let him or her check it to see if the agent's promises are in the contract. Remember, a contract is a legal document. You can't be too careful. If the sales rep won't allow you to do this, don't buy the land.

Try to get the agent to put an escape clause in the contract, too. This will allow you to cancel the sale within two weeks of the contract date. This gives you a chance to rethink the deal.

Be sure to find out what all the terms of the contract are. Remember that the contract obliges you to do certain things, too. You may have to do more than just make the payments. Don't be like the couple who bought two acres but found out that the contract forbade them to build a road to their land.

If you are careful to follow this advice, you will be able to buy a vacation homesite without being cheated. You, too, will be able to join the growing number of two-home families but without the problems which many people have to face.

IS (S-)
AS (AZ)
HIS (HEUZ)
Ex. RT-25 (Tape 2/A @ 125 wpm) & RT-25 (Tape 2/A @ 180 wpm)

His fame is widespread as a gardener. His house is surrounded by the most beautiful grounds in the area. His driveway is edged by roses as big as a man's fist. As one moves closer to the door, one sees his carefully trimmed shrubs which line his walkway.

The real showplace is the backyard. There are flowers in as many colors as one can imagine — roses, tulips, lilacs, and so forth. As I was passing the house one day, he was trimming the trees in front of his house. I had a chance to chat with him about his green thumb.

His gardening, he said, is a real relief from all the unpleasantness of the world. It is nice to come home from his job and look at his beautiful flowers and trees. It is also enjoyable to get out and work with his hands.

As I looked around at his yard, I asked if he was going to add any new plants to his garden.

"I sure am," he said. "As soon as I can clear a new area, I intend to plant some new rose bushes." His eyes sparkled as he described his plans. "Over there is where I will put them. They are a new kind, as big as small trees. Each flower is a very delicate shade of red.

"As long as you are here, let me show you something." He led me to the back of his house.

"This is my new Japanese garden. This area is made to look like the miniature gardens in Japan. Each tree is a perfect dwarf specimen. This one is my favorite." His hand pointed to a beautiful little tree. I had to agree with his opinion. It is surely the most beautiful thing I have seen.

Then, as we walked around the yard, his hands directed my gaze to various plants and flowers. His description of each one was delightful.

"This is a tea rose. Over there is a calla lily."

As I continued on his tour, I couldn't help but catch his enthusiasm. I had never realized how lovely nature is, but his description of his garden made it plain now.

Coming at last to a tree as high as his shoulder, he explained how it is the first peach tree he has planted. "When this tree produces peaches," he said, "they will be as sweet as honey." I could almost taste them, and I was sure to get his promise to let me try his peaches.

As I left his yard, I turned to wave at him. He gave me a smile and raised his hand. "Come back again," he called. "This garden is for everyone to enjoy."

That is one invitation I accepted gladly. I intend to visit his garden as soon as possible. It is just too beautiful not to enjoy often. I expect to be his most frequent visitor. That is a promise which I intend to keep as often as I can.

Step 2: High Frequency Words

WITH   (W-)
WERE   (W-R)
Ex. RT-26 (Tape 2/A @ 125 wpm) & RT-26 (Tape 2/A @ 180 wpm)

Some of the first cars were made with rather different materials than those of today. Instead of being made with steel and glass and plastic, these earliest cars were most often made with wood and iron.

Some of the first cars, which were made in Germany, were nothing more than modified carriages with wooden bodies. Most of these early cars were made with hand-built wooden bodies. The wheels were of wood with the outer rims surrounded with iron bands. The tops and the seats were made with canvas and with leather. The small engines, with only one or two cylinders, were made with cast iron and brass. There were no transmissions or brakes, only a chain drive. Steering was with a tiller, not with a wheel.

These very early cars were not fast. In fact, many were slower than carriages. They could never win a race with a horse. Their small, inefficient engines were no match for a thoroughbred.

With time, new developments were seen. Shortly after the turn of the century, there were racing cars which were capable of speeds of over 40 miles per hour. Cars were now equipped with transmissions, brakes, and steering wheels. Wooden bodies were still in evidence, but many cars were made with steel now.

Engines were, of course, much better. There were engines with four, six, and even more cylinders. The engines were more powerful and more efficient. Some cars were equipped with engines with 40 horsepower or more.

Many of these later cars were still very much like carriages, but the shapes with which we are familiar were beginning to appear. Cars were equipped with hoods and with fenders. Windshields were in evidence on some, and rubber tires were becoming common. Even colors besides black were available with some cars.

With the next decade, new changes were even more in evidence. Early attempts at streamlining were made with racing cars, and a number of new designs and ideas were tried. Cars were made with steam and electric motors. Electric headlights were added to some cars, with night driving made more practical.

Along with these changes, cars were becoming affordable. Henry Ford had set up his production line, and cars were being made in numbers. Anyone with a few hundred dollars could buy a car. People were rushing to buy these new machines and were beginning to motorize America.

In the span of about two decades, cars were changed from slow carriages with engines to reasonably quick and efficient machines with many of the features which were to be standard on cars from that time on.

The following decades were to see further changes. Cars would be equipped with sleeker bodies, with radios, with air conditioners, and with various power devices, but there were fewer real changes than those in the first two decades of the automobile's history. The basic concepts of the car of today were, with a few changes, established by 1910.

BE   (PW-)
BEEN   (PW-PB)
Ex. RT-27 (Tape 2/A @ 125 wpm) & RT-27 (Tape 2/A @ 180 wpm)

The old song says, "What will be, will be." Until recent times, this has been the attitude of many people. But this attitude can no longer be accepted. The uncontrolled growth we have been experiencing for several centuries must be replaced with a new attitude. This new attitude can be summed up as, "What will be, will be planned." This change of attitude has been brought into existence by two new types of people: urban planners and futurists.

Urban planners have to be a special breed of person. They have been trained in architecture, civil engineering, and sanitary engineering. They have often been trained in sociology and psychology as well so as to be able to understand the human problems which have been created in cities. An urban planner must be prepared to meet all difficulties which have been experienced by cities and which might be experienced in the future.

The urban planners have to be able to plan for the future growth and renewal of the city so that the haphazard growth which has been the past pattern will not be continued. Their goal must be to make the city a place which can be a safe, beautiful, and exciting home for people. They try to be sure that future growth will be directed toward this goal and that people's real needs in the city will be met. The urban planner has to be a person of rare skill to be able to direct the growth of the city.

The futurist has been another new arrival on the scene. Futurists attempt to project what will be from what has been. They look at what has been happening in some area of life and attempt to project what the results will be. Their goal is to be able to give people a picture of what their life will be like in the future so that they will be able to plan for it.

Futurists realize that the era when people have been surprised by changes in the world must be ended. Using the latest computers, they have been able to warn people of the dangers to be faced from pollution and abuse of resources. They have been able to show how new plans might be able to avert disaster.

Futurists have been a valuable source of information for urban planners as well. Using the projections of futurists, urban planners have been able to make plans which will be most effective on a long-term basis. They have thus been able to make the best choices from the plans that have been proposed or to see where new plans need to be created.

Urban planners and futurists, working together, can be extremely important to the future. Given a chance, they will be able to help make this a better world to live in than it has been. They will be able to make sure that future development will truly be in accordance with the best interests of society, which has not always been the case.

© 1993, 2001 *StenEd*®   **Step 2: High Frequency Words**

I   (EU)
EYE   (KWRAOEU)
Ex. RT-28 (Tape 2/A @ 125 wpm) & RT-28 (Tape 2/A @ 180 wpm)

He lost an eye as a child in a hunting accident, which explains the patch. His father's shotgun accidentally fired, and several pellets lodged in his face and eye.

"I guess I am lucky," he said, "that I wasn't closer, or I might have lost the other eye, too."

He has never let the loss of his eye get him down, though. Even with only one eye, he is a better man than most. In fact, he has come to regard his single eye as a rather distinctive feature and now wears the rakish patch over the eye.

I recently asked him to tell me the whole story of his childhood accident. He told me this story:

"I was only nine years old at the time. I had gone out into the woods with my father to hunt. I was trying to keep an eye out for rabbits. My father was looking for rabbits, too, and keeping his eye on me as well. Being a little boy, I ran ahead. I was perhaps 50 yards in front of him. I heard him yell and I turned. Just as I turned, I was struck in the right side of the face and eye by several shotgun pellets. I remember I screamed, and my father did, too. I remember that my eye hurt a lot, and then I fainted.

"I found out later that my father had tripped on a root and that the gun had fired as he fell, with the pellets striking my eye.

"The next thing I remember was that I woke up in the hospital. I could feel a large bandage over my eye. The doctor came in with my father and told me what had happened. He told me that he had tried to save the eye with a delicate eye operation but that there was too much damage to the eye. Finally, he had been forced to remove the eye since it might cause more serious problems.

"I don't think I really understood what had happened at first. I just didn't connect the bandage on my eye with what had happened. I think it took me a good 10 minutes to realize that I had really lost an eye. Then, I remember, I cried a lot.

"The doctor came back the next day and explained how I could get along quite well with one eye. He said that I would look like a young pirate — a thrilling idea for a little boy.

"I guess being young helped a lot. I think an older person would have had a harder time getting used to having just one eye. After I got over the first shock, I just never let it bother me.

"I think the hardest part was to get my father to realize that he was not to blame for the accident and the loss of the eye. It took a while, but he got over it, too.

"The one thing that I did learn from this is that eye care is important. Since I only have one eye, I always make sure I see the eye doctor often so I don't lose that other eye."

HAD (HAD)
DID (TKEUD)
Ex. RT-29 (Tape 2/B @ 125 wpm) & RT-29 (Tape 2/B @ 180 wpm)

Q   Mr. Gerber, did you say that you had occasion to visit Mr. Long in the course of your business?

A   I did. Mr. Long was a regular customer. He had been for some time.

Q   Did you visit his home on the morning in question?

A   Yes, I did. I had some items to bring him.

Q   Can you tell us what you did when you got to his house?

A   Yes, sir. I had to get the stuff out of the truck first. Then I had to walk up the front steps. I went to the door and knocked.

Q   Did you observe anything at that time?

A   I noticed that the front door had been left open. That did strike me as strange. Mr. Long did not make it a practice to leave his door open.

Q   What did you do next?

A   Well, I had been at the door a couple of minutes with no answer, so I yelled through the door.

Q   Did you get an answer?

A   No, sir. So then, I stuck my head in. That's something I did on occasion. That's when I saw what had happened.

Q   What did you see?

A   I saw Mr. Long on the floor. He had his head at a funny angle, and there was blood.

Q   What did you do then?

A   I did nothing for a minute. I had no idea what had happened. I was scared, I guess. Then I called to him. He did not move. Then I went closer. That's when I saw he had died.

Q   Mr. Long was dead? How did you know?

A   Well, I felt his pulse, but he did not have one. I had been a medic in the Army.

Q   What did you do next?

A   I called the police.

Q   How soon did the police come?

A   In just a few minutes.

Q   Did you stay at the scene after the police had come?

A   Yes, sir. I stayed until I had told the officers what I had seen and had given them my name and all.

Q   While you were waiting for the police, did you see anything unusual?

A   Well, I did see that the furniture was out of place. Mr. Long had always kept his house neat and had always had his furniture placed just so.

Q   You had been in the house before?

A   Yes, sir. I had been in the house several times making deliveries.

Q   What else did you notice?

A   I saw that some books had fallen or had been thrown to the floor and that the desk drawer had been left open.

Q   How was Mr. Long lying on the floor?

A   He had his face down, and he had his mouth open.

Q   Did you see anything besides blood around his body?

A   Yes, sir. I did see his wallet next to his body.

Q   Did it have anything in it?

A   I did not notice. I did see a piece of paper next to it.

Q   Did you pick up the paper?

A   No, sir. I had always heard that you shouldn't touch any clues.

Q   Did you see anything else?

A   No, sir. I did not.

    StenEd®   **Step 2: High Frequency Words**

HER (HER)
HERE (HAOER)
HEAR (HAER)

Ex. RT-30 (Tape 2/B @ 125 wpm) & RT-30 (Tape 2/B @ 180 wpm)

People have been coming here from miles around to hear Ms. Young's new band. They have been packing the hall to hear her and her fellow musicians playing her new music. Several critics, who arrived here last week, were astounded to hear such music coming from a woman. It seems that some male attitudes have not changed despite her obvious talent.

Her first show last night gave her a chance to have the public hear some new compositions for the first time. Such tunes as "Here and Now" and "You'll Hear From Us" were greeted with enthusiasm. Here, as in other towns where she plays, her music seems to always create great excitement, as also does her great ability to truly entertain an audience.

Unfortunately, there are not too many more days to hear this remarkable woman and her remarkable band here in town. On Sunday, she and her group will leave here for an engagement in New York where people have paid up to $75 to hear her and where all the tickets were sold out in two hours.

Unfortunately, it also seems unlikely that she will be back here for some time as there are plans for her to tour Europe and South America, where fans have been clamoring to hear her and her group. If you are lucky enough to have a ticket to one of her concerts while she is here in town, don't miss this opportunity to hear a rare and unique talent. You may never hear such music again here in town. Don't miss her.

THEIR   (THAEUR)
THERE   (THR-)
THERE IS (THR-S)   THERE ARE (THR-R)
THEY ARE   (THAEU/R- [THER])
Ex. RT-31 (Tape 2/B @ 125 wpm) & RT-31 (Tape 2/B @ 180 wpm)

There are many people who spend their lives as drug addicts. They are not the narcotics addicts you always read about. They are alcoholics. Alcoholism is the greatest drug problem there is. There are more alcoholics than there are narcotic addicts. More people lose their lives because of alcohol than lose their lives from narcotics. And, unlike the narcotics addict, alcoholics often take their families and their friends with them in bloody accidents and acts of violence.

Many people think that there are alcoholics only in the slums and skid rows of the nation. In fact, there are alcoholics in all walks of life. There are alcoholics who do their drinking in mansions, and there are those who do their drinking in alleys. There are women alcoholics, and there are men alcoholics. There are even teenage alcoholics.

Why do these people waste their lives in drink? No one knows for sure. There is some evidence that there are chemical imbalances in the body which make people susceptible to alcoholism. There is also evidence that people turn to drink to hide from their psychological problems. There are some researchers who believe that both elements are factors.

If there is one point of agreement, it is that alcoholism is a disease. Researchers who have spent their lives trying to discover how to help alcoholics are unanimous in their opinion that alcoholism is a sickness. Their evidence is sufficiently clear so that there is no longer a reason to consider alcoholism as a crime.

If there is a reason to believe alcoholism is a disease, what is there to be done to cure the alcoholic? How can one help these people to straighten out their lives and to rejoin their families and communities as productive citizens?

One of the most effective measures has been self-help. There are a number of organizations, such as Alcoholics Anonymous, which have spent their time and energies in helping the alcoholic. Their success has been gratifying in helping those alcoholics who have come to realize their problems and who were ready to seek to control their alcoholism.

Unfortunately, such groups can only help alcoholics who are prepared to face their problem. This is only a small percentage. These groups cannot force their help on the alcoholic. There must be a commitment on the alcoholic's part, and he must come seeking their help.

Increasingly, researchers are turning their attention toward true cures for alcoholics. There are intensive programs to find if there are psychological, psychiatric, or medical procedures which can permanently cure alcoholics.

Are there treatment methods, or are there medicines which can stop alcoholism? Are there ways of finding out potential alcoholics and preventing their ever becoming alcoholics? Researchers are now spending their time seeking answers to these questions. There is real hope that there are answers which will be found soon.

If there is to be a long-term solution to alcoholism, it must come from this research. There are just too many people wasting their lives and their money on alcohol for alcoholism to be allowed to continue its ravages.

       Step 2: High Frequency Words

AM (APL)
HIM (HEUPL)
MANY (PH-)

Ex. RT-32 (Tape 2/B @ 125 wpm) & RT-32 (Tape 2/B @ 180 wpm)

I am sure that you have seen him many times on television. He is that big actor who always plays a villain. I am certain that you would recognize him immediately.

I am not sure, though, that you would recognize him when he is away from the camera. When he is not working, you can find him surrounded by as many as 50 children. Despite his villainous roles, children naturally love him. I am positive that children know him for what he is—a kind and gentle man.

I am reminded of the time, many months ago, when we first met. I heard the excited voices of many children laughing near the pool. Going nearer, I saw him sitting in a chair making as many faces as he could think of. The children were laughing at him and having a grand time. Many of them were looking at him with what I am convinced was love.

I remember I said to him, "I am not disturbing you, am I?"

"Of course not," he said.

That is how I met him.

The next time I saw him, he was surrounded by so many children that he could hardly move. Many of the children were laughing so hard at him and his many stories that they were near tears.

He invited me over, and I sat down by him to enjoy his antics with the children. I generally am a serious person, but I was soon laughing at him, too.

I remember I later asked him if he was bothered by so many children. "Many," he said. "There are never too many. I am lost without children."

I am not aware of a single child who does not like him. I am again reminded of the little boy who was very sick in the hospital. This famous actor, when he heard about him, gathered up as many toys as he could and went to see him. I remember how he spent many long hours cheering him up.

I am trying not to sound silly, but I am unable to talk about him without praising him. He is, without a doubt, the finest person I am acquainted with. That is saying a lot, for I am acquainted with many people.

There is one other thing about him I am sure you would want to know. Despite his roles in films—and there are many—which require him to be mean, he is never cruel.

He says, "I know I am always a villain, but I am never a vicious one. I am never going to give a bad example to my many young friends. I always tell them that I am sure they know I am only acting on the screen."

I only wish you had the chance to know him as I know him. I am convinced that you would find him as wonderful as I do. It is too bad that many of his fans only know him as a bad man and do not know him as the best friend that many children will ever have.

THAN (THAPB)
THEN (THEPB)
Ex. RT-33 (Tape 2/B @ 125 wpm) & RT-33 (Tape 2/B @ 180 wpm)

Q   Mrs. Smith, will you describe what happened then?

A   I had just gotten off the bus not more than a second before. I remember it was a little later than I normally get home, but then the streets were covered with snow, and traffic was slower than usual. Then, as I turned to walk toward my house, I saw a car skidding toward me. When I first saw it, it was no farther than I am to the judge.

I tried to jump out of the way, but then my foot slipped. Then I remember the bumper of the car struck me.

Q   What happened then?

A   I really don't remember. I must have fainted then. When I woke up, there were more people around me than I could count. Then an ambulance pulled up and took me to the hospital.

Q   How long were you in the hospital?

A   I was in the hospital for more than two weeks. My back was injured, and I spent more than two months at home getting therapy.

Q   Just a moment. You spent more than two weeks in the hospital. How much more than two weeks?

A   Two or three days. Then they sent me home.

Q   Then you spent two months at home?

A   More than two months.

Q   Then what happened?

A   Then I had pains again, worse than ever. I went back to the hospital then. The doctors said a disk was rapidly deteriorating. All I know is I hurt more than I could stand.

Q   How long were you in the hospital this time, then?

A   More than a month.

Q   Then you were released?

A   Yes, sir.

Q   What was done in the hospital?

A   I had an operation.

Q   Then the condition was corrected?

A   No, sir. The pain is better than before. He couldn't do more than that.

Q   What is your condition now?

A   I am partially paralyzed. The doctor says I may recover, but it will take more than five years of treatment.

Q   How much will that cost?

A   More money than I have.

Q   How much more?

A   More than $200,000.

Q   Then you will need more than $200,000 and more than five years to recover?

A   Yes, but the doctor says that I may never be better than I am now.

Q   All of this was a result of being struck by the car, then?

A   Yes, sir.

Q   Did you work before the accident?

A   Yes. I was an office manager. I had been for more than 11 years.

Q   How long, then, since you have worked?

A   Since the accident. Better than a year now.

Q   How much were you making then?

A   Then I made $34,000 per year.

Q   Did you ever return to work?

A   No, sir. First there was the pain and then the paralysis. I can't do more than the simplest tasks and would need to do a lot better than I can now to be able to go back to work.

Q   Then you are unemployed?

A   Yes, sir. Other than some savings, I have no income. I would not have been eligible for a pension for more than three years.

          StenEd®   Step 2: High Frequency Words

STEP 3
INFLECTED ENDINGS

In pre-computer theories, the inflected endings "-(e)s," "-ed," and "-ing" were attached to the same stroke when possible. This created numerous conflicts. For realtime, conflict-free writing, these three inflected endings should be written as separate strokes.

-(e)s	/-S	-ed	/-D	-ing	/-G

Many experienced reporters initially resist this technique, feeling it will slow them down. Please give it a try. Many realtime writers, including captioners, have adopted this technique, solved hundreds of conflicts—without having to memorize new outlines—and have commented the speed loss was very temporary. It's an easy habit to get into, and most writers who adopt this technique are delighted with the results.

Following are examples of the types of word conflicts avoided by writing these inflected endings as separate strokes.

plays	PHRAEU/-S	banned	PWAPB/-D	sinning	SEUPB/-G
place	PHRAEUS	band	PWAPBD	sing	SEUPBG
tens	TEPB/-S	billed	PWEUL/-D	stabbing	STAB/-G
tense	TEPBS	build	PWEULD	stack	STABG

There are three common pre-computer briefs that cause a disproportionate amount of conflicts—both word and word boundary (where one word ends and another begins)—when writing for the computer. If you use /-S, /-D, or /-G for any high frequency words, you'll want to change your outline as soon as possible. (You may have already made some of these changes during *Step 2: High Frequency Words*.)

/-S	should only be used for the inflected ending "-(e)s."
	(is = S-, as = AZ, his = HEUZ)
/-D	should only be used for the inflected ending "-ed."
	(had = HAD, did = TKEUD)
/-G	should only be used for the inflected ending "-ing."
	(go = TKPWO, gone = TKPWOPB)

This will not only avoid many word conflicts, but many word boundary problems will also be solved.

ten is	TEPB/S-	fine had	TPAOEUPB/HAD	mob go	PHOB/TKPWO
tens	TEPB/-S	fined	TPAOEUPB/-D	mobbing	PHOB/-G
tense	TEPBS	find	TPAOEUPBD	mock	PHOBG

Using /-S, /-D, and /-G as separate strokes will also resolve conflicts resulting from some common writing techniques and briefs and phrases that are part of many reporter's styles.

rugs	RUG/-S	corrode	KROED	if I should	TPEURBD
Russian	RUGS	crowed	KROE/-D	fished	TPEURB/-D
twigs	TWEUG/-S	brig	PWREUG	so he could	SOEBGD
tuition	TWEUGS	bringing	PWREU/-G	soaked	SOEBG/-D

There are a few exceptions to making the /-S, /-D, and, -G a separate stroke:

It is recommended that you use -DZ for words ending in -ds since coming back for the /-S is awkward. (For example, grades = TKPWRAEUDZ, not TKPWRAEUD/-S.)

The inflected forms of <u>single stroke briefs with no vowels</u> are written by adding the -S, -D, or -G on the same stroke as the base word, if it fits. Similarly, multistroke outlines whose last stroke contains no vowels may add the inflected ending on that last stroke.

ask	SK-	have	SR-	battles	PWAT/-LS
asks	SK-S	having	SR-G	battled	PWAT/-LD
asked	SK-D	will	HR-	battling	PWAT/-LG
asking	SK-G	wills	HR-S	helps	HEL/-PS [H*EP/-S]
be	PW-	willed	HR-D	risked	REUS/-KD
being	PW-G	willing	HR-G	rumbles	RUPL/-BLS

Other words which do not require a separate stroke for an inflected ending:

doing	TKOEUPBG	does	TKUZ	laid	HRAEUD
going	TKPWOEUPBG	goes	TKPWOEZ	paid	PAEUD
				said	SAEUD

Words ending in **-ings** are written as follows:

buildings	PWEULD/-GS	feelings	TPAOEL/-GS	killings	KEUL/-GS
clippings	KHREUP/-GS	findings	TPAOEUPBD/-GS	meetings	PHAOET/-GS
dealings	TKAOEL/-GS	hearings	HAER/-GS	rulings	RAOUL/-GS

Note: -GS is also used for words ending with the -shun sound but not as a stroke by itself; e.g., portion = PORGS, division = TKEU/SREUGS [TKWEUGS]. /-GS as a stroke by itself represents -ings.

Other inflected endings will be covered in *Step 6: Suffixes and Word Endings.*

ACTION STEP
Since inflected endings will occur regularly in your daily taking, most of your practice for Step 3 will occur on the job. To get you started, take the practice exercises on pages 40-44.

The word exercise shows the types of conflicts resolved by using this technique. The sentence exercises use these words in sentences. The sentences are challenging, so don't become discouraged. You will probably want to review these sentences often until coming back for these endings becomes natural to you.

In Steps 1 and 2, it was suggested that you only change one outline at a time. For this step, it is suggested that you adopt this method of writing these three inflected endings at the same time since they all follow the same principle.

DICTIONARY MAINTENANCE
If you write long vowels, have eliminated all of your high frequency word conflicts, and are writing inflected endings "-(e)s," "-ed," and "-ing" as separate strokes, you will notice a remarkable improvement in your translations. But first, you have to update your CAT dictionary to reflect any changes in your writing style. As usual, changing your personal CAT dictionary, a principle or two at a time, to reflect the way you *want* to write, reinforces your change(s).

© 1993, 2001 *StenEd*®

It is recommended that you add these three inflected endings as suffixes in your CAT dictionary.

/-S	=	delete space s
/-D	=	delete space ed
/-G	=	delete space ing

You can then delete your old outlines that attach the inflected ending to the base word stroke. That is, you may delete PAEUS for pays since you will be writing PAEU/-S; PWAPBD for banned since you will be writing it PWAPB/-D, etc. This will make your dictionary smaller and more efficient.

Important: If the spelling of the base word is changed when adding an inflected ending (e.g., tax + s = taxes, not taxs; ban + ed = banned, not baned; hope + ing = hoping, not hopeing), you will have to add these words separately unless your CAT system has artificial intelligence that automatically corrects the spelling when inflected endings are added to a base word. If your CAT system does not have this capability, you will have to make a separate entry for each word in which there is a spelling change when an inflected ending is attached to the base word.

The following entries should be in your CAT dictionary in order for the base words "tax," "ban," and "hope" and their three inflected forms to translate correctly.

WITHOUT ARTIFICIAL INTELLIGENCE		WITH ARTIFICIAL INTELLIGENCE	
English	**Outline**	**English**	**Outline**
tax	TABGS	tax	TABGS
taxes	TABGS/-S		
ban	PWAPB	ban	PWAPB
banned	PWAPB/-D		
banning	PWAPB/-G		
hope	HOEP	hope	HOEP
hoped	HOEP/-D		
hoping	HOEP/-G		
~s	-S	~s	-S
~ed	-D	~ed	-D
~ing	-G	~ing	-G

Note: The symbol "~" represents delete space, making these entries suffixes. Use whatever symbol works with your CAT system.

If your CAT system does not have artificial intelligence but does allow you to replace a stroke for a word (without deleting the entire entry and then adding a new entry to represent your new outline), you may search for the old entry (e.g., banned = PWAPBD), save the English portion of the entry, and replace the old outline with the new outline (e.g., banned = PWAPB/-D).

Following are word and paragraph exercises reinforcing the material covered in Step 3. These exercises are also available on audio cassette.

Practice the exercises that cover the technique you are adopting. **Concentrate on coming back for the /-S, /-D, and /-G endings. Write other words the same as you normally would, even if they currently represent a conflict.** (They will be covered in a later step.)

STEP 3—EXERCISES

INFLECTED ENDINGS

Ex. RT-34 (Tape 2/B @ 60 wpm) & RT-34 (Tape 2/B @ 90 wpm)

pays	PAEU/-S	banned	PWAPB/-D	blabbing	PWHRAB/-G
pace	PAEUS	band	PWAPBD	black	PWHRABG
plays	PHRAEU/-S	warred	WAR/-D	stabbing	STAB/-G
place	PHRAEUS	ward	WARD	stack	STABG
rays	RAEU/-S	bayed	PWAEU/-D	mobbing	MOB/-G
race	RAEUS	bade	PWAEUD	mock	MOBG
trays	TRAEU/-S	brayed	PWRAEU/-D	robbing	ROB/-G
trace	TRAEUS	braid	PWRAEUD	rock	ROBG
curs	KUR/-S	stayed	STAEU/-D	sobbing	SOB/-G
curse	KURS	staid	STAEUD	sock	SOBG
fears	TPAOER/-S	swayed	SWAEU/-D	clubbing	KHRUB/-G
fierce	TPAOERS	suede	SWAEUD	cluck	KHRUBG
hers	HER/-S	billed	PWEUL/-D	dubbing	TKUB/-G
hearse	HERS	build	PWEULD	duck	TKUBG
peers	PAOER/-S	fined	TPAOEUPB/-D	subbing	SUB/-G
pierce	PAOERS	find	TPAOEUPBD	suck	SUBG
scares	SKAEUR/-S	mined	PHAOEUPB/-D	banning	PWAPB/-G
scarce	SKAEURS	mind	PHAOEUPBD	bang	PWAPBG
sours	SOUR/-S	wined	WAOEUPB/-D	sinning	SEUPB/-G
source	SOURS	wind	WAOEUPBD	sing	SEUPBG
tens	TEPB/-S	pried	PRAOEU/-D	thinning	THEUPB/-G
tense	TEPBS	pride	PRAOEUD	thing	THEUPBG
sins	SEUPB/-S	sighed	SAOEU/-D	winning	WEUPB/-G
since	SEUPBS	side	SAOEUD	wing	WEUPBG
dies	TKAOEU/-S	tied	TAOEU/-D	running	RUPB/-G
dice	TKAOEUS	tide	TAOEUD	rung	RUPBG
pries	PRAOEU/-S	rowed	ROE/-D	stunning	STUPB/-G
price	PRAOEUS	road	ROED	stung	STUPBG
pros	PROE/-S	toed	TOE/-D	sunning	SUPB/-G
prose	PROEZ	toad	TOED	sung	SUPBG
sacks	SABG/-S	bored	PWOER/-D	bashing	PWARB/-G
sax	SABGS	board	PWAORD	bark	PWARBG
tacks	TABG/-S	holed	HOEL/-D	dashing	TKARB/-G
tax	TABGS	hold	HOELD	dark	TKARBG
tucks	TUBG/-S	soled	SOEL/-D	gnashing	TPHARB/-G
tux	TUBGS	sold	SOELD	narc	TPHARBG
laps	HRAP/-S	tolled	TOL/-D	mashing	PHARB/-G
lapse	HRAPS	told	TOELD	mark	PHARBG
pulls	PUL/-S	rued	RAOU/-D	stashing	STARB/-G
pulse	PULS	rude	RAOUD	stark	STARBG

 Step 3: Inflected Endings

INFLECTED ENDINGS
Ex. RT-35 (Tape 2/B @ 125 wpm) & RT-35 (Tape 2/B @ 180 wpm)

1. This is the <u>place</u> they <u>hold</u> <u>plays</u> every Saturday.

2. All hope for their future <u>dies</u> with a toss of the <u>dice</u>.

3. She <u>pries</u> into everyone's business, but will have to pay the <u>price</u>.

4. It <u>scares</u> me that clean air and water are becoming more <u>scarce</u>.

5. It <u>pays</u> to <u>pace</u> yourself when first beginning an exercise program.

6. He thought he would <u>lapse</u> into a coma after <u>running</u> so many <u>laps</u>.

7. They <u>decided</u> to <u>race</u> down to the beach to catch the last <u>rays</u> of the sun.

8. Whiskey <u>sours</u> had been the <u>source</u> of his <u>sins</u> <u>since</u> he could remember.

9. She <u>sold</u> the shoes she had just had <u>re-soled</u>.

10. The <u>rude</u> man <u>rued</u> the day he <u>cursed</u> the police officer.

11. She <u>sighed</u> when she <u>realized</u> they were not on her <u>side</u>.

12. The mule <u>brayed</u> loudly as they <u>braided</u> his messy mane.

13. I <u>tied</u> the boat to the pier so it wouldn't drift with the <u>tide</u>.

14. The suspect, <u>holed</u> up in the old factory, knew he could never again <u>hold</u> up his head with <u>pride</u>.

15. The <u>band</u> was <u>banned</u> from <u>performing</u> because of their x-rated <u>lyrics</u>.

16. The <u>staid</u> gentlemen <u>stayed</u> calm even though he couldn't <u>find</u> his wallet.

17. We <u>rowed</u> the boat across the lake to where our car was <u>parked</u> on the dirt <u>road</u>.

18. The commercial <u>said</u> that if you are <u>bored</u> with your life, come <u>board</u> a cruise ship.

19. He <u>swayed</u> to and fro and <u>tapped</u> his blue <u>suede</u> <u>shoes</u>.

20. He <u>plays</u> the <u>sax</u> in a jazz <u>band</u> by night, but <u>sacks</u> <u>groceries</u> by day.

21. We did not <u>mind</u> when their <u>dogs</u> <u>bayed</u> all night, but when they <u>mined</u> all the <u>diamonds</u> and <u>rubies</u> from the mountain, we <u>bade</u> them goodbye.

22. His <u>thinning</u> hairline doesn't mean a <u>thing</u> to him.

23. Has the phone <u>rung</u> since I came back from <u>running</u>?

24. The <u>stabbing</u> victim put the <u>papers</u> to be <u>signed</u> in a separate <u>stack</u>.

25. The <u>stark</u> reality is that she's <u>stashing</u> money away that isn't <u>hers</u>.

26. He was <u>dashing</u> into the <u>dark</u> alley when he heard the police siren.

27. The <u>sobbing</u> boy <u>said</u> they were <u>blabbing</u> that his <u>black</u> <u>sock</u> was full of <u>holes</u>.

28. The old woman <u>pried</u> the lid off the jar, <u>glowing</u> with <u>pride</u> that she did not have to ask for help.

29. He was <u>stung</u> when <u>told</u> that the <u>sequined</u> <u>tucks</u> on his <u>rented</u> <u>tux</u> were not as <u>stunning</u> as he had thought.

30. <u>Gnashing</u> his teeth, the <u>fierce</u> drug dealer <u>aroused</u> <u>fears</u> in the woman <u>narc</u> that a <u>black</u> <u>hearse</u> would soon be <u>hers</u>.

31. Before <u>robbing</u> the store, they threw a <u>rock</u> through the window, <u>mashing</u> some <u>bananas</u>, but apparently <u>hitting</u> their <u>mark</u>.

32. We <u>wined</u> and <u>dined</u> the night away until I was <u>surprised</u> to <u>find</u> that I had forgotten to <u>wind</u> my watch and would be <u>fined</u> for <u>being</u> late.

33. The children <u>tolled</u> the church bell until the <u>tense</u> priest <u>told</u> them they were <u>sinning</u> and that they would not be <u>allowed</u> to <u>sing</u> in the choir.

INFLECTED ENDINGS

Ex. RT-36 (Tape 3/A @ 125 wpm) & RT-36 (Tape 3/A @ 180 wpm)

Only the potentially conflicting pairs of words are underlined in the following sentences. However, all inflected endings should be written according to the principles presented in this step.

1. He <u>fears</u> the attacks of the <u>fierce</u> animals in the cage.

2. He had little <u>flecks</u> of lint all over his blue serge suit.
George likes to <u>flex</u> his muscles and impress the girls.

3. He <u>lacks</u> the ambition to work hard, and his grades reflect his <u>lax</u> attitude.

4. Because of his <u>lapse</u> of memory, he couldn't remember how many <u>laps</u> he had run.

5. We ate <u>lox</u> and bagels for lunch.
The neighborhood ladies were expert at picking the <u>locks</u> on all their neighbors' doors.

6. The horse that runs the fastest <u>pace</u> around the track <u>pays</u> the largest amount of money to the bettor.

7. We had to <u>place</u> the props carefully for the <u>plays</u> we are having tomorrow.

8. He often <u>reflects</u> upon his success as a singer.
Putting your hand to your mouth is generally a <u>reflex</u> action whenever you cough.

9. They hid the <u>sacks</u> of gold coins in a hole in the basement wall.
He had played the <u>sax</u> for years, but he needed more practice.

10. David makes himself <u>scarce</u> when he sees the large, vicious dog that <u>scares</u> him.

11. The <u>tacks</u> fell out of the box.
Income <u>tax</u> is due April 15.

12. She always tells the children a story as she <u>tucks</u> them into bed.
The <u>tux</u> is too worn to wear any more.

13. He <u>bade</u> his family good-bye as he set out on his journey.
The bad dog <u>bayed</u> at the moon.

14. The little girl wore her hair in a long <u>braid</u>. Even though the mule <u>brayed</u> loudly, his owner still beat it.

15. The carpenter hired to <u>build</u> the furniture <u>billed</u> the homeowner immediately.

16. That big, old, <u>decayed</u> log has been there for almost a <u>decade</u>.

17. He was <u>fined</u> $10 when he could not <u>find</u> his registration.

18. I would not <u>mind</u> if you <u>mined</u> coal if you enjoyed your job.

19. His <u>mode</u> of operation was to first trim the hedge before he <u>mowed</u> the lawn.

20. The poet <u>owed</u> an <u>ode</u> to his friend for the brilliant tribute which had been given to his new work.

21. His <u>pride</u> was hurt when he <u>pried</u> his way into the vault and found all the money had already been stolen.

22. She <u>rued</u> the day she had been so <u>rude</u> to him.

23. The insomnia sufferer <u>sighed</u> and turned on his <u>side</u>, prepared for another sleepless night.

24. He <u>sold</u> the newly <u>soled</u> boots to the customer.

25. A <u>staid</u> and serious man <u>stayed</u> until the end of the boring lecture.

26. He <u>swayed</u> slightly in the wind as he closed his <u>suede</u> jacket to keep warm.

27. She <u>tied</u> the boat to the piling before the <u>tide</u> came in.

(continued)

Step 3: Inflected Endings

28. I was told the bell in the town square tolled mournfully when the war hero was killed.

29. The gangs of each ward often warred with each other.

30. As they wined and dined on the terrace, the wind caused so much havoc they had to wind down the umbrella and move inside.

31. Most pros are happy to cooperate, but this pro is different.

32. The pay is not as good as I'd like, but at least the job pays regularly.

33. Did you find that the steep fine had made him drive more carefully?

34. The war had been hard on him. Since returning home, he has become a ward of the state.

35. Did all members of the club go to the mock trial?

INFLECTED ENDINGS
Ex. RT-37 (Tape 3/A @ 125 wpm) & RT-37 (Tape 3/A @ 180 wpm)

Because reporters, stenocaptioners, and stenotranscriptionists generally take from the spoken word, you must develop an extremely refined sense of hearing. The following sentences contain words with inflected endings that are often confused with other words because of their similar sound.

Only the soundalikes and near soundalikes are underlined in the following sentences. However, all inflected endings should be written according to the principles presented in this step.

1. The accidence of the strange African language confused the student.
   There have been several accidents at that corner.

2. His acts with the ax landed him in jail.

3. The judge's strict adherence to the law won him much respect.
   The cause of human freedom has many adherents.

4. The adolescents were experiencing the typical problems of surviving adolescence.

5. The doctor and his assistants offered assistance to the injured when the factory exploded.

6. Attendants stationed by the door took attendance at the meeting.

7. Based on her questionable reputation as a cook, she shouldn't even be allowed to baste the turkey.

8. Though she was often chased, she was determined to remain chaste.

9. The little girl was coated with mud after her romp in the field.
   He coded the message so only the club members could understand it.

10. The coward cowered in a corner when the fight started.

11. The dens of the forest animals were hidden in the dense undergrowth.
    There were five dents in the car after the accident.

12. The overwhelming dependence of ten dependents was too great a burden for the poor working man.

13. The incidence of the burglary incidents in our neighborhood was decreasing.

14. Many people consider themselves independents rather than democrats or republicans because they prefer the independence of not belonging to a particular political party.

(continued)

15. The innocents knew that their innocence would finally be proven.

16. Scientists often deal with events that occur within extremely short instants of time.
For instance, the speed of computers is often measured in microseconds.

17. Bob was a very intense young man, and nothing could sway him from his intents once they were fixed in his mind.

18. They graphed the information they had gathered concerning governmental graft on a very revealing graph.

19. He leased his house from the least considerate man in town.
You had better hurry lest you miss the show.

20. The amateur astronomer often lends his telescope lens to fellow stargazers.

21. At the bottom of the mast, the crew of the sailboat massed the sail into a large but tidy bundle.

22. You mince the onions for the main dish, and I'll set out the after dinner mints.

23. In the minds of the legislators, the strike at the coal mines was harmful to the nation's economy.

24. He missed seeing the abduction of his fiancee as he walked through the mist.

25. He mows the field most of the time with the tractor.
The mouse scurried under the sofa to avoid being eaten by the cat.

26. I must freshen up because the wind has mussed my hair.

27. There was too much mustard on the ham sandwich.
They somehow mustered up the strength to continue.

28. He paced across the room making mea-

surements before he began to paste wallpaper on the wall.

29. Even though many students failed the course in the past, all passed this time.

30. The tedious procedure performed by the doctor often tested the patience of his patients.

31. When they realized that the pact would not be advantageous, they packed to go.

32. The precedents of the case took precedence over the lawyers' personal views.
The past presidents of the club were invited to an honorary dinner.

33. He was given presents in the presence of his sister, but she did not receive any.

34. He guessed that his guest did not care for the room he had been given.

35. The residents of the apartment had lived at that residence for many years.

36. The farmer was rigid in his belief that a ridged hillside was the best way to grow his crop.

37. There seems to be an infinite number of religious sects.
It is illegal to discriminate on the basis of sex.

38. The teacher didn't show much tact when she tacked the failing grades on the bulletin board.

39. He looked tense as the man paid his bill in tens and twenties.
The tents looked fragile as they swayed in the wind.

40. They tracked the sales of the tract homes on a chart.

41. They were at variance with one another about the spelling variants between American English and British English.

 Step 3: Inflected Endings

STEP 4
SOUNDALIKES

Ode To My Spell Checker

I have a spelling checker,
It came with my PC;
It plainly marks four my revue,
Mistakes eye cannot sea.
I've run this poem threw it,
I'm shore your please too no,
Its letter perfect inn it's weigh,
My checker tolled me sew.

(author unknown)

In the English language, there are several hundred words known as **HOMOPHONES**. Homophones, often called homonyms, are two or more words which are pronounced the same but are spelled differently; e.g., hear and here. In order to make the most efficient use of CAT, homophones need to be differentiated.

The StenEd theory of writing has eliminated potential homophone conflicts by giving a conflict-free outline for each word in a homophone set. A summary of these logical, consistent rules for differentiating homophones is presented below.

In general, stenotype is a phonetic language. When two or more words sound alike, StenEd uses the spelling, when possible, to distinguish the words. Since you use the spelling to differentiate these words when typing or writing longhand, it is the most natural way to distinguish them when stenotyping. When following the spelling will not resolve the soundalike, other StenEd techniques are used.

All instruction material for soundalikes is given first; all exercises are at the end of the chapter. There is also a summary of soundalike resolutions beginning on page 53. Some of the potential conflicts in the summary are covered in more detail in other steps. This is especially true for conflicts that are avoided by distinguishing between common words and prefixes (e.g., be = PW-/, be- = PWE/) and common words and suffixes (e.g., or = OR/, -or = /[c]OR). Some of these were covered in *Step 2: High Frequency Words*. Others will be covered in more detail in *Step 5: Prefixes & Other Word Beginnings* and *Step 6: Suffixes & Other Word Endings*.

ACTION STEP
This is one of the longest chapters in this text. Don't let it intimidate you. Just work on one group of words at a time. Start with the long a sound. Once you are comfortable with distinguishing fair/fare, flair/flare, mail/male, plain/plane, etc., tackle the next vowel sound.

Of course some soundalike groups have repercussions with another group (e.g., air/ere/err/heir/hare/hair/here/hear/ear). Sometimes you just have to memorize. Fortunately, most soundalikes can be solved by following logical, consistent principles.

DICTIONARY MAINTENANCE
As with other steps, it is recommended that you change your personal CAT dictionary as you change your writing style.

SOUNDALIKES WITH THE SAME VOWEL SOUND

SOUNDALIKES WITH LONG A SOUNDS

If one of the soundalikes has an **ai** in the spelling, use **AEU** in the outline. Use **AE** in the outline for the other word of the pair. E.g., f<u>ai</u>r = TPAEUR, f<u>a</u>re = TPAER.

bail	PWAEUL	lain	HRAEUPB	pain	PAEUPB	tail	TAEUL
bale	PWAEL	lane	HRAEPB	pane	PAEPB	tale	TAEL
fair	TPAEUR	maid	PHAEUD	plain	PHRAEUPB	waive	WA*EUF
fare	TPAER	made	PHAED	plane	PHRAEPB	wave	WA*EF
flair	TPHRAEUR	mail	PHAEUL	sail	SAEUL	waist	WA*EUS
flare	TPHRAER	male	PHAEL	sale	SAEL	waste	WA*ES
gait	TKPWAEUT	main	PHAEUPB	stair	STAEUR		
gate	TKPWAET	mane	PHAEPB	stare	STAER		

If neither of the words has an ai spelling, but one does have an **ea** spelling, use **AE** in the outline. Use **AEU** in the outline for the other word of the pair.

bare	PWAEUR	brake	PWRAEUBG	grate	TKPWRAEUT	stake	STAEUBG
bear	PWAER	break	PWRAEBG	great	TKPWRAET	steak	STAEBG

This technique works for the vast majority of **long a** soundalikes. There are some **long a** soundalikes, however, that don't follow normal spelling or are part of a three-member set. Some of these are logical; some have to be memorized.

aid	AEUD	faint	TPAEUPBT	rain	RAEUPB	vain	SRAEUPB
aide	AED	feint	TPAEPBT	rein	RAEPB	vane	SRAEPB
ade	A*ED		[TPEPBT]	reign	RA*EUPB	vein	SRA*EUPB
aids	AEUDZ						
aides	AEDZ	hay	HAEU	ray	RAEU		
ades	A*EDZ	hey	HA*EU	re	R*E		
AIDS	A*EUDZ			Ray	RA*EU		

SOUNDALIKES WITH LONG E SOUNDS

If one of the soundalikes has an **ee** spelling, use **AOE** in the outline. Use **AE** in the outline for the other word of the pair. E.g., t<u>ee</u> = TAOE, t<u>ea</u> = TAE.

beach	PWAEFP	feat	TPAET	knead	TPHAED	seam	SAEPL
beech	PWAOEFP	feet	TPAOET	need	TPHAOED	seem	SAOEPL
beat	PWAET	flea	TPHRAE	peace	PAES	shear	SHAER
beet	PWAOET	flee	TPHRAOE	piece	PAOES	sheer	SHAOER
breach	PWRAEFP	grease	TKPWRAES	peal	PAEL	steal	STAEL
breech	PWRAOEFP	Greece	TKPWRAOES	peel	PAOEL	steel	STAOEL
cheap	KHAEP	heal	HAEL	read	RAED	tea	TAE
cheep	KHAOEP	heel	HAOEL	reed	RAOED	tee	TAOE
creak	KRAEBG	hear	HAER	real	RAEL	team	TAEPL
creek	KRAOEBG	here	HAOER	reel	RAOEL	teem	TAOEPL
dear	TKAER	jeans	SKWRAEPBS	sea	SAE	weak	WAEBG
deer	TKAOER	genes	SKWRAOEPB/-S	see	SAOE	week	WAOEBG
cede	SAED	discrete	TKEUS/KRAET	scene	SAEPB	suite	SWAET
seed	SAOED	discreet	TKEUS/KRAOET	seen	SAOEPB	sweet	SWAOET

 Step 4: Soundalikes

This technique works for the vast majority of **long e** soundalikes. There are some long e soundalikes, however, that don't follow normal spelling or are part of a three-member set.

chic	SHAEBG	key	KAOE	peak	PAEBG
	[SHAO*EBG]	quay	KAE	peek	PAOEBG
sheik	SHAOEBG			pique	PAO*EBG
(shake	SHAEUBG)				

Since both long A and long E homonyms can have the **ea** spelling, care must be taken to avoid creating one conflict while solving another. When creating your own outlines using any rules given, be sure you think through any possible conflicts.

Below are some three-member sets with **LONG A and LONG E**.

ail	AEUL	grate	TKPWRAEUT	plait	PHRAEUT	stale	STAEUL
ale	AEL	great	TKPWRAET	plate	PHRAET	steal	STAEL
eel	AOEL	greet	TKPWRAOET	pleat	PHRAOET	steel	STAOEL
eight	AEUGT	grace	TKPWRAEUS	rail	RAEUL	tail	TAEUL
ate	AEUT	grease	TKPWRAES	real	RAEL	tale	TAEL
eat	AOET	Greece	TKPWRAOES	reel	RAOEL	teal	TAOEL
dare	TKAEUR	mail	PHAEUL	sail	SAEUL	tear (a)	TAEUR
dear	TKAER	male	PHAEL	sale	SAEL	tear (e)	TAER
deer	TKAOER	meal	PHAOEL	seal	SAOEL	tier	TAOER
fair	TPAEUR	pace	PAEUS	stair	STAEUR	waive	WA*EUF
fare	TPAER	peace	PAES	stare	STAER	wave	WA*EF
fear	TPAOER	piece	PAOES	steer	STAOER	weave	WAO*EF

NOTE: (a) = long a sound, (e) = long e sound
Tear (a) and tear (e) will translate correctly whether use write TAEUR or TAER since they are spelled the same. However, when you hear the long a tear, it is most likely that you will write TAEUR, rather than TAER. The same is true of similar words such as use (n, pronounced YAOU<u>S</u>) and use (v, pronounced YAOU<u>Z</u>).

Three-member sets pose no problem. It is the sets that have four or more words that must be carefully thought through, such as:

hear	HAER	here	HAOER	hair	HAEUR	hare	HA*ER

Following are examples of sets with **long a and long e** sounds which consist of four or more words. Many members of these sets follow the long a and long e principle. Those that don't generally include an asterisk to make the distinction unless they are resolved by another principle. (Contractions such as he'll [HE/AOEL] are covered in *Step 7: Punctuation*.)

air	AEUR	fate	TPAEUT	lain	HRAEUPB	pail	PAEUL
ere	*ER	feat	TPAET	lane	HRAEPB	pale	PA*EUL
err	A*ER	feet	TPAOET	lean	HRAOEPB	peal	PAEL
heir	HA*EUR	fete	TPET	lien	HRAO*EPB	peel	PAOEL
hare	HA*ER						
hair	HAEUR	hail	HAEUL	main	PHAEUPB	pair	PAEUR
here	HAOER	hale	HA*EUL	Maine	PHA*EUPB	pare	PA*EUR
hear	HAER	heal	HAEL		[PHEFPLT]	pear	PAER
ear	AOER	heel	HAOEL		[PH*E/PH*E]	peer	PAOER
		he'll	HE/AOEL	mane	PHAEPB	pier	PAO*ER
bait	PWAEUT		[HAO*EL]	mean	PHAOEPB		
bate	PWA*ET			mien	PHAO*EPB	sane	SAEUPB
bathe	PWA*EUT	laid	HRAEUD	mesne	PHA*EPB	seine	SA*EUPB
beat	PWAET	lade	HRA*ED			seen	SAOEPB
beet	PWAOET	lead (N)	HRAED	mate	PHAEUT	scene	SAEPB
		lead (V)	HRAOED	meat	PHAET		
bare	PWAEUR	led	HRED	meet	PHAOET	vail	SRAEUL
bear	PWAER			mete	PHAO*ET	vale	SRAEL
beer	PWAOER					veil	SRA*EUL
bier	PWEUR					veal	SRAOEL

SOUNDALIKES WITH LONG I SOUNDS

Because there is no definite spelling pattern for words with **long i** soundalikes, there is no consistent principle for all sets. An asterisk is used in one member of the set. If one of the words contains a y, use the asterisk in that outline.

bite	PWAOEUT	die	TKAOEU	isle	AOEUL	sign	SAOEUPB
byte	PWAO*EUT	dye	TKAO*EU	aisle	AO*EUL	sine	SAO*EUPB
				I'll	EU/AOEL		
quite	KWAOEUT	hi	HEU		[*EUL]	rime	RAOEUPL
quiet	KWAO*EUT	high	HAOEU			rhyme	RAO*EUPL
	[KWAOEU/ET]	hie	HAO*EU	vile	SRAOEUL		
				vial	SRAO*EUL	time	TAOEUPL
slight	SHRAOEUGT	lie	HRAOEU			thyme	TAO*EUPL
sleight	SHRAO*EUGT	lye	HRAO*EU				

SOUNDALIKES WITH LONG O SOUNDS

When possible, use something in the spelling to distinguish **long o** soundalikes. When that is not possible, use an asterisk for one member of the set.

load	HROED	groan	TKPWROEPB	doe	TKOE	sole	SOEL
lode	HRO*ED	grown	TKPWROUPB	dough	TKOU	soul	SOUL
loan	HROEPB	moan	PHOEPB	throe	THROE	pole	POEL
lone	HRO*EPB	mown	PHOUPB	throw	THROU	poll	POL
road	ROED	shone	SHOEPB	toe	TOE	role	ROEL
rode	RO*ED	shown	SHOUPB	tow	TOU	roll	ROL
rowed	ROE/-D						
		throne	THROEPB	oh	O*E		
		thrown	THROUPB	owe	KWROE		

SOUNDALIKES WITH LONG U SOUNDS

For words with **long u** soundalikes, if one of the words has an (i)ew spelling, use AOU in that outline. (Use AO*U or U for the other members of the set.)

blew	PWHRAOU	flew	TPHRAOU	pew	PAOU	review	RE/SRAOU
blue	PWHRAO*U	flu	TPHRU	pugh	PAO*U	revue	RE/SRAO*U
	[PWHRU]	flue	TPHRAO*U				[RE/SRU]
		dual	TKAOUL				
		duel	TKAO*UL				

Below are some three-member sets with **LONG O and LONG U**. Some also include a soundalike containing a diphthong.

lore	HROER	shore	SHOER	rote	ROET
lure	HRAOUR	sure	SHAOUR	route	RAOUT
lower	HROE/ER			root	RAOT
		sore	SOER	rout	ROUT
pore	POER	soar	SAOR		
pure	PAOUR			show	SHOE
poor	PAOR	mote	PHOET	shoe	SHAOU
pour	POUR	mute	PHAOUT	shoo	SHAO
power	POU/ER	moot	PHAOT		
	[PO*UR]	moat	PHO*ET		

 Step 4: Soundalikes

SOUNDALIKES WITH DIPHTHONGS
AND OTHER LONG VOWEL SOUNDS

As usual, use something in the English spelling in the outline to distinguish the soundalikes when possible. Remember, words with the "oo" spelling are always written AO.

bole	PWOEL	suit	SAOUT	bow (o)	PWOE	all	AUL
boll	PWOL	soot	SAOT	beau	PWO*E	awl	A*UL
bowel	PWOU/EL			bough	PWOUG	al-	AL
	[PWO*UL]	troupe	TRAOUP	bow (ou)	PWOU	-al	/(c)AL
bowl	PWOUL	troop	TRAOP			Al	A*L
				mow	PHOU		
bore	PWOER	cue	KAOU	mown	PHOUPB	ball	PWAL
boor	PWAOR	queue	KWAOU	moan	PHOEPB	bawl	PWAUL
boar	PWOR	coo	KAO	mode	PHOED		
		coop	KAOP	moo	PHAO	bald	PWALD
horde	HOERD	co-op	KO/OP	mood	PHAOD	baud	PWAUD
hoard	HAORD	coup	KOUP			bawled	PWAUL/-D
			[KAO*U]	row (o)	ROE	balled	PWAL/-D
boarder	PWAORD/ER	coupe	KAOUP	roe	RO*E		
border	PWORD/ER			row (ou)	ROU	hall	HAL
		chews	KHAOU/-S			haul	HAUL
hoarse	HAORS	choose	KHAOZ	foul	TPOUL	Hal	HA*L
horse	HORS			fowl	TPO*UL		
						mall	PHAL
coarse	KOERS [KAORS]			boy	PWOEU	maul	PHAUL
course	KOURS			buoy	PWO*EU		
						dawn	TKAUPB
bolder	PWOELD/ER					don	TKOPB
boulder	PWOULD/ER					done	TKOEPB
						dun	TKUPB
						Don	TKO*PB

NOTE: (o) = long o sound, (ou) = ou sound

SOUNDALIKES WITH SHORT VOWEL SOUNDS

ant	APBT	done	TKOEPB	altar	AL/TAR
aunt	AUPBT	dun	TKUPB	alter	AL/TER
		don	TKOPB		[ALT/ER]
bread	PWRAED	Don	TKO*PB		
bred	PWRED			capital	KAP/TAL
(breed	PWRAOED)	none	TPHUPB	capitol	KAP/TOL
		nun	TPH*UPB		
breadth	PWRED/*T	(known	TPHOEPB)	carat	KA/RAT
breath	PWR*ET	non-	TPHOPB	caret	KA/RET
(breathe	PWRAO*ET)			carrot	KAR/OT
		one	WUPB		
cash	KARB	won	WOPB	desert (N)	TKEZ/ERT
cache	KAERB			desert (V)	TKE/SERT
		some	SOPL	dessert	TKES/SERT
earn	ERPB	sum	SUPL		
urn	URPB			morning	PHORPB/-G [PHORPBG]
		son	SOPB	mourning	PHOURPB/-G
heard	HAERD	sun	SUPB		
herd	HERD			whether	WHR-
				weather	W*ET/ER

SOUNDALIKES WITH THE SAME CONSONANT SOUND
INITIAL CONSONANTS

SOUNDALIKES BEGINNING WITH WH- & WR-

whet	WHET	wrack	WRABG
wet	WET	rack	RABG
while	WHAOEUL	wrap	WRAP
wile	WAOEUL	rap	RAP
whine	WHAOEUPB	wrest	WR*ES
wine	WAOEUPB	rest	R*ES
whit	WHEUT	wring	WREUPBG
wit	WEUT	ring	REUPBG
(witness	W-PBS)		
		write	WRAOEUT [WREU]
whole	WHOEL	rite	RAOEUT
hole	HOEL	(right	RAOEUGT)
		(Wright	WRAOEUGT)
wholly	WHOEL/HREU		
holy	HOE/HREU	wrote	WROET
	[HOEL/HREU]	rote	ROET

SOUNDALIKES WITH S- AND SOFT C-

cell	KREL	decent	TKE/SEPBT	recede	RE/SAED
sell	SEL	descent	TKE/SKREPBT	reseed	RE/SAOED
		dissent	TKEUS/SEPBT		
cellar	KREL/HRAR			cereal	KRAOER/KWRAL
seller	SEL/ER	recent	RE/KREPBT	serial	SAOER/KWRAL
		resent	RE/SEPBT		
ceiling	KRAOEL/-G			cession	KREGS
seal	SAOEL	censer	SEPBS/ER	session	SEGS
sealing	SAOEL/-G	censor	KREPB/SOR		
		censure	SEPB/SHUR	cite	KRAOEUT
cent	KREPBT	sensor	SEPB/SOR	kite	KAOEUT
sent	SEPBT			site	SAOEUT
scent	SKREPBT	cease	SAOES	sight	SAOEUGT
		crease	KRAOES		
accent	ABG/SEPBT	seize	SAOEZ	incite	EUPB/SAOEUT
ascent	AS/KREPBT				[EUPB/KRAOEUT]
	[AEU/KREPBT]	cede	SAED	insight	EUPB/SAOEUGT
assent	AEU/SEPBT	creed	KRAOED	in sight	TPH-/SAOEUGT
		seed	SAOED		

SOUNDALIKES WITH OTHER BEGINNING CONSONANTS

choral	KHORL	colonel	KURPBL [KOL/TPHEL]
coral	KORL	kernel	KERPBL
corral	KRAL [KOR/RAL]		
		knight	TPHAO*EUGT
chord	KHORD	night	TPHAOEUGT
cord	KORD		

 Step 4: Soundalikes

SOUNDALIKES WITH THE
SAME CONSONANT SOUND

FINAL CONSONANTS

SOUNDALIKES ENDING IN -AL, -EL, -IL, -OL, -LE

bridal	PWRAOEU/TKAL	principal	PREUPBS/PAL	liable	HRAOEUBL
bridle	PWRAOEUD/-L	principle	PREUPBS/P-L	libel	HRAOEUB/EL
marital	PHAR/TAL	local	HROE/KAL	muscle	PHUS/-L
marshal	PHAR/-RBL	locale	HROE/KAEL	mussel	PHUSZ/EL
martial	PHART/-RBL	low-cal	HROE/H-F/KAL	muzzle	PHUZ/-L
medal	PHED/TKAL	moral	PHORL	peril	P*ERL
meddle	PHED/-L	morale	PHO/RAEL		[PER/REUL]
metal	PHET/TAL		[PHO/RAL]	pearl	PERL
met all	PHET/AUL			purl	PURL
mettle	PHET/-L	rational	RAGS/TPHAL [RARBL]		
		rationale	RAGS/TPHAEL	parol	PA/ROL [PARL]
mutual	PHAOU/KHAL			parole	PA/ROEL
mutuel	PHAOU/KHEL	counsel	KOUPB/SEL [KOUPBL]		
		council	KOUPB/SEUL	gamble	TKPWAPL/-BL
naval	TPHA*EUFL			gambol	TKPWAPL/PWOL
navel	TPHAEU/SREL	mantel	PHAPBT/EL		
		mantle	PHAPBT/-L	idle	AOEUD/-L
pedal	PED/TKAL	man tell	PHAPB/TEL	idol	AOEU/TKOL
peddle	PED/-L			idyll	AO*EUD/-L
petal	PET/TAL	Nobel	TPHOE/PWEL		
pet all	PET/AUL	noble	TPHOEBL		

SOUNDALIKES ENDING IN -ER, -OR

drier	TKRAOEU/ER	pair	PAEUR	sear	SAER
dryer	TKRAOEU/KWRER	pear	PAER	sere	SAOER
		pare	PA*EUR	seer	SAOE/ER
flier	TPHRAOEU/ER	payer	PAEU/ER		
flyer	TPHRAOEU/KWRER		[PAEU/KWRER]	sore	SOER
				soar	SAOR
friar	TPRAOEUR	hire	HAOEUR	suer	SAOU/ER
fryer	TPRAOEU/ER	higher	HAOEU/ER	sewer	SAOUR
	[TPRAOEU/KWRER]				[SOE/ER]
		flour	TPHROUR		
lair	HRAEUR	flower	TPHROU/ER [TPHRO*UR]	concur	KOPB/KUR
layer	HRAEU/ER			conquer	KOPB/KER
	[HRAEU/KWRER]	lore	HROER		
		lower	HROE/ER	licker	HREUBG/ER
mare	PHAEUR			liqueur	HREUBG/KUR
mayor	PHAEU/KWROR	pour	POUR	liquor	HREUBG/KOR
		power	POU/ER [PO*UR]		

SOUNDALIKES ENDING IN -GH(T)

ate	AEUT	nay	TPHAEU	lite	HRAOEUT	site	SAOEUT
eight	AEUGT	neigh	TPHAEUG	light	HRAOEUGT	sight	SAOEUGT
						cite	KRAOEUT
strait	STRAEUT	slay	SHRAEU	mite	PHAOEUT		
straight	STRAEUGT	sleigh	SHRAEUG	might	PHAOEUGT	taut	TAUT
						taught	TAUGT
wait	WAEUT	way	WAEU	rite	RAOEUT		
weight	WAEUGT	weigh	WAEUG	right	RAOEUGT		
				write	WRAOEUT [WREU]		

SOUNDALIKES WITH Z SOUND

advice	AD/SRAOEUS	face	TPAEUS	precedent	PRES/TKEPBT
advise	AD/SRAOEUZ	faze	TPAEUZ	president	PREZ/TKEPBT
		phase	TPAEZ		(brief = P-T)
brace	PWRAEUS				
braise	PWRAEUZ	fiscal	TPEUS/KAL	price	PRAOEUS
		physical	TPEUZ/KAL [TP-L]	prize	PRAOEUZ
bus	PWUS				
buss	PWUSZ	fuss	TPUSZ	race	RAEUS
buzz	PWUZ	fuzz	TPUZ	raise	RAEUZ
				raze	RAEZ
corps	KOERPZ	grace	TKPWRAEUS		
corpse	KORPS	graze	TKPWRAEUZ	rice	RAOEUS
				rise	RAOEUZ
device	TKE/SRAOEUS	mace	PHAEUS		
devise	TKE/SRAOEUZ	maize	PHAEUZ	vice	SRAOEUS
		maze	PHAEZ	vise	SRAOEUZ

SOUNDALIKES ENDING IN -Y

draftee	TKRAF/TAOE	warrantee	WARPB/TAOE	petit	PET/TAOE
drafty	TKRAF/TEU	warranty	WARPB/TEU	petite	PE/TAOET
				petty	PET/TEU
guarantee	TKPWARPB/TAOE	allay	AL/HRAEU		
guaranty	TKPWARPB/TEU		[AEU/HRAEU]	stationary	STAEUGS/TPHAEUR
		alley	AL/HRAOE	stationery	STAEUGS/TPHER/REU
levee	HR*EF/SRAOE	ally	AL/HREU		[STAEUGS/TPHA*EUR]
levy	HR*EF/SREU				
		chilly	KHEUL/HREU	summary	SUPL/REU
trustee	TRUS/TAOE	chili	KHEUL/HRAOE	summery	SUPL/ER/REU
trusty	TRUS/TEU	Chile	KH*EUL/HRAOE		
		holey	HOE/HRAOE		
		holly	HOL/HREU		
		holy	HOE/HREU		
		wholly	WHOEL/HREU		

SOUNDALIKES WITH OTHER ENDINGS

arc	A*RBG	as	AZ	genius	SKWRAOEPB/KWRUS
ark	ARBG	ass	ASZ	genus	SKWRAOE/TPHUS
bloc	PWHRO*BG	bus	PWUS	humerus	HAOUPL/RUS
block	PWHROBG	buss	PWUSZ	humorous	HAOUPL/ROUS
clique	KHR*EUBG	pus	PUS	mucus	PHAOU/KUS
click	KHREUBG	puss	PUSZ	mucous	PHAOU/KOUS
					[PHAOUBG/OUS]
doc	TKO*BG	bash	PWARB		
dock	TKOBG	barb	PWAR/-B	Venus	SRAOE/TPHUS
				venous	SRAOE/TPHOUS
disc	TKEUS/*BG	blush	PWHRURB		[SRAOEPB/OUS]
disk	TKEUS/-BG	blurb	PWHRUR/-B		
				currant	KUR/RAPBT
cannon	KAPB/TPHOPB	gash	TKPWARB	current	KURPBT
canon	KA/TPHOPB	garb	TKPWAR/-B		
				palate	PAL/HRAT
heroin	HER/ROEUPB [HAEURPB]	ad	A*D	palette	PAL/ET
heroine	HER/RO*EUPB	add	AD	pallet	PAL/*ET

Step 4: Soundalikes

SOUNDALIKE SUMMARY

Following is a summary of soundalike solutions following the StenEd theory. Also included are a few words that are not soundalikes but often cause conflicts in pre-computer stenotype theories. Briefs are used when available.

The list is arranged alphabetically. The soundalike words in each group are also arranged alphabetically. Therefore, to find the soundalike solution for to/too/two, look under "to" since that word occurs first in an alphabetical listing.

StenEd outlines are listed. Some optional outlines are also listed [in brackets]. Additional options for some words can be found in StenEd's *Volume I: Theory* and *Professional Dictionary*. If you make up your own outlines, be very careful not to create one conflict while solving another.

Some soundalikes are covered in more detail in other steps in this text. **THEY ARE ALL LISTED HERE TO GIVE ONE COMPREHENSIVE LISTING.** Don't memorize this list. Do use it for reference as needed.

The vast majority of these potential conflicts are resolved by principles presented throughout this text. Thus, most soundalikes are solved by following a principle, not memorizing a unique outline. Some principles have already been covered; other principles will be covered in subsequent steps.

SOUNDALIKES

a	A	advice	AD/SRAOEUS	airy	AEUR/REU
a- *(pre)*	AEU	advise	AD/SRAOEUZ	eerie	AOER/RAOE [E/RAOE]
				Erie	AO*ER/RAOE
accidence	ABGS/TKEPBS	adviser	AD/SRAOEUZ/ER		
	[STKEPBS]	advisor	AD/SRAOEU/SOR	aisle	AO*EUL
accidents	STKEPBT/-S			I'll	EU/AOEL [*EUL]
		aesthetic	AES/THET/EUBG	isle	AOEUL
acts	ABGT/-S	esthetic	ES/THET/EUBG	I will	EU/HR-
ax	ABGS			ill	EUL
		affect	AFBGT [AEU/TPEBGT]		
ad	A*D	effect	EFBGT [E/TPEBGT]	Al	A*L
add	AD			all	AUL
		affluence	AF/HRAOUPBS	awe	AU
addition	AEU/TKEUGS	effluence	EF/HRAOUPBS	awl	A*UL
edition	E/TKEUGS			al- *(pre)*	AL
		affluent	AF/HRAOUPBT	-al *(suf)*	(c)AL
ade	A*ED	effluent	EF/HRAOUPBT	ow	O*U
ades	A*EDZ			owl	OUL
aid	AEUD	ail	AEUL		
aide	AED	ale	AEL	alimentary	AL/-PLT/TAEUR
aides	AEDZ				[AL/-PLT/REU]
aids	AEUDZ	air	AEUR	elementary	EL/-PLT/TAEUR
AIDS	A*EUDZ	heir	HA*EUR		[EL/-PLT/REU]
		hair	HAEUR		
adherence	AD/HAOERPBS	hare	HA*ER	allay	AEU/HRAEU
adherents	AD/HAOERPBT/-S	hear	HAER	alley	AL/HRAOE
		here	HAOER	ally	AL/HREU
adieu	AEU/TKAOU	ear	AOER	-ally *(suf)*	(c)/HREU [(c)HREU]
ado	AEU/TKO	ere	*ER		
		err	A*ER	allowed	AEU/HROU/-D
adolescence	AD/HRES/EPBS	er- *(pre)*	*ER	aloud	AEU/HROUD
adolescents	AD/HRES/EPBT/-S	-er *(suf)*	ER	a loud	A/HROUD
		're	AO*ER		

allows	AEU/HROU/-S	assistance	AEU/SEUS/TAPBS [STA*PBS]	bald	PWAULD
a louse	A/HROUS			balled	PWAL/-D
		assistants	AEU/SEUS/TAPBT/-S [STA*PBT/-S]	baud	PWAUD
all ready	AUL/RED/TKEU			bawled	PWAUL/-D
already	HR-R	ate	AEUT		
		eight	AEUGT	ball	PWAL
all together	AUL/TOGT			bawl	PWAUL
altogether	AL/TOGT	attendance	AEU/TEPB/TKAPBS		
		attendants	AEU/TEPB/TKAPBT/-S	banc	PWAPB/*BG
allude	AEU/HRAOUD			bank	PWAPB/-BG [PWA*PBG]
elude	E/HRAOUD	aught	A*UGT		
		ought	AUGT	band	PWAPBD
allusion	AEU/HRAOUGS	auto- (pre)	AUT	banned	PWAPB/-D
elusion	E/HRAOUGS	auto	AU/TOE		
illusion	EUL/HRAOUGS			barb	PWAR/-B
		august	AUG/*US	Barb	PWA*RB
allusive	AEU/LAOUS/*EUF	August	AUG [A*UG/*US]	bash	PWARB
elusive	E/HRAOUS/*EUF				
illusive	EUL/HRAOUS/*EUF	aural	AURL	bard	PWARD
		oral	ORL	barred	PWAR/-D
alone	AEU/HRO*EPB				
a lone	A/HRO*EPB	auricle	AURBG/-L	bare	PWAEUR
a loan	A/HROEPB	oracle	ORBG/-L	bear	PWAER
altar	AL/TAR	away	AEU/WAEU	barren	[PWAEURPB] PWAEUR/-PB
alter	ALT/ER [AL/TER]	a way	A/WAEU		
		aweigh	AEU/WAEUG	baron	PWAR/ROPB
am	APL				
apple	AP/-L	awed	AU/-D	Barry	PWAR/REU
		odd	OD	berry	PWER/REU
amend	AEU/PHEPBD [APLD]			bury	PWUR/REU
emend	E/PHEPBD	awful	AUFL		
		offal	AUF/TPAL	basal	PWAEU/SAL
ant	APBT	of fall	OF/TPAUL	basil	PWAEU/SEUL
aunt	AUPBT				
		axel	ABGS/EL	base	PWAEUS
ante	APB/TAOE	axil	ABG/SEUL	bass (lg a)	PWAEUSZ
ante- (pre)	AEPBT	axle	ABGS/-L	bass (sh a)	PWASZ
anti	APB/TAOEU				
anti- (pre)	A*EPBT [APB/TEU]	aye	AO*EU	based	PWAEUS/-D
auntie	AUPB/TAOE	eye	KWRAOEU	baste	PWA*EUS
		I	EU		
appease	AEU/PAOEZ	i- (pre)	AOEU	bases	PWAEUS/-S [PWAEU/SAOEZ]
apiece	AEU/PAOES				
a peace	A/PAES	ayes	AO*EU/-S	basis	PWAEU/SEUS
a piece	A/PAOES	eyes	KWRAOEU/-S		
		ice	AOEUS	bayou	PWAOEU/KWRAOU
arc	A*RBG			by you	PWEU/KWROU
ark	ARBG	baa	PWA [PWAU]		
		bah	PWA* [PWA*U]	bazaar	PWA/SA*R
area	AEUR/KWRA			bizarre	PWEU/SA*R [PW*EU/SA*R]
aria	AR/KWRA	babble	PWABL		
		Babel	PWAB/EL		
as	AZ			be	PW-
ass	ASZ	bade	PWAEUD	bee	PWAOE
as- (pre)	AS	bayed	PWAEU/-D	be- (pre)	PWE/
ascent	AEU/KREPBT	bail	PWAEUL	beach	PWAEFP
assent	AEU/SEPBT	bale	PWAEL	beech	PWAOEFP
accent	ABG/SEPBT				
a cent	A/KREPBT	bait	PWAEUT	beat (see bait)	
a scent	A/SKREPBT	bate	PWA*ET		
as sent	AZ/SEPBT	bathe	PWA*EUT	Beatle(s)	PWAET/-L(S)
		beat	PWAET	beetle(s)	PWAOET/-L(s)
assay	AS/SAEU	beet	PWAOET		
essay	ES/SAEU				

 Step 4: Soundalike Summary

beau	PWO*E	bode	PWOED	Britain	PWREUT/TAEUPB
bo	PWO	bowed	PWOE/-D	Briton	PWREUT/TOPB
bow *(lg o)*	PWOE				
bough	PWOUG	bold	PWOELD	broach	PWROEFP
bow *(ou sd)*	PWOU	bowled	PWOUL/-D	brooch	PWRAOFP
bowel	PWOU/EL [PWO*UL]				
		bolder	PWOELD/ER	brows	PWROU/-S
beaus	PWO*EZ	boulder	PWOULD/ER	browse	PWROUZ
bows *(lg o)*	PWOE/-S				
		bole	PWOEL	buccal	PWUBG/KAL
been	PW-PB	boll	PWOL	buckle	PWUBG/-L
Ben	PW*EPB	bowl	PWOUL		
bin	PWEUPB			bur	PW*UR
bean	PWAOEPB	boogie	PWAOG/TKPWAOE	burr	PWUR
		boogy	PWAOG/TKPWEU		
beer	PWAOER			bus	PWUS
bier	PWEUR	boos	PWAO/-S	buss	PWUSZ
		booze	PWAOZ	buzz	PWUZ
bel	PW*L				
bell	PWEL	born	PWORPB	bussed	PWUSZ/-D
belle	PW*EL	borne	PWOERPB	bust	PW*US
		bourn	PWOURPB		
beet *(see bait)*				but	PWU
		borough	PWOR/ROEG	butt	PWUT
berg	PWERG	borrow	PWOR/ROE	butte	PWAOUT
burg	PWURG	burro	PWUR/ROE		
		burrow	PWUR/ROU	buy	PWAOEU
Bern	PWERPB			by	PWEU
burn	PWURPB	bouillon	PWOUL/KWROPB	bye	PWAO*EU
		bullion	PWUL/KWROPB	bi- *(pre)*	PW*EU
berth	PW*ERT				
birth	PW*EURT	boy	PWOEU	cache	KAERB
Bert	PWERT	buoy	PWO*EU	cash	KARB
				carb	KAR/-B
better	PWET/ER	brace	PWRAEUS		
bettor	PWET/TOR	braise	PWRAEUZ	callous	KAL/OUS
		brays	PWRAEU/-S	callus	KAL/HRUS
bight	PWAOEUGT	braze	PWRAEZ		
bite	PWAOEUT			calls	KAUL/-S
byte	PWAO*EUT	bracket	PWRABG/ET	cause	KAUZ
		bract	PWRABGT		
bill	PWEUL			can *(v)*	K-
Bill	PW*EUL	braid	PWRAEUD	can *(n)*	KAPB
		brayed	PWRAEU/-D	ken	KEPB
billed	PWEUL/-D			Ken	K*EPB
build	PWEULD	brake	PWRAEUBG	kin	KEUPB
		break	PWRAEBG		
bleu	PWHR*U			canape	KAPB/PAOE
blew	PWHRAOU	breach	PWRAEFP	canopy	KAPB/PEU
blue	PWHRAO*U [PWHRU]	breech	PWRAOEFP		
				cannon	KAPB/TPHOPB
bloc	PWHRO*BG	bread	PWRAED	canon	KA/TPHOPB
block	PWHROBG	bred	PWRED		
				can't	K-PBT
blurb	PWHRUR/-B	breadth	PWRED/*T	cant	KAPBT
blush	PWHRURB	breath	PWR*ET	cannot	K-/TPHOT
boar	PWOR	brewed	PWRAOU/-D	canter	KAPBT/ER
boor	PWAOR	brood	PWRAOD	cantor	KAPB/TOR
bore	PWOER				
		brews	PWRAOU/-S	canvas *n&j*	KAPB/SRAS
board	PWAORD	bruise	PWRAOUZ	canvass *(n&v)*	KAPB/SRASZ
bored	PWOER/-D	Bruce	PWRAO*US		
				capital	KAP/TAL
boarder	PWAORD/ER	bridal	PWRAOEU/TKAL	capitol	KAP/TOL
border	PWOERD/ER	bridle	PWRAOEUD/-L	Capitol	KA*P/TOL

caput	KAEU/PUT [KAP/UT]	cemetery	SEPL/TAEUR	chronical	KROPB/KAL
kaput	KA/PUT [KA/PAOUT]	symmetry	SEUPL/TREU	chronicle	KROPB/K-L
carat	KA/RAT	censer	SEPBS/ER	chute	SHAOUT
caret	KA/RET	censor	KREPB/SOR	shoot	SHAOT
carrot	KAR/OT	sensor	SEPB/SOR		
		censure	SEPB/SHUR	cirrus	SEUR/RUS
caress	KA/RESZ			serious	SAOER/KWROUS
cress	KRESZ	census	SEPB/SUS		[SAOERS]
		senses	SEPBS/-S	serous	SAOER/OUS
caressed	KA/RESZ/-D			series	SAOE/RAOEZ [SAOERZ]
crest	KR*ES	cent	KREPBT		
		sent	SEPBT	cite	KRAOEUT
caries	KAEU/RAOEZ	scent	SKREPBT	sight	SAOEUGT
carries	KAEUR/REU/-S			site	SAOEUT
		cents	KREPBT/-S		
Carl	KRARL	scents	SKREPBT/-S	claps	KHRAP/-S
Karl	KARL	sense	SEPBS	collapse	KHRAPS
carol	KAEURL	since	SEUPBS		
Carol	KA*EURL	sins	SEUPB/-S	clause	KHRAUZ
				claws	KHRAU/-S
cart	KART	cerate	KRE/RAEUT		
carte	KA*RT	serrate	SER/RAEUT	clef	KHREF
				cleft	KHREFT
cast	KA*S	cereal	KRAOER/KWRAL		
caste	KA*ES	serial	SAOER/KWRAL	click	KHREUBG
				clique	KHR*EUBG
caster	KA*S/ER	cession	KREGS		
castor	KAS/TOR	session	SEGS	climb	KHRAOEUPL
				clime	KHRAO*EUPL
caught	KAUGT [KAUT]	chance	KHAPBS		
cot	KOT	chants	KHAPBT/-S	climactic	KHRAOEU/PHABGT/EUBG
				climatic	KHRAOEU/PHAT/EUBG
cay	KAEU [KA*E]	chased	KHAEUS/-D		
key	KAOE	chaste	KHA*EUS	clone	KHROEPB
quay	KAE			cologne	KO/HROEPB
Kay	KA*EU	cheap	KHAEP	Colon	KO*/HROEPB
		cheep	KHAOEP		
cease	SAOES			close (v)	KHROEZ
seas	SAE/-S	check	KHEBG	clothes	KHRO*ET/-S
sees	SAOE/-S	cheque	KHEBG/-BG	close (j)	KHROES
seize	SAOEZ	Czech	KH*EBG		
				clued	KHRAOU/-D
cede	SAED	chews	KHAOU/-S	collude	KHRAOUD
seed	SAOED	choose	KHAOZ		
				coarse	KOERS [KAORS]
ceded	SAED/-D	chic	SHAEBG [SHAO*EBG]	course	KOURS
seeded	SAOED/-D	sheik	SHAOEBG	cores	KOER/-S
seated	SAOET/-D	shake	SHAEUBG	Coors	KAO*RS
		chick	KHEUBG		
ceding	SAED/-G			coated	KOET/-D
seeding	SAOED/-G	Chile	KH*EUL/HRAOE	coded	KOED/-D
seating	SAOET/-G	chili	KHEUL/HRAOE		
		chilly	KHEUL/HREU	code	KOED
ceil	KRAOEL			co-ed	KO/ED
seal	SAOEL	choir	KWOEUR		
		quire	KWAOEUR	coffer	KOFR [KOF/ER]
ceiling	KRAOEL/-G			cougher	KAUFR [KAUF/ER]
sealing	SAOEL/-G	choral	KHORL		
		coral	KORL	coif	KWOEUF
cell	KREL	corral	KRAL [KOR/RAL]	quaff	KWAUF
sell	SEL				
		chord	KHORD	colleague	KHRAOEG
cellar	KREL/HRAR	cord	KORD	klieg	KHRAO*EG
seller	SEL/ER	cored	KOER/-D		
cellular	KREL/KWRU/HRAR			collide	KHRAOEUD
		chow	KHOU	Clyde	KHRAO*EUD
		ciao	KHO*U		

Step 4: Soundalike Summary

colonel	KURPBL [KOL/TPHEL]	corespondents	KO/SPOPBT/-S [KO/SPOPBD/EPBT/-S]	cypress	SAOEUP/RESZ
kernel	KERPBL	correspondence	KOR/SPOPBD/EPBS	Cyprus	SAOEUP/RUS
		correspondents	KOR/SPOPBD/EPBT/-S	dad	TKAD
color	KO/HROR			Dad	TKA*D
colour	KO/HROUR	coroner	KOERPB [KOR/TPHER]		
		corner	KORPB/ER	dam	TKAPL
comedy	KOPL/TKEU			damn	TKA*PL
comity	KOPL/TEU	corporal	KORP/RAL	dapple	TKAP/-L
		corporeal	KOR/POEURL [KOR/POR/KWRAL]		
complacence	KOPL/PHRAEUS/EPBS			dawn	TKAUPB
complaisance	KOPL/PHRAEU/SAPBS			don	TKOPB
		corrode	KROED	Don	TKO*PB
		crowed	KROE/-D	done	TKOEPB
complacent	KOPL/PHRAEUS/EPBT			dun	TKUPB
complaisant	KOPL/PHRAEU/SAPBT	cosign	KO/SAOEUPB		
		cosine	KO/SAO*EUPB	days	TKAEU/-S
complainant	KPHRAEU/TPHAPBT			daze	TKAEUZ
complaint	KPHRAEUPBT	courtesy	KOURT/SEU		
		curtesy	KURT/SEU	deaf	TKEF
complement	KOFRP/HREPLT			deft	TKEFT
compliment	KOFRP/HREUPLT	cot (see caught)			
		coup (see coo)		dear	TKAER
concern	K-RPB	coupe (see coo)		deer	TKAOER
kern	KERPB				
		court	KOURT [KORT]	debit	TKEBT
concur	KOPB/KUR	Court	KO*URT [KO*RT]	debt	TKET
conquer	KOPB/KER				
		coward	KOU/WARD [KOURD]	decent	TKE/SEPBT [TKAOES/EPBT]
confer	KOPB/TPER [K-FR]	cowered	KOU/ER/-D [KOU/ERD]		
conifer	KOPB/TPHEU/TPER			descent	TKE/SKREPBT [TKES/KREPBT]
		crate	KRAEUT		
confirmation	KOPB/TPEUR/PHAEUGS	create	KRAET [KRAOE/KWRAEUT]	dissent	TKEUS/SEPBT
conformation	KOPB/TPOR/PHAEUGS				
		crater	KRAEUT/ER	demur	TKE/PHUR
consonance	KOPBS/TPHAPBS	creator	KRAET/TOR [KRAOE/KWRAEU/TOR]	demure	TKE/PHAOUR
consonants	KOPBS/TPHAPBT/-S				
				dens	TKEPB/-S
consul	KOPB/SUL	creak	KRAEBG	dense	TKEPBS
council	KOUPB/SEUL	creek	KRAOEBG	dents	TKEPBT/-S
counsel	KOUPBL [KOUPB/SEL]				
		cream	KRAOEPL	dependence	TKE/PEPBD/EPBS [TKPEPBD/EPBS] [TKPEPBS]
consular	KOPBS/HRAR	creme	KREPL [KRAO*EPL]		
councillor	KOUPB/SEU/HROR				
counselor	KOUPBS/HROR [KOURPBL]	crewel	KRAO*UL	dependents	TKE/PEPBD/EPBT/-S [TKPEPBD/EPBT/-S] [TKPEPBT/-S]
		cruel	KRAOUL		
contact	KOPB/TABGT [KABGT]				
Contac	KOPB/TABG	crewed	KRAOU/-D	depo	TKEP/POE
		crude	KRAOUD	depot	TKE/POE
continence	KOPBT/TPHEPBS				
continents	KOPBT/TPHEPBT/-S	crews	KRAOU/-S	depravation	TKEP/RA/SRAEUGS
countenance	KOUPBT/TPHAPBS	cruise	KRAOUZ	deprivation	TKEP/REU/SRAEUGS
coo	KAO	cue (see coo)		desert	TKE/SERT [TKEZ/ERT]
coop	KAOP			dessert	TKES/SERT
co-op	KO/OP	currant	KUR/RAPBT		
coup	KOUP [KAO*U]	current	KURPBT	deterrence	TKE/TERPBS
coupe	KAOUP			deterrents	TKE/TERPBT/-S
cue	KAOU	curs	KUR/-S		
queue	KWAOU	curse	KURS	Deutsche	TKOEUFP
				douche	TKAOURB
core	KOER	curser	KURS/ER	Dutch	TK*UFP
corps	KOERP [KOERPZ]	cursor	KUR/SOR	dutch	TKUFP
Corp.	KO*RP				
corpse	KOERPS	cymbal	SEUPL/PWAL	devest	TKE/SR*ES
		symbol	SEUPL/PWOL	divest	TKEU/SR*ES

---

deviance	TKAO*EF/KWRAPBS	draftee	TKRAF/TAOE	eminent	EPL/TPHEPBT
deviants	TKAO*EF/KWRAPBT/-S	drafty	TKRAF/TEU	imminent	EUPL/TPHEPBT
				immanent	EUPL/PHA/TPHEPBT
device	TKE/SRAOEUS	draw	TKRAU		
	[TKWAOEUS]	drawl	TKRAUL	emission	E/PHEUGS
devise	TKE/SRAOEUZ			omission	O/PHEUGS
	[TKWAOEUZ]	drier	TKRAOEU/ER		
		dryer	TKRAOEU/KWRER	empanel	EPL/PAPBL
dew	TKAO*U			impanel	EUPL/PAPBL
do	TKO	dual	TKAOUL		
due	TKAOU	duel	TKAO*UL [TKAOU/EL]	empress	EPL/PRESZ
				impress	EUPL/PRESZ
dice	TKAOEUS	duck	TKUBG		
dies	TKAOEU/-S	duct	TKUBGT	ensure	EPB/SHUR
dyes	TKAO*EU/-S	ducked	TKUBG/-D	insure	EUPB/SHUR
		dubbing	TKUB/-G		[STPHUR]
die	TKAOEU				
dye	TKAO*EU	dun (see dawn)		entrance	SPWRAPBS
di- (pre)	TKEU	ear (see air)		entrants	SPWRAPBT/-S
dine	TKAOEUPB	earn	ERPB	epic	EP/EUBG
dyne	TKAO*EUPB	urn	URPB	epoch	EP/OBG
dire	TKAOEUR	eastern	AO*ERPB	epitaph	EP/TAF
dyer	TKAO*EU/KWRER	east earn	AO*ES/ERPB	epithet	EP/THET
disburse	TKEUS/PWURS	eave	A*EF	ere, err, error (see air)	
disperse	TKEUS/PERS	eve	AO*EF	Erie (see airy)	
		Eve	K-P/AO*EF		
disc	TKEUS/*BG	've	AOEF [AO*EF, grpd]	especial	ES/PERBL
disk	TKEUS/-BG			special	SPERBL
		edition (see addition)			
discreet	TKEUS/KRAOET	eerie (see airy)		especially	ES/PERB/HREU
discrete	TKEUS/KRAET	effluence (see affluence)			[ES/PERBL/HREU]
		effluent (see affluent)		specially	SPERBL/HREU
discus	TKEUS/KUS	eight (see ate)			
discuss	TKEUS/KUSZ			essay (see assay)	
		either	E/THER [AOERT]	esthetic (see aesthetic)	
dissidence	TKEUSZ/TKEPBS	ether	AO*ET/ER		
dissidents	TKEUSZ/TKEPBT/-S			ewe	KWRAOU
		elementary (see alimentary)		yew	KWRAO*U
divers (n)	TKAO*EUFR/-S			you	KWROU
divers (j)	TKEU/SRERZ	eleven	HR*EFPB		
diverse	TKEU/SRERS	leaven	HR*EF/-PB	exalt	KPAULT
				exult	KPULT
doc	TKO*BG	elicit	E/HREUS/SEUT		
dock	TKOBG	illicit	EUL/HREUS/SEUT	exercise	KPER/SAOEUZ
					[KPERZ]
Doctor	TKR*	elude (see allude)		exorcise	KPOR/SAOEUZ
doctor	TKR-	elusion (see allusion)			
Dr.	TKR-FPLT	elusive (see allusive)		Expos	*EBGS/POE/-S
		emend (see amend)		expos	EBGS/POE/-S
doe	TKOE			expose (v)	EBGS/POEZ
Doe	TKO*E	emersion	E/PHERGS		
dough	TKOU	immersion	EUPL/PHERGS	extant	EBGS/TAPBT
DOE	TK-RBGS/O*E			extent	EBGS/TEPBT
		emigrant	EPL/TKPWRAPBT		
does (v)	TKUZ	immigrant	EUPL/TKPWRAPBT	eye (see aye)	
does (n, pl)	TKOE/-S				
dose	TKOES	emigrate	EPL/TKPWRAEUT	eyed	KWRAOEU/-D
doze	TKOEZ	immigrate	EUPL/TKPWRAEUT	I'd	EU/AOED [AO*EUD]
				I had	EU/HAD
done (see dawn)		emigration	EPL/TKPWRAEUGS		
		immigration	EUPL/TKPWRAEUGS	eyelet	KWRAOEU/HRET
draft	TKRAFT			islet	AOEU/HRET
draught	TKRAUFT	eminence	EPL/TPHEPBS	I let	EU/HRET
		imminence	EUPL/TPHEPBS		

Step 4: Soundalike Summary

face	TPAEUS	fleas	TPHRAE/-S	freeze	TPRAOEZ
faze	TPAEUZ	fleece	TPHRAOES	frieze	TPRAO*EZ
phase	TPAEZ	flees	TPHRAOE/-S	frees	TPRAOE/-S
facts	TPABGT/-S	flecks	TPHREBG/-S	friar	TPRAOEUR
fax	TPABGS	flex	TPHREBGS	fryer	TPRAOEU/ER
					[TPRAOEU/KWRER]
faint	TPAEUPBT	flew	TPHRAOU		
feint	TPAEPBT [TPEPBT]	flu	TPHRU	fuss	TPUSZ
		flue	TPHRAO*U	fuzz	TPUZ
fair	TPAEUR				
fare	TPAER	flier	TPHRAOEU/ER	gage	TKPWAEPBLG
		flyer	TPHRAOEU/KWRER	gauge	TKPWAEUPBLG
fairy	TPAEUR/REU				
ferry	TPER/REU	floe	TPHRO*E	Gail	TKPWAEUL
		flow	TPHROE	gale	TKPWAEL
farther	TPA*RT/ER				
further	TP*URT/ER [TPURT]	flour	TPHROUR	gait	TKPWAEUT
		flower	TPHROU/ER	gate	TKPWAET
fears	TPAOER/-S		[TPHRO*UR]		
fierce	TPAOERS			gallop	TKPWAL/OP
		foaled	TPOEL/-D	Gallup	TKPWAL/HRUP
feat	TPAET	fold	TPOELD		
feet	TPAOET			gamble	TKPWAPL/-BL
fete	TPET	for	TP-R	gambol	TKPWAPL/PWOL
		fore	TPOER(/SP-S)		
federal	TPED/RAL [TPRAL]	four	TPOUR	garb	TKPWAR/-B
Federal	TP*ED/RAL [TPRA*L]	for- (pre)	TPOR	gash	TKPWARB
		fore- (pre)	TPOER		
felon	TPHROPB			gays	TKPWAEU/-S
fell on	TPEL/OPB	force	TPORS [TPOERS]	gaze	TKPWAEUZ
		fours	TPOUR/-S		
fight	TPAOEUGT			gel	SKWR*EL
fite	TPAOEUT	ford	TPORD	jell	SKWREL
		Ford	TPO*RD		
filet	TPEU/HRAEU	forward	TPWARD	gene(s)	SKWRAOEPB(/-S)
fillet	TPEUL/ET	foreword	TPOER/WORD	jeans	SKWRAEPBS
	[TPEUL/HRAEU]			Gene	SKWRAO*EPB
		foremost	TPOER/PHO*ES	Jean	SKWRA*EPB
fill	TPEUL	for most	TP-R/PHO*ES		
Phil	TP*EUL			genius	SKWRAOEPB/KWRUS
		forgetting	TPERGT/-G	genus	SKWRAOE/TPHUS
finally	TPAOEUPBL/ HREU		[TPOR/TKPWET/-G]		
finely	TPAOEUPB/HREU	for getting	TP-R/TKPWET/-G	getaway	TKPWET/A*EU/WAEU
finale	TPEU/TPHAL/HRAOE			get away	TKPWET/AEU/WAEU
		forgiving	TPOR/TKPW*EUF/-G]	get a way	TKPWET/A/WAEU
find	TPAOEUPBD	for giving	TP-R/TKPW*EUF/-G]		
fined	TPAOEUPB/-D			ghost	TKPWO*ES
		form	TPORPL	goest	TKPWO/*ES
finish	TPEUPB/EURB	forum	TPOR/UPL		
Finnish	TP*EUPB/EURB			gibe	SKWRAO*EUB
		forth	TPO*RT	jibe	SKWRAOEUB
fir	TPEUR	fourth	TPO*URT		
fur	TPUR			gild	TKPW*EULD
		foul	TPOUL	guild	TKPWEULD
fiscal	TPEUS/KAL	fowl	TPO*UL		
physical	TPEUZ/KAL [TP-L]			gilt	TKPW*EULT
		franc	TPRAPB/*BG	guilt	TKPWEULT
flair	TPHRAEUR	frank	TPRAPB/-BG		
flare	TPHRAER	Frank	TPRA*PB/-BG	gist	SKWR*EUS
				jest	SKWR*ES
flamenco	TPHRA/PHEPB/KOE	frays	TPRAEU/-S	just	SKWR*US
flamingo	TPHRA/PHEUPB/TKPWOE	phrase	TPRAEUZ		
				glacier	TKPWHRAEU/SHER
flea	TPHRAE	freon	TPRAOE/KWROPB	glazier	TKPWHRAEUZ/KWRER
flee	TPHRAOE	free on	TPRAOE/OPB		

glance	TKPWHRAPBS	gross	TKPWROESZ	heed	HAOED
glans	TKPWHRAPBZ	grows	TKPWROU/-S	he'd	HE/AOED [HAO*ED]
	[TKPWHRAPB/-S]		[TKPWROE/-S]	he had	HE/HAD
glands	TKPWHRAOBDZ			head	HED
		guarantee	TKPWARPB/TAOE		
gnu	TPH*U	guaranty	TKPWARPB/TEU	heir (see air)	
knew	TPHAOU				
new	TPHU	guessed	TKPWESZ/-D	hence	HENS
nu	TPHAO*U	guest	TKPW*ES	hens	HEPB/-S
				Hen's	H*EPB/AOES
gofer	TKPWO*EFR	guise	TKPWAOEUZ		
gopher	TKPWOEFR	guys	TKPWAOEU/-S	herb	ERB [HERB]
				Herb	H*ERB
gorilla	TKPWREUL/HRA	gym	SKWREUPL		
guerrilla	TKPWER/EUL/HRA	Jim	SKWR*EUPL	here (see air)	
		gem	TKPWEPL		
grace	TKPWRAEUS			heroin	HER/ROEUPB
graze	TKPWRAEUZ	ha	HA		[HAEURPB]
grays	TKPWRAEU/-S	hah	HA*	heroine	HER/RO*EUPB
				heron	HER/ROPB
grade	TKPWRAEUD	hail	HAEUL	her on	HER/OPB
grayed	TKPWRAEU/-D	hale	HA*EUL	here on	HAOER/OPB
graded	TKPWRAEUD/-D	hair, hare (see air)		hertz	HERTS
grated	TKPWRAEUT/-D			Hertz	H*ERTS
		hairy	HAEUR/REU	hurts	HURT/-S
grader	TKPWRAEUD/ER	Harry	HA*R/REU		
grater	TKPWRAEUT/ER	harry	HAR/REU	hew	HAO*U
greater	TKPWRAET/ER			hue	HAOU
		Hal	HA*L	huge	HAOUPBLG
graft	TKPWRAFT	how	HOU	Hugh	HAOUG
graph	TKPWRAF	howl	HOUL		
graphed	TKPWRAF/-D	hall	HAL	hi	HEU
		haul	HAUL	hie	HAO*EU
gram	TKPWRAPL			high	HAOEU
grapple	TKPWRAP/-L	handsome	HAPBD/SPH-		
		hansom	HAPBS/OPL	hide	HAOEUD
grate	TKPWRAEUT	hand some	HAPBD/SOPL	Hyde	HAO*EUD
great	TKPWRAET				
		hangar	HAPB/TKPWAR	higher	HAOEU/ER
gray	TKPWRAEU	hanger	HAPBG/ER	hire	HAOEUR
grey	TKPWRA*EU				
		hardy	HAR/TKEU	him	HEUPL
grays (see grace)		hearty	HAR/TEU	hymn	H*EUPL
grease	TKPWRAES	hawk	HAUBG	hippie	HEUP/PAOE
Greece	TKPWRAOES	hoc	HO*BG	hippy	HEUP/PEU
	[TKPWRAO*ES]	hock	HOBG		
				his	HEUZ
grievance	TKPWRAOE/SRAPBS	hay	HAEU	hiss	HEUSZ
	[TKPWRAO*EFPBS]	hey	HA*EU		
grievants	TKPWRAOE/ SRAPBT/-S			ho	HO
	[TKPWRAO*EFPBT/-S]	heal	HAEL	hoe	HOE
		heel	HAOEL		
grip	TKPWREUP	he'll	HE/AOEL [HAO*EL]	hoar	HAOR
grippe	TKPWR*EUP	he will	HE/HR-	hoer	HOE/ER
		hell	HEL	whore	WHOER
grisly	TKPWREUS/HREU				
gristly	TKPWR*EUS/HREU	hear (see air)		hoard	HAORD
grizzly	TKPWREUZ/HREU			horde	HOERD [HORD]
		heard	HAERD	whored	WHOER/-D
groan	TKPWROEPB	herd	HERD		
grown	TKPWROUPB			hoarse	HAORS
		hearse	HERS	horse	HORS [HOERS]
grocer	TKPWROES/ER	hers	HER/-S	whores	WHOER/-S
grosser	TKPWROESZ/ER	herself	H*ERS	hoers	HOE/ERS

Step 4: Soundalike Summary

hoes	HOE/-S		indict	EUPB/TKAOEUT	kaput (see caput)	
hose	HOEZ			[TKAO*EUT]	Karl (see Carl)	
			indite	EUPB/TKAO*EUT	Kay, key (see cay)	
hold	HOELD				Ken, kin (see can)	
holed	HOEL/-D		indigence	EUPBD/SKWREPBS	kernel (see colonel)	
			indigents	EUPBD/SKWREPBT/-S	kern (see concern)	
hole	HOEL					
whole	WHOEL		inequity	EUPB/EBG/WEU/TEU	kill	KEUL
			iniquity	EUPB/EUBG/WEU/TEU	kiln	K*EUL
holey	HOE/HRAOE					
holy	HOE/HREU		ingest	EUPB/SKWR*ES	klieg (see colleague)	
wholly	WHOEL/HREU		in just	TPH-/SKWR*US		
holly	HOL/HREU				knave	TPHA*EUF
			innocence	TPHEPBS	nave	TPHAEUF
hostel	HO*S/EL [HOS/TEL]		innocents	TPHEPBT/-S		
hostile	HOS/TEUL				knead	TPHAED
			instance	EUPB/STAPBS	kneed	TPHAOE/-D
hour	HOUR		instants	EUPB/STAPBT/-S	need	TPHAOED
hr.	H*R					
our	OUR		insure (see ensure)		knees	TPHAOE/-S
					niece	TPHAOES
how (see Hal)			intense	SPWEPBS	Nice (France)	TPHAO*ES
			intents	SPWEPBT/-S		
humerus	HAOUPL/RUS				knew (see gnu)	
humorous	HAOUPL/ROUS		isle (see aisle)			
			islet (see eyelet)		knight	TPHAO*EUGT
I (see aye)					night	TPHAOEUGT
ice (see ayes)			its	EUTS		
I'd (see eyed)			it's	EUT/AOES [T*S]	knit	TPH*EUT
			it is	T-S	nit	TPHEUT
idle	AOEUD/-L		itself	*EUTS		
idol	AOEU/TKOL				knob	TPHOB
idyll	AO*EUD/-L		jam	SKWRAPL	nob	TPHO*B
			jamb	SKWRA*PL	nobody	TPHOEB
I'll (see aisle)					no body	TPHO/PWOD/TKEU
illicit (see elicit)			jack	SKWRABG		
illusion (see allusion)			Jack	SKWRA*BG	knot	TPHO*T
illusive (see allusive)					not	TPHOT
immersion (see emersion)			jam	SKWRAPL	naught	TPHAUGT [TPHAUT]
imminent (see eminent)			jamb	SKWRA*PL		
immigrant (see emigrant)					know	TPHOE
impanel (see empanel)			Jan	SKWRA*PB	no	TPHO
			January	SKWRAPB		
impatience	EUPL/PAEURBS				knows	TPHOE/-S
inpatients	EUPB/PAEURBT/-S		Jean (see gene)		nose	TPHOEZ
			jeans (see genes)		noes	TPHO/-S
impress (see empress)			jell (see gel)			
			jest (see gist)		labor	HRAEU/PWOR
in	TPH-				labour	HRAEU/PWOUR
inn	*EUPB		jewel	SKWRAOUL		
in- (pre)	EUPB/		joule	SKWRAO*UL	lace	HRAEUS
-in (suf)	(c)EUPB				lase	HRAEZ
			jewelry	SKWRAOUL/REU	lays	HRAEU/-S
Inc.	EUPB/*BG		Jewry	SKWRAOU/REU	laze	HRAEUZ
ink	EUPB/-BG [*EUPBG]					
I think	EUPBG		Jews	SKWRAOU/-S	lacks	HRABG/-S
			juice	SKWRAOUS	lax	HRABGS
incidence	EUPBS/TKEPBS					
incidents	EUPBS/TKEPBT/-S		jibe (see gibe)		lade	HRA*ED
			Jim (see gym)		laid	HRAEUD
incite	EUPB/SAOEUT				lead (n)	HRAED
insight	EUPB/SAOEUGT		john	SKWROPB	lead (v)	HRAOED
in sight	TPH-/SAOEUGT		John	SKWRO*PB	led	HRED
independence	EUPB/TKPEPBD/EPBS		juggler	SKWRUG/HRER		
	[EUPB/TKPEPBS]		jugular	SKWRUG/HRAR		
independents	EUPB/TKPEPBD/EPBT/-S					
	[EUPB/TKPEPBT/-S]		just (see gist)			

lain	HRAEUPB	levee	HR*EF/SRAOE	loot	HRAOT
lane	HRAEPB	levy	HR*EF/SREU	lute	HRAOUT
Lane	HRA*EPB				
lean	HRAOEPB	liable	HRAOEUBL	lore	HROER
lien	HRAO*EPB	libel	HRAOEUB/EL	lower	HROE/ER
				lure	HRAOUR
lair	HRAEUR	liar	HRAOEUR		
layer	HRAEU/KWRER	lier	HRAOEU/ER	lumbar	HRUPL/PWAR
	[HRAEU/ER]	lyre	HRAO*EUR	lumber	HRUPL/PWER
lam	HRAPL	lice	HRAOEUS	ma	PHA
lamb	HRA*PL	lies	HRAOEU/-S	Ma	PHA*
				maw	PHAU
laps	HRAP/-S	lichen	HREUFP/-PB		
lapse	HRAPS		[HRAOEU/KEPB]	mac	PHABG
		liken	HRAOEUBG/-PB	Mac	PHA*BG
lay	HRAEU			Mack	PHA*BG/-BG
lei	HRA*EU	licker	HREUBG/ER	Mc (pre)	PH*BG
		liqueur	HREUBG/KUR		
lays, laze (see lace)		liquor	HREUBG/KOR	mace	PHAEUS
				maize	PHAEUZ
lea	HRAE	lie	HRAOEU	maze	PHAEZ
lee	HRAOE	lye	HRAO*EU		
Lee	HRAO*E			mackintosh	PHABG/KEUPB/TORB
		lien (see lain)		Macintosh	PHABG/TORB
leach	HRAEFP				
leech	HRAOEFP	lieu	HRAOU	madam	PHAD/APL
		loo	HRAO	madame	PHA/TKAPL
lead (see lade)		Lou	HRAO*U		
				made	PHAED
leader	HRAOED/ER	light	HRAOEUGT	maid	PHAEUD
	[HRAED/ER]	lite	HRAOEUT		
liter	HRAOET/ER			mail	PHAEUL
		lightening	HRAOEUGT/-PBG	male	PHAEL
leads	HRAOEDZ	lightning	HRAOEUGT/TPHEUPBG		
Leeds	HRAO*EDZ			maim	PHAEUPL
		lime	HRAOEUPL	maple	PHAEUP/-L
leak	HRAEBG	Lyme	HRAO*EUPL		
leek	HRAOEBG			main	PHAEUPB
		line	HRAOEUPB	mane	PHAEPB
lean (see lain)		lion	HRAOEU/KWROPB	Maine	PHA*EUPB
				mean	PHAOEPB
leased	HRAOES/-D	links	HREUPB/-BGS	mien	PHAO*EPB
least	HRAO*ES		[HR*EUPBG/-S]	mesne	PHA*EPB
		lynx	HREUPBGS		
leaven (see eleven)				maize, maze (see mace)	
led (see lade)		lo	HRO		
		low	HROE	mall	PHAL
legend	HREPBLGD			maul	PHAUL
	[HREPBLG/EPBD]	load	HROED	moll	PHOL
ledge end	HREPBLG/SP-S/EPBD	lode	HRO*ED	mole	PHOEL
		lowed	HROE/-D		
lends	HREPBDZ			Mandarin	PHA*PBD/REUPB
lens	HREPBS [HREPBZ]	loan	HROEPB	mandarin	PHAPBD/REUPB
		lone	HRO*EPB	mandrin	PHAPB/TKREUPB
lessen	HRESZ/-PB				
lesson	HRES/SOPB	loath	HRO*T	mandate	PHAPBD/TKAEUT
less on	HRESZ/OPB	loathe	HRO*ET	man date	PHAPB/TKAEUT
lesser	HRESZ/ER	local	HROE/KAL	manner	PHAPB/ER
lessor	HRES/SOR	locale	HROE/KAEL	manor	PHA/TPHOR
less or	HRESZ/OR	low-cal	HROE/H-F/KAL	manure	PHA/TPHAOUR
less sore	HRESZ/SOER			man or	PHAPB/OR
		locks	HROBG/-S	man nor	PHAPB/TPH-R
lets	HRET/-S	lox	HROBGS		
let's	HRET/AOES [HR*ETS]			mantel	PHAPBT/EL
let us	HRET/US	loil	HRO*EUL	mantle	PHAPBT/-L
lettuce	HRET/TUS	loyal	HROEUL	man tell	PHAPB/TEL

 Step 4: Soundalike Summary

mar	PHAR	midst	PH*EUDZ [PHEUD/*S]	mood	PHAOD
march	PHAR/-FP	missed	PHEUSZ/-D	mooed	PHAO/-D
	[PHA*RPBLG]	mist	PH*EUS		
March	PHA*R [PHA*R/-FP]			moor	PHAOR
Marge	PHARPBLG	might	PHAOEUGT	more	PH-R
		mite	PHAOEUT	mor- (pre)	PHOR
marc	PHAR/*BG				
mark	PHARBG	mike	PHAOEUBG	moot (see moat)	
Mark	PHA*RBG	Mike	PHAO*EUBG		
mashing	PHARB/-G			moral	PHORL
		mil	PH*EUL	morale	PHO/RAEL [PHO/RAL]
mare	PHAEUR	mill	PHEUL		
mayor	PHAEU/KWROR	million	PH-L	morn	PHORPB
may or	PHAEU/OR			mourn	PHOURPB
		min	PHEUPB		
marks	PHARBG/-S	mint	PHEUPBT	morning	PHORPBG [PHORPB/-G]
Marx	PHARBGS	minute	PH*EUPB [PHEUPB/UT]	mourning	PHOURPB/-G
marital	PHAR/TAL	mince	PHEUPBS	mucous (j)	PHAOUBG/OUS
marshal	PHAR/-RBL	mints	PHEUPBT/-S	mucus (n)	PHAOU/KUS
martial	PHART/-RBL	minute	PH*EUPB/-S		
Marshall	PHA*R/-RBL		[PHEUPB/UT/-S]	muggee	PHUG/TKPWAOE
				muggy	PHUG/TKPWEU
marquee	PHAR/KAOE	mind	PHAOEUPBD		
marquis	PHAR/KWEUS	mined	PHAOEUPB/-D	muscle	PHUS/-L
				mussel	PHUSZ/EL
marry	PHAR/REU	miner	PHAOEUPB/ER	muzzle	PHUZ/-L
Mary	PHA*EUR/REU	minor	PHAOEU/TPHOR		
	[PHA*R/REU]	mine or	PHAOEUPB/OR	mussed	PHUSZ/-D
merry	PHER/REU	mine nor	PHAOEUPB/TPH-R	must	PH*US
massed	PHASZ/-D	miss	PHEUSZ	mustard	PH*US/ARD
mast	PHA*S	Miss	PH-S	mustered	PH*US/ERD
		mis- (pre)	PHEUS		
mat	PHAT	misc.	PHEUS/*BG	mute (see moat)	
matte	PHAT/-T	Ms.	PH-Z		
Matt	PHA*T/-T			mutual	PHAOU/KHUL
math	PHA*T	missal	PHEUS/SAL		[PHAOU/KHAL]
		missile	PHEUS/SEUL	mutuel	PHAOU/KHEL
may	PHAEU				
May	PHA*EU	missed, mist (see midst)		naught (see knot)	
Mae	PHA*E				
		misses	PHEUSZ/-S	naval	TPHA*EUFL
maybe	PHAEUB	missus	PHEUS/SUS	navel	TPHA*EUF/EL
may be	PHAEU/PW-	miss us	PHEUSZ/US		
		Mrs.	PHR-S	nave (see knave)	
mean (see main)					
		moan	PHOEPB	nay	TPHAEU
meant	PHEPBT	mown	PHOUPB	nee	TPHA*EU
-ment (suf)	/-PLT			neigh	TPHAEUG
		moat	PHO*ET		
meat	PHAET	moot	PHAOT	necks	TPHEBG/-S
meet	PHAOET	mote	PHOET	next	TPH*EBGS
mete	PHAO*ET	mute	PHAOUT		
				need (see knead)	
medal	PHED/TKAL	modal	PHOE/TKAL	new (see gnu)	
meddle	PHED/-L	model	PHOD/EL		
metal	PHET/TAL			news	TPHAOUZ
mettle	PHET/-L	mode	PHOED	noose	TPHAOS
met all	PHET/AUL	mowed	PHOE/-D [PHOU/-D]		
				nicks	TPHEUBG/-S
mental	PHEPB/TAL	mold	PHOELD	nix	TPHEUBGS
-mental (suf)	-PLT/TAL	mould	PHOULD		
				niece (see knees)	
mentally	PHEPBT/HREU	mole, moll (see ma)		night (see knight)	
-mentally (suf)	-PLT/HREU			nit (see knit)	
		mom	PHOPL	no (see know)	
		Mom	PHO*PL	nob (see knob)	

Nobel	TPHOEB/EL	pa	PA	passed	PASZ/-D
noble	TPHOEBL	Pa	PA*	past	PA*S
		paw	PAU		
nobody *(see knob)*				pat	PAT
noes *(see knows)*		PAC	PA*BG [P-RBGS/A*BG]	Pat	K-P/PAT
		pack	PABG	path	PA*T
none	TPHUPB				
nun	TPH*UPB	pace	PAEUS	patience	PAEURBS
non- *(pre)*	TPHOPB	pays	PAEU/-S	patients	PAEURBT/-S
northern	TPHO*RPB	paced	PAEUS/-D	pause	PAUZ
north earn	TPHO*RT/ERPB	paste	PA*EUS	paws	PAU/-S
nose *(see knows)*		pact	PABGT	pea	PAE
not *(see knot)*		packed	PABG/-D	pee	PAOE
nu *(see gnu)*		packet	PABG/ET		
				peace	PAES
oar	AOR	paddy	PAD/TKEU	piece	PAOES
or	OR	patty	PAT/TEU	peas	PAE/-S
ore	OER	Patty	PA*T/TEU	pees	PAOE/-S
or- *(pre)*	O*R				
-or *(suf)*	(c)OR	pail	PAEUL	peak	PAEBG
other	O*ER	pale	PA*EUL	peek	PAOEBG
		peal	PAEL	pique	PAO*EBG
odd *(see awed)*		peel	PAOEL		
				peal *(see pail)*	
odder	OD/ER	pain	PAEUPB		
otter	OT/ER	pane	PAEPB	pearl	PERL
				peril	P*ERL [PER/REUL]
ode	OED	pair	PAEUR	purl	PURL
owed	KWROE/-D	payer	PAEU/KWRER		
			[PAEU/ER]	peat	PAET
offal *(see awful)*		pare	PA*EUR	Pete	PAO*ET
		pear	PAER		
oh	O*E	peer	PAOER	pedal	PED/TKAL
owe	KWROE	pier	PAO*ER	peddle	PED/-L
				petal	PET/TAL
okay	O*EBG [O/KAEU]	pal	PAL	pet all	PET/AUL
o.k.	O*BG	POW	PO*U [P-RBGS/O*U]		
				peel *(see pail)*	
omission *(see emission)*		palate	PAL/HRAT	peer, pier *(see pair)*	
		palette	PAL/ET		
once	WUPBS	pallet	PAL/*ET	peers	PAOER/-S
ones	WUPB/-S	pal let	PAL/HRET	pierce	PAOERS
wants	WAPBT/-S			piers	PAO*ER/-S
		pall	PAUL		
one	WUPB	Paul	PA*UL	peg	PEG
won	WOPB			Peg	P*EG
		papa	PA/PA		
oracle *(see auricle)*		Papa	PA*/PA	penal	PAOEPBL
oral *(see aural)*		pawpaw	PAU/PAU	penile	PAOE/TPHEUL
ordinance	O*RD/TPHAPBS	parameter	PRAPL/TER	penance	PEPB/TPHAPBS
ordnance	ORD/TPHAPBS	perimeter	PREUPL/TER	pennants	PEPB/TPHAPBT/-S
otter *(see odder)*		parish	PAR/EURB	pend	PEPBD
ought *(see aught)*		perish	PER/EURB	penned	PEPB/-D
our *(see hour)*					
		parlay	PAR/HRAEU	pendant	PEPB/TKAPBT
overdo	O*FR/TKO	parley	PAR/HRAOE	pendent	PEPB/TKEPBT
overdue	O*FR/TKAOU				[PEPBD/EPBT]
		parol	PA/ROL [PARL]		
overseas	O*FR/SAE/-S	parole	PA/ROEL [PAERL]	per	PER
oversees	O*FR/SAOE/-S	payroll	PAEU/ROL [PAEURL]	purr	PUR
over seas	O*EFR/SAE/-S				
		partition	PAR/TEUGS		
ow, owl *(see Al)*		petition	PE/TEUGS		

 Step 4: Soundalike Summary

peremptory	PER/EFRPT/REU [PER/EFRP/TOEUR]	pool	PAOL	prophecy	PROF/S*EU
preemptory	PRE/EFRPT/REU [PRE/EFRP/TOEUR]	pull	PUL	prophesy	PROF/SEU
		poor	PAOR	pros	PROE/-S
persecute	PERS/KAOUT	pore	POER	prose	PROEZ
prosecute	PROS/KAOUT [PR-T]	pour	POUR		
		power	POU/ER [PO*UR]	protean	PROET/KWRAPB
personality	PERS/TPHAL/TEU [PERPBLT]	pure	PAOUR	protein	PRO/TAOEPB
personalty	P*ERS/TPHAL/TEU P*ERPBLT	poplar	POP/HRAR	proud	PROUD
		popular	POP/KWRU/HRAR [PO*P/HRAR]	prowled	PROUL/-D
petit	PET/TAOE			prow	PROU
petite	PE/TAOET	praise	PRAEUZ	prowl	PROUL
petty	PET/TEU	prays	PRAEU/-S		
		preys	PRA*EU/-S	psi	SAO*EU
pew	PAOU			sigh	SAOEU
pugh	PAO*U	pray	PRAEU		
		prey	PRA*EU	pulls	PUL/-S
phase (see face)				pulse	PULS
Phil (see fill)		prayer	PRAEUR [PRAEU/ER][PRAEU/KWRER]	purrs	PUR/-S
phrase (see frays)		preyer	PRA*EUR [PRA*EU/ER][PRA*EU/KWRER]	purse	PURS
physical (see fiscal)					
		precede	PRE/SAED	put	PUT
pi	PAO*EU	proceed	PRO/SAOED [PRAOED]	putt	P*UT
pie	PAOEU	preseed	PRE/SAOED		
				quaff (see coif)	
pier (see pare)		precedence	PRES/TKEPBS		
		precedents	PRES/TKEPBT/-S	quarts	KWART/-S
pidgin	PEUPBLG/SKWREUPB	presidents	P-TS [PREZ/TKEPBT/-S]	quartz	KWARTS
pigeon	PEUPBLG/SKWROPB				
		precedent	PRES/TKEPBT	quay (see key)	
pistil	PEUS/TEUL	president	P-T [PREZ/TKEPBT]	queue (see coo)	
pistol	PEUS/TOL	President	P*T		
				quiet	KWAO*EUT [KWAOEU/ET]
place	PHRAEUS	premier	PRE/PHAOER	quite	KWAOEUT
plays	PHRAEU/-S	premiere	PREPL/KWRAOER		
				quire (see choir)	
plain	PHRAEUPB	prescribe	PRE/SKRAOEUB		
plane	PHRAEPB	proscribe	PRO/SKRAOEUB	race	RAEUS
				raise	RAEUZ
plantar	PHRAPB/TAR	presence	PREPBS	rays	RAEU/-S
planter	PHRAPBT/ER	presents	PREPBT/-S	raze	RAEZ
				razz	RAZ
plat	PHRAT	price	PRAOEUS		
plait	PHRAEUT	pries	PRAOEU/-S	racer	RAEUS/ER
plate	PHRAET	prize	PRAOEUZ	raiser	RAEUZ/ER
				razor	RAEU/SO*R
pleas	PHRAOE/-S	pride	PRAOEUD		
please	PHRAOEZ	pried	PRAOEU/-D	rack	RABG
police	PHREUS			wrack	WRABG
		prince	PREUPBS		
plight	PHRAOEUGT	Prince	PR*EUPBS	racket	RABGT [RABG/ET]
polite	PHRAOEUT	prints	PREUPBT/-S	racquet	RABG/KET
plum	PHRUPL	princes	PREUPBS/-S	rail	RAEUL
plumb	PHR*UPL	princess	PREUPBS/ESZ	rale	RAL
		Princess	PR*EUPBS/ESZ	real	RAEL
polar	POE/HRAR			reel	RAOEL
poller	POL/ER	principal	PREUPBS/PAL	riyal	RAO*E/KWRAL
		principle	PREUPBS/P-L	rial	RAO*EL
pole	POEL			really	RAEL/HREU [RA*EL]
Pole	PO*EL	profit	PROFT		
poll	POL	prophet	PROF/ET	rain	RAEUPB
pol	PO*L			reign	RA*EUPB
				rein	RAEPB

ram	RAPL	recreation	REBG/RAEUGS	right	RAOEUGT
RAM	RA*PL	re-creation	RE/H-F/KRAOE/KWRAEUGS	rite	RAOEUT
			[RE/H-F/KRAEGS]	write	WRAOEUT [WREU]
rap	RAP			Wright	WRAOEUGT
wrap	WRAP	recur	RE/KUR	riot	RAOEU/OT
		reoccur	RE/O/KUR		[RAOEU/KWROT]
rappel	RA/PEL				
repel	RE/PEL	reefer	RAOEFR	rim	REUPL
		refer	REFR	ripple	REUP/-L
rapped	RAP/-D				
rapt	RAPT	reek	RAOEBG	ring	REUPBG
wrapped	WRAP/-D	wreak	WRAOEBG	wring	WREUPBG
rapper	RAP/ER	reel (see rail)		rise (see rice)	
wrapper	WRAP/ER				
		reflects	RE/TPHREBGT/-S	ritz	REUTS
rational	RAGS/TPHAL [RARBL]	reflex	RE/TPHREBGS	writs	WREUT/-S
rationale	RAGS/TPHAEL				
		reform	RE/TPORPL	riyal (see rail)	
ray	RAEU	re-form	RE/H-F/TPORPL		
Ray	RA*EU			road	ROED
re	R*E	regal	RE/TKPWAL	rode	RO*ED
re:	REFRPLT	regale	RE/TKPWAEL	rowed	ROE/-D
re- (pre)	RE				
		release	RE/HRAOES	roam	ROEPL
read	RAED	re-lease	RE/H-F/HRAOES	Rome	RO*EPL
reed	RAOED				
red	RED	residence	REZ/TKEPBS	roe	RO*E
		residents	REZ/TKEPBT/-S	row (o sd)	ROE
real (see rail)				row (ou sd)	ROU
		resign	RE/SAOEUPB		
realign	RE/AEU/HRAOEUPB	re-sign	RE/H-F/SAOEUPB	roil	RO*EUL
reline	RE/HRAOEUPB			royal	ROEUL
		resold	RE/SOELD		
rebait	RE/PWAEUT	resoled	RE/SOEL/-D	role	ROEL
rebate	RE/PWA*ET			roll	ROL
		resort	RE/SORT		
recede	RE/SAED	re-sort	RE/H-F/SORT	roomer	RAOPL/ER
reseed	RE/SAOED			rumor	RAOU/PHOR
		rest	R*ES		
receipt	RE/SAOEPT	wrest	WR*ES	roomie	RAO/PHAOE
reseat	RE/SAOET				[RAOPL/PHAOE]
		retch	REFP	roomy	RAO/PH*EU
recent	RE/KREPBT	wretch	WREFP		[RAOPL/PH*EU]
resent	RE/SEPBT				
		revelry	R*EFL/REU	root	RAOT
reck	REBG	reverie	R*EF/RAOE	rout	ROUT
wreck	WREBG			route	RAOUT
		review	RE/SRAOU		
recoil	RE/KOEUL	revue	RE/SRU	rose	ROEZ
re-coil	RE/H-F/KOEUL			Rose	RO*EZ
		rheum	RAOUPL	rows	ROE/-S
recollect	REBGT [REBG/HREBGT]	room	RAOPL		
re-collect	RE/H-F/KHREBGT			rot	ROT
		Rhodes	RO*EDZ	wrought	WRAUGT [WRAUT]
recommend	REPLD	roads	ROEDZ		
	[REBG/PHEPBD]			rote	ROET
rem	REPL	rhyme	RAO*EUPL	wrote	WROET [WRO]
REM	R*EPL	rime	RAOEUPL		
				rough	RUF
recount	RE/KOUPBT	rice	RAOEUS	ruff	R*UF
re-count	RE/H-F/KOUPBT	rise	RAOEUZ		
		ryes	RAOEU/-S	rude	RAOUD
recover	RE/KO*FR			rued	RAOU/-D
re-cover	RE/H-F/KO*FR	riffle	REUFL		
		rifle	RAOEUFL	rues	RAOU/-S
				ruse	RAOUZ

 Step 4: Soundalike Summary

ruin	RAOUPB	sea	SAE	sewer	SAOUR [SOE/ER]
rune	RAO*UPB	see	SAOE	soar	SAOR
				sore	SOER
ruinous	RAOUPB/OUS	seal (see ceil)		suer	SAOU/ER
ruin us	RAOUPB/US	sealing (see ceiling)		sour	SOUR
rung	RUPBG	seam	SAEPL	sewn	SOEPB
wrung	WRUPBG	seem	SAOEPL	sown	SOUPB
				zone	SO*EPB
rye	RAOEU	seamen	SAE/PHEPB		
wry	WRAOEU	see men	SAOE/PHEPB	shake (see chic)	
		semen	SAOEPL/-PB		
sac	SA*BG			shear	SHAER
sack	SABG	sear	SAER	sheer	SHAOER
		seer	SAOE/ER		
sacs	SA*BG/-S	sere	SAOER	sheik (see chic)	
sacks	SABG/-S				
sax	SABGS	seas (see cease)		shoe	SHAOU
		seated(ing) (see ceded[ing])		shoo	SHAO
said	SAEUD				
sed	SED	secede	SE/SAED [SE/SAOED]	shone	SHOEPB
		succeed	SUBG/SAOED	shown	SHOUPB
sail	SAEUL				
sale	SAEL	sects	SEBGT/-S	shoot (see chute)	
		sex	SEBGS		
Salk	SAUBG			shore	SHOER
sulk	SUL/-BG	seed (see cede)		sure	SHAOUR
		seeded(ing) (see ceded[ing])			
salt	SAULT	sees, seize (see cease)		shred	SH-/RED [SHR*ED]
sought	SAUGT [SAUT]	sell (see cell)		sled	SHRED
		seller (see cellar)			
sands	SAPBDZ			shrew	SH-/RAOU [SHRAO*U]
sans	SAPBS [SAPBZ]	seminal	SEPL/TPHAL	slew	SHRAOU
		Seminole	SEPL/TPHOEL		
sane	SAEUPB			shriek	SH-/RAOEBG
seine	SA*EUPB	sense (see cents)			[SHRAO*EBG]
Seine	K-P/SA*EUPB	senses (see census)		sleek	SHRAOEBG
		sensor (see censer)			
sat	SAT	sent (see cent)		shrink	SH-/REUPB/-BG
SAT	SA*T [S-RBGS/A*T]				[SHR*EUPB/-BG]
		Seoul	SO*EL		[SHR*EUPBG]
saver	SA*EUFR	sol	SOL	slink	SHREUPB/-BG
savor	SAEU/SROR	sole	SOEL	sling	SHREUPBG
savior	SA*EUF/KWROR	soul	SOUL		
safer	SAEUFR			shrug	SH-/RUG [SHR*UG]
save your	SA*EUF/KWROUR	serf	SER/-F	slug	SHRUG
		surf	SUR/-F		
scarce	SKAEURS			shrunk	SH-/RUPB/-BG
scares	SKAEUR/-S	serge	SERPBLG		[SHR*UPB/-BG]
		surge	SURPBLG	slunk	SHRUPB/-BG
scene	SAEPB			slung	SHRUPBG
seen	SAOEPB	serial (see cereal)			
		serious, serous (see cirrus)		sic	S*EUBG
scent (see cent)		serrate (see cerate)		sick	SEUBG
scents (see cents)		session (see cession)			
				sics	S*EUBG/-S
science	SAOEUPBS	settler	SET/HRER	six	SEUBGS
signs	SAOEUPB/-S	settlor	SET/HROR		
				side	SAOEUD
scion	SAOEU/KWROPB	sever	S*EFR [S*EF/ER]	sighed	SAOEU/-D
sign	SAOEUPB	zephyr	S*EF/TPER		
sine	SAO*EUPB		[S*EF/TPEUR]	sigh (see psi)	
scram	SKRAPL	sew	SOE	sighs	SAOEU/-S
scrapple	SKRAP/-L	so	SO	size	SAOEUZ
		sow (ou sd)	SOU		
scrip	SKREUP	sow (lg o)	SO*E	sight (see cite)	
script	SKREUPT			sign (see scion)	

silicon	SEUL/KOPB	spec	SP*EBG	tail	TAEUL
silicone	SEUL/KOEPB	speck	SPEBG	tale	TAEL
since, sins *(see cents)*		special(ly), *(see especial[ly])*		taught	TAUGT
sine *(see scion)*				taut	TAUT
		spice	SPAOEUS		
sink	SEUPB/-BG	spies	SPAOEU/-S	tea	TAE
sync	SEUPB/*BG			tee	TAOE
zinc	S*EUPB/-BG	staff	STAF		
		staph	STA*F	team	TAEPL
site *(see cite)*				teem	TAOEPL
		staid	STAEUD		
sits	SEUT/-S	stayed	STAEU/-D	tear *(a sd)*	TAEUR
sitz	SEUTS			tear *(e sd)*	TAER
		stair	STAEUR	tier	TAOER
slay	SHRAEU	stare	STAER	tare	TA*ER
sleigh	SHRAEUG				
		stake	STAEUBG	teas	TAE/-S
slew	SHRAOU	steak	STAEBG	tease	TAOEZ
slue	SHRU			tees	TAOE/-S
		stationary	STAEUGS/TPHAEUR		
slight	SHRAOEUGT	stationery	STAEUGS/TPHA*EUR	tens	TEPB/-S
sleight	SHRAO*EUGT			tense	TEPBS
		steal	STAEL	tends	TEPBDZ
sloe	SHRO*E	steel	STAOEL	tents	TEPBT/-S
slow	SHROE				
		steam	STAOEPL	tenser	TEPBS/ER
soar *(see sewer)*		steeple	STAOEP/-L	tensor	TEPB/SOR
soared	SAOR/-D	stile	STAO*EUL	tern	TERPB
sword	SOERD [SWORD]	style	STAOEUL	turn	TURPB
socks	SOBG/-S	straight	STRAEUGT	testee	TES/TAOE
sox	SOBGS	strait	STRAEUT	testy	TES/TEU
sold	SOELD	succor	SUBG/KOR	theater	THAOET/ER
soled	SOEL/-D	sucker	SUBG/ER	theatre	THAOET/*ER
sole *(see Seoul)*		sue	SAOU	their	THAEUR
		Sue	SAO*U	there	THR-
some	SOPL			they're	THAEU/AO*ER
sum	SUPL	suede	SWAEUD		[THA*EUR]
some- *(pre)*	SPH-, S-	swayed	SWAEU/-D	they are	THER [THAEU/R-]
-some *(suf)*	/SPH-			there are	THR-R
supple	SUP/-L	suite	SWAET		
		sweet	SWAOET	theirs	THAEURS
son	SOPB			there's	THR-/AOES [THR*S]
sun	SUPB	summarize	SUPL/RAOEUZ	there is	THR-S
		summerize	SUPL/ER/AOEUZ		
soot	SAOT			therefor	THR*FR
suit	SAOUT	summary	SUPL/PHAEUR	therefore	THR-FR
		summery	SUPL/REU	there for	THR-/TP-R
sore *(see sewer)*					
soul *(see Seoul)*		sundae	SUPB/TKAE	thigh	THAOEU
		Sunday	SUPBD [SUPB/TKAEU]	thy	THAO*EU
sores	SOER/-S				
source	SOURS	symbol *(see cymbal)*		threw	THRAOU
sours	SOUR/-S	symmetry *(see cemetery)*		through	THRU
southern	SO*RPB	syntax	SEUPB/TABGS	throe(s)	THROE(/-S) [THROES]
south earn	SO*UT/ERPB	sin tax	SEUPB/SP-S/TABGS	throw(s)	THROU(/-S)
spade	SPAEUD	tack	TABG	throne	THROEPB
spayed	SPAEU/-D	tact	TABGT	thrown	THROUPB
		tacked	TABG/-D		
spars	SPAR/-S			thyme	TAO*EUPL
sparse	SPARS	tacks	TABG/-S	time	TAOEUPL
		tax	TABGS		

tic	T*EUBG	trussed	TRUSZ/-D	vigor	SREU/TKPWOR
tick	TEUBG	trust	TR*US	vigour	SREU/TKPWOUR
tidal	TAOEU/TKAL	trustee	TRUS/TAOE	vindictive	SREUPB/TKEUBGT/*EUF
title	TAOEUT/-L	trusty	TRUS/TEU	vindicative	SREUPBD/KAEUT/*EUF
tide	TAOEUD	tucks	TUBG/-S	violence	SRAOEUL/EPBS
tied	TAOEU/-D	tux	TUBGS		[SRAOEUPBLS]
				violins	SRAOEU/HREUPB/-S
timber	TEUPL/PWER	turban	TUR/PWAPB		
timbre	TEUPL/PWRE	turbine	TUR/PWAOEUPB	Wac	WABG
			[TUR/PWEUPB]	whack	WHABG
to	TO				
too	TAO	udder	UD/ER	Wacs	WABG/-S
two	TWO	utter	UT/ER	wax	WABGS
				whacks	WHABG/-S
toad	TOED	unceded	UPB/SAED/-D		
toed	TOE/-D	unseated	UPB/SAOET/-D	wade	WAEUD
towed	TOU/-D	unseeded	UPB/SAOED/-D	weighed	WAEUG/-D
toe	TOE	undo	UPB/TKO	wail	WAEUL
tow	TOU	undue	UPB/TKAOU	whale	WHAEUL
				Wales	WAELS [WAELZ]
told	TOELD	unreal	UPB/RAEL		
tolled	TOL/-D	unreel	UPB/RAOEL	waist	WA*EUS
				waste	WA*ES
tole	TOEL	urn (see earn)			
toll	TOL			wait	WAEUT
		vail	SRAEUL	weight	WAEUGT
ton	TOPB	Vail	K-P/SRAEUL		
tun	TUPB	vale	SRAEL	waive	WA*EUF
		veil	SRA*EUL	wave	WA*EF
tooter	TAOT/ER	veal	SRAOEL	waif	WAEUF
tutor	TAOU/TOR				
		vain	SRAEUPB	waiver	WA*EUFR
tort	TORT	vane	SRAEPB	waver	WA*EFR
torte	TO*RT	vein	SRA*EUPB	wafer	WAEUFR
tortuous	TOR/KHOUS	variance	SRAEURPBS	walk	WAUBG
tortious	TOR/-RBS	variants	SRAEURPBT/-S	wok	WOBG
torturous	TOR/KHUR/OUS				
		vary	SRAEUR	want	WAPBT
trace	TRAEUS	very	SR-R	wont	WOPBT
trays	TRAEU/-S			won't	WOEPBT
		vas	SRAS	wasn't	WUPBT
track	TRABG	vast	SRA*S	was not	WUZ/TPHOT
tract	TRABGT				
tracked	TRABG/-D	vender	SREPBD/ER	wants (see once)	
		vendor	SREPB/TKOR		
trance	TRAPBS			war	WAR
trans	TRAPBZ	venous	SRAOEPB/OUS	wore	WOER
trans- (pre)	TRA*PBS	Venus	SRAOE/TPHUS		
				ward	WARD
transience	TRA*PBS/KWREPBS	veracious	SRE/RAEURBS	warred	WAR/-D
transients	TRA*PBS/KWREPBT/-S	voracious	SRO/RAEURBS		
				ware	WAEUR
tray	TRAEU	verses	SRERS/-S	wear	WAER
trey	TRA*EU	versus	SRER/SUS	where	WR-
		vs.	SR*S		
trim	TREUPL	v.	SR-RS [SR*PD]	warn	WARPB
triple	TREUP/-L			worn	WORPB
		vial	SRAO*EUL		
troop	TRAOP	vile	SRAOEUL	warrantee	WARPB/TAOE
troupe	TRAOUP			warranty	WARPB/TEU
		vice	SRAOEUS		
trooper	TRAOP/ER	vise	SRAOEUZ	watt	WAT
trouper	TRAOUP/ER	vies	SRAOEU/-S	what	WHA

---

way	WAEU		wry (see rye)	
weigh	WAEUG			
whey	WHAEU		yaw	KWRAU
			yawl	KWRAUL
we	WE		y'all	KWRA*UL
wee	WAOE			
			yea	KWRAE
weak	WAEBG		yeah	KWRA*E
week	WAOEBG			
			yew (see ewe)	
weaken	WAEBG/-PB			
weakened	WAEBG/-PBD		yoke	KWRO*EBG
weekend	WAOEBG/EPBD		yolk	KWROEBG
	[WAOEBGD]			
week end	WAOEBG/SP-S/EPBD		yore	KWROER
			your	KWROUR
weal	WAOEL		you're	KWROU/AO*ER
wheel	WHAOEL			[KWRO*UR]
we'll	WE/AOEL [WAO*EL]		you are	UR [KWROU/R-]
we will	WE/HR-			
well	WEL		you (see ewe)	
weather	W*ET/ER		you'll	KWROU/AOEL
whether	WHR-			[KWRO*UL]
			yule	KWRAOUL
weave	WAO*EF		you will	KWROU/HR-
we've	WE/AO*EF [W*EF]			
we have	WEF [WE/SR-]		zephyr (see sever)	
			zinc (see sink)	
weed	WAOED		zone (see sewn)	
we'd	WE/AOED [WAO*ED]			
we had	WE/HAD			
wed	WED			

whine	WHAOEUPB			
wine	WAOEUPB			
whined	WHAOEUPB/-D			
wind (v)	WAOEUPBD			
wined	WAOEUPB/-D			
whirl	WHEURL			
whorl	WHORL			
whirled	WHEURL/-D			
world	WORLD			
whiskey	WHEUS/KAOE			
whisky	WHEUS/KEU			
whit	WHEUT			
wit	WEUT			
whither	WH*EUT/ER			
wither	W*EUT/ER			
whiz	WHEUZ			
wiz	WEUZ			
whoa	WHOE			
woe	WOE			

whole (see hole)
wholly (see holy)
whore (see hoar)
whored (see hoard)
whores (see hoarse)

whose	WHOZ
who's	WHO/AOES [WHO*S
who is	WHOS]

wig (see Whig)

will	HR-
Will (name)	W*EUL
wince	WEUPBS
wins	WEUPB/-S
wolf	WOL/-F
woof	WAOF

won (see one)

wood	WAOD
would	WOULD

wrack (see rack)
wrap (see rap)
wrapped (see rapt)
wrapper (see rapper)
wreak (see reek)
wreck (see reck)
wrest (see rest)
wretch (see retch)
wring (see ring)
write (see right)
writs (see ritz)
wrote (see rote)
wrought (see rot)
wrung (see rung)

we'll, well (see weal)

were	W-R
we're	WE/AO*ER [WAO*ER]
we are	WER
whir	WHEUR
western	W*ERPB
west earn	W*ES/ERPB
wet	WET
whet	WHET

wheel (see weal)

whence	WHEPBS
when's	WHEPB/AOES [WH*S]
when is	WH-S [WHEPB/S-]
which	KH-
witch	WEUFP
Whig	WHEUG
wig	WEUG
while	WHAOEUL
wile	WAOEUL
whiled	WHAOEUL/-D
wild	WAOEULD

© 1993, 2001 *StenEd*® **Step 4: Soundalike Summary**

STEP 4—EXERCISES

SOUNDALIKES WITH THE SAME VOWEL SOUND

SOUNDALIKES WITH LONG A
Ex. RT-38 (Tape 3/A @ 125 wpm) & RT-38 (Tape 3/A @ 180 wpm)

1. The paramedic administered first <u>aid</u> to the accident victim.
   A presidential <u>aide</u> has many important duties to perform.
2. He would not <u>ail</u> so much if he would temper his intake of <u>ale</u>.
3. The judge set a high <u>bail</u> for the release of the criminal.
   The farmer sold the man a <u>bale</u> of hay for his garden.
4. The land was <u>bare</u> of trees and flowers.
   A large grizzly <u>bear</u> was captured for the city zoo.
5. The mechanic sent by the garage to repair the <u>brake</u> on the car took a long lunch <u>break</u>.
6. She was afraid she would <u>faint</u> at the sight of the accident victim.
   He attempted to <u>feint</u> a blow to the boxer's weak side in order to gain an advantage.
7. Ten cents is a <u>fair</u> bus <u>fare</u> for the three-block trip.
8. She has a <u>flair</u> for giving dinner parties.
   The <u>flare</u> warned the motorist of the impending danger.
9. The horse maintained its <u>gait</u> as it moved through the <u>gate</u>.
10. The <u>hair</u> of the frightened <u>hare</u> had been singed in the fire.
11. He was feeling <u>hale</u> and hearty on that beautiful spring day as he went to <u>hail</u> a cab.
12. <u>Hey</u>, did you see that pile of <u>hay</u> over by the horses?
13. Father asked us to <u>lade</u> the wagons with hay before we <u>laid</u> down our tools for the day.
14. The accident victim had <u>lain</u> in the <u>lane</u> for many hours before someone found him.

15. She turned <u>pale</u> when she saw the snake in the <u>pail</u>.
16. When the window <u>pane</u> fell on his head, he suffered great <u>pain</u>.
17. The highjacker's <u>plan</u> to seize the <u>plane</u> as they flew over the <u>plain</u> failed.
18. It was all the coachman could do to <u>retain</u> the <u>rein</u> when the horses ran away.
   The king was unable to begin his <u>reign</u> because it began to <u>rain</u> in the middle of his coronation parade.
19. He had to <u>rebait</u> his hook after the fish grabbed the worm.
   If you buy the equipment this week, you can get a <u>rebate</u>.
20. The <u>ray</u> of light made a beautiful path through the trees.
   A memo was written <u>re:</u> Employee Benefits.
21. As we put the last <u>stake</u> in the tent, Mother announced that the <u>steak</u> was ready to eat.
22. Three men tried in <u>vain</u> to find a <u>vein</u> of gold under the shadow of the weather <u>vane</u>.
23. The <u>waif</u> tried to <u>wave</u> and smile as she left on the ship that was returning her to her homeland after she had been deported.
   He chose to <u>waive</u> his right to read the transcript.
24. She signed a <u>waiver</u> relinquishing her previous claim.
   He continued to <u>waver</u> back and forth on the issue.
25. Even though she regretted her expanding <u>waist</u>, she hated to see food go to <u>waste</u>.

SOUNDALIKES WITH LONG E

Ex. RT-39 (Tape 3/A @ 125 wpm) & RT-39 (Tape 3/A @ 180 wpm)

1. The vegetarian claimed that, as far as taste was concerned, it was hard to beat the beet.
2. There were beech trees lining the beach.
3. He wanted just one more beer before retiring for the night.
   The bier was gently lowered into the ground.
4. The young woman sued the man for breach of promise when he broke their engagement.
   The breech of the rifle was cracked.
5. If she wasn't so cheap, she could have gotten a bird with a more melodic cheep.
6. The sheik didn't particularly care whether the women looked chic.
7. The warm water of the creek cured the creak in the old man's bones.
8. She was the dear daughter of a famous architect.
   The couple hit a deer as they were driving on the dark, deserted highway.
9. It is important to be discreet when conducting delicate foreign negotiation.
   The two discrete units were joined in the new operating system.
10. It will be quite a feat if he can stay on his feet after drinking champagne at the wedding fete.
11. Rover wished the flea would flee and stop pestering him.
12. With their genes, they're bound to have a blue-eyed baby.
    Her tight-fitting jeans drew much attention.
13. The people of Greece fry much of their food in grease.
14. The wound on his heel would not heal properly.
    He'll have to go back to the doctor to have it checked.
15. She brought her brother here to the clinic to find out why he could not hear.
16. She was quite indiscreet about her feelings on the subject.
    The chemical compound could not be further broken down into any more indiscrete components.
17. He was accidentally kneed in the head when he fell during a soccer game.
    You will need to knead the dough twice in order to make good bread.
18. He liked to lean against the wall and watch the girls.
    The bank put a lien on his house when his business failed.
19. In order to meet rationing requirements, the butcher had to mete out a certain portion of meat to each customer.
20. He reached the summit of the mountain peak in time for lunch.
    The boy likes to peek out the window and watch the birds peck at the seeds in the feeder.
    His tasteless comments always seem to pique her.
21. They couldn't get the lad to eat one single pea.
    The pee of the anchor was badly chipped.
22. He made peace with his brother by giving him a piece of candy.
23. His musical talent peaked at an early age.
    She was piqued when her friend peeked at her diary.
24. The captain's glance as he gazed at his men on the piers could pierce the heart of the bravest of his peers.
25. She heard the peal of the bell as she started to peel the potatoes.
26. Pete spread the peat moss on the garden.
27. They waited at the quay while the boat owner went to get the key.
28. Learning to reel in a fish can be a real problem.
29. The newlyweds could see the sea from their window.
30. The seam of the dress didn't seem strong enough.
31. The hit-and-run driver was seen at the scene of the accident.
32. The blouse was made of a sheer material which Jean bought with the money she earned by learning to shear sheep.
33. The bandit was unable to steal the diamonds because they were locked in a steel vault.
34. The hotel suite was filled with heavy, sweet perfume.
35. They had some tea in the clubhouse before they prepared to tee off.
36. She had been invited to many luncheon teas during the years.
    They decided to tease the obnoxious player by hiding his golf tees.
37. The gymnasium began to teem with excitement as the basketball team came out on the floor for the championship game.
38. He was too weak to walk after having spent a week in the hospital.

SOUNDALIKES WITH LONG A/LONG E
Ex. RT-40 (Tape 3/A @ 125 wpm) & RT-40 (Tape 3/A @ 180 wpm)

1. The city air was smoggy ere the pollution control devices were installed.
   She tried not to err when preparing her income tax return.
   The wealthy man left his heir $3 million.
2. We greet winter by building a great fire on the grate.
3. The kidnappers led the Secretary of State into their hideout and threatened to hit him with a lead pipe.
   The male lead in the play won acclaim for his performance.
4. The girl received an invitation for a meal from a male in the mail.
5. The mean horse's mane got wet when the main water main broke on his owner's farm in Maine.
6. The boy learned to pare a pear by watching his mother.
   He would peer through the window at the boy on the pier who was watching a pair of ducks splashing in the water.
7. Her long hair was in a beautiful plait flowing down her back.
   The plat showed the lot to be over two acres.
   She filled her plate with tempting offerings from the buffet.
   The pleat in his trousers was uneven.
8. We were able to seal the sale of the boat by agreeing to provide a new sail.
9. The warning stare of his mother kept the boy from teasing the steer.
   The small infant fell off the bottom stair but was not hurt.
10. They heard the tale of the donkey with the teal blue tail.
11. Changing the tire caused a tear in the tier of her gown which brought a tear to her eye.
12. The cottages were clustered in the vale.
    The veal was prepared to perfection.
    The bridal veil was too extravagant.

SOUNDALIKES WITH LONG I
Ex. RT-41 (Tape 3/A @ 125 wpm) & RT-41 (Tape 3/A @ 180 wpm)

1. When debugging her program, she was forced to bite the bullet and examine every last byte of source code.
2. His fortune was lost on a toss of the dice.
   New dies were made to produce the metal parts for the automobile.
   She says she practically dies every time she gives a presentation.
   The dyes in the cloth were found to be dangerous to the health of the users.
3. Dye injected under the skin caused the animal to die.
4. "Hi," the young lad shouted to his father from high up in the tree.
   He found it necessary to hie himself to the lawyer's office.
5. "I'll walk down the aisle with you," said the bride-to-be.
   The ship's passengers were stranded on a desert isle.
6. He felt it best to lie about where he had put the lye.
7. I was quite tempted to quit my job when it became impossible to work in peace and quiet.
8. The poet was working on a rhyme to aptly describe the rime gently coating the ground.
9. Give me a sign when you've figured out the sine of the angle.
10. His knowledge of sleight of hand made him a slight favorite of the youngsters at a party.
11. The vial contained a vile smelling substance.

SOUNDALIKES WITH LONG O
Ex. RT-42 (Tape 3/B @ 125 wpm) & RT-42 (Tape 3/B @ 180 wpm)

1. Her beau tried to impress her with his expertise with the bow and arrow.
2. The doe and her fawns ran lightly across the field.
   She used the leftover dough to make a pie.
3. He let out a groan when he found he had grown an inch.
4. They load the wagons daily with high quality silver from the lode.
   The cows lowed as they walked by the fence.
5. The Lone Ranger obtained a loan using his silver bullets as collateral.
6. The moat around the castle kept trespassers away.
   There was not one mote of dust left after the cleaning crew was finished.
7. "Oh, how will I pay the money I owe," cried the desperate woman.
8. A poll was taken to determine if the pole vaulter should go to the Olympics.
9. Wyatt Earp rode his horse down the road.
   He rowed the boat to the nearby island.
10. His role in the party was to provide a jelly roll.
11. The star which had shone in the sky on Christmas night had shown the wise men the way to the manger.
12. The hobo practically had to sell his soul in order to have the sole of his shoe repaired.
13. Prince Charles may inherit the British throne some day.
    His knee was thrown out of joint during the game.
14. He throws the ball so hard that the catcher sounds like he's going through his death throes when he catches it.
15. Pat broke her leg when she got her toe caught in the tow rope while water skiing.
16. The toad seemed to croak endlessly.
    The girl was terribly pigeon-toed.
    The wrecked car was towed to the garage.
17. The yoke of the dress contrasted with the rest of the garment.
    The egg's yolk was not quite firm enough.

SOUNDALIKES WITH LONG U
Ex. RT-43 (Tape 3/B @ 125 wpm) & RT-43 (Tape 3/B @ 180 wpm)

1. When they were given the cue, the fans formed a queue in front of the theater to see the star arrive for the premier of her movie.
2. A strong wind blew over the blue spruce in our yard.
3. The man had a dual personality; one side of him was dull and colorless while the other was an adventurous fellow who loved to fight a duel.
4. The patient flew from the doctor's office when told he had the flu.
   Mama forgot to open the flue when she lit the fire in the fireplace.
   All his influence could not change the teacher's mind about the boy's grades.
5. The critic went to review the gala revue.

SOUNDALIKES WITH LONG O & LONG U
Ex. RT-44 (Tape 3/B @ 125 wpm) & RT-44 (Tape 3/B @ 180 wpm)

1. The moat around the castle kept trespassers away.
   There was not one mote of dust left after the cleaning crew was finished.
2. It was a moot point whether or not John would remain mute.
3. The invalid had to pour pure water on his poor crippled legs in order to regain the power to walk.
   An important cure for acne is to be sure that every pore is free of dirt and oil.
4. When the battle along the unfamiliar route turned into a rout, the general searched for the root of the problem.
5. She had to shoo a caterpillar out of her new shoe in order to show it to her friend.
6. He was sure that the shore was made of the whitest sand he had ever seen.

 Step 4: Soundalikes

SOUNDALIKES WITH DIPHTHONGS
& OTHER VOWEL SOUNDS
Ex. RT-45 (Tape 3/B @ 125 wpm) & RT-45 (Tape 3/B @ 180 wpm)

1. The <u>boar</u> slowly moved toward the food. The <u>boor</u>, because of his bad manners, quickly became a <u>bore</u> to the other guests.
2. The man became quite <u>bold</u> as he <u>bowled</u> his third strike in a row.
3. The <u>bolder</u> of the two boys climbed over the large <u>boulder</u> blocking the entrance to the cave in which they were trapped.
4. Soon after he crossed the <u>border</u>, he became a <u>boarder</u> in a run-down rooming house.
5. Joe <u>bored</u> a large hole in the <u>board</u>.
6. The <u>bole</u> of the old elm tree was diseased. The entire cotton crop was destroyed by the <u>boll</u> weevil. The students studied the function of the <u>bowel</u> in health class. Billy ate a <u>bowl</u> of soup and four sand-wiches for lunch.
7. The subject was requested to <u>bow</u> before the queen as she stood beneath the <u>bough</u> of the tree.
8. The tough drill sergeant with the <u>coarse</u> voice had been a member of the Marine <u>Corps</u> for 20 years. The <u>core</u> of his training <u>course</u> was to teach the young recruit who <u>cowers</u> from fright at the sound of gunfire how to avoid becoming a <u>corpse</u>. When they finish their training, they will be true fighting men and women to the very <u>cores</u> of their beings.
9. When the lawn was <u>mown</u>, a buried box of <u>money</u> was discovered, and a <u>moan</u> was heard from the thief who had put it there.
10. It took <u>more</u> energy than the man was willing to exert to move the lawn <u>mower</u> around his yard.
11. Shad <u>roe</u> is considered a delicacy in many areas. They had a <u>row</u> over who could <u>row</u> the boat the fastest. All the prizes were lined up in a <u>row</u>.

12. The dog <u>chews</u> the bones given to him by the butcher. He was forced to <u>choose</u> between college and a military career.
13. The feed flowed down the <u>chute</u>. He was excited about going to his first turkey <u>shoot</u>.
14. The two doves <u>coo</u> contentedly in their <u>coop</u>. The marketing <u>co-op</u> was part of the <u>coup</u> to lower food prices. The old <u>coupe</u> had over 150,000 miles, but it was still running.
15. She didn't appreciate the <u>rumor</u> that was going around town about her <u>roomer</u>.
16. The boy always seemed to <u>lose</u> all his <u>loose</u> change.
17. His <u>suit</u> was covered with <u>soot</u> and <u>sweat</u> from his long train trip.
18. The <u>troop</u> of soldiers hoped they would be going home soon. The <u>troupe</u> of actors collapsed after their long journey.
19. The students were not <u>allowed</u> to speak <u>aloud</u> during exams.
20. There was a <u>foul</u> smell coming from the dead <u>fowl</u> that was thrown in the gar-bage.
21. The <u>boy</u> warned his father when their boat got too close to the <u>buoy</u>.
22. She had to <u>don</u> warm clothes in order to go on the ski trip at <u>dawn</u>.
23. The young boy was <u>bawled</u> out for throw-ing the <u>balled</u>-up candy wrapper at the <u>bald</u> man in the row in front of him.
24. It was difficult to <u>haul</u> the grand piano through the narrow <u>hall</u>.
25. The shopping <u>mall</u> was bewitchingly decorated for Halloween. The trainer took precautions so the lion wouldn't <u>maul</u> him.

 StenEd®

SOUNDALIKES WITH SHORT VOWELS
Ex. RT-46 (Tape 3/B @ 125 wpm) & RT-46 (Tape 3/B @ 180 wpm)

1. The couple wanted to <u>alter</u> the <u>altar</u> before their wedding ceremony.
2. My <u>aunt</u> killed an <u>ant</u> which was crawling up her leg.
3. After much deliberation, the code breaker thought that the missing character <u>ought</u> to be an <u>aught</u>.
4. She returned to her <u>berth</u> to get a good night's sleep.
   The <u>birth</u> of the kittens was an unexpected event.
5. There were some extremely <u>bizarre</u> trinkets for sale at the <u>bazaar</u>.
6. Homemade <u>bread</u> is delicious served warm with butter and jam.
   The germs on the rotten meat <u>breed</u> disease.
   Farmers in Kentucky have <u>bred</u> thoroughbred race horses for years.
7. It was at least five minutes before he could <u>breathe</u> normally again after losing his <u>breath</u> while attempting to run the whole <u>breadth</u> of the stadium.
8. There was a <u>cache</u> of <u>cash</u> hidden at the bottom of the well.
9. The porter's <u>cap</u> fell off as he lifted the heavy suitcases.
   The tour group was awed by the grandeur of the <u>capitol</u> building when they visited the <u>capital</u> city.
10. Tom gave Mary a one <u>carat</u> diamond ring.
    The important passages in the speech were indicated with a <u>caret</u>.
    We fed a <u>carrot</u> to the horse on the farm.
11. He was <u>cast</u> out of the tribe when he married above his level in the <u>caste</u> system.
12. The girl was given a <u>compliment</u> on what a beautiful <u>complement</u> her new mink coat was to her ensemble.
13. The <u>decease</u> of his grandfather from the dread <u>disease</u> caused the boy much sorrow.
14. He wanted to <u>desert</u> when he realized he'd be spending the next six months in the <u>desert</u>.

That <u>dessert</u> is the best she's made yet.
15. Nothing was <u>done</u> to <u>dun</u> the gambler for payment of his debts.
16. She hoped she would <u>earn</u> enough to be able to afford an antique <u>urn</u> she had been admiring.
17. <u>For the</u> <u>fourth</u> time, the cavalry was forced to ride <u>forth</u> to protect the <u>fort</u>.
18. She tore her <u>fur</u> coat on the large <u>fir</u> tree in the yard.
    <u>Fewer</u> people attended the fireworks than ever before in the history of the July 4th celebration.
19. When the <u>herd</u> of cattle <u>heard</u> the sound of gunfire, they began to run across the open plain.
20. The <u>gorilla</u> was used for <u>guerrilla</u> warfare.
21. I was <u>just</u> trying to get at the <u>gist</u> of the matter.
    He always seems to <u>jest</u> about his lack of education.
22. <u>More than</u> ever, he was moved to <u>mourn</u> for his dead wife on a lovely summer <u>morn</u>.
23. This is the third <u>morning</u> she's been in <u>mourning</u> for her lost cat.
24. A <u>non</u>-Catholic girl cannot become a <u>nun</u>.
    <u>No one</u> had seen the <u>known</u> criminal when he arrived in town, and <u>none</u> of us knew he had left.
25. Those oranges only cost $1.00 <u>per</u> dozen.
    The cat liked to <u>purr</u> when she was fed.
26. The famous <u>prophet</u> predicted the faltering business would earn a large <u>profit</u> that year.
27. They <u>read</u> the story of the prince who found a magical <u>red</u> <u>reed</u>.
28. The <u>serf</u> temporarily escaped from his chores to relax on the <u>surf</u>.
29. The <u>sun</u> shone brightly on the day the couple's first <u>son</u> was born.
30. As we took the <u>turn</u> that led to the shore, we saw a <u>tern</u> sitting on a rock.
31. The <u>urbane</u> gentleman preferred the country to the <u>urban</u> life.
32. We wondered <u>whether</u> the <u>weather</u> would be fair for our picnic tomorrow.

SOUNDALIKES WITH THE SAME CONSONANT SOUND

INITIAL

SOUNDALIKES WITH WH- AND WR-
Ex. RT-47 (Tape 3/B @ 125 wpm) & RT-47 (Tape 3/B @ 180 wpm)

1. The little girl began to <u>wail</u> when she saw the <u>whale</u> at Marineland.
2. She hated to <u>wax</u> the floor.
   It took many <u>whacks</u> to fell that huge tree.
3. <u>Weal</u> is a word which refers to a healthy state, and this term cannot be used when referring to the bent <u>wheel</u> of my car. <u>We'll</u> have to get it fixed quickly.
4. The cutlery expert decided to <u>whet</u> the knife which had gotten <u>wet</u> when it fell in the lake.
5. The <u>Whig</u> wore a long, curly, white-powdered <u>wig</u>.
6. <u>While</u> he was on vacation, he lost his money to a girl with a coquettish <u>wile</u>.
7. Her husband asked her not to <u>whine</u> when she spilled the <u>wine</u>.
8. The <u>wit</u> of the <u>witness</u> was not worth a <u>whit</u>.
9. "<u>Whither</u> thou goest, I will go," are lines from an old, popular song.
   The cherry blossoms are sure to <u>wither</u> because of the late frost.
10. He put his <u>whole</u> savings into a <u>hole</u> in his backyard and covered it with dirt.
11. The <u>holy</u> man's robe was made <u>wholly</u> of burlap and was very <u>holey</u> and worn.
12. Unsure of what the future would bring, they decided to <u>hoard</u> a <u>horde</u> of groceries.
    Many thought that he had <u>whored</u> away his good name by taking the bribes.
13. The old man, withered and <u>hoar</u> with age, confided to the <u>whore</u> that he had had big dreams once.

The <u>hoer</u> worked on his garden diligently.
14. He grew <u>hoarse</u> from screaming at the <u>whores</u> who stole his <u>horse</u>.
15. Even though he <u>racked</u> his brain, he couldn't remember where he put the <u>rack</u>. The old, dilapidated <u>wrack</u> had been quite a ship in its day.
16. When she heard a <u>rap</u> on her door, the girl had to quickly <u>wrap</u> a robe around her in order to answer it.
17. A <u>rapt</u> reader, she was so <u>wrapped</u> up in the novel that she was startled when someone loudly <u>rapped</u> on the door.
18. He tried not to <u>wreak</u> his anger at the owner of the tower that always seemed to <u>reek</u> of offensive fumes.
19. He had to <u>rest</u> after attempting to <u>wrest</u> the canoe paddle from the hungry shark.
20. The poor, old <u>wretch</u> quietly staggered into the alley to <u>retch</u>.
21. She cried until she could <u>wring</u> the water out of her handkerchief when she lost her wedding <u>ring</u>.
22. He felt it was his <u>right</u> to <u>write</u> about the <u>riot</u>, including the <u>rite</u> of purification performed over the ruins of the damaged buildings.
23. He <u>wrote</u> the paragraph until he could recite it by <u>rote</u>.
24. He <u>wrung</u> out the towel which had been hanging on the <u>rung</u> of the ladder.
25. He gave a <u>wry</u> smile at the sight of the <u>rye</u> bread on the table.

SOUNDALIKES WITH S- AND SOFT C-
Ex. RT-48 (Tape 3/B @ 125 wpm) & RT-48 (Tape 3/B @ 180 wpm)

1. He needed his father's <u>assent</u> in order to participate in the <u>ascent</u> of the balloon.
2. He would not <u>cede</u> the treasure without a fight.
   They followed the <u>creed</u> they were taught in their childhood.
   A beautiful flower bloomed from the <u>seed</u> they planted last year.
3. The soldiers were ordered to <u>cease</u> and desist when they tried to <u>seize</u> the fort.
   The <u>crease</u> in his suit gave the speaker a rumpled appearance.
   He <u>sees</u> the motorboat cruising across the open <u>seas</u> every day.
4. The defective <u>sealing</u> substance on the roof allowed water to drip onto the <u>ceiling</u>.
5. He was asked to <u>sell</u> his scientific findings on <u>cell</u> growth to a magazine.
6. He stared at the walls of his <u>cell</u>, wishing he had never been so stupid as to <u>sell</u> the stolen goods.
7. The <u>seller</u> of the house decided he had better clean the <u>cellar</u> if he expected someone to buy.
8. The fragrance from the <u>censer</u> was unusual but pleasant.
   The <u>censure</u> of the <u>censor</u> forced the play to close after one night.
   A <u>sensor</u> was placed at the bottom of the ocean to detect sharks.
9. The <u>scent</u> of the skunk <u>sent</u> the boys running from the cave.
10. Since he had no <u>sense</u> of money management, he lost all his dollars and <u>cents</u> gambling in Las Vegas.
    She finally decided which of the <u>scents</u> she preferred and made her purchase.
    He was afraid he would not be forgiven for his <u>sins</u>.
11. The boy wanted that particular <u>cereal</u> so he could read the <u>serial</u> on the back of the box.
12. The <u>cession</u> of the territory taken during the war came after a long negotiating <u>session</u>.
13. He could <u>cite</u> a dozen reasons why children shouldn't be allowed on the construction <u>site</u> since one worker lost his <u>sight</u> in an accident.
14. His untimely <u>descent</u> from his important position gave rise to much <u>dissent</u> among the <u>decent</u> people of the community.
15. He got some <u>insight</u> into the methods used to <u>incite</u> riots by watching films of student protest demonstrations.
    The end of the trip was <u>in sight</u>.
16. The water will <u>recede</u> from the boardwalk when the storm ends.
    They had to <u>reseed</u> the lawn after the hurricane.
17. Her most <u>recent</u> complaint is that he seems to <u>resent</u> her success.

He was given one <u>cent</u> for helping the elderly lady across the street.

OTHER INITIAL SOUNDS
Ex. RT-49 (Tape 3/B @ 125 wpm) & RT-49 (Tape 3/B @ 180 wpm)

1. After being hit in the <u>chin</u>, the boy kicked his opponent in the <u>shin</u>.
2. The <u>choral</u> group wore <u>coral</u>-colored robes for their concert.
   The horses jumped over the fence in the <u>corral</u>.
3. The pianist could not play that <u>chord</u>.
   A package tied with <u>cord</u> was left on the porch.
4. The <u>colonel</u> politely removed the <u>kernel</u> of corn that had fallen on his lap.
5. He <u>needed</u> to rest and catch his breath after being <u>kneed</u> in the stomach.
6. He <u>knew</u> that the <u>new</u> kid would get tired of his antics.
7. The daring <u>knight</u> waited till <u>night</u> to rescue the distressed damsel.
8. I was <u>not</u> able to untie the <u>knot</u>.

 Step 4: Soundalikes

SOUNDALIKES WITH THE SAME CONSONANT SOUND

FINAL

SOUNDALIKES WITH (v)L, -LE

Ex. RT-50 (Tape 3/B @ 125 wpm) & RT-50 (Tape 4/A @ 180 wpm)

1. The bridal party was nervous but excited.
   After putting on his bridle and saddle, she mounted the horse and they rode away.
2. They tried to console the American consul after the unsuccessful kidnap attempt.
   The legal counsel for the citizens' council won the case against discrimination.
3. The council reprimanded the habitually late councillor.
   The counselor for the defendant was worried about the outcome.
4. He tried not to gamble too much money away.
   The puppy wanted to gambol about all day long.
5. His new wife appeared to be quite genteel.
   Though she was a gentile, she had many Jewish friends.
   He was a thoughtful and gentle man.
6. They thought he was just being idle and wasting time, but he was actually writing an idyll for his idol.
7. She is liable to be sued for libel for her story about the celebrity.
8. Their marital spat was over some silly, unimportant thing.
   The parade marshal approved of the martial music the band played.
9. Because of her tendency to meddle, the gossip met all the newcomers to the neighborhood before anyone else.
   The medal on his chest, which was made of shiny metal, proved the hero's mettle.
10. He learned the modal split theory in his engineering class.
    The old sailor built a model of the ship on which he had sailed.

11. His morale was low because he thought his friend's behavior was not very moral.
12. The young boy flexed his arm, but his muscle was unimpressive.
    The mussel had washed up on the sand.
    The dog's owner insisted the muzzle was a necessary precaution.
13. The feeling was mutual that the pari-mutuel betting had ruined their budget for the month.
14. In early times, in order to prevent scurvy, navel oranges were typically kept on the ship as part of standard naval procedure.
15. The tramp would pedal his bicycle through the town, stopping to peddle his wares.
    The petal of the fragile flower was blown off by the wind.
16. The seeds of a flower are located in the pistil.
    This is the pistol that is the alleged murder weapon.
17. Through parol sources, they learned the prisoner was about to be released on parole.
    The company could barely make its payroll.
18. In his personal judgment, the personnel of the company could work harder.
19. The principal interest of most home buyers is the economic principle which gives them a tax advantage.
20. The principals of the play were taught the principles of good acting by looking at prints of The Prince and the Pauper.
21. What was your rationale for your decision?
    Being a rational person, he decided not to get upset.

SOUNDALIKES WITH -ER, -OR
Ex. RT-51 (Tape 4/A @ 125 wpm) & RT-51 (Tape 4/A @ 180 wpm)

1. That particular bettor did better than anyone else here.
2. The two armies concur it will be necessary to conquer the enemy before ending the war.
3. John was a doer of good deeds, and his door was always open to those in need.
4. After making the cake from natural flour, she then decorated it with an artificial flower.
5. The friar has been a member of the order for over 50 years.
   She had a delicious smelling fryer in the oven.
6. After the plane was safely in the hangar, the pilot took his hanger of clothes and left for home.
7. In order to hire the nurse, the doctor had to pay her a higher wage than anyone else in the office.
8. The lessor of the property decided to charge the lesser of the two advertised rents.
9. The mailing operation was organized all the way down to the licker of the stamps.
   He couldn't decide whether he wanted a drink of hard liquor or a more mellow after dinner liqueur.
10. The lord of the manor, who claimed he was not afraid of either man or beast, lost his haughty manner when he stepped in the manure.
11. The mare may or may not belong to the mayor.
12. Whether it was dangerous in the mine or not was a minor consideration to the miner.
    The money is neither mine nor yours; it belongs to the bank.
13. Not only does he love to savor fine wines, but he's quite a saver of corkscrews as well.
    She turned out to be the savior of the fumbling company.
14. The seer predicted the man would sear his hands and face in a fire which would destroy his house.
    The sere and wrinkled face of the old sea captain was the result of many long years of exposure to the elements.
15. He was sore from trying to soar over the sewer and sorry he broke his skateboard. Who is the suer in this case?
16. We accepted succor from the Red Cross after the tornado blew away our home.
    The little boy was licking an all-day sucker.

SOUNDALIKES WITH -GH(T)
Ex. RT-52 (Tape 4/A @ 125 wpm) & RT-52 (Tape 4/A @ 180 wpm)

1. He ate ten apples and eight pears before dinner.
2. "Anchors aweigh," they shouted as the boat pulled away from the dock.
3. The troops are expected to invade tomorrow.
   The teacher inveighed against the students' behavior.
4. That mite might carry dangerous disease, so it must be destroyed.
5. As he sped down the hill on his sleigh, he was careful not to slay the deer that ran across his path.
6. They steered carefully as they headed straight for the narrow strait.
7. The Boy Scouts were taught how to make a rope taut.
8. They loved to wade in the water.
   She weighed over 200 pounds before her diet.
9. They had to wait in line to find out their height and weight.
10. What is the best way to weigh a kangaroo?
    The cheese makers threw the whey away while making cheese.

 Step 4: Soundalikes

SOUNDALIKES WITH -Z

Ex. RT-53 (Tape 4/A @ 125 wpm) & RT-53 (Tape 4/A @ 180 wpm)

1. It was the lawyer's job to advise the company executives, and he was noted for his wise legal advice.

2. The brace enabled the crippled woman to walk.
   The chef will braise the meat for his famous French recipe.
   The donkey brays when he is hungry.

3. The witch carefully brews her love potion in the kettle.
   The bruise on his leg wouldn't go away.

4. The man's bushy brows looked stern as he continued to browse through the debris.

5. A clause in the local law prohibited cats to have claws.

6. Three crews were required to sail the cruise ship.

7. "That vote was close," she said at the close of the meeting.
   Her closet was so full of clothes that she couldn't close the door.
   They found some old cloths for washing the car.

8. The king spent his days sitting on his throne on the dais staring out the window in a daze.

9. He was able to devise a device to prevent burglary of his property.

10. During one phase of the fight, he was hit in the face, but the blow did not seem to faze him.

11. If you freeze the strawberries, it frees you to use them whenever you like.

12. The glacier caused much concern to the sailors.
    The glazier produced some beautiful pottery.

13. I admire the woman who grays with grace.
    The cattle were let out in the field to graze.

14. After he hoes the garden, he'll water it well with the hose.

15. She carried mace in her purse to stop muggers from accosting her.
    Walking through the rows of maize, the girl felt as though she were lost in a maze.

16. "No, sir, my nose knows when there is gold in the area," said the old prospector, "and there is none to be found here."

17. During a pause in the battle, George noticed one of his dog's paws was bleeding.

18. Her pleas to the police to please help her went unheeded.

19. The man prays to God to help him overcome the evil that preys on his soul.
    Such praise was unexpected.

20. A prize will be given to the first man who pries the lid off the jar.
    No price is too great to pay for good health.

21. She carefully studied the pros and cons of voting for that man.
    He generally prefers prose to poetry.

22. They drink at least three quarts of milk a week.
    The quartz had crystallized into a beautiful specimen.

23. He knew it would raise his spirits if he could just win the race.
    The rays of the sun were blinding.
    The wrecking crew was assigned to raze any unsafe buildings.

24. The rice in the Orient grows well in areas where rivers often rise.

25. The roes escaped the hunter by running through the forest.
    She had rows of every color rose in her exquisite garden.

26. Because of the tiny size of the child, he amazed people with his loud sighs.

27. He used a vise when he was repairing the toy.
    Smoking was his only vice, but he refused to try to quit.

SOUNDALIKES WITH -Y
Ex. RT-54 (Tape 4/A @ 125 wpm) & RT-54 (Tape 4/A @ 180 wpm)

1. They tried to <u>allay</u> his fears by reassuring him of the safety of the situation.
   The gang members knew they'd find an <u>ally</u> in the dark <u>alley</u>.
2. It was hard to decide her favorite <u>canape</u> from all the varieties served under the colorful <u>canopy</u> at the garden party.
3. They're leaving for <u>Chile</u> tomorrow.
   <u>Chili</u> is a nice hot dish for a <u>chilly</u> day.
4. She drove the car up to the <u>levee</u>.
   She only had two days left to pay the <u>levy</u> on the property.
5. The <u>petit</u> jury had been deliberating for hours.

Though she was <u>petite</u> and quite cute, her constant complaining over <u>petty</u> things made her less than charming.
6. I wrote a thank you note on my best <u>stationery</u>.
   The train remained in a <u>stationary</u> position while it was in the station.
7. In <u>summary</u>, the tour group concluded it had been a beautiful <u>summery</u> day, and the trip had been very pleasant and educational.
8. The eldest daughter was named <u>trustee</u> of the father's estate.
   His <u>trusty</u> dog followed him everywhere.

OTHER FINAL SOUNDS
Ex. RT-55 (Tape 4/A @ 125 wpm) & RT-55 (Tape 4/A @ 180 wpm)

1. She rushed to <u>add</u> her <u>ad</u> to the circular before the deadline.
2. The rainbow formed a colorful <u>arc</u> across the summer sky as the animals were led into the <u>ark</u>.
3. The <u>baron</u> appeared to have a mind as <u>barren</u> as his fields.
4. The <u>basis</u> for my believing that they'll win is that the <u>bases</u> are loaded and it's the bottom of the 9th inning.
5. The <u>base</u> of the lamp was broken by careless children.
   <u>Bass</u> jumped in the clear water of the lake.
   George Smith sang <u>bass</u> in the community chorus.
   That dog <u>bays</u> mournfully every time his owners go away.
6. All faithful members followed each <u>canon</u> of the church.
   The soldiers fired the <u>cannon</u> into the forest.
7. The tent was made of treated <u>canvas</u> to make it water repellent.
   Students were hired to <u>canvass</u> the neighborhood on behalf of the candidate.
8. A <u>census</u> was taken of the population of the community.
   The odors and smoke in the room offended his <u>senses</u>.
9. She felt insulted when she heard the <u>click</u> of the receiver.
   "I don't want to be part of that <u>clique</u> anyway," she thought to herself.
10. His grandmother's <u>currant</u> jam was his <u>current</u> favorite.
11. The governor felt it necessary to <u>damn</u> the engineering company when the <u>dam</u> collapsed.
12. He feared the <u>draft</u> would be reinstated by the time he came of age.
    August's <u>drought</u> had caused him to increase his consumption of <u>draught</u> beer.
13. When asked what he wanted as his final <u>epitaph</u>, he requested that they simply use his <u>epithet</u>, Ivan the Terrible.
14. They were sure their youngest was a true <u>genius</u>.
    What <u>genus</u> does this belong to?
15. The <u>heroine</u> of the story overcame her addiction to <u>heroin</u>.
16. He had an <u>ingenious</u> way of being able to decipher the latest tax laws.
    His <u>ingenuous</u> remark offended the hostess.
17. He was on the <u>lam</u> after stealing the farmer's <u>lamb</u>.
18. His geometry <u>lesson</u> did not <u>lessen</u> his confusion with math.
19. Her dinner was most pleasing to the <u>palate</u>.
    The artist's <u>palette</u> was a painting in itself.
    They improvised a make-shift <u>pallet</u> for their overnight guest.
20. The <u>stature</u> of the <u>statue</u> was imposing but impressive.
    They were careful to adhere to every <u>statute</u> of the law.

StenEd®   **Step 4: Soundalikes**

STEP 5
PREFIXES & OTHER WORD BEGINNINGS

Many potential conflicts have already been solved in *Steps 1* through *4*. These solutions are briefly reviewed below.

PRINCIPLES ALREADY COVERED

STEP 1: THE ALPHABET
(See Pages 5, 6, 8 & 9 for Review)

LETTER		LETTER		EXAMPLES	
s-	S-	z-	S* [STK-]	sip = SEUP	zip = S*EUP
c-	K, S-, or KR-	s-	S-	(see page 74)	

STEP 2: HIGH FREQUENCY WORDS
(See Pages 18-23 for Review)

WORD		PREFIX		EXAMPLES	
a	A	a-	AEU	a long	A/HROPBG
				along	AEU/HROPBG
after	AF	after-	AFR	after math	AF/MA*T
				aftermath	AFR/MA*T
Al	A*L	al-	AL	Al buy	A*L/PWAOEU
all	AUL			alibi	AL/PWAOEU
as	AZ	as-	AS	as nine	AZ/TPHAOEUPB
				asinine	AS/TPHAOEUPB
be	PW-	be-	PWE	be calm	PW-/KAUPL
				becalm	PWE/KAUPL
by	PWEU	bi-	PW*EU	by plane	PWEU/PHRAEPB
				biplane	PW*EU/PHRAEPB
could	KOULD	co-	KO	could exist	KOULD/KP*EUS
				coexist	KO/KP*EUS
for	TP-R	for-	TPOR	for giving	TP-R/TKPW*EUF/-G
				forgiving	TPOR/TKPW*EUF/-G
I	EU	i-	AOEU	ideal	AOEU/TKAOEL
				I deal	EU/TKAOEL
in	TPH-	in-	EUPB	in different	TPH-/TKEUFRPBT
				indifferent	EUPB/TKEUFRPBT
or	OR	or-	O*R	or deal	OR/TKAOEL
				ordeal	O*R/TKAOEL
over	OEFR [O*EFR]	over-	O*FR	over age	OEFR/AEUPBLG
				overage	O*FR/AEUPBLG

Note: AS/ is used for words beginning with as- when the s is pronounced in the first syllable (e.g., asinine = AS/TPHAOEUPB). If the first syllable is pronounced a, use AEU/ as the first stroke (e.g., assail = AEU/SAEUL).

STEP 4: SOUNDALIKES
(See Pages 50, 77, 78 for Review)

INITIAL CONSONANT		INITIAL CONSONANT		EXAMPLES	
w-	W-	wh-	WH-	witch	WEUFP
				which	WHEUFP
w-	W-	wr-	WR-	rap	RAP
				wrap	WRAP
c- (soft)	KR-	s-	S-	cell	KREL
				sell	SEL
c-	K-	ch-	KH-	cord	KORD
				chord	KHORD

Note: Remember that KR- is only used for soft c- when a conflict would result when using S-. (E.g., KREL = cell because SEL = sell; civic = S*EUFBG, not KR*EUFBG, since there is no word spelled sivic.)

Additional practice material for these principles already covered is given after the instructional material for this step. If you have not already solved any of the above conflicts in your writing style, it is suggested you do so before covering the new material in this step.

THINGS TO REMEMBER

There are three important things to remember.

1. Spelling differences can be used to distinguish between homophones which start with the same consonant sound.
   E.g., wrap = WRAP, rap = RAP.

2. The same stenotype representation should not be used for different beginning letter combinations if it would result in a conflict.
   E.g., sled = SHRED, shred = SHR*ED or SH-/RED.
   E.g., compile = KOPL/PAOEUL, exile = KPAOEUL.

3. High frequency words that can also be a prefix should be differentiated. E.g., TPH-/ABGT/*EUF = in active, EUPB/ABGT/*EUF = inactive.

Items 1 and 2 are generally concerned with **single word conflicts**. Item 1 has been covered in detail in *Step 4: Soundalikes*. Item 2 will be covered in this step.

Item 3 deals with word boundary conflicts. **Word boundary conflicts** refer to those mistranslations where the computer confuses where one word ends and the other begins; e.g., in different/indifferent, broke entire/broken tire, my normal/minor mall, former maids/for mermaids.

The bulk of this step will deal with resolving word boundary conflicts.

ACTION STEP

After you have reviewed the "Principles Already Covered," concentrate on any single-word conflicts that can be resolved by differentiating the initial consonants. Once you have mastered these, practice any word boundary conflicts in your writing style. Don't try to change too much at once.

StenEd outlines have been given for all words and word parts covered in this step. Because StenEd has chosen outlines that are conflict free within the entire StenEd framework, it is best if you can follow the suggestions given. However, if the StenEd solution conflicts with something else you write that you are not going to change, choose another solution.

Potential conflicting prefixes are grouped by type. A summary of StenEd outlines for all major prefixes and word beginnings is given at the end of the instructional material for this step. (Note: There are optional StenEd outlines, including briefs, for some of the words and prefixes given in this step. For more information, see *Volume I: Theory* and/or the *Professional Dictionary*.)

DICTIONARY MAINTENANCE

It is recommended that you update your CAT dictionary as you update your writing style so you can get the full benefit of your evolving conflict-free writing style.

When changing a single word outline, you should replace the old outline with the new outline. Thus, if you currently write SHRED for both sled and shred and you are going to begin writing SHR*ED for shred, replace that outline in your CAT dictionary. Leave SHRED in your dictionary for sled.

When changing the way you write a prefix, you can often add the outline as a prefix in your CAT dictionary. For example, if you used to write EUPB for both the word "in" and the prefix "in-" and you are now going to use TPH-/ for the word and continue using EUPB/ for the prefix, you would do the following.

- Delete the outline EUPB for the word "in."

- Enter the outline TPH- for the word "in."

  If your system allows, you may replace the outline for the word "in" rather than having to delete it and then add it with the new outline.

- Enter the stroke EUPB as the prefix "in-." Use the delete space symbol for your CAT system. This will attach the prefix to the base words already in your dictionary.

- Delete any words beginning with in- that will now translate automatically. That is, if you have words such as indifferent = EUPB/TKEUFRPBT, incomplete = EUPB/KPHRAOET, indeed = EUPB/TKAOED, etc., you may delete them from your CAT dictionary.

  Do not delete any words that would not translate correctly without being an individual entry. For example, influence (EUPB/TPHRAOUPBS) should remain in your CAT dictionary since fluence is not a word. Similarly, ingress (EUPB/TKPWRESZ) should remain since gress is not a word by itself.

Warning: Do not add any words as prefixes that can also represent an individual word. E.g., *ER = both the prefix "er-" and the word "ere" in StenEd, thus all er- words are entered separately in the StenEd CAT dictionary.

POTENTIAL PREFIX/WORD BEGINNING CONFLICTS

INITIAL CONSONANTS

The following prefixes and word beginnings include techniques for avoiding conflicts found in many non-StenEd theories. Often a short vowel is used in the prefix outline to distinguish a prefix from a suffix. This will be explained in more detail in *Step 6: Suffixes*. Prefixes which can also be a word (e.g., be- or be) are covered in this step.

PREFIX		**WORD(S)**		
coll-	KHR-	collect	KHREBGT	when the l is doubled
col-	KOL	colic	KOL/EUBG	when the l is not doubled (KHREUBG = click)
comm-	KPH-	common	KPHOPB	when the m is doubled
comp-	KOPL/P-	compact	KOPL/PABGT	when the vowel is not doubled (KPABGT = exact)
	Note:	There are some briefs available for words beginning with "comp" (e.g., compare = KOPL/PAEUR or KPAEUR). Just make sure any briefs you use do not create a conflict.		
corr-	KR-	correct	KREBGT	when the r is doubled and the second syllable is accented
	KOR/	correspond	KOR/SPOPBD	when the second syllable is unaccented
con-	KOPB/	conflict	KOPB/TPHREUBGT	whether or not the n is doubled
	con	KOPB (no conflicts)		
de-	TKE/	decode	TKE/KOED	TKAOE is reserved for endings
en-	EPB/	enforce	EPB/TPORS	optional outline = EPB/TPOERS
int-	SPW-	intend	SPWEPBD	optional outline = EUPB/TEPBD
ent-	SPW-	entrance	SPWRAPBS	optional outline = EPB/TRAPBS
intra-	SPWRA	intrastate	SPWRA/STAEUT	
intro-	SPWRO	introduce	SPWRO/TKAOUS	
er-	*ER/	error	*ER/ROR	err = A*ER, ere = *ER (no conflicts) /ER is reserved for endings
	E/R-	erupt	E/RUPT	first syllable = long e, not er sound
ex-	KP-	exam	KPAPL	before vowels, h, s sound
	EBGS/	explain	EBGS/PHRAEUPB	before other consonants
		ex-teacher	EBGS/TAOEFP/ER	hyphen may be omitted if no conflict
para-	PAR/	paradise	PAR/TKAOEUS	PAEUR = pair, PAER = pear,
		par	PAR (no conflicts)	PA*EUR = pare
pre-	PRE/	predate	PRE/TKAEUT	PRAOE is reserved for endings
shr-	SHR*	shrug	SHR*UG	when SHR- would cause a conflict
	SH-/R-	shrug	SH-/RUG	option for shr-
	SHR-	shrill	SHREUL	use SHR- for sl-
sl-	SHR-	slug	SHRUG	use SHR- for shr- when there is no conflict with sl-
un-	UPB/	unjust	UPB/SKWR*US	(If you want to phrase "you know," use KWRO*UPB, not UPB.)

     Step 5: Prefixes

WORDS BEGINNING WITH VOWELS

Words beginning with vowels should be outlined as follows.

PREFIX		WORD(S)				
a-	AEU/	a = A		accuse	AEU/KAOUZ	first syllable = long or short a
	AEU(c)			alias	AEUL/KWRAS	first syllable = long a + consonant
	A(c)			atlas	AT/HRAS	first syllable = short a + consonant
e-	E/	he = HE		elect	E/HREBGT	first syllable = long e
	AOE(c)			easier	AOEZ/KWRER	first syllable = long e + consonant
	E(c)			escape	ES/KAEUP	first syllable = short e + consonant
i-	AOEU/	I = EU		icon	AOEU/KOPB	first syllable = long i
	AOEU(c)			isolate	AOEUS/HRAEUT	first syllable = long i + consonant
	I(c)			impart	EUPL/PART	first syllable = short i + consonant
o-	O/	oh = O*E		ozone	O/SO*EPB	first syllable = long o
	OE(c)	on = OPB		orient	OER/KWREPBT [OEURPBT]	first syllable = long o + consonant
	O(c)			opposite	OP/SEUT	first syllable = short o + consonant
u-	KWRAOU/	you = KWROU		usurp	KWRAOU/SURP	first syllable = long u
	KWRAOU(c)			urine	KWRAOURPB	first syllable = long u + consonant
	U(c)			ultimate	ULT/PHAT	first syllable = short u + consonant

PREFIXES THAT ARE ALSO WORDS
(or Sometimes Used as Words)

Following are prefixes that can also stand alone as words. In most cases, both the prefix and the independent word should have unique outlines. (If a unique outline is not necessary, it is so noted.)

PREFIX		WORD		PREFIX EXAMPLE	
a-	AEU/	a	A	ahead	AEU/HED
after-	AFR/	after	AF	aftermath	AFR/PHA*T
		aft	AFT		
al-	AL/	Al	A*L	alibi	AL/PWAOEU
ante-	AEPBT/	ante	APB/TAOE	antedate	AEPBT/TKAEUT
anti-	A*EPBT/	anti	APB/TAOEU	antisocial	A*EPBT/SOERBL
as-	AS/	as	AZ	aspect	AS/PEBGT
		ass	ASZ		
	AEU/S-			assault	AEU/SAULT
be-	PWE/	be	PW-	befit	PWE/TPEUT
		bee	PWAOE		
bi-	PW*EU/	by	PWEU	biannual	PW*EU/APB/KWRUL
by-	PW*EU/	buy	PWAOEU	bypass	PW*EU/PASZ
		bye	PWAO*EU		
co-	KO/	could	KOULD	coexist	KO/KP*EUS
		company	KPAEPB		
counter-	KO*UPBT/	counter	KOUPBT/ER	countersign	KO*UPBT/SAOEUPB
		count	KOUPBT		

PREFIX		WORD		PREFIX EXAMPLE	
. di-	TKEU/	die	TKAOEU	dilate	TKEU/HRAEUT
dia-	TKAOEU/	dye	TKAO*EU	diarrheal	TKAOEU/RAOEL
extra-	EBGS/TRA [KPRA]	extra	EBGS/TRA	(no conflicts)	
for-	TPOR/	for	TP-R	forgive	TPOR/TKPW*EUF
fore-	TPOER/	fore	TPOER/SP-S		
		four	TPOUR		
hyper-	HAO*EUP/	hyper	HAOEUP/ER	hypertension	HAO*EUP/TEPBGS
		high per	HAOEU/PER		
il-	EUL/	ill	EUL (no conflicts)	illegal	EUL/LAOEL
		I'll	EU/AOEL [*EUL]		
im-	EUPL/	I'm	EU/AOEPL [AO*EUPL]	impatient	EUPL/PAEURBT
in-	EUPB/	in	TPH-	inactive	EUPB/ABGT/*EUF
		inn	*EUPB		
inter-	SPWER/	inter	EUPB/TER	interchange	SPWER/KHAEUPBG
enter-	SPWER/	enter	SPWR- [EPBT/ER]	enterprise	SPWER/PRAOEUZ
		into	SPWAO		
mega-	PHEG/	Meg	PH*EG	megaphone	PHEG/TPOEPB
mis-	PHEUS/	miss	PHEUSZ	misgiving	PHEUS/TKPW*EUF/-G
		Miss	PH-S		
		Ms.	PH-Z		
multi-	PHULT/	multi	PHUL/TAOE	multivitamin	PHULT/SRAOEUT/PHEUPB
			PHUL/TAOEU		
or-	O*R/	or	OR	ordeal	O*R/TKAOEL
out-	O*UT/	out	OUT	outstanding	O*UT/STAPBD/-G
over-	O*FR/	over	OEFR	overstate	O*FR/STAEUT
			O*EFR		
post-	PO*S/	post	PO*ES	postgraduate	PO*S/TKPWRAPBLG/WAT
re-	RE/	re	R*E	replay	RE/PHRAEU
se-	SE/	see	SAOE	secure	SE/KAOUR [SKUR]
		sea	SAE		
self-	SEFL/	self	SEL/-F	self-discipline	SEFL/TKEUS/PHREUPB
semi-	SEPL/	semi	SEPL/PHAOE	semicircle	SEPL/SEURBG/-L
			SEPL/PHAOEU		
sub-	SUB/	sub	SUB	(no conflicts)	
super-	SAO*UP/	super	SAOUP/ER	superman	SAO*UP/PHAPB
trans-	TRA*PBS/	trance	TRAPBS	transact	TRA*PBS/ABGT
		trans	TRAPBZ		
tri-	TR*EU/	try	TRAOEU	tricolor	TR*EU/KO/HROR
				TREU is reserved for endings	
under-	UPBDZ/	under	URPBD	underworld	UPBDZ/WORLD

   Step 5: Prefixes

PREFIXES ENDING IN O

Prefixes ending in the letter "o" should be written with a short o whether the o is pronounced short or long. This avoids any confusion as to whether the outline represents a prefix or a word in itself. It also avoids any prefix/suffix word boundary problems. (Suffixes are covered in Step 6.) If all sounds but the "o" can be covered in one stroke, you can generally write the prefix in one stroke.

This principle is also used in medical terminology when the medical root and combining form are used as a prefix. However, when the o is part of the suffix, you may use either the long or short o form (e.g., arteriosclerosis = AR/TAOER/KWRO/SKHRE/ROE/SEUS or AR/TAOER/KWRO/SKHRE/RO/SEUS). For more information on medical terms, see StenEd's *Medical Dictionary for Stenotypists* and/or *Medical Terminology for Stenotypists*.

PREFIX		WORD	PREFIX EXAMPLE	
arterio-	AR/TAOER/KWRO		arteriolith	AR/TAOER/KWRO/HR*EUT
audio-	AUD/KWRO	AUD/KWROE	audiophile	AUD/KWRO/TPAOEUL
auto-	AUT/	AU/TOE	autopilot	AUT/PAOEUL/OT
bio-	PWAOEU/KWRO	PWAOEU/KWROE	biology	PWAOEU/KWROLG
carcino-	KARS/TPHO		carcinogenic	KARS/TPHO/SKWREPB/EUBG
cardio-	KARD/KWRO		cardiogram	KARD/KWRO/TKPWRAPL
chemo-	KAOEPL [KAOE/PHO]	KAOE/PHOE	chemotherapy	KAOEPL/THER/PEU [KAOEPL/THAEURP} KAOE/PHO/THER/PEU
ego-	E/TKPWO	E/TKPWOE	egotist	E/TKPWO/T*EUS
electro-	HREBG/TRO		electronic	HREBG/TROPB/EUBG
gastro-	TKPWAS/TRO		gastropexy	TKPWAS/TRO/PEBG/SEU
hetero-	HET/RO-	HET/ROE	heterosexual	HET/RO/SEBGS/KWRUL [HET/RO/SWAUL]
homo-	HOEPL/ [HOE/PHO]	HOE/PHOE	homogenic	HOEPL/SKWREPB/EUBG HOE/PHO/SKWREPB/EUBG
hydro-	HAOEU/TKRO	HAOEU/TKROE	hydropower	HAOEU/TKRO/POU/ER {PO*UR]
hypo-	HO*EUP/	HAOEU/POE	hypothetical	HO*EUP/THET/KAL
intro-	SPWRO	SPWROE	introvert	SPWRO/SRERT [SPWRO*EFRT]
micro-	PHAOEU/KRO	PHAOEU/KROE	microphone	PHAOEU/KRO/TPOEPB
mono-	PHOPB/	PHOPB/TPHOE	monoplane	PHOPB/PHRAEPB
neo-	TPHAOE [TPHAOE/KWRO]		neoplasm	TPHAOE/PHRAFPL TPHAOE/KWRO/PHRAFPL
neuro-	TPHAOUR [TPHAOU/RO]		neuropathic	TPHAOUR/PA*T/EUBG TPHAOU/RO/PA*T/EUBG
photo-	TPOET/	TPOE/TOE	photostatic	TPOET/STAT/EUBG
physio-	TPEUZ/KWRO		physiochemical	TPEUZ/KWRO/KEPL/KAL
pro-	PRO/	PROE	protest	PRO/T*ES
proto-	PROET/		prototype	PROET/TAOEUP
pseudo-	SAOUD/	SAOU/DOE	pseudonym	SAOUD/TPHEUPL
psycho-	SAOEUBG/	SAOEU/KOE	psychopath	SAOEUBG/PA*T
pyro-	PAOEUR [PAOEU/RO]	PAOEU/ROE	pyromaniac	PAOEUR/PHAEUPB/KWRABG PAOEU/RO/PHAEUPB/KWRABG
radio-	RAEUD/KWRO	RAEUD/KWROE	radioactive	RAEUD/KWRO/ABGT/*EUF
retro-	RET/RO		retroactive	RET/RO/ABGT/*EUF
socio-	SOERB/KWRO		sociopath	SOERB/KWRO/PA*T
stereo-	STER/KWRO	STER/KWROE	stereotype	STER/KWRO/TAOEUP
video-	SREUD/KWRO	SREUD/KWROE	videotape	SREUD/KWRO/TAEUP [SRAOP]

SUMMARY OF PREFIXES & WORD BEGINNINGS

Following is a summary of major prefixes and word beginnings.

a-	AEU/		ego-	E/TKPWO		OE(c)
	AEU(c)		electro-	HREBG/TRO		O(c)
	A(c)		en-	EPB/	or-	O*R/
after-	AFR/		ent-	SPW-		OR(c)
al-	AL/		enter-	SPWER/	out-	O*UT/
ante-	AEPBT/		er-	*ER	over-	O*FR/
anti-	A*EPBT/			E/R-	para-	PAR/
arterio-	AR/TAOER/KWRO		ex-	EBGS/	photo-	TPOET/
as-	AS/			KP-	physio-	TPEUZ/KWRO
	AEU/S-		extra-	EBGS/TRA [KPRA]	post-	PO*S/
audio-	AUD/KWRO		for-	TPOR/	pre-	PRE/
auto-	AUT/		fore-	TPOER/	pro-	PRO/
be-	PWE/		gastro-	TKPWAS/TRO	proto-	PROET/
bi-	PW*EU/		hetero-	HET/RO-	pseudo-	SAOUD/
bio-	PWAOEU/KWRO		homo-	HOEPL/	psycho-	SAOEUBG/
by-	PW*EU/			HOE/PHO	pyro-	PAOEUR/
c-	K-		hydro-	HAOEU/TKRO		PAOEU/RO
	S-		hyper-	HAO*EUP/	radio-	RAEUD/KWRO
	KR-		hypo-	HO*EUP/	re-	RE/
carcino-	KARS/TPHO		i-	AOEU/	retro-	RET/RO
cardio-	KARD/KWRO			AOEU(c)	se-	SE/
ch-	KH-			EU(c)	self-	SEFL/
	K-		il-	EUL/	semi-	SEPL/
chemo-	KAOEPL/		im-	EUPL/	shr-	SH-/R-
	KAOE/PHO		in-	EUPB/		SHR*
co-	KO/		int-	SPW-		SHR-
col-	KOL/		inter-	SPWER/	sl-	SHR-
coll-	KHR-		intra-	SPWRA	socio-	SOERB/KWRO
comb-	KOPL/PW-		intro-	SPWRO	stereo-	STER/KWRO
comm-	KPH-		ir-	EUR/	sub-	SUB/
comp-	KOPL/P-		mega-	PHEG/	super-	SAO*UP/
con-	KOPB/		micro-	PHAOEU/KRO	trans-	TRA*PBS/
corr-	KR-		mis-	PHEUS/	tri-	TR*EU/
	KOR/		mono-	PHOPB/	u-	KWRAOU/
counter-	KO*UPBT/		multi-	PHULT/		KWRAOU(c)
de-	TKE/		neo-	TPHAOE/		U(c)
di-	TKEU/			TPHAOE/KWRO	un-	UPB/
dia-	TKAOEU		neuro-	TPHAOUR	under-	UPBDZ/
dis-	TKEUS/			TPHAOU/RO	video-	SREUD/KWRO
e-	E/		non-	TPHOPB/	wh-	WH-
	AOE(c)		o-	O/	wr-	WR-
	E(c)					

 Step 5: Prefixes

STEP 5—EXERCISES
PREFIXES

PRINCIPLES ALREADY COVERED
Ex. RT-56 (Tape 4/A @ 125 wpm) & RT-56 (Tape 4/A @ 180 wpm)

1. She zipped down to the cellar to check on the laundry.

2. The seller of the house promised that the ceiling fan cord would be replaced before final inspection.

3. The senator was anxious for Congress to adjourn so she and her family could begin a journey—a long journey home.

4. A long time ago she decided to go along with his plans.

5. We'll take a long walk after math class.

6. The aftermath of the earthquake was devastating.

7. That was a real zinger of an alibi. Did Al buy it?

8. She tried all ways possible to try to make him happy, but it didn't always work.

9. The actors were all ready for the play that they had already performed three times before.

10. They were altogether convinced that they would succeed if they just stuck all together.

11. It was asinine to think he would be an asset.

12. He resented the man trying to belittle him as nine of his friends looked on.

13. The flight attendant tried to becalm the passengers that were traveling by plane for the first time.

14. The company could exist indefinitely if it continues to make this many sales bi-weekly.

15. They coexist peacefully for most of the year.

16. I concluded that I would forgive her for giving me a hard time.

17. I ran into the next room to tell my mom the news about Iran.

18. He was indifferent about the prospect of having branch offices in different states.

19. I think the day when most people believe in organic gardening is in sight.

20. I know this is an informal game, but do you intend to talk all night or deal the cards?

21. The orphans didn't care whether the Christmas presents were wrapped in plain or fancy paper.

22. We've told her over and over that she tends to overdo that scene.

23. The library book was three weeks over-due.

24. He often comes over due to the fact that he has a crush on my sister.

25. He oversees the overseas branch of the company. In fact, he has overseen it for over four years now.

THE WORD "A" &
THE PREFIX "A-"
Ex. RT-57 (Tape 4/A @ 125 wpm) &
RT-57 (Tape 4/A @ 180 wpm)

The rush of <u>a</u> few years <u>ago</u> to <u>attend</u> college seems to be over. Rather than <u>attempting</u> to stay in school as long as possible, many young people are more <u>aware</u> of the job market and more concerned with <u>acquiring</u> <u>a</u> trade or job skill. <u>Apparently</u> financial security and success have become the major <u>areas</u> of interest for the young <u>adults</u>.

This new interest has created an <u>amazing</u> growth in trade and technical schools which promise to <u>address</u> the new-found needs of modern students. <u>Among</u> these schools, there have <u>also</u> <u>arisen</u> numerous fly-by-night <u>associations</u> and schools which are <u>attuned</u> more to separating the students from their money than they are in <u>affording</u> them the career training desired. Due to lax laws which <u>allow</u> such schools to be set up with little or no backing and which do not require them to be <u>accredited</u>, such schools have been <u>able</u> to <u>achieve</u> <u>a</u> remarkable record in bilking ill-<u>advised</u> young people.

Fortunately, recent laws and consumer groups have <u>allowed</u> the <u>abused</u> young person to <u>avail</u> himself or herself of legal remedies to <u>avoid</u> the clutches of these unscrupulous and <u>avaricious</u> "educators" and to <u>allow</u> the <u>authorities</u> to <u>arrest</u> the growth of such <u>alarming</u> institutions which <u>attack</u> the foundations of vocational education.

WH- = WH-
WR- = WR-
Ex. RT-58 (Tape 4/A @ 125 wpm) &
RT-58 (Tape 4/A @ 180 wpm)

The <u>wrath</u> of many home gardeners is the <u>whimsy</u> dandelion. But weep no more! The dandelion has proven to be one of the most healthful foods around. In fact, almost the <u>whole</u> dandelion plant can be used for eating.

<u>Whether</u> or not it can ever replace <u>wheat</u> or <u>whiskey</u>, it can at least <u>whet</u> your appetite <u>when</u> you prepare some of the salads, <u>wholesome</u> vegetable dishes, and <u>wine</u> made from this weed. <u>What</u> was once a <u>whim</u> of the health food enthusiasts is now finding its <u>way</u> to the suburbs.

<u>When</u> you see the dandelions sprouting this spring, <u>rest</u>—relax. Even if your neighbors think you have lost your <u>wits</u>, it'll not bother you one <u>whit</u>. <u>While</u> they're working hard trying to find a <u>way</u> to <u>whip</u> this weed, you'll be relaxing with your glass of homemade dandelion <u>wine</u>.

KR- FOR SOFT C-
(See Pages 50 & 78)

© 1993, 2001 *StenEd*®

POTENTIAL PREFIX/WORD
BEGINNING CONFLICTS

INITIAL CONSONANTS

COLL- = KHR-
COMM- = KPH-
CORR- = KR-
OTHERS = WRITE OUT
(UNLESS BRIEF)
Ex. RT-59 (Tape 4/A @ 125 wpm) &
RT-59 (Tape 4/A @ 180 wpm)

Recent <u>computer</u> technology has made it possible to <u>compile</u> a model of the earth as it existed 18,000 years ago. Though the findings are not totally <u>complete</u>, scientists using sophisticated <u>computers</u> have been able to <u>compute</u> past sea and land temperatures from the <u>composition</u> of fossil plankton <u>collected</u> from the ocean floor.

During the last glacial period, much of the northern hemisphere was <u>composed</u> of ice. New York City, in <u>combination</u> with many neighboring regions, was under ice hundreds of yards thick.

It is difficult to <u>comprehend</u> the land characteristics <u>common</u> during this period. Much of the North Atlantic region was under ice, and the existing land surfaces were <u>comprised</u> of very sparse vegetation. The <u>combination</u> of dried climates and shorter growing seasons <u>commonly</u> caused forests to shrink and deserts to expand. In <u>comparison</u>, during the peak of the last glacial period, Death Valley, almost <u>completely</u> barren today, was <u>complemented</u> by a freshwater lake <u>composed</u> of melted snow from nearby mountains.

Water frozen in land-based glaciers caused the sea level to be <u>comparatively</u> low, exposing <u>continental</u> shelves and land bridges. Scientists have <u>collected</u> data showing that Alaska and Siberia were <u>connected</u>, as were England and France. In fact, many extremely <u>competent</u> scientists have worked to <u>corroborate</u> the <u>complex</u> theory that America, Asia, Europe, and Africa once formed a single, massive <u>continent</u>.

Perhaps the major reason for <u>collecting</u> data on the last ice age and <u>comparing</u> this information to current climatic <u>conditions</u> is to see whether another glacial period is likely. If only natural forces are <u>compared</u>, another ice age should <u>commence</u> within the next couple of thousand years. However, the <u>complex</u> activity of human existence <u>complicates</u> natural climatic forces.

The <u>combinations</u> of the overuse of natural resources, which cools the atmosphere, and widely-used heat producing processes, which warm the atmosphere, <u>complicate</u> climatic <u>conditions</u>. What scientists hope to determine is whether this altering of the atmosphere can eliminate the possibility of another ice age, cause other unexpected climatic problems, or have no noticeable effect whatsoever.

EX = KP-, EBGS/
Ex. RT-60 (Tape 4/B @ 125 wpm) &
RT-60 (Tape 4/B @ 180 wpm)

The exploits of your favorite football team may provide excitement enough to make you ignore the expenses involved. Even if you only watch games on television, from the exhibition season to the extra playoff games, the expanding advertising expenses exceed network budgets. This means higher prices for the public. For the fan who exhorts his team at the ball park, the ticket prices grow more exorbitant.

The explanation for this is the extent of exaggerated contracts that are extended to men who excel in this sport. With an expert lawyer or agent, these people can exert pressure on an owner and expect an extremely good deal.

An exuberant college senior who exults in signing with a pro team will not likely take exception to an agent who extorts a large percentage. The star may not pass his exams, but his explosive talent and ability to excite the fans will get him good marks with coaches and owners.

The owners explain that the reason they expend such excessive amounts of money is to win games. Though it may bring a title, exponents of large payrolls who expound upon its advantages may be forced to explore the sea and exhume a sunken treasure to meet the expenses extant in the sport.

Don't think the owners do not express interest in the games. Every touchdown and extra point is important to them. When the time expires and the fans are heading toward the exits, he will either extol the virtues of his team or threaten to expel them from the league.

If his stars exude the will to win and exclaim their desire to reach the exalted position of first place, that is not enough. Only when revenues exceed expenses will the owner exhale a sigh of relief and exuberate at the excellence of his team.

Perhaps nothing exasperates a football executive more than an expensive player who gets injured. An expert player with an extraordinary record may be benched due to an injury he suffered during exercises. The owner may choose to export him to another team or even exile him to the minor leagues. The only thing that could exonerate the player would be an explosive return to action where he could exhibit his talent to the excited fans.

While the fans may express only modest contempt for these business details, they are quick to execrate the role of television. While expanding coverage has matched expansion of the leagues, many feel network expedience has brought a drop in the quality of sports shows.

Many viewers have experienced the announcer who, upon delivering a moving explicative of a star's career, will exclude any mention of the big play that was just executed on the field. Except for a few, most announcers exhibit an extreme lack of knowledge of the game.

The effect of the pressure exerted on the game by television is most explicit in the case of the television time-out. This device is used purely to let networks meet expenses with extra advertising, and it exists for that express purpose.

Despite the business details that lie beneath the exterior of pro football, the excitement and exhilaration make an excellent excuse to follow the sport.

OTHER
INITIAL CONSONANTS
Ex. RT-61 (Tape 4/B @ 125 wpm) &
RT-61 (Tape 4/B @ 180 wpm)

1. What is the <u>exact</u> price of this <u>compact</u> car?

2. The principal was <u>compelled</u> to <u>expel</u> them from school.

3. The <u>entrance</u> was <u>designed</u> so that tight security could be easily <u>enforced</u>.

4. I <u>enjoy</u> being <u>introduced</u> to new people.

5. She was <u>extremely</u> <u>introverted</u> during her <u>entire</u> childhood and, though quite <u>intellectual</u>, would become easily <u>intimidated</u>.

6. The team was <u>delighted</u> that the starting time for the <u>intramural</u> games had been <u>delayed</u>.

7. I tried to <u>erase</u> all my <u>errors</u> <u>ere</u> the teacher thought I <u>erred</u> too much.

8. The <u>paramedic</u> was <u>precluded</u> from running the rest of his <u>errands</u> by the sound of the emergency bell.

9. The <u>paralegal</u> helped <u>prepare</u> the papers for the <u>preliminary</u> hearing.

10. It is an ideal day for <u>sledding</u> for those who don't <u>shrink</u> from the cold.

11. The tall, <u>sleek</u> model let out a loud <u>shriek</u> when the mugger grabbed her purse, pushed her to the ground, and threatened to <u>slug</u> her.

12. You know it is <u>unwise</u> to <u>shrug</u> off as <u>unimportant</u> an annoying, <u>unrelenting</u> cough.

WORDS BEGINNING
WITH VOWELS
Ex. RT-62 (Tape 4/B @ 125 wpm) &
RT-62 (Tape 4/B @ 180 wpm)

1. Now that he had <u>a new</u> identity and <u>a new</u> home, he could start his life <u>anew</u>.

2. There must be <u>a way</u> to make this feeling go <u>away</u>.

3. Is this <u>a proven</u> way to get a desperate man off <u>a ledge</u>?

4. He showed no <u>emotion</u> as <u>he motioned</u> to the ambulance driver to pull over.

5. <u>He merged</u> into the main traffic lane, mumbling, <u>as he rode</u>, that the road had become so <u>eroded</u>, it was difficult to pass.

6. <u>I ran</u> all the way home <u>irate</u> that <u>I rated</u> so low in final test scores.

7. <u>I dine</u> <u>alone</u> almost every night.

8. <u>I concluded</u> that that was the best <u>icon</u> available.

9. On <u>occasion</u> she has given talks about the <u>oppressing</u> problems of the <u>ozone</u> layer.

10. Though usually <u>opposing</u> any change in land use, he was intent <u>on zoning</u> this piece of property as commercial.

11. They are <u>usually</u> divided into <u>unique</u> categories.

12. It's my job to teach <u>you phonics</u>.

PREFIXES THAT ARE ALSO WORDS

(or Sometimes Used as Words)
Ex. RT-63 (Tape 4/B @ 125 wpm) &
RT-63 (Tape 4/B @ 180 wpm)

1. She felt so <u>alone</u> when she walked into the bank to apply for <u>a loan</u>.

2. When you said to meet you this <u>after-noon</u>, I though you meant at any time <u>after noon</u>.

3. <u>Al</u> can be quite a smart <u>aleck</u> at times.

4. <u>Ante</u> up so we can proceed with the game.
   This fabulous <u>antebellum</u> home actually <u>antedates</u> the Civil War.
   I'm afraid there is no <u>antidote</u> for her <u>antisocial</u> behavior. She just seems to thrive on being <u>anti</u> everything and <u>anti</u> everybody.

5. The <u>asterisk</u> is a very useful, and often underused, key on the stenotype machine.

6. It won't <u>be long</u> <u>before</u> the house will <u>belong</u> to me.

7. <u>By</u> <u>buying</u> gifts at the <u>bimonthly</u> crafts show, I am helping the school <u>buy</u> new playground equipment.
   They waved <u>bye</u> as they headed toward the <u>bypass</u>.

8. The <u>co-counsel</u> hoped the <u>corespondents</u> would <u>cooperate</u>.

9. Her <u>counterpart</u> at the home office told her to <u>count part</u> of it as inventory.

10. The <u>dietitian</u> <u>displayed</u> her <u>diploma</u> on the wall.
    People who take care of themselves tend to <u>die later</u>.

11. The murder suspect was <u>extradited</u> to the United States.

12. She was never <u>forgiven</u> <u>for warning</u> her <u>four</u> friends about the <u>foreman's</u> <u>formidable</u> temper.

13. The <u>hypersensitive</u> patient became <u>hyper</u> about her <u>hypertension</u>.
    The cost of the medicine is quite <u>high per</u>

usual standards.

14. <u>I'll</u> prove to you that it's no <u>illusion</u> that I've been <u>ill</u>.

15. <u>I'm</u> not usually <u>impatient</u>, but I can't wait to finish this task.

16. He has been quite successful <u>in most</u> of the <u>enterprises</u> he has <u>entered</u> <u>into</u>.
    The <u>international</u> spy was shot as he <u>entered</u> the country. Shortly thereafter, he was <u>interred</u> at the military hospital.

17. <u>Meg</u> shouted the school cheer loudly into the <u>megaphone</u>.

18. Because little <u>Miss</u> Janie <u>misbehaved</u>, her nanny, <u>Ms.</u> Graves, said she would have to <u>miss taking</u> her afternoon walk.

19. This <u>multiprocessor</u> has a <u>multitude</u> of uses.

20. After the fire, most of our furniture was either soaked <u>or charred</u>.
    The apples in the <u>orchard</u> looked tempting.

21. He was so <u>outraged</u> he decided to go <u>out</u> <u>looking</u> for the perpetrator himself.

22. She <u>overheard</u> them saying he would get <u>over</u> it <u>over time</u>.

23. People shopping at the <u>post paid</u> lower prices for their weekly groceries.
    She plans to begin her <u>postgraduate</u> studies in environmental law next year.

24. The boss wanted <u>Ray</u> to <u>reschedule</u> his talk <u>re:</u> the company <u>restructure</u>.

25. Did you <u>see men</u> driving away from that <u>secluded</u>, old farmhouse?

26. <u>Self-discipline</u> and <u>self-confidence</u> can help one improve one's own <u>self</u>.

27. He drives that <u>semi</u> full of oranges out of Florida <u>semiannually</u>.

28. I just <u>subleased</u> an apartment over the <u>sub</u> shop.

29. Did the <u>super intend</u> to <u>supersede</u> the owner's wishes?

30. They appeared to be in a <u>trance</u> after that most unfavorable <u>transaction</u>.

31. I will <u>try</u> to do better this <u>trimester</u>.

32. Most of the <u>undergraduates</u> in this college are <u>under age</u> 22.

PREFIXES ENDING IN O
Ex. RT-64 (Tape 4/B @ 125 wpm) & RT-64 (Tape 4/B @ 180 wpm)

1. Her <u>biography</u> is now available on <u>audio</u>-<u>tape</u>.
2. He has an awfully large <u>ego</u> for such a <u>neophyte</u>.
3. We saw some very advanced <u>electronic</u> wizardry at the <u>auto</u> show.
4. She asked if they could make a <u>photocopy</u> of the <u>electrocardiogram</u>.
5. She had much <u>gastrointestinal</u> discomfort as a result of the <u>chemotherapy</u> treatments.

6. There was just some disturbing news about the <u>hydropower</u> plant on the <u>radio</u>.
7. The <u>neurologist</u> felt that the patient had <u>psychological</u> as well as <u>physiological</u> symptoms.
8. The <u>professional</u> was delighted when he learned that the raise was <u>retroactive</u>.
9. The <u>psychologist</u> agreed that the defendant had <u>sociopathic</u> tendencies.
10. We saw an extremely graphic <u>video</u> showing the destruction the <u>pyromaniac</u> had caused.

EN- & IN-
Ex. RT-65 (Tape 4/B @ 125 wpm) & RT-65 (Tape 4/B @ 180 wpm)

There are a number of species whose existence has become <u>endangered</u> in recent years. Despite the best <u>endeavors</u> of naturalists, conservationists, and others <u>interested</u> in animal life, there are many animals which face the same fate as the passenger pigeon. Among the beasts <u>involved</u> are the whales, elephants, the bald eagle, the puma, and numerous other creatures.

Whenever one <u>investigates</u> the reasons for the <u>endangering</u> of such animals, a single <u>enemy</u> emerges: man. It is man who has <u>encroached</u> on the <u>environment</u> of these animals; hunted them for gain, "protection," or "<u>enjoyment</u>"; and <u>introduced</u> new diseases and pollution.

In spite of <u>incredible</u> problems, there is hope that many of these animals can be saved. The recent case of the <u>enlargement</u> of the American bison population is an <u>encouraging</u> development. The American bison (also <u>incor</u>-rectly referred to as buffalo) once roamed America in vast herds. They were a principal source of food and materials for <u>innumerable</u> American <u>Indians</u>. Toward the end of the last century, <u>inhumane</u> and excessive hunting threatened to exterminate the bison. Thanks to the <u>enactment</u> of laws and the careful attempt to <u>increase</u> the size of the herds, there are again numerous bison in many <u>enclaves</u> across the country.

If the story of the bison is any <u>indication</u>, there is real hope that the <u>enervation</u> and destruction of animal species can be <u>inhibited</u> or stopped. All those who see the protection and <u>enlargement</u> of animal populations as an <u>enhancement</u> of the human condition are <u>engaged</u> in <u>endeavors</u> to <u>insure</u> that the example of the bison will be followed with other creatures in the <u>ensuing</u> years. Let us hope that their efforts and <u>energies</u> will not be met with <u>indifference</u>.

IN- = EUPB
IN = TPH-/

**Ex. RT-66 (Tape 4/B @ 125 wpm) &
RT-66 (Tape 4/B @ 180 wpm)**

It was a crisp, <u>inviting</u>, sunny day <u>in</u> early autumn. The birds were singing, and the ground was covered with brightly-covered leaves. Mrs. Ann Caldwell, an elderly <u>infirm</u> lady, was on her way to the <u>institute</u> <u>incognito</u> to receive her <u>injection</u> and treatment for the <u>insidious</u> illness which continually threatened to <u>incapacitate</u> her.

<u>Indeed</u>, every week, she traveled to this <u>institute</u> <u>in</u> her <u>inexpensive</u> disguise hoping no one would see her and <u>inform</u> her relatives that she was ill. It would <u>infuriate</u> her if anyone <u>in</u> her family began treating her like an <u>invalid</u>.

It was <u>incredible</u> to her that this <u>infernal</u> disease should <u>inflict</u> itself upon her, but she was grateful that a recent <u>increase</u> <u>in</u> her <u>income</u> had enabled her to <u>include</u> these <u>inescapable</u> weekly treatments <u>in</u> her budget. The extra <u>increment</u> had come, fortunately, just as her illness began two months earlier.

While at the <u>institute</u>, Mrs. Caldwell would undergo a complete medical <u>inspection</u> by the doctors and receive <u>inhalation</u> therapy to <u>inflate</u> her <u>infected</u> lungs. It was <u>ingrained</u> <u>in</u> her personality to obey the doctor's <u>instructions</u> even though she <u>inevitably</u> suffered an <u>inward</u> aversion to the drugs that it seemed necessary for them to <u>inject</u> <u>into</u> her arm. She was sure that they would someday <u>invent</u> a treatment where she would have to <u>ingest</u> a frog while sitting in an <u>inverted</u> position.

However, she knew that medicine was an <u>inexact</u> science, and she had <u>invested</u> too much money <u>in</u> treatment to do herself <u>inexcusable</u> harm through <u>indolence</u> by not taking the <u>inconvenient</u> but prescribed medicine. She only hoped that the doctor's seemingly <u>insightful</u> diagnosis would not be <u>incorrect</u> and that she would be well <u>in</u> no time.

The only pleasure Mrs. Caldwell derived from being at the institute was becoming <u>involved</u> <u>in</u> the children's ward. The children <u>instantly</u> cheered up when they saw her coming, and she loved all the little ones. She especially enjoyed visiting the <u>infants</u> and felt it was an <u>injustice</u> for small children to suffer from <u>infectious</u> diseases.

Nevertheless, every week during her visits, she always brought the children shiny, <u>interesting</u> presents wrapped <u>in</u> <u>inexpensive</u> paper and ribbons and <u>insisted</u> that soon they would no longer be <u>indoors</u> but <u>instead</u> would be home running, jumping, and playing <u>in</u> <u>active</u> games.

She told the children <u>incredible</u> stories <u>in</u> verse which she, herself, had written. She spoke <u>in</u> a voice full of <u>inflection</u>, and her stories, gifts, and — most important — her kindness made everyone feel <u>infinitely</u> better.

© 1993, 2001 *StenEd*® **Step 5: Prefixes**

ENT-, INT- = SPW-
ENTER- = SPWER
INTER- = SPWER
ENTER = SPW-R or
EPBT/ER
INTER = EUPB/TER
Ex. RT-67 (Tape 4/B @ 125 wpm) &
RT-67 (Tape 4/B @ 180 wpm)

Carl Jackson was an <u>intellectual</u>, <u>intense</u>, and <u>enterprising</u> spy. His <u>interest</u> in <u>international</u> affairs and foreign governments had led him <u>into</u> much exciting <u>interaction</u> with enemy agents. Only his quick thinking and <u>intensive</u> planning had allowed him to escape almost <u>entirely</u> unharmed from his many <u>intriguing</u> adventures.

Because he had solved many <u>intricate</u> problems <u>integral</u> to the foreign policy of the United States, Jackson had been <u>enthusiastically</u> praised by the President for his bravery and <u>intellect</u>.

Upon his <u>entrance</u> <u>into</u> the spy game as a young <u>intern</u>, Carl had <u>interconnected</u> with an <u>interracial</u> group of agents who were planning to steal the gold in Fort Knox. While among them, he <u>intercepted</u> and <u>interpreted</u> their special code and managed to notify the police so they could <u>intervene</u> before the agents could carry off their scheme successfully.

Another time, he had been <u>entrusted</u> with the mission of <u>enticing</u> several foreign spies to turn over to him a top secret document they had stolen from the Defense Department files. It contained an <u>interview</u> giving some specifications for the latest United States missile program.

It was the enemy's <u>intention</u> to <u>entomb</u> the document underground. After the <u>interment</u>, they planned to <u>interface</u> with the United States Government and demand a large ransom. The plan would <u>entail</u> the payment of $1 billion to the enemy. However, once the enemy agents had the money in hand, they had no <u>intention</u> of returning the file but would turn it over to their own <u>internal</u> government.

Because it was Carl's <u>intent</u> to return the document <u>intact</u>, he <u>intermixed</u> with the enemy spies. During an <u>interlude</u> before the document was buried, he <u>entrapped</u> the group by <u>interrupting</u> their communications. He crept <u>into</u> the radio room and, by <u>interfering</u> with the wires, destroyed their <u>intercom</u> system. Because of his <u>intervention</u>, the agents lost communication with each other, and their plan failed.

The President, who was <u>intolerant</u> of the schemes of the enemy, provided an <u>entire</u> evening of <u>entertainment</u> in Jackson's honor. During an <u>intermission</u> in the <u>entertainment</u>, a late <u>entrant</u> to the party approached Carl. The man <u>entreated</u> Jackson to meet him in the hallway.

It was Carl's <u>intention</u> to ignore this <u>intruder</u>, but the man was so <u>insistent</u> that Carl finally joined him in the darkened hall for an <u>intimate</u> conversation. Upon his return to the party, Jackson announced that the enemy was suffering from a disease of the <u>intestines</u>, and therefore all spy activity had been temporarily canceled.

UN- = UPB or
KWRAOUPB
UNDER- = UPBDZ
UNDER = URPBD
Ex. RT-68 (Tape 4/B @ 125 wpm) &
RT -68 (Tape 4/B @ 180 wpm)

The <u>undercurrent</u> was <u>unusually</u> strong and the waves <u>unceasing</u>. This was their last day here and, <u>unless</u> the <u>uninviting</u> winds died down, they would be <u>unable</u> to enjoy the water.

<u>Under</u> normal conditions, their <u>undersized</u> boat was not <u>unsafe</u>. But today's <u>unwieldy</u> winds would make their small craft <u>unnavigable</u>. They were not <u>unschooled</u> in the art of boating. They <u>understood</u> the dangers of the sea and knew better than to <u>underestimate</u> its <u>unrestrained</u> powers.

It was <u>unfortunate</u> that they could not enjoy the pleasure of the sea for this last day of their vacation, but it would be even more <u>unpleasant</u> if they <u>underemphasized</u> the <u>unquestionable</u> warnings and ventured out. They agreed that nothing could be more <u>undesirable</u> than ending up <u>underneath</u> these <u>unpredictable</u> waters. As beautiful as the <u>undersea</u> world can be, it cannot be appreciated if you are <u>under</u> water fighting the <u>undertow</u> and struggling for your life.

They decided to leave the <u>uncertain</u> waters <u>unchallenged</u>, their boat <u>undamaged</u>, and themselves <u>unscathed</u>. A day on land, they agreed <u>unanimously</u>, was not that <u>unappealing</u> after all.

 Step 5: Prefixes

STEP 6

SUFFIXES & OTHER WORD ENDINGS

Many potential conflicts have already been solved in *Steps 1* through *5*. These solutions are briefly reviewed below.

PRINCIPLES ALREADY COVERED

STEP 1: THE ALPHABET
(See Pages 5, 8, 9 for Review)

LETTER		LETTER		EXAMPLES
-f	-F	-v	*F	safe = SAEUF save = SA*EUF
		-ive	*EUF	active = ABGT/*EUF or ABG/T*EUF

STEP 2: HIGH FREQUENCY WORDS
(See Pages 18, 19, 20-23 for Review)
STEP 3: INFLECTED ENDINGS
(See Pages 37, 40-44 for Review)

WORD		SUFFIX		EXAMPLES	
as	AZ	-s	/-S	pay as	PAEU/AZ
his	HEUZ			pay his	PAEU/HEUZ
is	S-			pay is	PAEU/S-
				pays	PAEU/-S
				(pace	PAEUS)
did	TKEUD	-ed	/-D	mine did	PHAOEUPB/TKEUD
had	HAD			mine had	PHAOEUPB/HAD
				mined	PHAOEUPB/-D
				(mind	PHAOEUPBD)
I	EU	-y	/(c)EU	risk I	REUS/-BG/EU
eye	KWRAOEU			risk eye	REUS/-BG/KWRAOEU
				risky	REUS/KEU
or	OR	-or	/(c)OR	save or	SA*EUF/OR
oar	AOR			save oar(s)	SA*EUF/AOR(/-S)
ore	OER			save ore	SA*EUF/OER
other	O*ER			save other	SA*EUF/O*ER
				savor	SAEU/SROR
all	AUL	-al	/(c)AL [-L]	or all	OR/AUL
awl	A*UL			or awl	OR/A*UL
Al	A*L			or Al	OR/A*L
awe	AU			or awe	OR/AU
				oral	ORL
				formal	TPOR/PHAL

WORD		SUFFIX		EXAMPLES	
some	SOPL	-some	SPH-	hand some	HAPBD/SOPL
sum	SUPL			handsome	HAPBD/SPH-
				two sum(s)	TWO/SUPL(/-S)
over	OEFR [O*EFR]	-over	OFR	more over	PH-R/OEFR
offer	AUFR			more offer(s)	PH-R/AUFR(/-S)
				moreover	PHROFR [PHOR/OFR]

STEP 4: SOUNDALIKES
(See Pages 51, 52, 53-70, 79-82 for Review)

FINAL CONSONANT		FINAL CONSONANT		EXAMPLES	
-ght	-GT	-t	-T	ate	AEUT
				eight	AEUGT
(c)ee	/(c)AOE	(c)y	/(c)EU	trustee	TRUS/TAOE
(c)ey	/(c)AOE			trusty	TRUS/TEU
-s sound	-S	-z sound	-Z	rice	RAOEUS
				rise	RAOEUZ
		-ize	AOEUZ	specialize	SPERBL/AOEUZ
-s	-S	-ss	-SZ	bus	PWUS
				buss	PWUSZ
				buzz	PWUZ

Other potentially conflicting endings mentioned in *Step 4: Soundalikes* will be covered in more detail in this step.

THINGS TO REMEMBER

There are three important things to remember.

1. Spelling differences can be used to distinguish between homophones which end with the same consonant sound.
   E.g., right = RAOEUGT, rite = RAOEUT (write = WRAOEUT, Wright = WRAOEUGT).

2. The same stenotype representation should not be used for different ending letter combinations if it would result in a conflict.
   E.g., liable = HRAOEUBL, libel = HRAOEUB/EL.
   E.g., barely = PWAEUR/HREU, barrel = PWAEURL.

3. A suffix that is also a high frequency word should not stand alone if a conflict would result.
   E.g., actor = ABG/TOR, act or = ABGT/OR.
   E.g., lucky = HRUBG/KEU, luck I = HRUBG/EU.

Items 1 and 2 are generally concerned with **single word conflicts**. Item 1 has been covered in detail in *Step 4: Soundalikes*. Some Item 2 words have been covered in Step 4. These will be reviewed here; others will be introduced.

Item 3 deals with word boundary conflicts. **Word boundary conflicts** refer to those mistranslations where the computer confuses where one word ends and the other begins; e.g., meta<u>l</u>/met <u>all</u>, triple/trip <u>will</u>, hope<u>less</u>/hope <u>less</u>, short<u>en list</u>/short <u>enlist</u>, export<u>ation</u>/export <u>Asian</u>.

These word boundary conflicts will be covered in detail in this step.

ACTION STEP

After you have reviewed the "Principles Already Covered," concentrate on any single word conflicts that can be resolved by differentiating the final consonants. Once you have mastered these, practice eliminating any word boundary conflicts in your writing style. Don't try to change too much at once.

Don't let the large number of suffixes and word endings presented scare you. We have included all major and most minor endings because different reporters have different problem areas, and we would rather give you too much information than too little.

StenEd outlines have been given for all words and word parts covered in this step. Because StenEd has chosen outlines that are conflict free within the entire StenEd framework, it is best if you can follow the suggestions given. However, if the StenEd solution conflicts with something else you write that you are not going to change, choose another solution.

Potential conflicting suffixes are grouped by type. A summary of StenEd outlines for all major suffixes and word endings is given at the end of the instructional material for this step.

DICTIONARY MAINTENANCE

It is recommended that you update your CAT dictionary as you update your writing style so you can get the full benefit of your evolving conflict-free writing style.

When changing a single word outline, you should replace the old outline with the new outline. Thus, if you currently write HRAOEUBL for both liable and libel and you are going to begin writing HRAOEUB/EL or HRAOEU/PWEL for libel, replace that outline in your CAT dictionary. Leave HRAOEUBL in your dictionary for liable.

When changing the way you write a suffix, you can often add the outline as a suffix in your CAT dictionary. For example, if you used to write HRES for both the word "less" and the suffix "-less" and you are now going to use HRESZ for the word and continue using HRES for the suffix, you would do the following.

- Delete the outline HRES for the word "less."

- Enter the outline HRESZ for the word "less."

  If your system allows, you may replace the outline for the word "less" rather than having to delete it and then add it with the new outline.

- Enter the stroke HRES as the prefix "-less." Use the delete space symbol for your CAT system. This will attach the suffix to the base words already in your dictionary.

- Delete any words ending with -less that will now translate automatically. That is, if you have words such as blameless, helpless, harmless, etc., you may delete them from your CAT dictionary since the suffix "-less" will now automatically attach to these root words.

  Do not delete any words that would not translate correctly without being an individual entry. If the spelling of the base word is changed when adding an ending, do not delete that entry unless your CAT system has artificial intelligence that will change the spelling (e.g., penny + less = penniless, not pennyless.)

Warning: Do not add any words as suffixes that can also begin a word or represent an individual word. E.g., TKPWRAF = both the suffix "graph" and the word "graph."

POTENTIAL SUFFIX/WORD ENDING CONFLICTS

ADDITIONAL INFLECTED ENDINGS

In addition to -s, -ed, and -ing, other inflected endings should be written distinctively to differentiate them from prefixes and individual words.

SUFFIX		SUFFIX EXAMPLES		NOTES	
-er	/ER	bigger	PWEUG/ER	er-	*ER/
	/(c)ER	banker	PWAPB/KER	err	A*ER
			PWA*PBG/ER	air	AEUR
-ier	/KWRER	busier	PWEUZ/KWRER	ere	*ER
-(v)fer	-FR, -F/ER	briefer	PWRAOEFR		
			PWRAOEF/ER		
-(v)ver	*FR, *F/ER	braver	PWRA*EUFR		
			PWRA*EUF/ER		
-ener	/-TPHER	softener	SOF/TPHER		
-erer	/RER	loiterer	HROEUT/RER		
-rver	-FRB/ER, -R/SRER	server	SEFRB/ER		
			SER/SRER		
-est	/*ES	biggest	PWEUG/*ES	-st	*S
-iest	/KWR*ES	busiest	PWEUZ/KWR*ES		
-st	*S	test	T*ES	-st	*S
-sts	*S/-S	tests	T*ES/-S		
-sted	*S/-D	tested	T*ES/-D		
-sting	*S/-G	testing	T*ES/-G		
-sten	-S/-PB	glisten	TKPWHREUS/-PB	the t is silent	
-ster	*S/ER	toaster	TO*ES/ER		
	/STER, -S/TER, *S/ER	sinister	SEUPB/STER	to match the pronunciation	
			SEUPBS/TER		
			S*EUPBS/ER		
-ist	*EUS	realist	RAEL/*EUS		
-stic	*S/EUBG	realistic	RAEL/*EUS/EUBG		
-ic	EUBG	plastic	PHRA*S/EUBG	do not use EUBG for "I can"	
-en	/-PB	blacken	PWHRABG/-PB	en- = EPB/	
-ens	/-PBS	blackens	PWHRABG/-PBS		
-ened	/-PBD	blackened	PWHRABG/-PBD		
-ening	/-PBG	blackening	PWHRABG/-PBG		
-(v)ven	*FPB, *F/-PB	driven	TKR*EUFPB [TKR*EUF/-PB]		
-(v)vern	*FRPB	govern	TKPWO*FRPB		

As mentioned earlier in this text, everything builds on everything else. The outlines presented in this text are conflict free based on the entire StenEd theory. If you are following StenEd outlines throughout, everything will fit together. If you are creating your own outlines for the conflicts listed that you have in your writing style, be very careful not to create a new conflict when solving an old one.

In the following examples, when more than one way is given to write an ending it is either because some words with the same endings have a different ending sound (e.g., liter<u>ary</u> = HREUT/<u>RAEUR</u>, sal<u>ary</u> = SAL/<u>REU</u>) or because that ending has options (e.g., sta<u>mp</u> = STA<u>FRP</u> or STA<u>PL</u>/-P).

                                       Step 6: Suffixes

WORDS ENDING WITH VOWELS

Words ending with vowels should be outlined as follows. Always include a consonant on the stroke with the vowel ending.

SUFFIX		WORD(S)		NOTES
-a	/(c)A	quota	KWOE/TA	KWOET/A = quote a
-e	/(c)AOE	escapee	ES/KAEU/PAOE	E = the prefix e-; AOE = ' (apostrophe)
-i (i snd)	/(c)AOEU	rabbi	RAB/PWAOEU	AOEU = the prefix i-; I = I
-i (e snd)	/(c)AOE	taxi	TABG/SAOE	AOE = ' (apostrophe)
-o	/(c)OE	cargo	KAR/TKPWOE	O = the prefix o-; TKPWO = go
-u	/(c)AOU	menu	PHEPB/KWRAOU	men you = PHEPB/KWROU
-(c)ee	/(c)AOE	draftee	TKRAF/TAOE	drafty = TKRAF/TEU
-(c)ie	/(c)AOE	yuppie	KWRUP/PAOE	
-(c)ey	/(c)AOE	holey	HOE/LAOE	holy = HOE/LEU
-(c)y	/(c)EU	lucky	HRUBG/KEU	luck I = HRUBG/EU

SUFFIXES THAT ARE ALSO WORDS

Following are suffixes that can also stand alone as words. In most cases, both the suffix and the independent word should have unique outlines. (If a unique outline is not necessary, it is so noted.)

Some compound words are included in the examples below (e.g., dropout). Additional compound words are covered in *Step 10: Special Considerations*.

SUFFIX		WORD		SUFFIX EXAMPLE	
-an	(c)APB	an	APB	Roman	ROE/PHAPB
-ance	-PBS	answer	APBS	nuance	TPHAOUPBS
	(c)APBS			nuisance	TPHAOU/SAPBS
-ant	-PBT	ant	APBT	reliant	RE/HRAOEUPBT
	(c)APBT			gallant	TKPWAL/HRAPBT
-as	(c)AS	as	AZ	menace	PHEPB/TPHAS [PHEPBS]
-at	(c)AT	at	AT	format	TPOR/PHAT
-(c)ful	/-FL	full	TPUL	youthful	KWRAO*UT/-FL
-(v)ful	-FL			lawful	HRAUFL
-if	(c)EUF	if	TP-	bailiff	PWAEU/HREUF [PWHR-F]
-(c)il	(c)IL	ill	EUL	council	KOUPB/SEUL
	(c)L			sterile	STERL
-in	(c)EUPB	in	TPH-	raisin	RAEU/S*EUPB
-it	/(c)EUT	it	EUT	bandit	PWAPB/TKEUT
-less	/HRES	less	HRESZ	jobless	SKWROB/HRES
-ment	-PLT	meant	PHEPBT	payment	PAEUPLT
				placement	PHRAEUS/-PLT
-on	(c)OPB	on	OPB	lesson	HRES/SOPB
-or	(c)OR	or	OR	exhibitor	KPEUB/TOR
-out	/O*UT	out	OUT	dropout	TKROP/O*UT
-over	/OFR	over	OEFR [O*EFR]	takeover	TAEUBG/OFR
-self	*S	self	SEL/-F	yourself	KWRO*URS
-some	/SPH-	some	SOPL	gruesome	TKPWRAOU/SPH-
-us	(c)US	us	US	sinus	SAOEU/TPHUS

FINAL CONSONANTS

The following suffixes and word endings include techniques for avoiding conflicts found in many non-StenEd theories. Many of these suffixes deal with consonants that cannot be written on the final side in the same stroke.

Except for conflict-free briefs, it is not recommended that you omit sounded letters (e.g., bulb = PWUL/-B, not PWUL or PWUB) or that you invert letters (e.g., help = HEL/-P, not HEPL, HEP, or HEL). Omitting and inverting letters causes many conflicts.

SUFFIX		WORD(S)		NOTE
-lb	-L/-B	bulb	PWUL/-B	
-lch	-L/-FP	belch	PWEL/-FP	
-lf	-L/-F	golf	TKPWOL/-F [TKPWOF]	sounded l
-lf	-F	half	HAF	silent l
-lge	-L/-PBLG	bulge	PWUL/-PBLG	lj sound
-lk	-L/-BG	bulk	PWUL/-BG	sounded l
-lk	-BG	talk	TAUBG	silent l
-lm	-L/-PL	film	TPEUL/-PL	sounded l
-lm	-PL	calm	KAUPL	silent l
-ln	*L	kiln	K*EUL	kill = KEUL
-lp	-L/-P	help	HEL/-P [H*EP]	
-lve	-L/*F	solve	SOL/*F [SO*F]	sounded l
-lve	*F	halve	HA*F	silent l
-mb	-PL	bomb	PWOPL	silent b
	*PL	lamb	HRA*PL	lam = HRAPL
-mn	*PL	damn	TKA*PL	dam = TKAPL
-mp	-FRP	stamp	STAFRP	
	-PL/-P	stamp	STAPL/-P	option
-mpt	-FRPT	exempt	KPEFRPT	
	-PLT	exempt	KPEPLT	option
-nch	-PB/-FP	bench	PWEPB/-FP	
	-FRPBLG	bench	PWEFRPBLG	option
-nge	-PB/-PBLG	lunge	HRUPB/-PBLG	-nj sound, HRUPBG = lung
-nk	-PB/-BG	sink	SEUPB/-BG	SEUPBG = sing
-nx	-PBGS	jinx	SKWREUPBGS	
-rb	-RB	verb	SRERB	
	-R/-B	blurb	PWHRUR/-B	if conflict with -SH
(-sh	-RB	blush	PWHRURB)	
-rch	-R/-FP	search	SER/-FP	
	*RPBLG	search	S*ERPBLG	option
-rf	-R/-F	surf	SUR/-F	
-rv(e)	-FRB	serve	SEFRB	
	-R/V-	serve	SER/*F	option
-sk	-S/-BG	risk	REUS/-K	
-sm	-FPL	realism	RAEL/EUFPL	
-sp	-S/-P	grasp	TKPWRAS/-P	
-ss	-SZ	buss	PWUSZ	bus = PWUS
-st	*S	past	PA*S	pass = PASZ
-th	*T	both	PWO*ET	boat = PWOET
-arial	AEURL	secretarial	SEBG/TAEURL	
-orial	OEURL	tutorial	TAOU/TOEURL	
-arian	AEURPB	veterinarian	SRET/TPHAEURPB	
-orian	OEURPB	historian	HEUS/TOEURPB	
-itis	(c)AOEUTS	dermatitis	TKERPL/TAOEUTS	
-(v)tient	(v)RBT	patient	PAEURBT	

WORDS ENDING WITH -Y

Generally, an I is used to represent the -y. Always attach a consonant to I (EU) when it is used for a -y at the end of a word. EU as a stroke by itself is only used for the word "I."

-LY

-ly	/HREU	briefly	PWRAOEF/HREU
-ily	/HREU	happily	HAP/HREU
-(c)ally	(c)/HREU	socially	SOERBL/HREU
-(i)cally	/KHREU	typically	TEUP/KHREU
-stically	*S/KHREU	statistically	STA/T*EUS/KHREU
-arily	(c)AEUR/HREU	arbitrarily	ARB/TRAEUR/HREU
-bly	/PWHREU	capably	KAEUP/PWHREU
	-B/HREU	doubly	TKUB/HREU
-edly	/TKHREU	crookedly	KRAOBG/TKHREU
-fully	/TPHREU	hopefully	HOEP/TPHREU
-ingly	/TKPWHREU	exceedingly	KPAOED/TKPWHREU
-(i)ously	-RBS/HREU	cautiously	KAURBS/HREU
	OUS/HREU	generously	SKWREPB/ROUS/HREU
	/SHREU	nervously	TPHEFRB/SHREU
-lessly	/HRES/HREU	aimlessly	AEUPL/HRES/HREU
-mentally	-PLT/HREU	environmentally	EPB/SRAOEURPLT/HREU

-TY

-ty	/TEU	empty	EPL/TEU [EFRP/TEU]
-ity	/TEU	majority	PHA/SKWROR/TEU

OTHERS

-bility	-BLT	mobility	PHOEBLT	
-ary	(c)AEUR	literary	HREUT/RAEUR	
	/REU	salary	SAL/REU	when no "airy" sound
-by	/PWEU	flabby	TPHRAB/PWEU	
-chy	/KHEU	itchy	EUFP/KHEU	
-cy	/SEU	policy	POL/SEU	s sound
-dy	/TKEU	study	STUD/TKEU	
-fy	/TPEU	trophy	TROE/TPEU	long e sound
	/TPEU	certify	SERT/TPEU	long i sound
-gy	/TKPWEU	baggy	PWAG/TKPWEU	g sound
	/SKWREU	strategy	STRAT/SKWREU	j sound
-ky	/KEU	lucky	HRUBG/KEU	monarchy PHOPB/AR/KEU
-my	/PH*EU	enemy	EPB/PH*EU	PHEU is reserved for "my"
-ny	/TPH*EU	felony	TPEL/TPH*EU	TPHEU is reserved for "any"
-ory	(c)OEUR	category	KAT/TKPWOEUR	
-py	/PEU	copy	KOP/PEU	
-ry	/REU	forgery	TPORPBLG/REU	
-shy	/SHEU	fishy	TPEURB/SHEU	
-sy	/SEU	bossy	PWOS/SEU	s sound
	/S*EU	noisy	TPHOEU/S*EU	z sound
	-Z/SEU, -Z/S*EU	noisy	[TPHOEUZ/SEU] [TPHOEUS/S*EU]	
-thy	/TH*EU	healthy	HEL/TH*EU	THEU is reserved for "think"
-vy	/SREU	envy	EPB/SREU	
-wy	/WEU	showy	SHOE/WEU	
-xy	-BG/SEU, -BGS/SEU	proxy	PROBG/SEU	proxy PROBGS/SEU
-zy	/S*EU	crazy	KRAEU/S*EU	
	-Z/SEU, -Z/S*EU	crazy	KRAEUZ/SEU	crazy KRAEUZ/S*EU

WORDS ENDING IN -L(E)

The following suffixes and word endings include techniques for avoiding conflicts found in many non-StenEd theories. Using these techniques and others previously covered in this text, conflicts such as bridal/bridle, medal/meddle/metal/mettle/met all, council/counsel are avoided.

SUFFIX		WORD(S)	NOTES

Always precede -al with a consonant. AL as a stroke by itself is only used for prefixes.

SUFFIX		WORD(S)		NOTES
-(c)al	(c)AL	brutal	PWRAOU/TAL	
	(v)L	loyal	HROEUL	
	(c)L	rival	RAO*EUFL	
-(c)ally	(c)/HREU	brutally	PWRAOUT/HREU	
-(i)cally	/KHREU	surgically	SURPBLG/KHREU	
-mental	-PLT/TAL	environmental	EPB/SRAOEURPLT/TAL	
-mentally	-PLT/HREU	environmentally	EPB/SRAOEURPLT/HREU	
-stical	*S/KAL	statistical	STA/T*EUS/KAL	
-stically	*S/KHREU	statistically	STA/T*EUS/KHREU	
-el	-L	panel	PAPBL	use -L if it fits and "el" is not accented
	EL	model	PHOD/EL	use EL if -L doesn't fit
		propel	PRO/PEL	to match the sound
-pel	PEL	lapel	HRA/PEL	HRAPL = lam
	-P/EL	chapel	KHAP/EL	to match the sound

Always precede -il with a consonant. EUL as a stroke by itself is used for prefixes and for the word "ill."

-il	-L	civil	S*EUFL	use -L if it fits and "il" is not accented
	/(c)EUL	pencil	PEPB/SEUL	

Do not use -L for the word "will." -L should be reserved for word endings.

-ble	-BL	payable	PAEUBL	attach -BL to same stroke if it fits
		scribble	SKREUBL	
		favorable	TPA*EUFRBL	
	/-BL	legible	HREPBLG/-BL	use -BL as a separate stroke if it doesn't fit on the same stroke
-cle	-K/-L	recycle	RE/SAOEUBG/-L	
	/K-L	miracle	PHEUR/K-L	
-dle	-D/-L	middle	PHEUD/-L	
-fle	-FL	rifle	RAOEUFL	
-gle	-G/-L	haggle	HAG/-L	
-kle	-K/-L, /K-L	wrinkle	WREUPB/K-L	
-mple	-PL/P-L	ample	APL/P-L	
	FRP/-L	ample	AFRP/-L	
-ple	-P/-L	triple	TREUP/-L	TREUPL = trim
	/P-L	multiple	PHULT/P-L	if -P doesn't fit on previous stroke
-scle	-S/-L	muscle	PHUS/-L	
-sle	-S/-L	hassle	HAS/-L	
-stle	-S/-L	hustle	HUS/-L	silent t
-tle	-T/-L	battle	PWAT/-L	
-xle	-BGS/-L	axle	ABGS/-L	
-zle	-Z/-L	puzzle	PUZ/-L	

OTHER WORD ENDINGS

The following summarizes the remaining suffixes and word endings. The major optional outlines for these endings have also been included.

A more detailed explanation of these word endings can be found in StenEd's *Volume I: Theory*. A summary of StenEd outlines is contained in StenEd's *Professional Dictionary*.

SUFFIX		WORD(S)	
-ct	-BGT	act	ABGT
-nct	-PBGT	precinct	PRE/SEUPBGT [PREUPBGT]
-nction	-PBGS	function	TPUPBGS
-nctional	-PBGS/TPHAL	functional	TPUPBGS/TPHAL
-nctionally	-PBGS/HREU	functionally	TPUPBGS/HREU
-x	-BGS	fix	TPEUBGS
-xt	*BGS	text	T*EBGS
-xion	*BGS	flexion	TPHR*EBGS
-ction	*BGS	fiction	TP*EUBGS
-ctional	*BGS/TPHAL	fictional	TP*EUBGS/TPHAL
-ctionally	*BGS/HREU	fictionally	TP*EUBGS/HREU
-(v)sion	(v)GS	fusion	TPAOUGS
-(c)sion	(c)GS	version	SRERGS
-lsion	-LGS	convulsion	KOPB/SRULGS
-ssion	-GS	profession	PRO/TPEGS [PROFGS]
-ssional	-GS/TPHAL	professional	PRO/TPEGS/TPHAL
-ssionally	-GS/HREU	professionally	PRO/TPEGS/HREU
-(v)tion	(v)GS	education	EPBLG/KAEUGS [EGS]
-(v)tional	(v)GS/TPHAL	educational	EPBLG/KAEUGS/TPHAL [ELGS]
-(v)tionally	(v)GS/HREU	educationally	EPBLG/KAEUGS/HREU
-mption	-PLGS, -FRPGS	gumption	TKPWUPLGS [TKPWUFRPGS]
-ntion	-PBGS	convention	KOPB/SREPBGS
-ption	-PGS	exception	KPEPGS
-rtion	-RGS	portion	PORGS
-stion	*GS	congestion	KOPB/SKWR*EGS
	-GS	congestion	KOPB/SKWREGS
-cious	-RBS	conscious	KOPB/-RBS [KORBS]
-ciously	-RBS/HREU	consciously	KOPB/-RBS/HREU
-ciousness	-RBS/*PBS	consciousness	KOPB/-RBS/*PBS [KORBS/*PBS]
-tious	-RBS	ambitious	APL/PWEURBS
-tiously	-RBS/HREU	ambitiously	APL/PWEURBS/HREU
-tiousness	-RBS/*PBS	ambitiousness	APL/PWEURBS/*PBS
-ish	EURB	punish	PUPB/EURB
-ishment	/SH-PLT	punishment	PUPB/SH-PLT [PUPLT]
-ishness	/SH*PBS	foolishness	TPAOL/SH*PBS
-ous	-RBS	when sounded as in -cious and -tious above	
	OUS	generous	SKWREPB/ROUS
-us	(c)US	sinus	SAOEU/TPHUS
-cial	-RBL	social	SOERBL
-cially	-RBL/HREU	socially	SOERBL/HREU
-tial	-RBL	impartial	EUPL/PAR/-RBL
-tially	-RBL/HREU	impartially	EUPL/PAR/-RBL/HREU

-tual	/KHUL	factual	TPABG/KHUL
-tually	/KHUL/HREU	factually	TPABG/KHUL/HREU
-ture	/KHUR	feature	TPAOE/KHUR [TPAOEFP]
-gram	/TKPWRAPL	diagram	TKAOEU/TKPWRAPL
-(o)graph	/TKPWRAF	stenograph	STEPB/TKPWRAF
-(o)graphic	/TKPWRAFBG	stenographic	STEPB/TKPWRAFBG
-(o)grapher	(O)G/TPER	stenographer	STEPB/OG/TPER
-(o)graphy	(O)G/TPEU	stenography	STEPB/OG/TPEU
-(o)logical	/HROPBLG/KAL	ecological	EBG/HROPBLG/KAL
-(o)logically	/HROPBLG/KHREU	ecologically	EBG/HROPBLG/KHREU
-(o)logist	(O)*LGS	criminologist	KREUPL/TPHO*LGS
-(o)logy	(O)LG	criminology	KREUPL/TPHOLG
-ness	*PBS	darkness	TKARBG/*PBS
-fulness	/TPHR*PBS	carefulness	KAEUR/TPHR*PBS
-ishness	/SH*PBS	childishness	KHAOEULD/SH*PBS
-lessness	/HRES/*PBS	carelessness	KAEUR/HRES/*PBS [KAEURLS/*PBS]
-iveness	*EUF/*PBS	forgiveness	TPOR/TKPW*EUF/*PBS
	*EUFPBS	forgiveness	TPOR/TKPW*EUFPBS
-someness	/SPH*PBS	gruesomeness	TKPWRAOU/SPH*PBS

SUMMARY
SUFFIXES

There is a lot of information in this step. All major suffixes and word endings have been included—not just those that commonly cause conflicts—because everything builds on everything else. As mentioned throughout this text, all suggested outlines are based on the StenEd theory.

Even if you choose not to use the StenEd solution, this text will still help you identify your conflict areas by illustrating the causes of individual word and word boundary conflicts. Many reporters, skeptical at first, have opted to adopt StenEd outlines because they have been designed to be as logical and consistent as the English language allows.

If you are unsure of what conflicts or mistranslations may be in your writing style, we suggest you take the practice sentences using CAT (realtime, if possible). Your translation will tell you which areas you should work on.

A summary of all major suffixes and words endings is given on pages 111-112. Dictation exercises covering the most common conflict areas found in traditional stenotype theories begin on page 113.

SUMMARY OF
SUFFIXES AND WORD ENDINGS

Following is a summary of major suffixes and word endings.

The following abbreviations are used in this list.

(c)	=	any consonant	(n pl)	=	plural form of noun	(snd)	= sound
(v)	=	any vowel	(v sing)	=	singular form of verb	(past)	= past tense of verb

-a	(c)A	-ction	*BGS	-gy *(j snd)*	/SKWREU
-ability	-BLT	-ctional	*BGS/TPHAL	-i *(i snd)*	(c)AOEU
	(v)BLT	-ctionally	*BGS/HREU	-i *(e snd)*	(c)AOE
-able	/-BL	-cy *(s snd)*	/SEU	-ibility	/-BLT
	(v)BL	-dle	-D/-L		(v)BLT
-ably	/PWHREU	-down	TKO*UPB	-ible	/-BL
-ache	/A*EUBG		KWROUPB		(v)BL
-ad	(c)AD	-ds	-DZ	-ibly	/PWHREU
-age	APBLG	-dy	/TKEU	-ik	EUBG
-ak	(c)ABG	-e	(c)AOE	-id	EUD
-(c)al	(c)AL	-eau	(c)OE	-(c)ie	(c)AOE
	-(c)L	-eaux	(c)OEZ	-ier	/KWRER
-(c)ally	(c)/HREU	-(c)ee	(c)AOE	-iest	/KWR*ES
	(c)HREU	-(e)d *(V past)*	/-D	-if	(c)EUF
-an	(c)APB	-edly	/TKHREU	-(c)il	(c)EUL
-ance	(c)APBS	-el	-L		(c)L
-ant	(c)APBT		EL	-ily	/HREU
	-PBT	-em	(c)EPL	-in	(c)EUPB
-ar	(c)AR	-en	/-PB		KWREUPB
-ard	ARD	-ened	/-PBD	-ing	/-G
-arial	AEURL	-ener	/TPHER	-ingly	/TKPWHREU
-arian	AEURPB	-ening	/-PBG	-ings	/-GS
-arily	(c)AEUR/HREU	-ens	/-PBS	-is	(c)EUS
-ary	(c)AEUR	-ent	-NT	-ish	/EURB
	/REU		ENT		EURB
-as	(c)AS	-er	/ER	-ishment	/SH-PLT
-at	(c)AT		(c)ER	-ishness	/SH*PBS
-away	/A*EU/WAEU	-erer	/RER	-ism	EUFPL
-back	/PWA*BG	-est	(c)*ES	-ist	*EUS
-bility	-BLT		/*ES	-istic	*EUS/EUBG
	/-BLT	-et	/ET		EUS/TEUBG
-ble	-BL		(c)ET	-it	(c)EUT
	/-BL	-(c)ey	(c)AOE	-itis	(c)AOEUTS
-bly	/PWHREU	-(v)fer	-FR	-ity	/TEU
	-B/HREU		-F/ER	-ive	*EUF
-by	/PWEU	-fle	-FL	-iveness	*EUF/*PBS
-(i)cally	/KHREU	-(c)ful	/-FL		*EUFPBS
-ces *(e snd)*	/SAOEZ	-(v)ful	-FL	-ize	AOEUZ
-ch	-FP	-fully	/TPHREU	-izer	AOEUZ/ER
-chy	/KHEU	-fulness	/TPHR*PBS	-kle	-K/-L
-cial	-RBL	-fy	/TPEU		/K-L
	/-RBL	-g(e) *(j snd)*	-PBLG	-kshun snd	*BGS
-cially	-RBL/HREU	-ght	-GT	-ky	/KEU
	/-RBL/HREU	-gle	-G/-L	-lb	-L/-B
-cious	-RBS	-gram	/TKPWRAPL	-lch	-L/-FP
	/-RBS	-(o)graph	/TKPWRAF	-less	/HRES
-ciousness	-RBS/*PBS	-(o)grapher	OG/TPER	-lessly	/HRES/HREU
-cket	-BGT	-(o)graphic	/TKPWRAFBG	-lessness	/HRES/*PBS
	-BG/ET		/TKPWRAF/EUBG	-lf *(snd'd l)*	-L/-F
-cle	-K/-L	-(o)graphy	(O)G/TPEU	-lf *(silent l)*	-F
	/K-L	-gt	-GT	-lge *(-lj snd)*	-L/-PBLG
-ct	-BGT	-gy *(g snd)*	/TKPWEU	-like	/HRAO*EUG

Suffix	Steno	Suffix	Steno	Suffix	Steno
-lk *(snd'd l)*	-L/-BG	-(i)ously	-RBS/HREU	-stle *(silent t)*	-S/-L
-lk *(silent l)*	-BG		OUS/HREU	-sts	*S/-S
-lm *(snd'd l)*	-L/-PL		/SHREU	-sy *(s snd)*	/SEU
-lm *(silent l)*	-PL	-ousness	-RBS/*PBS	-sy *(z snd)*	/S*EU
-ln	*L		OUS/*PBS		-Z/SEU
-(o)logical	/HROPBLG/KAL	-out	/O*UT		-Z/S*EU
-(o)logically	/HROPBLG/KHREU		KWROUT	-tch	-FP
-(o)logist	(O)*LGS	-over	/OFR	-th	*T
-(o)logy	OLG		KWRO*EFR	-thy	/TH*EU
-lp	-L/-P	-ple	-P/-L	-tial	-RBL
-lsion	-LGS		/P-L		/-RBL
-lve *(snd'd l)*	-L/*F	-ption	-PGS	-tially	-RBL/HREU
-lve *(silent l)*	*F	-ptional	-PGS/TPHAL		/-RBL/HREU
-ly	/HREU	-ptionally	-PGS/HREU	-(v)tient	(v)RBT
-mb *(silent b)*	-PL	-py	/PEU	-(v)tion	(v)GS
	*PL	-rb	-RB	-(v)tional	(v)GS/TPHAL
-ment	-PLT		-R/-B	-(v)tionally	(v)GS/HREU
	/-PLT	-rch	-R/-FP	-tious	-RBS
-mental	/-PLT/TAL		*RPBLG		/-RBS
-mentally	/-PLT/HREU	-rf	-R/-F	-tiously	-RBS/HREU
-mn	*PL	-rtion	-RGS		/-RBS/HREU
-mp	-FRP	-rtional	-RGS/TPHAL	-tiousness	-RBS/*PBS
	PL/-P	-rtionally	-RGS/HREU		/-RBS/*PBS
-mple	-PL/P-L	-rv(e)	-FRB	-tive	-T/*EUF
	-FRP/-L		-R/*F		T*EUF
-mpt	-FRPT	-rver	-FRB/ER	-tle	-T/-L
	-PLT		-R/SRER	-tual	/KHUL
-mption	-FRPGS	-ry	/REU	-tually	/KHUL/HREU
	-PLGS	-s (-es) *(n pl)*	/-S	-ture	/KHUR
-my	/PH*EU	-s (-es) *(v sing)*	/-S	-ty	/TEU
-nch	-PB/-FP	-s *(z snd)*	-Z	-u	/(c)AOU
	-FRPBLG	-scle	-S/-L	-um	UPL
-nct	-PBGT	-self	*S	-up	/*UP
-nction	-PBGS	-ses *(e snd)*	/SAOEZ		KWRUP
-nctional	-PBGS/TPHAL	-sh	-RB	-us	(c)US
-nctionally	-PBGS/HREU	-shal snds	-RBL	-v(e)	*F
-ness	/*PBS	-shun snds	-GS *(except -kshun)*	-vel	*FL
-nge *(-nj snd)*	-PB/-PBLG	-shus snds	-RBS		/SREL
-nk	-PB/-BG	-shy	/SHEU	-(v)ven	*FPB
-nker	-PB/KER	-(v)sion	(v)GS		*F/-PB
-ntion	-PBGS	-(c)sion	(c)GS	-(v)ver	*FR
-ntional	-PBGS/TPHAL	-sive	-S/*EUF		*F/ER
-ntionally	-PBGS/HREU		S*EUF	-(v)vern	*FRPB
-nx	-PBGS	-sk	-S/-BG	-vy	/SREU
-ny	/TPH*EU	-sle	-S/-L	-ward	/WA*RD
-o	(c)OE	-sm	-FPL	-way	/WA*EU
-ock	OBG	-some	/SPH-	-wise	/WAO*EUZ
-off	/A*UF	-someness	/SPH*PBS	-work	/WO*RBG
	KWRAUF	-sp	-S/-P	-wy	/WEU
-(o)logical	HROPBLG/KAL	-ss	-SZ	-x	-BGS
-(o)logically	HROPBLG/KHREU	-ssion	-GS	-xion	*BGS
-(o)logist	O*LGS	-ssional	-GS/TPHAL	-xle	-BGS/-L
-(o)logy	OLG	-ssionally	-GS/HREU	-xt	*BGS
-om	OPL	-st	*S	-xy	-BG/SEU
-on	(c)OPB	-sted	*S/-D		-BGS/SEU
	/O*PB	-sten	-S/-PB	-(c)y	/(c)EU
	KWROPB	-ster	*S/ER	-z(e)	-Z
-op	OP		-S/TER	-zle	-Z/-L
-or	(c)OR		/STER	-zy	/S*EU
-orial	OEURL	-stic	*S/EUBG		-Z/S*EU
-orian	OEURPB		-S/TEUBG		-Z/SEU
-ory	(c)OEUR	-stical	*S/KAL		
-ot	OT	-stically	*S/KHREU		
-ous	-RBS	-sting	*S/-G		
	(c)OUS	-stion	*GS		
	OUS		-GS		

© 1993, 2001 *StenEd*®

STEP 6—EXERCISES

SUFFIXES

PRINCIPLES ALREADY COVERED
Ex. RT-69 (Tape 5/A @ 125 wpm) & RT-69 (Tape 5/A @ 180 wpm)

1. The two <u>trains</u> <u>pulled</u> into the station at the same time.

2. The <u>locks</u> on the chest were <u>rusted</u> and could easily be broken.

3. Her <u>fears</u> for the safety of her son <u>caused</u> her many anxious <u>moments</u>.

4. The <u>nurses</u> <u>administered</u> the <u>shots</u> to the <u>patients</u> in Ward C.

5. When are the <u>girls</u> <u>leaving</u> on their trip to New York City?

6. The <u>boxes</u> were <u>padded</u> to protect the fragile glass <u>bowls</u> inside.

7. A flock of <u>birds</u> was <u>flying</u> south for the winter.

8. <u>Running</u> is good exercise, and many women are now <u>jogging</u> to stay healthy.

9. The <u>thieves</u> <u>dashed</u> out of the store, <u>clutching</u> their <u>bags</u> of loot.

10. <u>Oranges</u>, <u>pineapples</u>, <u>lemons</u>, and <u>limes</u> are four <u>fruits</u> grown in warm <u>climates</u>.

11. He <u>finds</u> <u>working</u> tedious and <u>climbs</u> <u>mountains</u> for recreation.

12. <u>Eating</u> an apple, Billy <u>rushed</u> out of the house and <u>jumped</u> on the school bus just as it <u>arrived</u> at his stop.

13. Her daughter's <u>friends</u> were <u>concerned</u> about the <u>problems</u> the girl <u>caused</u> her mother.

14. The <u>boys</u> in the park spent the day <u>playing</u> baseball and <u>flying</u> <u>kites</u>.

15. He <u>limped</u> down the <u>stairs</u> on his <u>crutches</u> and <u>escaped</u> the fire <u>burning</u> in his bedroom.

16. David <u>slipped</u> on the ice while <u>walking</u> to school and broke both <u>arms</u>.

17. We <u>laughed</u> at the sight of two <u>clowns</u> <u>sliding</u> on <u>mounds</u> of <u>shaving</u> cream.

18. The <u>pay is</u> good here, but the <u>pace is</u> a bit hectic.

19. I know it's <u>risky</u>, but it is a <u>risk I</u> am <u>prepared</u> to take.

20. There are <u>eight</u> <u>more over</u> there.

21. Did you decide to <u>save or</u> spend the money the <u>trustee</u> said you would be getting?

22. If I win a <u>prize</u>, it will certainly be worth the <u>price</u> of the ticket.

23. I've had <u>more offers</u> since I decided to <u>specialize</u> in <u>primitive</u> cultures.

24. Did you go to the <u>formal</u> with that <u>handsome</u> new guy <u>or Al</u>?

25. It <u>pays</u> to pay attention to the <u>instructor</u>.

26. The <u>supervisor</u> of the <u>mine had</u> a strict safety code that he <u>insisted</u> the <u>operators</u> heed so they would not <u>risk eye</u> <u>injuries</u>.

27. Did her job <u>pay as</u> well as <u>mine did</u>?

28. Please <u>hand some</u> <u>potatoes</u> to me, if you don't <u>mind</u>.

29. Did he just forget to <u>pay his</u> VISA bill <u>or all</u> his <u>bills</u>?

30. He <u>taught</u> his <u>trusty</u> dog to understand <u>oral</u> <u>commands</u>.

-S = -S
-SS = -SZ

ass	class	mass	puss
bass	cuss	miss	address
boss	less	moss	compass
buss	loss	pass	repress
bus	canvas	discus	grocer
buss	canvass	discuss	grosser

-S = -S
-Z = -Z

For suggested StenEd outlines for the following words, see pages 53-70, Soundalike Summary.

advice	device	fuss	price
advise	devise	fuzz	prize
brace	diverse	grace	race
braise	divers	graze	raise
			raze
bus	face	loose	
buzz	faze	lose	rice
			rise
cease	fiscal	mace	
seize	physical	maze	vice
	fizz	maize	vise

-S = -S
-Z = -Z
Ex. RT-70 (Tape 5/A @ 125 wpm) & RT-70 (Tape 5/A @ 180 wpm)

The <u>emphasis</u> among radicals in recent <u>days</u> has been on violence. Where <u>once</u> such people only stood on a <u>dais</u> and shouted angry words at the human <u>race</u>, now they <u>seize</u> airplanes and buildings with poison <u>gas</u> and <u>mace</u> and other <u>devices</u>. Where <u>once</u> they were content to live on exotic diets of <u>maize</u> and <u>rice</u>, they now <u>terrorize</u> whole nations with <u>mass</u> terror.

As these acts continue to <u>rise</u> and the radicals succeed or fail, new <u>ones</u> seem to be ready to take their <u>place</u>. <u>As</u> each new act <u>plays</u> out its <u>course</u>, another follows quickly. The fact is that societies which <u>prize</u> life and liberty have been reluctant to pay the <u>price</u> for ending terrorism. Rather, to save the innocent, they have tried to <u>devise</u> <u>ways</u> to <u>appease</u> the radicals. <u>As</u> a result, they have paid millions of dollars <u>apiece</u> to ransom kidnap victims.

There seems no easy solution to the <u>maze</u> of problems terrorism has <u>raised</u>. One can only <u>emphasize</u> preventive measures and vigilance in the face of this latest <u>phase</u> of worldwide violence which is <u>amassing</u> new victims daily.

 Step 6: Suffixes

POTENTIAL SUFFIX/WORD ENDING CONFLICTS

ADDITIONAL INFLECTED ENDINGS
Ex. RT-71 (Tape 5/A @ 125 wpm) &
RT-71 (Tape 5/A @ 180 wpm)

1. George is <u>bigger</u> than Joe but <u>smaller</u> than Sam.
2. The cross-country <u>runners</u> chose the <u>fastest</u> route to the finish line.
3. Oscar felt his rabbit's foot was <u>luckier</u> than John's four-leaf <u>clover</u>.
4. They thought it would be <u>safer</u> to use the same <u>caterer</u> as last time.
5. The <u>golfer</u> asked the <u>butler</u> to put less <u>softener</u> in his <u>winter</u> whites.
6. The <u>giraffes</u> and <u>elephants</u> are the <u>largest</u> <u>animals</u> in the zoo.
7. This problem was the <u>easiest</u> one on the page.
8. John Jones was the <u>strongest</u> of all the <u>wrestlers</u> on his high school team.
9. All of the <u>ladies</u> won blue <u>ribbons</u> for <u>having</u> the <u>tastiest</u> <u>pies</u> at the fair.
10. Though she had <u>fasted</u> since yesterday afternoon, she couldn't <u>resist</u> <u>tasting</u> the <u>feast</u> prepared by the <u>caterers</u>.
11. <u>Listen</u>, I'm a <u>realist</u>, and I know I can't ace both <u>tests</u> unless I study all night.
12. The <u>plastic</u> apple was so <u>realistic</u> that I almost bit into it.
13. I'm not <u>loitering</u>; I'm just <u>resting</u> here for awhile.
14. As it so <u>happens</u>, our <u>server</u> is the <u>best</u> this restaurant has to <u>offer</u>.
15. The <u>rooms</u> of the house were <u>blackened</u> by the fire, and all of them are <u>going</u> to be <u>repainted</u>.

16. What <u>happened</u> to the <u>seven</u> <u>broken</u> <u>toasters</u>?
17. The <u>sinister</u> <u>youngster</u> was <u>loosening</u> the catch on the <u>chicken</u> coop.
18. He has <u>proven</u> that he can <u>govern</u> with strength.

WORDS ENDING WITH VOWELS
Ex. RT-72 (Tape 5/A @ 125 wpm) &
RT-72 (Tape 5/A @ 180 wpm)

1. After analyzing all the <u>data</u>, I decided to <u>date a</u> younger man.
2. While planning the <u>escape, he</u> warned the others not to underestimate the <u>rookie</u>.
3. With a little <u>luck I</u> should be out of here before midnight.
4. I am <u>lucky</u> that this is all the <u>tax I</u> have to pay this year.
5. They wanted to <u>get opposing</u> viewpoints before finalizing the plans for cleaning up the <u>ghetto</u>.
6. Are these the <u>men you</u> were <u>arguing</u> with about the prices on the <u>menu</u>?
7. The <u>draftee</u> sipped some warm <u>coffee</u> as she sat in the <u>drafty</u> barracks.
8. <u>Yup, he</u> enjoys being a <u>yuppie</u>.
9. This <u>book equals</u> , even surpasses, his earlier works.
10. The <u>holy</u> man was dressed in tattered, <u>holey</u> garb.

SUFFIXES THAT ARE ALSO WORDS

GENERAL
Ex. RT-73 (Tape 5/A @ 125 wpm) &
RT-73 (Tape 5/A @ 180 wpm)

1. He <u>knew answers</u> to all the questions.
2. The talent of the young <u>men aston</u>ished everyone.
3. The <u>diplomat</u> knew it was unwise to <u>insult an</u> enemy.
4. The <u>playful</u> boys knew better than to <u>defy Aunt</u> Jane.
5. The <u>powerful tyrant</u> was determined to <u>gain full</u> control of the country.
6. She will pay the <u>bail if</u> the <u>sheriff</u> so advises.
7. Because many of their members were <u>ill</u>, the <u>council</u> logically decided to postpone the meeting.
8. The <u>evil</u> twin has the annoying <u>habit</u> of sticking <u>raisins</u> up her nose.
9. They <u>visited</u> the <u>palace</u> nine days ago.
10. The <u>joyful</u> 50-year-old seems to <u>age less</u> every year.
11. Did you notice he has a <u>mind full</u> of <u>useless</u> facts?
12. Having <u>less pay meant</u> that I would have to be <u>ruthless</u> in sticking to my budget.
13. The <u>lesson</u> seemed to <u>drag on</u> and on.
14. As the <u>investor</u> made another <u>investment</u>, he thought ahead to his <u>retirement</u> years which he expected to be <u>full</u> of <u>cheerful</u> pursuits.
15. Neither <u>man nor</u> beast could live in such a <u>manner</u> for long.
16. Was that just an <u>act or</u> does he really plan to <u>drop out</u> of school?
17. The cold <u>climate</u> turned <u>out</u> to be a real <u>nuisance</u>, making the <u>turnout</u> much <u>less</u> than expected.
18. The <u>glutton</u> scarfed down eight apple <u>turnovers</u>.
19. The diver showed such excellent <u>form at the tryouts</u> that they were sure they would <u>win some</u> meets.
20. He agreed to <u>take over</u> the <u>irksome</u> task <u>himself</u>.
21. The <u>raise</u> included an unexpected $1,000 <u>bonus</u>.
22. Did you <u>sign us</u> up for the <u>Roman</u> tour?

-EN, -IN & -ON
Ex. RT-74 (Tape 5/A @ 125 wpm) &
RT-74 (Tape 5/A @ 180 wpm)

While much has been <u>written</u> about the romance of the <u>cotton</u> plantation, <u>cotton</u> is an extremely difficult crop to grow. The <u>cotton</u> planter must be constantly aware of the problems that can <u>happen</u>. The crop may be <u>eaten</u> by a horde of boll weevils, or <u>cotton</u> ripe for picking may be <u>dampened</u> and destroyed by a <u>sudden</u> rainstorm or wiped out in a flash flood from a <u>swollen</u> river. There have <u>even</u> been cases where <u>arson</u> was responsible for the destruction of an entire field.

<u>Given</u> the <u>dozens</u> of calamities which <u>threaten</u> the planter, it is amazing that <u>cotton</u> growing has continued to be such an important activity in the American South. Another amazing fact is that the <u>cotton</u> industry would still be small were it not for a single invention, the <u>cotton engine</u>, or <u>cotton gin</u> as it came to be known.

Until Eli Whitney invented this remarkable device, <u>cotton</u> was a luxury material like silk and <u>satin</u> and much prized for its lightness and coolness. The problem was that the tiny seeds had to be removed by hand, a labor which took long hours of work.

What Whitney developed was a machine which could comb out the seeds from the <u>swollen</u> clumps of <u>cotton</u> very quickly. Thanks to this device, a whole industry has <u>arisen</u>. Now a <u>legion</u> of things are made quickly and economically from <u>cotton</u>, such as shirts, pants, dresses, <u>ribbons</u>, coverings, and hosts of others. <u>Cotton</u> displaced <u>linen</u> as the everyday material of the average man.

It was not until synthetic fibers such as <u>nylon</u>, <u>Dacron</u>, <u>Orlon</u> and others came on the <u>horizon</u> and manufacturers were <u>bitten</u> by the synthetics fever that <u>cotton</u> lost its standing as the <u>chosen</u> fiber for most uses.

© 1993, 2001 *StenEd*®

TECHNIQUES TO AVOID

Following are some techniques that were often taught in precomputer theories. They are extremely conflicting and should not be used.

Some of these groupings may seem like they don't go together, but all are conflicts collected from various writing styles through the years.

If you don't use any of these techniques or if you learned StenEd and are using this text for theory review, just skip this section. You may wish, however, to take the word lists and two narratives to make sure you do not have any of the conflicts made evident in the text.

POSSIBLE CONFLICTS
WHEN USING INVERTED -R for ER or OR

bailor	clatter	heater	major	pepper	sinner
barrel	clarity	hearth	marriage	perpetrate	siren
baker	clobber	honor	maker	pewter	sober
bark	closure	horn	mark	purity	association
better	cutter	jitter	meter	propeller	water
berate	curt	gyrate	merit	properly	wart
briber	dealer	jobber	neighbor	regulator	
British	dearly	josh	gnash	regularity	
captor	fiber	labor	pallor	rubber	
carpet	fish	lash	particle	rush	

POSSIBLE CONFLICTS WHEN USING -S for ER

cheaper	fatter	livelier	paler	queerer	summer
cheeps	father	lifeless	pales	queers	sums
closer	freer	lovelier	pallor	sicker	temper
closes	frees	loveless	pals	six	temperatures
commoner	gayer	merrier	pepper	slyer	truer
commons	gaze	marries	peps	slice	truce
cooler	homier	newer	phonier	soggier	
cools	homes	news	phones	social	
copper	leaner	oftener	purer	sorer	
cops	leans	offense	purse	source	

-S = -S
-ER = /ER or /cER
-OR = /cOR
(Don't use inverted R)
Ex. RT-75 (Tape 5/A @ 125 wpm) &
RT-75 (Tape 5/A @ 180 wpm)

Sails down, the old cutter steamed into port. Her creaking hull was covered with barnacles and bits of foreign matter. Only one letter of her name was visible under the rust on her sides. She looked as if she had taken a few hits in some battle, and her tiller was somewhat askew. Two curt blasts of the horn announced her arrival.

Almost as soon as she was docked, her crew scrambled to have the honor of being first ashore. Some rats on the dock were scrambling also to find a way aboard. The captain, wearing a red sash, with a saber at his side, gave the crew a brief speech. He told each sailor to watch for dishonest towns-people and not to dishonor the ship's name while in port. Then he let them go.

Each man rushed eagerly down the mats on the way. Even the mascot, an old setter, raced ashore in search of fun. Each sailor had some goal in mind: a pewter mug full of ale, some bets on a game of chance, or just an excuse to waste enormous sums of money.

A bitter wind could not chill their inner enthusiasm. They acted like boys on the beach in summer. Soon they filled the inns and the innkeepers' tills. Thoughts of purity were far away. They had "better things" to do.

Meanwhile, the captain stood at the railing idly scratching a wart on his hand. He looked out across the water and thought of the voyages hither and yon he had made. "The sea," he thought, "lets all people find their own way." He again sniffed the sea odor and felt a certain satisfaction in the order of his life. He was a man who could understand the sea.

-ER, -OR & -URE
Ex. RT-76 (Tape 5/A @ 125 wpm) &
RT-76 (Tape 5/A @ 180 wpm)

Going exploring with a metal detector can be a great pleasure. You never quite know what you will discover. There is always the hope that some treasure will be found or that some strange artifact will turn up.

A friend of mine, who is normally a bank director, spends much of his leisure time out in the hinterlands, with his metal detector in hand, looking for silver or copper trinkets buried in the earth. From time to time, he discovers something out of the ordinary which he is eager to show any visitor.

Recently, he showed me an old badge belonging to a police inspector around the latter part of the last century. It was found in a sector of land which was scattered with the remains of several old campfires. The badge itself had a coating of rust on the exterior but one could still see the careful engraving of the fabricator or creator.

Among some of the other items in his collection is the key to some old manor house, a phosphor-coated salver, and some beautiful pieces of old pewter. Among the coins which he has found are some shillings and piasters left by travelers from other lands in their journeys. There is also a saucer-shaped coin whose age and origin are unknown.

My friend, this intrepid explorer of fields and heather, is now in the process of obtaining a special extractor device designed to quickly and easily remove metal from surrounding material. He is also getting some chemical vapor cleaners to use in polishing his finds.

Of course, among all these wonderful things, he has also found things such as old radiators and car distributors and pieces of erector sets. So one can't always expect to find some major or even minor treasure.

 Step 6: Suffixes

FINAL CONSONANTS

Sentences—Ex. RT-77 (Tape 5/A @ 125 wpm) & RT-77 (Tape 5/A @ 180 wpm)

The following suffixes and word endings include techniques for avoiding conflicts found in many non-StenEd theories. Many of these suffixes deal with consonants that cannot be written on the final side in the same stroke.

1. With a little <u>help</u>, I can finish planting the <u>bulk</u> of these <u>bulbs</u> before <u>lunch</u>.

2. He let out a loud <u>belch</u> after <u>gulping</u> down a large <u>brunch</u> and a quart of <u>milk</u>.

3. <u>Half</u> wanted to play <u>golf</u> while the other <u>half</u> just wanted to <u>talk</u> about it.

4. He tried to hide the stolen <u>film</u>, but the <u>bulge</u> in his shirt pocket was a dead giveaway.

5. She tried to remain <u>calm</u> as the doctor applied the soothing <u>salve</u> on her injured <u>palm</u>.

6. She was careful not to let the heat from the <u>kiln</u> <u>singe</u> her hand.

7. They hope to <u>solve</u> the problems caused by the leaking <u>dam</u> by nightfall.

8. It's amazing that the <u>bomb</u> didn't <u>kill</u> anyone.

9. On the <u>lam</u> from the law and hiding out in the old barn, he didn't give a <u>damn</u> about the poor little <u>lamb</u> that was almost <u>numb</u> from the cold.

10. We all know that Jack put in his <u>thumb</u> and pulled out a <u>plum</u>.

11. The colonists wanted to be <u>exempt</u> from the <u>stamp</u> tax.

12. The <u>risk</u> of <u>lung</u> cancer was enough to make <u>him</u> stop smoking.

13. She <u>flung</u> her books on the sofa, <u>thinking</u> that if she didn't study harder she would surely <u>flunk</u> her <u>test</u>.

14. Whenever they start to <u>sing</u> that <u>song</u>, my heart <u>sinks</u> and my mind

goes <u>blank</u>.

15. I have a <u>hunch</u> he must be a <u>jinx</u> because every company he works for ends up making <u>zilch</u> in profits.

16. The <u>gash</u> on her leg resulted from trying to scale the <u>barbed</u> wire fence.

17. The <u>search</u> for the missing girl came to a sad end when they discovered she had been left in the woods with her head <u>bashed</u> in.

18. The <u>rancher</u> shouted that the <u>stranger</u> had some <u>nerve</u> trespassing on his private <u>turf</u>.

19. He sat on the far <u>bench</u> where he could <u>observe</u> the entire game uninterrupted.

20. They sat on the <u>porch</u>, sipping their <u>drink</u>, and enjoying the cool, <u>brisk</u> fall day.

21. The communist could not easily <u>grasp</u> the concept of <u>capitalism</u>.

22. As the <u>bus</u> came into sight, <u>both</u> Mom and Dad gave me a <u>buss</u> on the cheek and told me to work hard.

23. I don't mean to <u>skimp</u>, but if you <u>carve</u> the <u>roast</u> into smaller pieces, it will <u>serve</u> more people.

24. The <u>librarian</u> wrote an <u>editorial</u> about the prevalent practice of utilizing nouns as <u>verbs</u>.

25. The <u>patient</u>, who had long suffered with <u>dermatitis</u>, was <u>tempted</u> to change doctors.

-S = -S
-ST = *S

Following are some conflicts common in precomputer theories that result from not distinguishing -s, -ss, and -st endings. Practice writing these words before taking the dictation exercse.

baste	chest	haste	lost	quest
base	chess	haze	loss	questions
bass				
bays	crest	host	mast	roast
	cress	hose	mass	rose
beast		hoes		rows
bees	cyst		mist	
	sis	last	miss	toast
boast		lass		toes
bows	east		past	
	ease	least	pass	trust
boost		lease		truss
booze	fist		paste	
boos	fizz	lest	pace	worst
		less	pays	worse
bust	guest			
bus	guess	locust	post	
buss		locus	pose	

-ST = *S
Ex. RT-78 (Tape 5/A @ 125 wpm) & RT-78 (Tape 5/A @ 180 wpm)

Our highways are becoming more and more <u>congested</u>. The <u>exhaust</u> fumes from cars are choking all of us. One would think this would be a big <u>boost</u> for public transportation. So far, it has not been. There is one reason for this: <u>cost</u>. The <u>cost</u> has <u>just</u> been too high. Now, though, this is changing. New methods promise to reduce <u>costs</u>.

New fears of pollution have brought a new <u>crest</u> to public demand. We have come to see that a <u>capitalist</u> nation needs public transportation, too. We need it fast. We can no longer <u>exist</u> in the <u>midst</u> of a traffic jam.

Now, all over the land, crews are <u>blasting</u> rock for new subways. <u>Dust</u> is flying as workers <u>cast</u> concrete rail beds. Commuters now <u>pester</u> politicians to speed up construction. Work is going forward with great <u>haste</u>.

The <u>quest</u> is now on for even better ways. The <u>thrust</u> is toward new methods. <u>Urbanologists</u> and <u>scientists</u> are working for solutions. Helicopters, monorails, and air cushion cars are all being <u>tested</u>. A <u>host</u> of other devices are planned.

If this work <u>persists</u>, <u>motorists'</u> anger will subside. Instead of traffic jams, we will have <u>fast</u> trains or buses to take us to and from work. Cars may be left to gather <u>dust</u>.

 Step 6: Suffixes

-T = -T
-TH = *T

Following are some conflicts common in precomputer theories that result from not distinguishing -t, -gt, and -th endings. Practice writing these words before taking the dictation exercise.

bath	broth	feather	lithe	pith	tithe
bat	brought	fetter	light	pit	tight
bathe	cloth	forth	math	scythe	tooth
bate	clot	fort	mat	site	toot
blithe	death	hearth	myth	sheathe	width
blight	debt	heart	mitt	sheet	wit
booth	eighth	lathe	oath	soothe	
boot	eight	late	oat	soot	
both	faith	length	path	swath	
boat	fate	lent	pat	swat	

-T = -T
-TH = *T

Ex. RT-79 (Tape 5/A @ 125 wpm) & RT-79 (Tape 5/B @ 180 wpm)

Giving his <u>faithful</u> dog a friendly <u>pat</u>, <u>Bret Booth</u> set <u>forth</u> down the <u>path</u> to the <u>heath</u>. There was little <u>light</u> as yet, and a <u>sheet</u> of mist covered the ground. Nearing a section of the <u>path</u> where various <u>worts</u> and weeds blocked his way, he took out his <u>scythe</u>. With a few <u>lithe</u> movements, he slashed away the <u>growth</u>.

Soon he was at the <u>heath</u>, and his goal was in <u>sight</u>. There stood the old <u>fort</u> <u>bathed</u> in the early morning <u>light</u>. Quickly now, and with <u>bated</u> <u>breath</u>, he moved toward it.

As he reached the door, he tugged his knife from its <u>sheath</u> and used it to pry open the old lock. The <u>fort</u> was now his, and he had dreams of restoring it and making it a museum. He could already picture where the <u>booths</u> would go at which souvenirs would be sold.

His <u>boots</u> crunched on the dry grass as he moved to the old main building and took a <u>seat</u> on the porch. His <u>heart</u> was now beating wildly with excitement, and he tried to <u>soothe</u> his nerves for a minute before entering.

Finally, he went in. There he saw the old <u>hearth</u> covered with black <u>soot</u>. "What <u>fateful</u> events occurred here?" he wondered. He also wondered if all the work and money would be <u>worth</u> it. "It would," he <u>thought</u>. "It sure would."

© 1993, 2001 *StenEd®*

WORDS ENDING WITH -Y

Ex. RT-80 (Tape 5/B @ 125 wpm) & RT-80 (Tape 5/B @ 180 wpm)

1. Her <u>family</u> was <u>properly</u> impressed with her <u>highly</u> developed writing skills.

2. <u>Academically</u>, he was superior to most, but <u>socially</u>, he was a little self-conscious.

3. <u>Ordinarily</u>, their figures are <u>statistically</u> accurate.

4. With her <u>bubbly personality</u>, she <u>capably</u> and <u>memorably</u> led the choir.

5. She was <u>decidedly</u> nervous at the beginning but, <u>hopefully</u>, she will become more relaxed as the concert progresses.

6. She'll <u>undoubtedly</u> be the last one to leave, he said <u>jokingly</u>.

7. He <u>cautiously</u> and <u>suspiciously</u> followed the man into the back room.

8. They thanked her <u>rigorously</u> for <u>generously</u> giving so much of her time.

9. She <u>carelessly</u> and <u>shamelessly</u> refused to use <u>environmentally</u> correct gardening techniques.

10. It's a <u>pity</u> they were just <u>empty</u> promises.

11. The <u>majority</u> did not appreciate the <u>gravity</u> and <u>intensity</u> of this <u>deformity</u>.

12. The <u>probability</u> of his keeping this job depends on his <u>capability</u>, <u>reliability</u>, and emotional <u>stability</u>.

13. Due to <u>budgetary</u> constraints, the <u>library</u> will be <u>temporarily</u> closed on weekends.

14. He was <u>weary</u> of making the same low <u>salary</u>.

15. The <u>baby</u> was <u>itchy</u> and <u>grouchy</u> because of the diaper rash.

16. Because she was so <u>tidy</u>, she <u>quickly</u> tired of <u>messy</u> roommates.

17. You may think I'm <u>goofy</u>, but I like <u>baggy</u> clothes.

18. Losing the <u>trophy</u> was a minor <u>tragedy</u>, but it doesn't <u>justify</u> your being so <u>edgy</u>.

19. You're <u>lucky</u> you're at the top of the <u>hierarchy</u>.

20. It's hard to believe he's now my <u>enemy</u> since we used to be so <u>chummy</u>.

21. Has he been arrested for <u>any felony</u>?

22. Living in the <u>dormitory</u> isn't much <u>fun any</u> time exams are looming.

23. She was not <u>happy</u> when she learned her <u>copy</u> of the rare print was a <u>forgery</u>.

24. The <u>fish she</u> prepared tasted <u>terribly mushy</u>.

25. Because she was so <u>noisy</u> and <u>bossy</u>, she had trouble keeping friends.

26. It is our <u>policy</u> to encourage our employees to be <u>healthy</u>, <u>wealthy</u>, and wise.

27. With that new car, you would <u>think</u> she'll be the <u>envy</u> of the neighborhood.

28. Not wanting to show <u>apathy</u>, I decided to read the position statements and send in my <u>proxy</u>.

29. It was a <u>snowy</u>, <u>foggy</u>, <u>hazy</u> day, so I decided I had <u>plenty</u> of work to keep me <u>busy</u> inside.

30. These sentences are <u>slowly</u> driving me <u>crazy</u>.

POSSIBLE CONFLICTS WHEN USING -L FOR -LY

Following are some conflicts common in precomputer theories that result from not distinguishing -l and -ly endings and/or from using an inversion technique.

Some of these groupings may seem like they don't go together, but all are conflicts collected from various writing styles through the years.

barely	early	keenly	powerfully
barrel	earl	kennel	powerful
beautifully	faithfully	lawfully	probably
beautiful	faithful	lawful	probable
carefully	gratefully	locally	properly
careful	grateful	local	propeller
doubly	gravely	manly	purposely
double	gravel	manual	purple
doubtfully	heavily	playfully	rashly
doubtful	helpful	playful	racial
dully	highly	possibly	severely
dull	hill	possible	several

-L = -L
-LY = /HREU
**Ex. RT-81 (Tape 5/B @ 125 wpm) &
RT-81 (Tape 5/B @ 180 wpm)**

In the early morning, Earl was already out carefully loading the barrel onto his truck. The sun was barely up, but his manly body was covered with perspiration from the manual labor. Several barrels remained to load, and he was severely pressed for time. He had to get to the local brewery which sat on the hill outside of town. He needed fresh refills of the powerful brew so highly esteemed locally.

Working his muscles powerfully with double effort, he finished the job and got into the truck. He was doubly pleased with himself today as he had managed to finish ahead of schedule and could go home early. He was quick but careful as he set off down the old gravel road gravely reflecting on what he would do later that day.

POSSIBLE CONFLICTS WHEN USING -T FOR -TY

Following are some conflicts common in precomputer theories that result from not distinguishing -t and -ty endings and/or from using an inversion technique.

Some of these groupings may seem like they don't go together, but all are conflicts collected from various writing styles through the years.

acuity	charity	fealty	laity
acute	chart	felt	late
affinity	comity	gaiety	levity
affiant	comment	gate	left
anxiety	county	gravity	liberty
antic	count	graft	libelant
beauty	disparity	guilty	mighty
butte	disparate	guilt	mite
brevity	empty	identity	parity
bereft	eminent	it	part
certainty	entreaty	infirmity	unity
cerate	entreat	environment	unit

-T = -T
-TY = /TEU
**Ex. RT-82 (Tape 5/B @ 125 wpm) &
RT-82 (Tape 5/B @ 180 wpm)**

He felt rather bad. He had an acute pain in the muscles around his left eye, and it was affecting his normal visual acuity. He was certainly in no mood for levity. Rather, his pain and anxiety made any antics of others in his environment highly undesirable.

Still, he did not want to let on about the gravity of his infirmity, and so he tried to feign gaiety as he entered the gate. He did not want to do anything which might damage the fealty of his employees or affect the security of his operation. Even at seventy, he intended to remain executor of the seventh largest bank, even if he had to use deception and graft. One could count on the fact that no little ache would affect his position in the county.

WORDS ENDING IN -L(E)

Ex. RT-83 (Tape 5/B @ 125 wpm) & RT-83 (Tape 5/B @ 180 wpm)

The following sentences contain potentialconflicts common in precomputer theories that result from not distinguishing -al, -il, and -el from each other and/or from single words, prefixes, and suffixes.

1. That <u>brute almost</u> caused me to have a <u>fatal</u> accident.

2. He hoped this would be the <u>final</u> time he would have to <u>tote all</u> his <u>dental</u> records to a new location.

3. <u>Usually</u> I look at things more <u>logically</u>, but I <u>irrationally</u> thought I could do it.

4. At least one <u>governmental</u> agency has allowed this product to be used <u>experimentally</u>.

5. That's not a very <u>realistic</u> conclusion <u>statistically</u>.

6. Was the <u>panel</u> on the <u>level</u> when they said <u>travel</u> expenses would not be covered?

7. The judge pounded his <u>gavel</u>, stating that he would be <u>compelled</u> to <u>expel</u> from the courtroom anyone who continued to be disruptive.

8. She will pay the bail if <u>counsel</u> so advises.

9. He hoped he could find a friendly way to <u>repel weasels</u> from destroying his garden.

10. The <u>Council</u> on <u>Civil</u> Disobedience decided it was <u>futile</u> to ignore the wishes of the <u>hostile</u> audience.

11. The <u>pupil</u> sharpened all his <u>pencils</u> before sitting down to take the math test.

12. It is <u>preferable</u> to make the check <u>payable</u> to me personally.

13. Don't <u>scribble</u>; your signature should be <u>legible</u>.

14. The earth will be in quite a <u>pickle</u> if we don't <u>recycle</u> whenever possible.

15. I had to <u>chuckle</u> when I saw what a <u>spectacle</u> she had made of the Christmas tree.

16. It got so cold in the <u>middle</u> of the night we had to <u>bundle</u> up to keep warm.

17. I was <u>baffled</u> when I heard about the <u>scuffle</u> with the <u>rifle</u>.

18. Be careful when you <u>mingle</u> at the <u>singles</u> bar or you may end up a <u>strangle</u> victim.

19. The <u>couple</u> insisted that a <u>simple</u> meal would be more than <u>ample</u>.

20. An <u>apple</u> a day will help keep you <u>trim</u>.

21. The school <u>principal</u> expected all students to abide by certain <u>principles</u>.

22. It was becoming a <u>hassle</u> to have to work out every day to build up his <u>muscles</u>.

23. It was good to be <u>able</u> to <u>nestle</u> by the fire with a cup full of hot chocolate after surviving the <u>hustle</u> and <u>bustle</u> of Christmas shopping.

24. I was <u>startled</u> when I learned the <u>battle</u> had been lost.

25. She wondered if the <u>rattle</u> had anything to do with the cracked <u>axle</u>.

26. It was a <u>puzzle</u> to her why he always seemed to <u>guzzle</u> down his drink so quickly.

27. The city <u>council</u> met to decide which firm to use for legal <u>counsel</u>.

28. He had the <u>mettle</u> to try to <u>meddle</u> in my affairs.

29. Did that <u>man tell</u> you he kept his <u>medals</u> on the <u>mantel</u>?

30. While <u>pedaling</u> my bike down the street, I <u>met almost</u> the entire <u>bridal</u> party, who were strewing rose <u>petals</u> on the front steps of the church.

31. She is <u>liable</u> to be sued for <u>libel</u> if she keeps trying to <u>peddle</u> that story to the newpapers.

OTHER WORD ENDINGS

Ex. RT-84 (Tape 5/B @ 125 wpm) & RT-84 (Tape 5/B @ 180 wpm)

The following summarizes the remaining suffixes and word endings. A more detailed explanation of these endings can be found in StenEd's *Volume I: Theory*. A summary of StenEd outlines is contained in StenEd's *Professional Dictionary*.

1. I expect this precinct to serve with distinction.
2. Though dysfunctional now, I suspect the car will be functionally sound tomorrow.
3. According to the fax, no action will be taken on the proposed reduction of staff until next year.
4. The fictional heroine had a perfect figure and a flawless complexion.
5. The protection provided by the now defunct security firm was only fractionally effective.
6. There was much tension in the room as the discussion on professional ethics was nearing its conclusion.
7. Professionally speaking, and I feel passionately about this, an admission of guilt would cause an explosion in the department.
8. At the completion of the examination, the physician asked me to wait in the reception area.
9. He didn't have enough gumption to make an exception to this portion of the question.
10. The seminars at the convention were exceptionally educational.
11. Though it is educationally sound, I do have one small suggestion.
12. Though dinner was delicious, she ate with cautiousness, knowing that her punishment for overeating would be a nervous stomach.
13. He temporarily lost consciousness after feeling nauseous for quite some time.
14. Being ambitious, he judiciously learned to be conscientious about his studies.
15. She convinced him that it was foolish to take those bogus census figures seriously.
16. She ambitiously courted all the VIPS in town, but people soon tired of her pretentiousness and snobbishness.
17. She sells both residential and commercial properties and potentially stands to make a substantial amount of money this year.
18. It would be very beneficial to his career in special services if he could be a little more adept socially.
19. Though initially culturally illiterate, she gained much worldliness as she matured.
20. He knew being punctual was a virtue that would nurture his future career.
21. "They see" is an anagram of "the eyes"; "it ran" is an anagram of "train."
22. Demographically, this geographical region is unique.
23. The lexicographer added stenographic outlines to all words in the dictionary.
24. The typography on this lithograph is extremely ornate.
25. The criminologist had taken many classes in psychology and sociology in college.
26. Meteorological studies support the importance of everyone being ecologically aware of the needs and health of our planet.
27. In all fairness, I must say I feel she handled the whole thing with foolishness, impulsiveness and carelessness.
28. In addition to their singing talent, the wholesomeness and cheerfulness of the young singing troupe is bound to impress the judges.

-C = -BG
-CT = -BGT
-X = -BGS
-CTION = *BGS

acts	sect	contracts	distracts	intersects
ax	sex	contraction	distraction	intersection
action	sects			
	section	contradicts	deducts	recollects
complex		contradiction	deduction	recollection
complexion	affects		duck	
	affection	convicts	duct	selects
convex		conviction		selection
convection	collects		inducts	
	collection	defects	induction	subtracts
facts		defection		subtraction
fax	connects		infects	
faction	connection	deflects	infection	tracts
		deflection		traction
fix	corrects		inflicts	
fiction	correction	directs	infliction	
		direction		
flex	constructs		instructs	
flexion	construction	dissects	instruction	
		dissection		
reflex	constricts		interacts	
reflection	constriction		interaction	

-C = -BG
-CT = -BGT
-X = -BGS
-CTION = *BGS

Ex. RT-85 (Tape 5/B @ 125 wpm) & RT-85 (Tape 5/B @ 180 wpm)

One of the latest additions to the endangered species list is the <u>aquatic</u> manatee. These sea cows have been quietly moving closer to <u>extinction</u> for the last century.

Various <u>acts</u> and treaties have been <u>enacted</u> to <u>protect</u> the various creatures that have suffered from human <u>neglect</u> and exploitation. A healthy <u>respect</u> for all living creatures is slowly <u>instructing</u> people to <u>reject</u> the earlier <u>characteristic</u> behavior of indiscriminate killing for sport and profit. The <u>stark</u> realization that this <u>erratic</u> <u>action</u> was having a detrimental <u>effect</u> on the survival of the earth's plants and animals has <u>directed</u> our <u>actions</u> toward a more <u>constructive</u> appreciation of the earth's inhabitants.

No complete plan of <u>protection</u> can be devised for the manatee, however, until the <u>exact</u> ecology of this massive sea cow is understood. One <u>project</u> is now under way using an <u>acoustic</u> <u>tracking</u> device to <u>detect</u> the <u>direction</u> of travel, the <u>climatic</u> conditions, and the section of the ocean preferred by these <u>gigantic</u> yet gentle creatures.

We realize that we have been <u>lax</u> and are now taking steps to <u>correct</u> this. We can <u>expect</u> that we will not let this legendary mermaid of days past disappear from our oceans.

© 1993, 2001 *StenEd*®

STEP 7
PUNCTUATION

It is very important that punctuation be included in your notes. Not only is punctuation often essential to the meaning of the sentence (was it "No shots were fired." or "No. Shots were fired."), but many hours of scoping can be saved if you or your scopist doesn't have to add commas and other punctuation marks when proofing/editing the transcript.

Punctuation is even more important for realtime, captioning, and text entry.

Following are the major punctuation symbols. Many of these are the same in all stenotype theories (e.g., -FPLT = the period, -RBGS = the comma). Others vary. StenEd outlines are given below.

STANDARD PUNCTUATION

-FPLT	.	period
STPH-	?	question mark
STKPWHR-FPLT	!	exclamation point
-RBGS	,	comma
-FRBGS	;	semicolon
-FRPLT	:	colon
H-F	-	hyphen
TK-RB	—	dash
SHR-RB	/	slash
AOE	'	apostrophe
KW-T	"	opening quotes
KW-TS	"	closing quotes
STPH-FPLT	(	opening parenthesis
STPH-FPLD	)	closing parenthesis
P-F		begin new paragraph

End marks (period, question mark, etc.) should be included in your notes unless they will occur automatically. (CAT software automatically puts a period after the last sentence when you stroke the Q bank and an interrog [question mark] after the last sentence when you stroke the A bank unless you have overridden this by including punctuation in your notes.)

The more internal punctuation you use (comma, semicolon, quotation marks, etc.), the cleaner your translation will be. Your job situation(s) will help determine how strict (or lax) you can be with punctuation. Just remember that the more you can "fit in" while taking, the more easily and accurately your translation will be read by your audience and/or your scopist.

CONTRACTIONS & POSSESSIVES

When you include the apostrophe in your notes, it make transcription easier and eliminates many conflicts. (E.g., I'll = EU/AOEL, ill = EUL; she'd = SHE/AOED, shed = SHED; they're = THAEU/AO*ER, their = THAEUR, there = THR-; books = PWAOBG/-S, book's = PWAOBG/AOES.) Conflicts that result from not writing contractions distinctly are listed in *Step 9*: "Potential Short Form Conflicts."

Also be sure to write the contraction and its two-word counterpart differently. (E.g., they're = THAEU/AO*ER, they are = THAEU/R- or THER; it's = EUT/AOES, it is = EUT/S-, its = EUTS.)

Use AOE unless the stroke translation already includes the apostrophe or unless you choose to use the optional one-stroke, conflict-free, brief forms listed in [brackets] below.

POSITIVE CONTRACTIONS

I'd	EU/AOED [AO*EUD]	he'd	HE/AOED [HAO*ED]	we'd	WE/AOED [WAO*ED]
I'll	EU/AOEL [*EUL]	he'll	HE/AOEL [HAO*EL]	we'll	WE/AOEL [WAO*EL]
I'm	EU/AOEPL [AO*EUPL]	he's	HE/AOES [HAO*ES]	we're	WE/AO*ER [WAO*ER]
I've	EU/AO*EF [AO*EUF]			we've	WE/AO*EF [W*EF]
	[EU/AOEF]	she'd	SHE/AOED [SHAO*ED]		[WE/AOEF] [WAOEF]
		she'll	SHE/AOEL [SHAO*EL]		
you'd	KWROU/AOED [KWRO*UD]	she's	SHE/AOES [SHAO*ES]	they'd	THAEU/AOED [THA*EUD]
you'll	KWROU/AOEL [KWRO*UL]			they'll	THAEU/AOEL [THA*EUL]
you're	KWROU/AO*ER [KWRO*UR]	it'd	EUT/AOED [T*D]	they're	THAEU/AO*ER [THA*EUR]
you've	KWROU/AO*EF [KWRO*UF]	it'll	EUT/AOEL [T*L]	they've	THAEU/AO*EF [THA*EUF]
	[KWROU/AOEF]	it's	EUT/AOES [T*S]		[THAEU/AOEF]

here's	HAOER/AOES [HAO*ERS]			
let's	HRET/AOES [HR*ETS]			
that's	THA/AOES [THA*S]	that'll	THA/AOEL [THA*L]	
there's	THR-/AOES [THR*S]	there'll	THR-/AOEL [THR*L]	
what's	WHA/AOES [WHA*S]	who'll	WHO/AOEL [WHO*L]	
when's	WHEPB/AOES [WH*S]			
where's	WR-/AOES [WR*S]			
who's	WHO/AOES [WHO*S]			

NEGATIVE CONTRACTIONS

ain't	AEUPBT	hasn't	HAPBT [HAZ/-PBT]
aren't	R-PBT	haven't	SR-PBT
can't	K-PBT	isn't	S-PBT
couldn't	KOULD/-PBT [KO*PBT]	shouldn't	SHOULD/-PBT [SHO*PBT]
didn't	TK-PBT	wasn't	WUPBT [WUZ/-PBT]
doesn't	TKUPBT [TKUZ/-PBT]	weren't	W-RPBT
don't	TKOEPBT	won't	WOEPBT
hadn't	H-PBT	wouldn't	WOULD/-PBT [WO*PBT]

POSSESSIVES

singular	the book's cover	T-/PWAOBG/AOES/KO*FR
regular plural	the books' covers	T-/PWAOBG/-S/AOE/KO*FR/-S
irregular plural	the children's parents	T-/KHEURPB/AOES/PARPBT/-S

Note: AOE should be in your CAT dictionary as a suffix *apostrophe* ('); AOES should be in your dictionary as a suffix *apostrophe s* ('s). In this way, possessives will attach automatically.

SPECIAL PUNCTUATION

In stenoscription, Captioning, and other realtime applications, there will be times when you need more than the normal punctuation encountered in Q&A type material. *All* punctuation is summarized below for reference. You'll just want to pick and choose what is appropriate for your needs.

Punctuation/Symbol	Sample Use	Outline
Ampersand (space before and after)	Q & A	PH-PBD
Ampersand (prefix/suffix)	Q&A	PH*PBD
Apostrophe (suffix)	writers'	AOE
Apostrophe + s (suffix)	writer's	AOES
Apostrophe Used for Omitted Years (prefix)	'97	AO*E
Asterisk (space before and after)	use * to	STR-BG
Asterisk (suffix)	Note 1* is	STR*BG
At Symbol (space before and after)	shirts @ $5	T-T
At Symbol (prefix/suffix)	jcr@aol	T*T
Backslash (prefix/suffix)	c:\wp51	PWHR-RB
Bracket, Opening (prefix)	[start	PWR-BG
Bracket, Closing (stop)(suffix)	stop]	PWR-BGS
Bullet	•	PWHRET
Cent(s) Symbol (suffix)	2¢	S-TS
Colon (suffix, one space following)	follows:	-FRPLT
Colon (suffix, two spaces following, cap next)	follows:	KHR-PB
Colon in Time (prefix/suffix)	5:30	KHR*PB
Comma (suffix)	stop,	-RBGS
Comma Used with Numbers (prefix/suffix)	1,000	-RBGZ
Comma + End Quotes (suffix)	,"	KW-RBGTS
Dash (prefix/suffix)	one—not two	TK-RB
Decimal Point (prefix/suffix)	2.1	P*PBT
Decimal Point (prefix)	.01	P-PBT
Degree Symbol (suffix)	32°	TK-RG
Division Symbol (space before and after)	4 ÷ 2	TKW-D
Dollar Sign (prefix)	$5	TKHR-R
Ellipsis (suffix, periods connected)	but...	HR-PS
Ellipsis (suffix, periods separated)	but. . .	HR-PZ
Equal Sign (space before and after)	a = b	KW-L
Equal Sign (prefix/suffix, used with List Files)	a=b	KW*L
Exclamation Point (suffix, two spaces, cap next)	stop!	STKPWHR-FPLT
Greater Than (space before and after)	2 > 1	TKPWR*PB
Hyphen (prefix/suffix)	ex-teacher	H-F
Hyphen (space before and after)	2 - 1	H-FS
Hyphen (suffix)	2- and	H*F
Less Than (space before and after)	1 < 2	HR*PB
Minus Sign (space before and after)	2 - 1	PH-PBS
Minus sign (prefix)	and -2	PH*PBS
Multiplication Symbol (times)(space before and after)	2 x 2	T-PLZ
Number Symbol (pound sign)(prefix)	#1	TPH-B
One-Half Symbol (suffix)	5½	HAFS
One-Quarter Symbol (suffix)	5¼	KWARS
Parenthesis, Opening (prefix)	(start	STPH-FPLT
Parenthesis, Closing (suffix)	stop)	STPH-FPLD
Percent (suffix)	99%	P-BGT
Period (suffix, two spaces, cap next)	stop.	-FPLT
Period + End Quote (suffix, two spaces, cap next)	stop."	KW-FPLTS
Plus Sign (space before and after)	2 + 2	P-LS
Plus Sign (suffix)	2+	P*LS
Question Mark (suffix, two spaces, cap next)	stop?	STPH-
Quotation Mark, Beginning (prefix)	"start	KW-T
Quotation Mark, Ending (stop)(suffix)	stop"	KW-TS
Quotation Mark, Single, Beginning (prefix)	'start	SKW-T
Quotation Mark, Single, Ending (stop)(suffix)	stop'	SKW-TS
Semicolon (suffix)	stop;	-FRBGS
Slash (prefix/suffix)	1/2	SHR-RB
Tilde (no space before and after)	~	T*LD
Times (space before and after)	2 x 2	T-PLZ

Be sure you use the punctuation outline that gives the spacing desired (e.g., a comma requiring a space following is written -RBGS; a comma in numbers [as in 1,000] is written -RBGZ). (Note: For more information on numbers, see *Step 8: Numbers*.)

There are two other special commands that are worth noting. They do not work for all translation systems, but they are invaluable when available. (For more information on joining words, see *Step 10: Special Considerations—Compound Words*.)

SP-S	space command (forces a space between two words)
SKWR-PB	join command (joins two words)

ACTION STEP

The main thing to remember about punctuation is to use it.

You probably already use the standard punctuation listed on page 117. If any of your outlines differ from the recommended StenEd outlines, you may continue using your own (assuming they cause no conflicts) or you may decide to change. For example, some theories teach OE for the hyphen and OE/OE for the dash. StenEd uses H-F for the hyphen and TK-RB for the dash. We find these outlines more descriptive and, thus, easier to remember and just as easy to stroke. (Plus, some text entry systems cannot handle a two-stroke outline for punctuation, thus OE/OE would not be appropriate for the dash.)

If you currently don't include punctuation when taking, begin including it with your notes. Once you are comfortable writing the standard punctuation, start incorporating any of the special purpose punctuation (page 119) that is appropriate for your job situation(s).

DICTIONARY MAINTENANCE

It is recommended that you update your CAT dictionary as you update your writing style so you can get the full benefit of your evolving conflict-free writing style.

Much punctuation requires special formatting symbols when added to your translation dictionary. You probably already have many punctuation entries in your dictionary (the period, comma, etc.). When adding additional punctuation, be sure you use the proper formatting symbols for your CAT system.

There are some variations in punctuation usage. For example, Q&A may be written with or without spaces around the ampersand (i.e., Q & A or Q&A); a colon may be followed by one or two spaces depending on the style manual used (though two spaces is generally preferred).

To review, punctuation may be added as

a prefix	KW-T	an "opening quote
	TKHR-R	costs $45.00
a suffix	KW-TS	closing quote" of
	-RBGS	the comma, the
a prefix & suffix	H-F	hyphen-hyphen
	KHR*PB	11:45 a.m.
a suffix, two spaces & forced cap	-FPLT	period. The
	STPH-	question mark? The

STEP 7—EXERCISES

PUNCTUATION

STANDARD PUNCTUATION

Ex. RT-86 (Tape 5/B @ 125 wpm) & RT-86 (Tape 5/B @ 180 wpm)

1. Be sure to include the period at the end of the sentence.
2. What if it will occur automatically?
3. Then you can omit it.
4. The same with the question mark?
5. The same with the question mark.
6. Watch out!
7. Drop that gun now!
8. Sam, Bart, and Fred are all in a good mood.
9. I wanted to go, but she wanted to stay.
10. I will stay; you will leave.
11. Mom wanted the van; George wanted the truck.
12. I like them all: steak, chicken, and fish.
13. Be sure to bring the following to class: paper, a pen, and a blank disk.
14. The 6-year-old child was too scared to testify.
15. He wanted the ex-police officer to testify.
16. I hate her type—loud and crude.
17. They are expected to be here—Ellie and her daughter—at 5 p.m.
18. Tell him/her the job is filled.
19. I wanted Jim and/or his brother to be here for this.
20. The team's coach is expected to retire this year.
21. Did you say all the girls' moms were here?
22. "You can leave now," I told her.
23. The attorney asked again, "When did you last see him?"
24. This is your last (and only) chance.
25. Please check items (1), (2), and (3) below.

Notes: #15 Write the hyphen after the ex unless it will occur automatically. (It will occur automatically if you have a separate entry "ex-police officer" or a separate prefix "ex-" [with the hyphen] in your dictionary.)

#17. Include a separate period after the p.m., even though p.m. has a period, so the computer will know to follow p.m. with two spaces and to cap the next word. You should have entries in your dictionary to accommodate this. (E.g., If you write P*PL for p.m. and -FPLT for the period, enter P*PL/-FPLT for p.m. Format it so that two spaces and a cap follow. The same should be done for words like a.m., etc., et al., and so forth.)

CONTRACTIONS

Ex. RT-87 (Tape 5/B @ 125 wpm) & RT-87 (Tape 5/B @ 180 wpm)

1. I'd go if I thought he wouldn't be there.

2. I'll tell you what's wrong—it won't work.

3. I'm afraid he's not right for the job.

4. I've often said it isn't perfect, but it'll do.

5. He wouldn't get in so much trouble if he'd behave himself.

6. He'll feel better after they've diagnosed the problem.

7. They couldn't believe what we'd done.

8. After we've eaten, we'll relax by the fire.

9. Isn't that what we're supposed to do?

10. We've never eaten snake before, but don't let that stop you.

11. You'd think it's the first time she's made a mistake.

12. We'll try again if you'll just be patient.

13. You're the first one who hasn't complained.

14. If you've got an answer, let's hear it.

15. She'd rather believe they're real, and that's why she's upset.

16. She'll feel better after they've gone.

17. She's the only one who didn't understand.

18. It'd been too long, and there wasn't any turning back.

19. It'll be okay if you can't make it.

20. It's a real surprise that they haven't solved the problem.

21. She'd make it if they'd just give her a chance.

22. They'll want to know why you weren't there.

23. They're the only ones he'll talk to.

24. They've often wondered why it doesn't work the way it's supposed to.

25. I ain't going and that's that.

26. Aren't you surprised at the way he's dressed?

27. Did he say he can't or he wouldn't?

28. I'm sad because I couldn't get it right.

29. You're mad because you didn't even try.

30. Doesn't he know it won't work?

31. Don't let them know there's any left.

32. Since he hadn't been there before, he wasn't sure what to do.

33. He hasn't any reason to believe they weren't there.

34. Haven't you any faith that they'll arrive on time?

35. Here's what I'd like to do.

36. Let's not forget what's important.

37. You've said they shouldn't do that many times.

38. There'll be a lot more sold if you'll advertise more.

39. I'll bet there's only one that wasn't broken.

40. Where's the list of those who aren't coming?

41. I've never understood why they'd want it.

42. If he'd insisted—if you'd insisted—we'd have done it.

43. She'll try harder when we're here again.

44. It'd been a long day.

45. Here's the first thing we'll want to do.

46. He ain't no saint, but he's never hurt anyone.

47. They hadn't even been there an hour before they'd gotten in trouble.

48. Shouldn't they go where they're told to go?

49. There'll be an investigation of this.

50. Where's the best place to stop?

CONTRACTIONS & POSSESSIVES
INCLUDING SOUNDALIKES
Ex. RT-88 (Tape 5/B @ 125 wpm) & RT-88 (Tape 6/A @ 180 wpm)

1. I'd like to study more about the ego and the id.

2. I'd show my ID if I had remembered to bring it.

3. I'll join you when you go on your cruise to the isle if I'm not too ill.

4. I'll walk down the aisle when I'm good and ready.

5. I know I'm mature enough to go, even though she insists I'm immature.

6. I've given him all the money I have, even if he denies it.

7. You'll have to put another yule log on the fire if you want it to last.

8. Your dad said you're going to Europe this summer.

9. He'd like to be head of his own company some day.

10. He'd do better if he would just heed his mentor's words.

11. He'll preach about heaven and hell to all who'll listen.

12. He'll have to change his ways if he doesn't want to be thought of as a heel.

13. If he wants his leg to heal properly, he'll have to go to the doctor.

14. She said she'd be out in the shed potting some seedlings.

15. She'll show you her shell collection after lunch.

16. It's been five days since the cat hurt its paw.

17. He said we'd wed in the spring.

18. The persistent weed was the healthiest thing in the garden.

19. Well, we'll go if we have to.

20. We're a bit concerned that we haven't been feeling well for over a week.

21. We were ailing with the flu, but we are fine now.

22. We've wanted to learn how to weave for some time.

23. They're going to take their business to the new shop over there in the mall.

24. Here's the man who hears strange sounds.

25. Let's see if his teacher lets him take the exam over.

26. There's a controversy over whether theirs was the first entry.

27. Where's the woman who always wears black?

28. Whose dog is responsible for this mess, and who's going to clean it up?

29. Who'll be the first to finish the whole thing?

30. I can't understand that beggar's cant.

31. She is wont to be late, but she promised she won't be late today.

32. Several of my friends' children are graduating this year.

33. The expert witness's testimony was not as technical as I had anticipated.

34. Mr. Jones' son was arrested for trespassing.

35. The jury's verdict is expected any minute.

36. All the witnesses' stories supported the plaintiff's claim.

Note: #34 For words ending in -s, an 's may be added if an extra s is heard (e.g., Jones's); Jones' is also correct.

SPECIAL PUNCTUATION
Ex. RT-89 (Tape 6/A @ 100 wpm) & RT-89 (Tape 6/A @ 160 wpm)

Practice is given below for all punctuation covered in this step. Most of these punctuation symbols occur in court work; some of these symbols will only occur in specialized situations. You may want to take all of these sentences now "just for fun." You can then refer to this step, as needed, in the future.

You may want to take this exercise from sight before taking it from audio.

1. Most of the material I take is Q&A.

2. She will soon begin working in the R & D Department for Bates & Associates.

3. The two witnesses' testimonies were contradictory.

4. Items marked with an * are described below.

5. They sold 50 raffle tickets @ $2 each.

6. To return to the root directory, type cd\ and press the enter key.

7. The note says that the check's in the male [sic].

8. She only paid 25¢ for this paperback.

9. The schedule is as follows: John, 8:30 a.m.; Pat, 11:30 a.m.; and Chuck, 2:30 p.m.

10. There were over 2,000 posters made for the political rally.

11. He had but one vice — smoking.

12. Only .09 percent of the respondents were under 21 years of age, but 25.5 percent were under 30.

13. Her 101.6° temperature had her parents worried.

14. $20 ÷ 2 = $10 and $30 ÷ 3 = $10.

15. They wanted to go but . . .

16. Fire!

17. 10 > 9 but < 12.

18. It is a well-known fact that 2- and 3-year olds are very active.

19. -5 + 3 = -2.

20. 7 - 5 = 2.

21. 5 x 3 = 15.

22. Item #14 can be written different ways.

23. The recipients (2% of the total) were elated.

24. Are you a member of the 40+ generation?

25. "I can't go home," she insisted, "until I have finished this transcript."

26. He said, "She said 'No.'"

27. There are options when writing a comma followed by an ending quote; there are options when writing a period followed by an ending quote.

28. We visited Vienna, Virginia; Atlanta, Georgia; and Melrose, Florida.

29. Her blood pressure was 140/80.

30. Each person has turned in his/her ballot.

STEP 8

NUMBERS

It is strongly recommended that you use the number bar when you want the translation to be a digit (e.g., 3 = 3). Use the shorthand outline when you want the number to be written out as a word (e.g., THRAOE = three).

Some reporters prefer to always write numbers as words and to edit them during the scoping phase. This will not work for realtime applications. Some reporters have devised separate outlines for the digits (e.g., WUPB = one, W*UPB = 1). All such lists we have seen have contained conflicts and/or were not consistent (i.e., too much memorization).

Again, it is strongly *recommended* that you use the number bar when you want the translation to be a digit. A review follows for those of you who are not familiar with the number bar.

NUMBER BAR

The long bar across the top of the stenotype machine is the number bar. When combined with a letter, it prints out the following numbers.

S-	+	bar	=	1	A	+	bar	=	5	-F + bar = 6
T-	+	bar	=	2	O	+	bar	=	0	-P + bar = 7
P-	+	bar	=	3						-L + bar = 8
H-	+	bar	=	4						-T + bar = 9

Another way of looking at this follows.

```
 1  2  3  4  5  0           6  7  8  9
    T  P  H                 F  P  L  T  D
 S                 *        
    K  W  R                 R  B  G  S  Z
          A  O        E  U
```

When figures appear in the same sequence as those on the keyboard, a multi-digit number can be written in one stroke.

13   14   15   20   30   123   159

When figures of a multi-digit number do not appear in the same sequence as those on the keyboard, multiple strokes will be needed.

31 = 3/1   51 = 5/1   231 = 23/1   951 = 9/5/1

For numbers with three or more digits, there are often alternatives. For example, 236 may be written 236, 2/36, 23/6, or 2/3/6. Whichever way chosen is equally correct. Generally, it is easiest to write the number as spoken. That is, if the number is spoken *two-thirty-six*, write 2/36 or 236; if the number is spoken *two-three-six*, write 2/3/6, 23/6, 2/36, or 236.

Following is a review of cardinal and ordinal numbers in digits and in words. Larger, more complicated numbers are covered on pages 140-141. (There are often options for larger numbers.)

CARDINAL NUMBERS
DIGITS & WORDS

Digit	Outline		Word	Outline
1	1		one	WUPB
2	2		two	TWO
3	3		three	THRAOE
4	4		four	TPOUR
5	5		five	TPAO*EUF
6	6		six	SEUBGS
7	7		seven	S*EFPB
8	8		eight	AEUGT
9	9		nine	TPHAOEUPB
10	10		ten	TEPB
11	1/1		eleven	HR*EFPB
12	12		twelve	TW*EFL
13	13		thirteen	THEUR/TAOEPB
14	14		fourteen	TPOUR/TAOEPB
15	15		fifteen	TPEUF/TAOEPB
16	16		sixteen	SEUBGS/TAOEPB
17	17		seventeen	S*EFPB/TAOEPB
18	18		eighteen	AEUGT/TAOEPB
19	19		nineteen	TPHAOEUPB/TAOEPB
20	20		twenty	TWEPBT
21	2/1		twenty-one	TWEPBT/WUPB
30	30		thirty	THEURT
32	3/2		thirty-two	THEURT/TWO
40	40		forty	TPOURT
45	45		forty-five	TPOURT/TPAO*EUF
50	50		fifty	TPEUFT
56	56		fifty-six	TPEUFT/SEUBGS
60	6/0		sixty	SEUBGT
66	6/6		sixty-six	SEUBGT/SEUBGS
70	7/0		seventy	S*EFT
78	78		seventy-eight	S*EFT/AEUGT
80	8/0		eighty	AEUBGT
83	8/3		eighty-three	AEUBGT/THRAOE
90	9/0		ninety	TPHAOEUPBT
91	9/1		ninety-one	TPHAOEUPBT/WUPB
100	10/0		one hundred	WUPB/HUPB
			1 million	1/PH-L
			1 billion	1/PW-L
			1 trillion	1/TR-L
			1 zillion	1/S*L

© 1993, 2001 *StenEd*®   **Step 8: Numbers**

ORDINAL NUMBERS
DIGITS & WORDS

Digit	Outline		Word	Outline
1st	1/*S		first	TP*EURS
2nd	2/*PB		second	SEBGD
3rd	3/-RD		third	THEURD
4th	4/*T		fourth	TPO*URT
5th	5/*T		fifth	TP*EUFT
6th	6/*T		sixth	S*EUBGS
7th	7/*T		seventh	S*EFPBT
8th	8/*T		eighth	A*EUGT
9th	9/*T		ninth	TPHAO*EUPBT
10th	10/*T		tenth	T*EPBT
11th	1/1/*T		eleventh	HR*EFPBT
12th	12/*T		twelfth	TW*EFLT
13th	13/*T		thirteenth	THEUR/TAO*EPBT
14th	14/*T		fourteenth	TPOUR/TAO*EPBT
15th	15/*T		fifteenth	TPEUF/TAO*EPBT
16th	16/*T		sixteenth	SEUBGS/TAO*EPBT
17th	17/*T		seventeenth	S*EFPB/TAO*EPBT
18th	18/*T		eighteenth	AEUGT/TAO*EPBT
19th	19/*T		nineteenth	TPHAOEUPB/TAO*EPBT
20th	20/*T		twentieth	TWEPBT/KWR*ET
21st	2/1/*S		twenty-first	TWEPBT/TP*EURS
30th	30/*T		thirtieth	THEURT/KWR*ET
32nd	3/2/*PB		thirty-second	THEURT/SEBGD
40th	40/*T		fortieth	TPOURT/KWR*ET
45th	45/*T		forty-fifth	TPOURT/TP*EUFT
50th	50/*T		fiftieth	TPEUFT/KWR*ET
56th	56/*T		fifty-sixth	TPEUFT/S*EUBGS
60th	6/0/*T		sixtieth	SEUBGT/KWR*ET
66th	6/6/*T		sixty-sixth	SEUBGT/S*EUBGS
70th	7/0/*T		seventieth	S*EFT/KWR*ET
78th	78/*T		seventy-eighth	S*EFT/A*EUGT
80th	8/0/*T		eightieth	AEUBGT/KWR*ET
83rd	8/3/-RD		eighty-third	AEUBGT/THEURD
90th	9/0/*T		ninetieth	TPHAOEUPBT/KWR*ET
91st	9/1/*S		ninety-first	TPHAOEUPBT/TP*EURS
100th	10/0/*T		one hundredth	WUPB/H*UPBT
			1 millionth	1/PH*LT
			1 billionth	1/PW*LT
			1 trillionth	1/TR*LT
			1 zillionth	1/S*LT

Note: *S   =   -st   -RD   =   -rd
        *PB =   -nd   *T   =   -th

In the StenEd CAT dictionary, the hyphen is automatic for words such as twenty-first, twenty-one, etc. You may want to add these entries if they are not already in your dictionary.

TIMES & DATES

Number + :00

	:00	=	K- or -BG	1:00	1-BG
				9:00	K-9
				10:00	10-BG
				11:00	1/1-BG

Note: Use -BG (-K) for 1:00 through 5:00; use K- for 6:00 through 9:00. Enter 1:00 (1-BG) through 12:00 (12-BG) in your CAT dictionary.

Number + o'clock

	o'clock	=	KHRO*BG	1 o'clock	1/KHRO*BG
				9 o'clock	9/KHRO*BG
				12 o'clock	12/KHRO*BG

Note: Enter KHRO*BG for o'clock in your CAT dictionary.

Number Colon

	:	=	KHR*PB	1:30	1/KHR*PB/30
				9:45	9/KHR*PB/45

Note: KHR-PB and -FRPLT are only used when you want the colon followed by space(s). Enter KHR*PB in your CAT dictionary as a prefix/suffix colon.

a.m. & p.m.

	a.m.	=	A*PL	6 a.m.	6/A*PL
	p.m.	=	P*PL	6 p.m.	6/P*PL

Note: These outlines should be entered in your CAT dictionary. As mentioned in *Step 7: Punctuation*, you will also want to enter them with an -FPLT in the outline so they will translate correctly when they occur at the end of a sentence. (E.g., A*PL/-FPLT = a.m., with two spaces following and a forced cap for the next word.)

Days of the Week

Monday	=	PHOPBD	Friday	=	TPREUD
Tuesday	=	TAOUZ	Saturday	=	SATD [SARD]
Wednesday	=	WEPBZ	Sunday	=	SUPBD
Thursday	=	THURZ			

Note: If you already have nonconflicting outlines for days of the week, continue using them.

Months of the Year

January	=	SKWRAPB	July	=	SKWRUL
February	=	TPEB	August	=	AUG
March	=	PHA*R	September	=	SEPT
April	=	PREUL	October	=	OBGT
May	=	PHA*EU	November	=	TPHO*F
June	=	SKWRAOUPB [SKWRUPB]	December	=	TKES

Note: If you already have nonconflicting outlines for months of the year, continue using them.

Dates Written Out

September 9, 1979	=	SEPT/9/-RBGS/19/79
June 15, 1984	=	SKWRAOUPB/15/-RBGS/19/8/4
Tuesday, August 1, 1994	=	TAOUZ/-RBGS/AUG/1/-RBGS/19/9/4

Dates with Slashes

9/9/79	=	9/SHR-RB/9/SHR-RB/79
6/15/84	=	6/SHR-RB/15/SHR-RB/8/4

Dates with Century Omitted

'93	=	AO*E/9/3 (a prefix apostrophe that attaches to the next word or number)

Note: StenEd does not recommend inverting numbers; e.g., using 39 for 93, with or without an accompanying letter in the stroke. It's confusing and prone to error in taking and/or in transcribing.

NUMBER SYMBOLS & PUNCTUATION

Plural of Numbers   's   =   AOES   1900's   19/0/0/AOES
                                       10's   10/AOES
                         -s   =   /-S   1900s   19/0/0/-S
                                        10s   10/-S

> Note: Both 's and -s are acceptable ways of forming the plural of a number. AOES should be in your CAT dictionary as a suffix 's; -S should be in your dictionary as the suffix s.

Fractions   /   =   SHR-RB   1/2   1/SHR-RB/2 or 1/HAF
                                  99/100   9/9/SHR-RB/10/0
                                  9/9/79   9/SHR-RB/9/SHR-RB/79

> Note: Small fractions (1/2, 2/3, 1/4) may be written as a digit followed by a word if that outline is in your translation dictionary. Large, complicated fractions (e.g., 23/50, 99/100) should always be written with the slash. SHR-RB should be entered in your CAT dictionary as a prefix/suffix.

Decimals   .#   =   P-PBT   .5   P-PBT/5
                                .01   P-PBT/0/1
               #.# =   P*PBT   99.9   9/9/P*PBT/9
                                89.5   89/P*PBT/5

> Note: # denotes any number. Do not use -FPLT for decimals. -FPLT is only used for a period at the end of a sentence (when you want two spaces and the next word capped.) Enter P-PBT as a prefix; enter P*PBT as a prefix/suffix.

Percent   %   =   P-BGT   50%   50/P-BGT
                               98.6%   9/8/P*PBT/6/P-BGT
            percent = PER/SEPBT   50 percent   50/PER/SEPBT
                                    99.6 percent   9/9/-P*PBT/6/PER/SEPBT

> Note: P-BGT should be in your CAT dictionary as a suffix.

Number Comma   ,   =   -RBGZ   1,000   1/-RBGZ/0/0/0
                                    10,250   10/-RBGZ/250
                                    150,000   150/-RBGZ/0/0/0
                                    23,475   23/-RBGZ/47/5

> Note: -RBGZ for the number comma will work with all CAT systems. Enter it in your CAT dictionary as a prefix/suffix comma. For an easier way to write numbers that will work with "some" CAT systems, see pages 140-141.

Dollars & Cents $ =   TKHR-R $10   TKHR-R/10
                  dollar(s) = TKHRAR   10 dollars   10/TKHRAR/-S
                                        ten dollars TEPB/TKHRAR/-S
                      .   =   P*PBT $23.25   TKHR-R/23/P*PBT/25
                      ¢   =   S-TS   25¢   25/S-TS
                  cent(s) = KREPBT   25 cents   25/KREPBT/-S
                                       two cents   TWO/KREPBT/-S

> Note: TKHR-R for the $ symbol will work with all CAT systems. (For an easier, more realistic way to write dollar amounts that will work with "some" CAT systems, see page 141.) TKHR-R should be in your CAT dictionary as prefix $; ST-S as a suffix ¢.

Spaces in Numbers   =   SP-Z   1 5-foot pole   1/SP-Z/5/H-F/TPAOT/POEL
                                   2 10-year-olds 2/SP-Z/10/H-F/KWRAOER/OELDZ
                                                   [2/SP-Z/10/H-F/KWRAOERLDZ]

> Note: SP-Z does not work on all CAT systems. If you can't enter an outline to equal a single space in your dictionary, ask your CAT system rep if this capability will be part of their next update. (If enough people request it, they will do it.)

You should write numbers according to how you want them to translate. Sometimes you will want all words (e.g., one million), sometimes all digits (e.g., 1,000,000), and sometimes a combination of digits and words (e.g., 1 million). Different usages are appropriate for different types of jobs. Both words and digits for 1 through 99 have already been covered in this step.

NUMBERS OVER 100

When writing numbers in which part of the number should be transcribed as a word, use the following outlines in conjunction with a digit or word.

HUPB	=	hundred		PW-L	=	billion
THOU	=	thousand		PH-L	=	million
				TR-L	=	trillion

ALL WORDS			**DIGIT + WORD**	
one hundred	WUPB/HUPB		1 hundred	1/HUPB
one thousand	WUPB/THOU		1 thousand	1/THOU
one million	WUPB/PH-L		1 million	1/PH-L
one billion	WUPB/PW-L		1 billion	1/PW-L
one trillion	WUPB/TR-L		1 trillion	1/TR-L
one hundredth	WUPB/H*UPBT		1 hundredth	1/H*UPBT
one thousandth	WUPB/THO*UT		1 thousandth	1/THO*UT
one millionth	WUPB/PH*LT		1 millionth	1/PH*LT
one billionth	WUPB/PW*LT		1 billionth	1/PW*LT
one trillionth	WUPB/TR*LT		1 trillionth	1/TR*LT

ALL DIGITS

As mentioned earlier, large numbers may be written using the number bar and the special number comma (e.g., 10,000 = 10/-RBGZ/0/0/0). The drawback of this method is that numbers are not always heard in the way they are to appear in the transcript. This is especially true with very large numbers.

For example, the number 1,013 is usually pronounced "one thousand thirteen" or "one thousand and thirteen." (Note: Never include the "and" when writing numbers, no matter which method you use). If written using digits alone, this number would be written 1/-RBGZ/0/13. As you can see, this does not very closely follow the way the number is spoken.

Large numbers are best written as they are heard because the bottom line is to "get down what was said," and this very often does not leave time to format numbers using special symbols, reorder the numbers, etc. The method for writing large numbers presented below more closely follows the way numbers are "spoken" and thus "heard" by the stenotypist.

OPTIONS FOR NUMBERS OVER 100

CAT systems have different ways of dealing with numbers. The "number comma" presented on page 129 will work with all CAT systems. However, this is not the most efficient way to write numbers because it is not the way you usually hear them. Generally, you will hear "one thousand," not "one-comma-zero-zero-zero."

Some CAT systems will translate numbers perfectly using the following methods, while others will inevitably have a few glitches. By assigning the outlines presented in this section to dictionary

---

entries specific to each CAT system, however, you should be able to get a workable number translation. Since some CAT systems already accommodate the methods presented in this section, most, if not all, should develop the technology in the near future. (Note: All CAT systems have been given a typed copy of the logic that makes this number system work. We have also talked to representatives of each CAT company in person and will continue doing so. We expect most systems to have this capability in the near future.)

If your CAT system cannot handle numbers in this manner, ask them to include this capability in their next update. If enough people ask, they will answer.

When writing numbers to be translated entirely as digits, use the following outlines in conjunction with the digits.

HURBGS	=	*for hundred*	HURBGS/PHEURBGS	=	*for hundred million*
THOURBGS	=	*for thousand*	PWEURBGS	=	*for billion*
HURBGS/THOURBGS	=	*for hundred thousand*	TREURBGS	=	*for trillion*
PHEURBGS	=	*for million*			

In the following examples, the shortest way to write numbers will be shown; e.g., 123 = 123, not 1/2/3. You can always write each digit separately if you so desire.

100	1/HURBGS
525	5/HURBGS/25

1,000	1/THOURBGS
* 1,001	1/THOURBGS/1

100,000	1/HURBGS/THOURBGS
550,000	5/HURBGS/50/THOURBGS
1,000,000	1/PHEURBGS
* 1,000,001	1/PHEURBGS/1
1,525,250	1/PHEURBGS/5/HURBGS/25/THOURBGS/2/HURBGS/50
4,500,000	4/PHEURBGS/5/HURBGS/THOURBGS
1,000,000,000	1/PWEURBGS
10,600,000,000	10/PWEURBGS/6/HURBGS/PHEURBGS
1,000,000,000,000	1/TREURBGS
5,500,000,000,000	5/TREURBGS/5/HURBGS/PWEURBGS

* Zeros are not included when not spoken. In the asterisked examples above, a number occurs after zero(s). Some CAT systems can accommodate this, others cannot. If your CAT system cannot translate numbers correctly using the outlines shown, you will need to include the 0's when writing.

WRITING DOLLARS & CENTS AS SPOKEN

Some, <u>but not all</u>, CAT systems can accommodate the following method of writing dollar figures. If yours can't, encourage them to incorporate it. In the meantime, you will have to write dollars and cents as described on page 129.

This method involves writing the dollar ($) symbol when it is heard. Never write "and" when writing dollar figures, even if spoken (e.g., $1.02 would be written 1/TKHR-RS/2/S-PBTS, not 1/TKHR-RS/APBD/2/S-PBTS).

$10	10/TKHR-RS
$275	2/HURBGS/7/5/TKHR-RS
$477,500	4/HURBGS/7/7/THOURBGS/
	5/HURBGS/TKHR-RS

$10.99	10/TKHR-RS/9/9/S-PBTS
$32.02	3/2/TKHR-RS/2/S-PBTS
$6,999.99	6/THOURBGS/9/HURBGS/
	9/9/TKHR-RS/9/9/S-PBTS

ACTION STEP

If you don't yet use the number bar, you should first concentrate on using it when you want a digit to appear in the translation. Use the word outline when you want the word to appear in your translation.

If you do not already have an efficient, conflict-free way to represent any of the times and dates illustrated on page 138, work on them next.

Then, review the number symbols and punctuation on page 139. Incorporate any techniques that would be helpful to you.

Finally, review the numbers over 100 on pages 140-141. Incorporate whatever is useful into your writing style—including the "Options for Numbers Over 100" if your CAT system so allows.

DICTIONARY MAINTENANCE

It is recommended that you update your CAT dictionary as you update your writing style so you can get the full benefit of your evolving conflict-free writing style.

Add any principles you adopt from pages 135 through 140 to your dictionary. Be sure to add items as a prefix or suffix when needed. (Hints are given throughout this step for updating your dictionary.)

If your CAT system can handle the "Numbers Over 100 Option" (HURBGS, THOURBGS, etc.) add them to your CAT dictionary following the instructions from your CAT company.

If practical, we hope to include specific CAT system instructions in the appendix in subsequent editions of this text.

STEP 8—EXERCISES
NUMBERS

Write the numbers in the following sentences the way you would want them to translate; e.g., the number bar for digits, word outlines for words, KHRO*BG for o'clock, K- or -BG for :00, etc. You may want to alter the way some numbers are shown for additional practice (e.g., 10-year anniversary/ten-year anniversary, 10%/ten percent, 8 p.m./8:00 p.m., 3 o'clock/three o'clock, 1990's/1990s).

NUMBER BAR

1. Practice writing the numbers 1 through 100 using the number bar.
2. Then, practice writing the ordinal numbers 1st through 100th using the number bar.
3. Practice larger numbers; e.g., 123, 321, 476.
4. Make up simple sentences containing numbers. Substitute different cardinal numbers in the sentences. E.g.,

   She has ___ cats.   It's only ___ days until Christmas.
   10   364
   15   25

5. Make up simple sentences containing numbers. Substitute different ordinal numbers in the sentences. E.g.,

   He lives on ___ Street.   Meet me at the corner of ___ and ___.
   1st   3rd   23rd
   12th   45th   2nd

CARDINALS & ORDINALS
Ex. RT-90 (Tape 6/A @ 125 wpm) & RT-90 (Tape 6/A @ 180 wpm)

1. The author wrote <u>87</u> short stories, <u>43</u> plays, and <u>8</u> novels.
2. In <u>45</u> days, the company will celebrate its <u>10</u>-year anniversary.
3. The vote was as follows: <u>20</u> voted yea, <u>5</u> dissented.
4. The <u>10</u>-year-old wanted to go to the movies with her <u>two</u> older sisters.
5. Please make <u>four</u> copies of all <u>three</u> transcripts.
6. The <u>second</u> and <u>third</u> prize winners did not receive trophies.
7. <u>First</u>, you have to get his attention.
8. Turn right at the <u>third</u> traffic light.
9. The penthouse is on the <u>44th</u> floor.
10. My office is on the <u>23rd</u> floor.
11. At the <u>16th</u> Winter Olympics, the U.S. won <u>5</u> gold, <u>4</u> silver, and <u>2</u> bronze for a total of <u>11</u> metals.
12. At the <u>25th</u> Summer Olympics, the U.S. won <u>37</u> gold, <u>34</u> silver, and <u>37</u> bronze for a total of <u>108</u> metals.

TIMES & DATES

Ex. RT-91 (Tape 6/A @ 100 wpm) & RT-91 (Tape 6/A @ 160 wpm)

You may want to take this dictation from sight before taking it from audio.

:00

1. Class starts promptly at <u>8:00</u>.
2. Dinner is served at <u>7:00</u> sharp, so don't be late.
3. She expects everyone to be here by <u>9:00</u>.
4. If he doesn't show up by <u>10:00</u>, we'll leave without him.
5. The sun rises at <u>6:00</u> tomorrow.

O'clock

6. School is out at <u>4 o'clock</u>.
7. The library opens at <u>8 o'clock</u>.
8. I'll be ready at <u>5 o'clock</u>, and not a minute sooner.
9. I was told to meet her at <u>12 o'clock</u> in the lobby.
10. I have an appointment at <u>2 o'clock</u>.

Colon

11. His appointment was for <u>1:30</u> in the afternoon.
12. I'll be home by <u>6:45</u>.
13. Set the alarm for <u>7:15</u> so you won't be late.
14. There is a <u>1:5 </u>chance he won't survive the operation.
15. The <u>800</u>-meter run was won with a speed of <u>01:43:00</u>.

a.m./p.m.

16. They will both be home by <u>7 p.m.</u>
17. I catch the bus at <u>7:30 a.m.</u> every morning.
18. My last class of the day is over at <u>5:00 p.m.</u>
19. The deposition will begin at <u>9 a.m.</u>
20. The hearing reconvened at <u>1:15 p.m.</u>

Days

21. <u>Monday</u>, <u>Tuesday</u>, and <u>Friday</u> are the days our office is open.
22. She was willing to babysit on the <u>first</u> <u>Thursday</u> of every month from <u>10:30 a.m.</u> to <u>4:30 p.m.</u>
23. The <u>70-year-old</u> woman always took her <u>six</u> cats and <u>seven</u> dogs for a walk on <u>Sunday</u>.
24. He works late every <u>Wednesday</u>.
25. The study group meets every other <u>Saturday</u>.

Months

26. The <u>fourth</u> quarter of the fiscal year runs through <u>June</u>, <u>July</u>, and <u>August</u>.
27. We try to spend a week with the folks every <u>February</u> or <u>March</u> and each <u>November</u>.
28. On the <u>twenty-fifth</u> of <u>December</u>, we celebrate Christmas.
29. The quarters end the last day of <u>April</u>, <u>July</u>, <u>October</u>, and <u>January</u>.
30. They had a <u>May-September</u> relationship.

Dates

31. My sister was born on <u>Tuesday, January 17, 1977</u>.
32. <u>April</u> and <u>May</u> were warmer in <u>'90</u> than in <u>'89</u>.
33. On <u>February 7, 1990</u>, Soviet leaders agreed to surrender the Communist Party's <u>72</u>-year monopoly on power.
34. On <u>10/3/89</u>, Germany reunited after <u>43</u> years of separation.
35. Iraq set fire to <u>two</u> Kuwaiti oil refineries on <u>January 22, 1991</u>. By war's end, <u>732</u> Kuwaiti wells were ablaze.

Step 8: Numbers

NUMBER SYMBOLS & PUNCTUATION

Ex. RT-92 (Tape 6/A @ 100 wpm) & RT-92 (Tape 6/A @ 160 wpm)

You may want to take this dictation from sight before taking it from audio.

Plurals
1. The pies were divided into 12's, and each person had at least one piece.
2. The 1960's has proved to be an extremely influential decade.
3. The 1990's will be an exciting time.
4. Most of the guests are in their 30's.
5. Only people in their 60's and 70's and beyond will clearly remember the 1940's.

Fractions
6. One-half of the class saw the show on Wednesday, and the rest saw it on Saturday.
7. British Prime Minister Margaret Thatcher was Britain's prime minister for 11 1/2 years.
8. The infant was only 8 1/2 months old.
9. The approval of two-thirds of the membership is needed to change the date.
10. He owns half of everything I have.

Decimals
11. The world population has risen from approximately 4.5 billion in the early 1980's to 5.5 billion in the early 1990's.
12. In 1991, China's population topped 1.15 billion for a population density of 409 people per square mile.
13. In the U.S., annual beef consumption per capita in 1960 was 85.1 lbs.; 1971, 113 lbs.; 1976, 128.5 lbs.
14. The Tokyo metropolitan area has 27 million people, Mexico City, 23; New York, 14; Los Angeles, 10; Cairo, 9.8; Teheran, 9.3; London, 9; Paris, 8.7.
15. They found a .30 caliber gun at the bottom of the pond.

Percent
16. During the study, it was found that 95 percent of the class already used the product regularly.
17. Two-thirds of the group visited the museum while the remaining 33 percent went to the theater.
18. In the early 1990's, the age distribution of the U.S. population was as follows: 0-14 years of age, 21.7%; 15-59 years of age, 61.4%; over 60, 16.9%.
19. In 1990, 80% of college undergraduates attended public universities; 20% attended private institutions.
20. The following price increases from 1983 to 1991 were recorded: apparel, 9%; entertainment, 28%; food, 34%; rent, 35%; and medical care, 56%.

Comma
21. Earthquakes in northern Iran on June 21 and 24, 1990, killed an estimated 50,000, injured 200,000, and left 500,000 homeless.
22. On March 24, 1989, the Exxon Valdez ran aground releasing 240,000 barrels of oil into Prince William Sound.
23. In 1849, 7,000 "Forty-Niners" rushed to California in search of gold.
24. In the 7 years following 1849, California's population jumped from 15,000 to 300,000.
25. There were some 4,000-odd people at the celebration.

Dollars & Cents
26. All items in this store cost between $1 and $10.
27. I think $50 is too much for this product.

---

28. This book costs $45.25 plus $2.72 sales tax for a total of $47.97.

29. In 1991, some average per pound food prices in the U.S. included: bread, 70.5¢; eggs, $1.10; chicken, 89¢; and ground beef, $1.65.

30. In 1974, some average per pound food prices in the U.S. included: bread, 34.5¢; potatoes, 24.9¢; sugar, 32.3¢; rice, 44¢; and coffee, $1.28.

31. In 1933, some average food prices in the U.S. included: bread, $.05 per 20-ounce loaf; eggs, $.29/dozen; butter, $.28/lb.; coffee, $.26/lb.; chicken, $.22/lb.; rice, $.06/ lb.; sugar, $.06/lb.; potatoes, $.02/lb.

Spaces

32. He brought in 15 2-foot boards to use in building the roof.

33. Five 200-pound rocks fell on the truck, causing the accident.

34. I can only find three 10-room houses on the multiple listing.

35. I paid the man $4.54 each for the 10 3-gallon potted plants.

36. Those 13 22-ton trucks carried produce worth $98,470.66.

NUMBERS OVER 100

Ex. RT-93 (Tape 6/A @ 100 wpm) & RT-93 (Tape 6/A @ 160 wpm)

You may want to take this dictation from sight before taking it from audio.

1. There were 5,982 people at the football game.

2. The well produced 6,795 barrels of oil every four hours.

3. Her jewelry collection was valued at $14,652,394 and consisted of 50 diamond necklaces, 79 rings, 26 brooches, 41 earrings, and 14 watches.

4. The $10,500 reward was divided, and 20 percent of it was given to 35 people.

5. Each child gave $1.75 to the Red Cross, bringing the total funds to $8,343.

6. On October 17, 1989, at 5:04 p.m.,an earthquake shook San Francisco measuring 7.1 on the Richter scale and causing $6 billion in damage.

7. In 1988, U.S. S&L's lost $13.44 billion.

8. In 1988, the following median annual incomes were reported: lawyer, $47,528; physician, $37,232; college teacher, $35,152; registered nurse, $26,832; mechanic, $22,048; secretary, $15,548; cashier, $9,984.

9. In November, we traveled 3,000 miles on our vacation and spent two weeks sightseeing.

10. He left $5 million to charity when he died.

11. In 1991, there were 773,000 college and university teachers: 457,000 men and 316,000 women.

12. In the same year, there were 626,000 men and 146,000 women employed as lawyers or judges for a total of 772,000.

13. The aggregate U.S. national income for 1991 was $4,542.2 billion (over 4.5 trillion); in 1980, it was $2,203.5 billion (2.2 trillion); in 1970, $832.6 billion (.83 trillion); and in 1960, $424.9 billion (.42 trillion).

14. Of the total population in 1990 of 248,709,873, 127,470,455 were female, 121,239,418 were male.

15. In 1990, 75,331,300 were 20 years of age or younger, 95,765,733 were 21-44, 46,371,009 were 45-64, and 31,241,831 were 65 or older.

STEP 9

SHORT FORMS

Six general writing principles were itemized on page 1 of this text. Three of those principles merit repeating here.

- Do not use the same outline for more than one word or phrase regardless of how frequent or infrequent a particular word may be.

- Use only briefs and phrases that do not conflict with another word or phrase.

- Use only briefs and phrases that you can easily remember.

BRIEFS & PHRASES

Short forms (also called briefs, arbitraries, phrases, abbreviations) are permitted as long as no conflicts are created. Many briefs and phrases are conflict free. The key is to never use an outline for a brief or phrase that can also represent another word or phrase or is a common word beginning or word ending.

If you use lots of briefs and phrases, we strongly recommend that you start writing out (or find an alternative non-conflicting outline for) any that can also represent another word. E.g., DUG should not be used for "did you go" because it can also represent the word "dug." WIT should not be used for "witness" because it can also represent the word "wit."

Only use short forms that are conflict free and easy to remember. Many realtime reporters prefer to "write it out," reasoning that it is easier to just write a longer form than to try to remember whether a particular brief or phrase would result in a conflict. Other reporters continue to use many short forms but eliminate or alter those that cause conflicts. Do whatever is most natural for you.

A list of potential short form conflicts begins on page 151. This list mainly contains conflicts that are caused by outlining a word or phrase with a short form (brief or phrase) that can also stand for another word.

Conflicts caused by soundalikes, prefixes, suffixes (including inflected endings), and other principles covered elsewhere in this text are not included unless they are part of a short form conflict set.

Similarly, StenEd medical outlines and text entry commands are included if they are part of a short form conflict set. If you do not do medical work and/or do not expect to use text entry, you need not be concerned with these. (Note: Currently, text entry software is rarely used in court work. However, text entry software will continue to become more sophisticated and may, quite possibly, become the software of choice for many court reporters in the future.)

If you have followed the first eight steps covered in this text, most of your conflicts will have already been resolved.

These first eight steps are "briefly" summarized below. Some examples of the types of conflicts avoided are listed for each step. As mentioned before, these types of potential conflicts are not listed in the conflict summary for this step unless they potentially conflict with a brief or phrase.

STEP	DESCRIPTION	SAMPLE POTENTIAL CONFLICTS ALREADY RESOLVED	
1	The Alphabet	sip = SEUP zip = S*EUP	safe =SAEUF save =SA*EUF
		pan =PAPB pain =PAEUPB	cot = KOT coat = KOET
2	High Frequency Words	the = T- it = EUT at = AT	is = S- as = AZ his = HEUZ
		be = PW- been = PW-PB about = ABT	of = OF if = TP- have = SR-
3	Inflected Endings	pays = PAEU/-S pace = PAEUS	tied = TAOEU/-D tide = TAOEUD
		rays = RAEU/-S race = RAEUS raise = RAEUZ	stabbing = STAB/-G stack = STABG
4	Soundalikes	pain = PAEUPB pane =PAEPB	ant = APBT aunt = AUPBT
		be = PW- bee = PWAOE	hire = HAOEUR higher = HAOEU/ER
5	Prefixes	along = AEU/HROPBG a long = A/HROPBG	asinine = AS/TPHAOEUPB as nine = AZ/TPHAOEUPB
		write = WRAOEUT rite = RAOEUT (right = RAOEUGT)	benign = PWE/TPHAOEUPB be nine = PW-/TPHAOEUPB (bee = PWAOE)
6	Suffixes	pace = PAEUS paste = PA*EUS	action = A*BGS ax = ABGS acts = ABGT/-S
		mayor = PHAEU/KWROR may or = PHAEU/OR (mare = PHAEUR)	lesson = HRES/SOPB less on = HRESZ/OPB

 Step 9: Short Forms

7	Punctuation	(= STPH-FPLT	he'd = HE/AOED [HAO*ED]
		) = STPH-FPLD	head = HED
			heed = HAOED
		" = KW-T	Ed = E*D [or ED]
		" = KW-TS	(he would = HE/WOULD)
			(held = HELD)

8	Numbers	1 = 1	1:00 = 1-BG
		one = WUPB	1:30 = 1/KHR*PB/30
		3rd = 3/-RD	.5 = P-PBT/5
		third = THEURD	1.5 = 1/P*PBT/5

Many conflict solutions are interrelated. This is one of the main reasons it is so difficult to solve one conflict without causing another. For example, some writers write "pay as," "pay his," "pay is," and "pays" the same. Other writers write "pays," "pace," and "paste" the same. If you decide to distinguish between "pays" and "pace" by writing /-S as a separate stroke for plurals and then discover that you also use /-S for "is" and/or "as" and/or "his," it can become very confusing and discouraging.

The steps in this text build on one another, giving a systematic approach to solving potential conflicts by using consistent principles that can be applied to large groups of related words.

If you have followed the recommendations presented in this text:

> Step 2: High Frequency Words for the words "as," "his," and "is";
> Step 3: Inflected Endings for the inflected ending "-s"; and
> Step 6: Suffixes for the suffix "-st";

you are already writing the words mentioned above in a conflict-free manner and are developing a consistent way of writing that solves most potential conflicts.

pay as	PAEU/AZ		pays	PAEU/-S
pay his	PAEU/HEUZ		pace	PAEUS
pay is	PAEU/S-		paste	PA*EUS

ACTION STEP
Pace through the Potential Short Form Conflicts beginning on page 151, writing each word the way you normally would (using realtime if available). Your translation will tell you what conflicts you have. If your conflict can be solved by following a StenEd principle for a particular type of word, refer to the proper step in this text. If your conflict is a result of using a conflicting brief or phrase, either begin writing out one of the conflicts or chose a non-conflicting short form.

Use memorization as a last resort, and only use short forms that are easy to remember. The time you think you will save in shortening an outline is often lost when you can't immediately remember what the short form is or whether it is safe.

DICTIONARY MAINTENANCE
It is recommended that you update your CAT dictionary as you update your writing style so you can get the full benefit of your changes.

POTENTIAL SHORT FORM CONFLICTS

Following are common conflicts involving short forms often used by non-StenEd writers.

Suggested StenEd outlines are given. You can adapt the StenEd stroke(s) or choose your own non-conflicting outline.

Generally, only one StenEd outline has been listed per word. Often there are options. (Any options given in this list are shown in brackets.) For additional conflict-free StenEd outlines (including briefs and phrases), see the *Professional Dictionary* and/or *Volume I: Theory*.

Generally, a brief has been given if one is available. Words can also be written out as long as no conflict is created (e.g., soundalikes are written out within the confines of soundalike principles).

When perusing this list, it may seem that the StenEd theory involves writing it out when traditional writing would have used a phrase. That is because we have only included those phrases that are potentially conflicting. There are hundreds of safe phrases. Safe phrases are not listed (unless they are part of a larger set which contains a potential conflict). Remember, this is a list of potential conflicts. If a brief or phrase you use is not listed, it is probably safe. Let your own translation be your guide.

ORDER OF LIST

The list is alphabetized by the first word of each group. If there is a phrase in the group, it is generally listed first. Otherwise, the word most often briefed is listed first.

Any word in a particular group is a potential conflict with at least one other word in that group, not necessarily with all other words. For example, the word "about" may conflict with "absent," the word "absent" may conflict with "absence," but "about" and "absence" are rarely conflicts. Some groups are long and may contain seemingly unrelated words. But each word in a group is a potential conflict with at least one other word in that group.

Some word parts that often cause word boundary conflicts have been included. If it is a word ending, *(suffix)* follows whether the word part is technically a suffix, an inflected ending, or the last letter(s) in the word. Similarly, word parts that are word beginnings are followed by *(prefix)*.

Because it is intended that you do *Step 9* after completing *Steps 1 through 8*, many of these potential conflicts should have already been resolved. Also, many conflicts have already been covered in *Steps 1 through 8* and are not included here unless they are part of a short form conflict set.

Don't be alarmed by the size of this list. The list was compiled from many different theories and styles of writing. No one has all of these conflicts. Conversely, there may be a conflict we missed. Again, let your translation be your guide.

Pace through the potential conflict word groups, writing the words (or word part) as you normally would. Check your translation to see what, if any, conflicts you have for the group. Choose alternate outlines for any of your conflicts. (Recommended StenEd outlines have been given.)

Do not try to change too much at once. Once you have discovered two or three additional conflicts to resolve, work on them before continuing with the list.

POTENTIAL SHORT FORM CONFLICTS

ability	ABLT [AEUBLT]
-ability *(suffix)*	-BLT
built	PWEULT

about	ABT
absence	AB/SEPBS
absent	AB/SEPBT
-b *(suffix)*	-B
be	PW-
be- *(prefix)*	PWE
bee	PWAOE
been	PW-PB
Ben	PW*EPB
benefit	PWEPB/TPEUT

about a	ABT/A
about an	ABT/APB
baa	PWA [PWAU]
bah	PWA* [PWA*U]

about the	ABT/T-
about it	ABT/EUT
bit	PWEUT
bite	PWAOEUT
by the	PWEU/T-
byte	PWAO*EUT

about us	ABT/US
bus	PWUS
but it is	PWU/T-S
buts	PWU/-S
butts	PWUT/-S

about you	ABT/KWROU
but	PWU
but it	PWU/EUT
but the	PWU/T-
butt	PWUT

about your	ABT/KWROUR
burr	PWUR

absolute	AB/SHRAOUT
salute	SLAOUT
slut	SHRUT

-abuse	AEU/PWAOUZ
boos	PWAO/-S
booze	PWAOZ

accept	SEP [ABG/SEPT]
except	KPEPT
receive	SEF [RE/SAO*EF]
receiver	SEFR [RE/SAO*EFR]
reef	RAOEF
ref	REF
rev	R*EF
self	SEL/-F
self- *(prefix)*	SEFL
-self *(suffix)*	*S (e.g., H*ERS, H*EUPLS)
September	SEPT
seven	S*EFPB [SEFPB]
7	7
sever	S*EFR
Sever *(medical)*	SAO*EFR
severe	SE/SRAOER
sheriff	SHR-F

accident	STKEPBT
act	ABGT
cope	KOEP
copy	KOP/PEU
descent	TKE/SKREPBT
dissent	TKEUS/SEPBT

accuse	AEU/KAOUZ
cues	KAOU/-S

active	ABGT/*EUF
act if	ABGT/TP-
tiff	TEUF

addition	AEU/TKEUGS
digs	TKEUG/-S

adjudication	AEU/SKWRAOUD/KAEUGS
jugs	SKWRUG/-S

administer	AD/PHEUPB/STER [AD/PH*R]
add more	AD/PH-R
add Mr.	AD/PHR-

advance	AD/SRAPBS [SRAPBS]
have a	SR-/A
have an	SR-/APB
van	SRAPB
vans	SRAPB/-S

advertise	TEUZ
ties	TAOEU/-S
-tize *(suffix)*	TAOEUZ

---

advice	AD/SRAOEUS
advise	AD/SRAOEUZ
vice	SRAOEUS
vies	SRAOEU/-S
vis	SREUS
vise	SRAOEUZ
viz	SREUZ

---

advisability	AD/SRAOEUZ/-BLT
advisable	AD/SRAOEUZ/-BL
visibility	SREUZ/-BLT
visible	SREUZ/-BL

---

afraid	AEU/TPRAEUD
a frayed	A/TPRAEU/-D
frayed	TPRAEU/-D

---

after the	AF/T-
aft	AFT
after	AF
after- *(prefix)*	AFR
after it	AF/-EUT
avenue	A*F

Alabama	AL/PWA/PHA [A*L/A*L]
Al	A*L
al- *(prefix)*	AL
-al *(suffix)*	(c)AL
all	AUL
and you will	APBD/KWROU/HR- [SKPUL]
awl	A*UL

---

and he will	APBD/HE/HR- [SKPEL]
ail	AEUL
ailing	AEUL/-G
ale	AEL
allegation	AL/TKPWAEUGS
alley	AL/HRAOE
ally	AL/HREU
and I will	APBD/EU/HR- [SKPEUL]
and I would	APBD/EULD [SKPEULD]
eel	AOEL
he will	HE/HR-
he'll	HE/AOEL [HAO*EL]
heal	HAEL
heel	HAOEL
hell	HEL

---

also	ALS
a letter	A/HRET/ER
alert	AEU/HRERT
always	AULS

letter	HRET/ER
-l *(suffix)*	-L
-ls *(suffix)*	-LS
will	HR- [WEUL]
Will	W*EUL
wills	HR-S

---

a.m.	A*PL
am	APL
apple	AP/-L
him	HEUPL
hymn	H*EUPL
main	PHAEUPB
Maine	PHA*EUPB [PH*E/PH*E]
mane	PHAEPB
many	PH-
Miami	PHAOEUPL/PHAOE

---

ambulance	PWHRAPBS
balance	PWAL/HRAPBS [PWHRA*PBS]
balanced	PWAL/HRAPBS/-D [PWHRA*PBS/-D]
bald	PWAULD [PWALD]
ball	PWAL
balled	PWAL/-D
bawl	PWAUL
bawled	PWAUL/-D

---

amputation	AFRP/TAEUGS [APL/PAOU/TAEUGS]
imputation	EUFRP/TAEUGS [EUPL/PAOU/TAEUGS]

---

analyze	APBL/AOEUZ
anal	AEUPBL
annals	APBL/-S
annual	APB/KWRUL

---

ancient	AEUPB/SHEPBT
anxious	APBGS

---

and he had	APBD/HE/HAD [SKPED]
ad	A*D
add	AD
address	AEU/TKRESZ
a dress	A/TKRESZ
adds	ADZ
ads	A*DZ
aid	AEUD
aide	AED
and I had	APBD/EU/HAD [SKPEUD]

---

and I	APBD/EU [SKPEU]
a	A
a- *(prefix)*	AEU

  Step 9: Short Forms

acknowledge	ABG/TPHOPBLG		[SKPEURBG]
age	AEUPBLG	aircraft	AEURBGT
-aj (suffix)	APBLG		

---

an	APB
and	APBD [SKP-]
Arizona	AR/SO*E/TPHA [A*Z/A*Z]

and I say	APBD/EU/SAEU [SKPEUBZ]
ace	AEUS

---

as	AZ
as- (prefix)	AS
ass	ASZ

and is	APBD/S- [SKP-S]
answer	APBS

---

ate	AEUT
ate I	AEUT/EU
ate one	AEUT/WUPB
ate two, etc.	AEUT/TWO

and she	APBD/SHE [SKPHE]
and she is	APBD/SHES [SKPHES] [APBD/SHE/S-]
ash	ARB
ashes	ARB/-S

---

aye	AO*EU
ayes	AO*EU/-S
eight	AEUGT
8	8
eight one	AEUGT/WUPB
eight two	AEUGT/TWO
eighth	A*EUGT
8th	8/*T
eighty	AEUBGT
80	8/0
eighty-one	AEUBGT/WUPB
81	8/1
eighty-two, etc.	AEUBGT/TWO
82	8/2
eye	KWRAOEU
eyes	KWRAOEU/-S
his	HEUZ
hiss	HEUSZ
I	EU
i- (prefix)	AOEU
ice	AOEUS
is	S-
-ize (suffix)	AOEUZ
-j (suffix)	-PBLG
knowledge	TPHOPBLG
no knowledge	TPHO/TPHOPBLG
-(e)s (suffix)	/-S
sincerely	SEUPB/SAOER/HREU
-uate (suffix)	KWRAEUT
yea	KWRAE
yeah	KWRA*E

and the	APBD/T- [SKP-T]
airplane	AEURP
ant	APBT
ante	APB/TAOE
ante- (prefix)	AEPBT
anti	APB/TAOEU
anti- (prefix)	A*EPBT [APB/TEU]
anticipate	APB/TEUS/PAEUT
ape	AEUP
appear	AEU/PAOER
appearance	AEU/PAOERPBS
appears	AEU/PAOER/-S
April	PREUL
aunt	AUPBT
pair	PAEUR
pare	PA*EUR
pear	PAER
peer	PAOER
pier	PAO*ER
prep	PREP
prepare	PRE/PAEUR

---

and I am	APBD/EU/APL [SKPEUPL]
aim	AEUPL

and you believe	APBD/UBL [SKPUBL]
automobile	AUBL
audible	AUD/-BL

---

and I believe	APBD/EUBL [SKPEUBL]
able	AEUBL
-bl(e) (suffix)	-BL

and you feel	APBD/UFL [SKPUFL]
awful	AUFL
offal	AUF/TPAL
of fall	OF/TPAUL

---

and I can	APBD/EU/K- [SKPEUBG]
ache	AEUBG
ached	AEUBG/-D
and I could	APBD/EUBGD [SKPEUBGD]

and you go	APBD/KWROU/TKPWO [SKPUG]
August	AUG
august	AU/TKPW*US

---

and I recollect	APBD/EU/REBGT

and you have	APBD/UF [SKPUF]
ever	-FR [*FR]
every	EFR [*EFR]
eyed	KWRAOEU/-D

-f *(suffix)*	-F		previous	PRAO*EF/KWROUS
fie	TPAOEU			[PRAO*EFS]
-fy *(suffix)*	TPEU		previous to	PR*EFT
have	SR-			
I did	EU/TKEUD		------------------	
I had	EU/HAD		appeal	AEU/PAOEL
I have	EUF		a peal	A/PAEL
I have had	EUFD		a peel	A/PAOEL
I was	EUFS		pail	PAEUL
I'd	EU/AOED [AO*EUD]		pale	PA*EUL
I've	EU/AO*EF [AO*EUF]		peal	PAEL
id	EUD		peel	PAOEL
ID	*EUD [EURBGS/TK*RBGS]			
identified	AOEUD/TPEU/-D [AOEUF/-D]		------------------	
identifies	AOEUD/TPEU/-S [AOEUF/-S]		appoint	AEU/POEUPBT
identify	AOEUD/TPEU [AOEUF]		a point	A/POEUPBT
if I	TP-/EU		appoints	AEU/POEUPBT/-S
if	TP-		poi	POEU
ifs	TP-S		point	POEUPBT
-ive *(suffix)*	*EUF		points	POEUPBT/-S
of	OF		poise	POEUZ
off	AUF			
vary	SRAEUR [SRAEUR/REU]		------------------	
very	SR-R		appraise	AEU/PRAEUZ
			praise	PRAEUZ
------------------			prays	PRAEU/-S
and you recall	APBD/URL [SKPURL]		preys	PRA*EU/-S
aural	AURL			

------------------			appreciates	PRAOERBT/-S
and you remember	APBD/URPL [SKPURPL]		appreciation	PRAOERBGS
aurem *(medical)*	AUR/EPL [AURPL]		precious	PRERBS
aurum *(medical)*	AUR/UPL		presentation	PREGS
------------------			------------------	
announce	AEU/TPHOUPBS		are	R-
nouns	TPHOUPB/-S		respectfully	R-PT/TPHREU
------------------			------------------	
anybody	TPHEUB		are not	R-/TPHOT
any body	TPHEU/PWOD/TKEU		aren't	R-PBT
nib	TPH*EUB		reason	R-PB
			reasoned	R-PBD
------------------			reasons	R-PBS
anybody else	TPHEUB/ELS [TPHEUBLS]		region	RE/SKWROPB
nibbles	TPHEUBL/-S		residence	REZ/TKEPBS
			resident	REZ/TKEPBT
------------------			residents	REZ/TKEPBT/-S
apartment	PARPLT		Rhone	RO*EPB
apt	APT		right hand	RAOEUGT/HAPBD
apart	AEU/PART		right-hand *(j)*	RAOEUGT/H-F/HAPBD
a part	A/PART			[R*PBD]
			roan	ROEN
------------------				
apparent	AEU/PAEURPBT		------------------	
a parent	A/PAEURPBT		area	AEUR/KWRA
paren	PREPB		air	AEUR
parens	PREPB/-S		anterior	APB/TAOER/KWROR
parent	PARPBT [PAEURPBT]		aria	AR/KWRA
pre- *(prefix)*	PRE		Ayr *(medical)*	A*EUR
presence	PREPBS		ear	AOER
present	PREPBT		er- *(prefix)*	*ER
prevent	PRE/SREPBT [PR*EFPBT]		-er *(suffix)*	ER

 Step 9: Short Forms

ere	*ER		seasons	S-PBS
err	A*ER		seen	SAOEPB
hair	HAEUR		sent	SEPBT
hairy	HAEUR/REU		signe (medical)	SAO*EPB
Harry	HAR/REU		sin	SEUPB
hear	HAER		sing	SEUPBG
heir	HA*EUR		singe	SEUPB/-PBLG
here	HAOER		sink	SEUPB/-BG
			sinned	SEUPB/-D
			sinning	SEUPB/-G
are you able	R-/KWROU/AEUBL		Skene (medical)	SKAOEPB
rubble	RUBL		sone (medical)	SOEN
			zing	S*EUPBG
			zone	SO*EPB
are you ever	R-/KWROU/-FR			
rougher	RUFR		as much	S-FP
			is much	S-/PHUFP
			as such	AZ/SUFP
are you sure	R-/KWROU/SHAOUR		is such	S-/SUFP
rush	RURB			
			as near as	AZ/TPHAOER/AZ
				[STPHAOERS]
Arkansas	ARBG/SAU [A*R/A*R]		sneers	STPHAOER/-S
arc	A*RBG			
ark	ARBG		as the	AZ/T-
			as it	AZ/EUT
			does it	TKUZ/EUT
arrest	AEU/R*ES [A*EURS]		does the	TKUZ/T-
a rest	A/R*ES		exit	KPEUT
ar- (prefix)	AR		is it	S-/EUT
-ar (suffix)	(c)AR		is the	S-T
			saint	SAEUPBT
			signature	SEUGT
arrival	AEU/RAO*EUFL		sit	SEUT
a rival	A/RAO*EUFL		sitting	SEUT/-G
arrive	AEU/RAO*EUF		skit	SKEUT
riff	REUF		St.	ST-FPLT
riffle	REUFL		-st (suffix)	*S
rifle	RAOEUFL		Street	STRAO*ET
			street	STRAOET
			zit	S*EUT
as far as	STPARS			
far as	TPAR/AZ			
farce	TPARS		as well	AZ/WEL
so far as	SO/TPAR/AZ [SOFRS]		as well as	SWELS
			swell	SWEL
			swells	SWEL/-S
as I had	AZ/EU/HAD			
acid	AS/EUD			
			as you could	AZ/UKD
			save and exit (wp cmd)	S-BGS
as I understand	SEUPBDZ		sec	SEBG [S*EBG]
cent	KREPBT		second	SEBGD
disown	TKEUS/OEPB		secretaries	SEBG/TAEUR/-S
is in	S-/TPH-		secretary	SEBG/TAEUR
? (question mark)	STPH-		sect	SEBGT
scene	SAEPB		section	S*EBGS
scent	SKREPBT		sex	SEBGS
science	SAOEUPBS		skied	SKAOE/-D
screen	SKRAOEPB			
season	S-PB			

succeed	SUBG/SAOED
succeeded	SUBG/SAOED/-D
success	SUBG/SESZ
successes	SUBG/SESZ/-S
suck	SUBG
sucked	SUBG/-D
sucks	SUBG/-S
suction	S*UBGS

ask you to	SK-/KWROU/TO
discussion	TKEUS/KUGS
exec	KPEBG
execute	EBGS/KAOUT
execution	EBGS/KAOUGS
executive	KPEBG/T*EUF
scuff	SKUF

ask your	SK-/KWROUR
secure	SKUR
skewer	SKAOU/ER

assurance	AEU/SHURPBS
assure	AEU/SHUR
-cial (suffix, shal snd)	-RBL
-tial (suffix, shal snd)	-RBL
insurance	EUPB/SHURPBS [STPHURPBS]
insure	EUPB/SHUR [STPHUR]
shall	SHAL
shore	SHOER
shower	SHOU/ER [SHO*UR]
sure	SHAOUR

at a	AT/A
take	TAEUBG
tea	TAE
tee	TAOE

at all	AT/AUL
-tal (suffix)	TAL
tall	TAUL

at another time	AT/AOT/TAOEUPL
toot	TAOT

at any rate	AT/TPHEU/RAEUT
treat	TRAOET [TRAET]
trait	TRAEUT

at that time	TA*T
tat	TAT

at the present time	TEPT
the President	T*PT
the president	T-PT

at this	AT/TH-
-ty (suffix)	TEU

at this time	T*EUT
tit	TEUT

at what time	TWHAT
twat	TWAT

at which time	TKH-T
twit	TWEUT

attention	AEU/TEPBGS
a tension	A/TEPBGS
continuance	KOPBT/KWRAPBS
continue answer	KONT/APBS
continue	KOPBT
continuing	KOPBT/-G
couldn't	KOULD/-PBT [KO*PBT]
ten	TEPB
10	10
Tennessee	T-PB [T*PB/T*PB]
tin	TEUPB
ting	TEUPBG

barely	PWAEUR/HREU
barrel	PWAEURL [PWARL]

barrier	PWAEUR/KWRER [PWAR/KWRER]
bare	PWAEUR
bear	PWAER

because	PWAUZ
cause	KAUZ

before a	PW-FR/A
bra	PWRA

before I	PW-FR/EU
brig	PWREUG
bring	PWREUPBG [PWREU]
bringing	PWREUPBG/-G [PWREU/-G]

begun	PWE/TKPWUPB [TKPW-PB]
bun	PWUPB
go	TKPWO
gone	TKPWOPB
good	TKPWAOD
gotten	TKPWOT/-PB
gun	TKPWUPB
-ing (suffix)	/-G

 StenEd®

behind	PWE/HAOEUPBD [PWHAOEUPBD]		bomb	PWOPL
hind	HAOEUPBD			
			brother	PWROER
-being	PW-G		bro	PWROE
beg	PWEG			
can	K-		bulb	PWUL/-B
-k (suffix)	-BG		blub	PWHRUB
			bub	PWUB
below	PWE/HROE [PWHRO*E]		bull	PWUL
be low	PW-/HROE			
blow	PWHROE		burden of proof	PWR-P
			bop	PWOP
better	PWET/ER		burp	PWURP
Bert	PWERT			
berth	PW*ERT		but she	PWU/SHE
birth	PW*EURT		bush	PWURB
beyond a reasonable doubt	KWR-RD		can do	K-/TKO
yard	KWRARD		can go	K-/TKPWO [K-G]
			canned	K-D
bill of lading	PWEUL/OF/HRAEUD/-G [PWOFLG]		canning	KAPB/-G
			kg	K*G
backspace (wp cmd)	PW-S			
bill	PWEUL		can he go	K-/HE/TKPWO
Bill	PW*EUL		keg	KEG
bill of sale	PWEUL/OF/SAEL [PWOFS]			
billed	PWEUL/-D		can he understand	KEPBDZ
billion	PW-L		calendar	KAL/EPB/TKAR [KAL/TKAR]
billion dollar	PW-LD			
billion dollars	PW-LDZ		calender	KAL/EPBD/ER
B.S.	PW-FPLT/S*FPLT		colander	KOL/APB/TKER
build	PWEULD			
			can I tell	K-/EU/TEL
binge	PWEUPB/-PBLG		account	K-T
bing	PWEUPBG		can it	K-/EUT
			can the	K-/T-
body	PWOD/TKEU		can't	K-PBT
bode	PWOED		cannot	K-/TPHOT
			cant	KAPBT
bony	PWOE/TPH*EU [PWOEPB/TPH*EU]		count	KOUPBT
			county	KOUPB/TEU
bone	PWOEPB		County	KO*UPB/TEU
Bonn	PWOPB		kit	KEUT
Bonnie	PWOPB/TPHAOE			
bonny	PWOPB/TPH*EU		can we	K-/WE
			confess	KOPB/TPESZ
bother	PWO*T/ER		quest	KW*ES
boar	PWOR		question	KWE
boor	PWAOR		questions	KWES [KWE/-S]
bore	PWOER			
			can you be	K-/KWROU/PW-
bottom	PWOT/OPL		cub	KUB
balm	PWAUPL		KUB (medical)	K*UB

can you do	K-/KWROU/TKO
cud	KUD
custody	K*US/TKEU

---

can you have	K-/UF
cuff	KUF
curve	KUFRB

---

can you mean	K-/KWROU/PHAOEPB
all caps command	K-PS
cap next word cmd	K-P
chi	KAOEU
Chicago	SHEU/KA/TKPWOE [KHEUG]
clock	KHROBG
co- *(prefix)*	KO
Co.	KOFPLT
coast	KO*ES
come	KOPL
companies	KPAEPB/-S
company	KPAEPB
coo	KAO
cost	KO*S
could	KOULD
could he	KOULD/HE
could I	KOULD/EU
could you	KOULD/KWROU
couple	KUP/-L
cow	KOU
coy	KOEU
cue	KAOU
cum	KUPL
indicate	EUPBD/KAEUT
indication	EUPBD/KAEUGS
Kate	KAEUT
Kay	KAEU
key	KAOE
# o'clock *(number preceding)*	#/KHRO*BG (e.g., 1/KHRO*BG)
#:00 *(number preceding)*	K# or #BG (e.g., 1BG, K9, 12BG)
o'clock	KHRO*BG [O/KHROBG]
o.k.	O*BG
o.k.s	O*BG/-S
o.k.'s	O*BG/AOES
oak	OEBG
objecting	OBT/-G
objection	O*BGS [OB/SKWR*EBGS]
objects	OBT/-S
observing	OB/SEFRB/-G
occasion	O/KAEUGS
October	OBGT
okay	O*EBG
okays	O*EBG/-S
Oklahoma	OEBG/HOE/PHA [O*BG/O*BG]
on account	OPB/K-T
ox	OBGS
quay	KAE
queue	KWAOU
which I	KH-/EU [KH*EU]

---

can you recall	K-/KWROU/RAUL [K*URL]
curl	KURL

---

can you remember	KURPL
can your	K-/KWROUR
cordially yours	KORPBLG/HREU/KWROURS
cur	KUR
curd	KURD
curs	KUR/-S
curse	KURS
occur	O/KUR
occurred	O/KUR/-D
occurs	O/KUR/-S

---

can you say	K-/KWROU/SAEU
cuss	KUSZ
customer	K*US/PHER

---

can you tell	K-/KWROU/TEL
cut	KUT

---

can you tell us	K-/KWROU/TEL/US
cuts	KUT/-S

---

cash on delivery	KARB/OPB/TKHR*EUF/REU
cod	KOD
c.o.d.	KR*PD/O*PLD/TK*PLD
C.O.D.	KR-FPLT/O*D [KR-FPLT/O*FPLT/TK*FPLT]
COD	KR-RBGS/O*D [KR-RBGS/O*RBGS/TK*RBGS] [KROD]

---

central nervous system	STRAL/TPHEFRB/OUS/S-PL [STRAL/TPHEFRBS/S-PL]
conditions	K-PBS

---

certify	SERT/TPEU
certification	SERT/TPEU/KAEUGS

---

charge	KHARPBLG
which	KH-

---

clothes	KHRO*ET/-S [KHRO*ETS]
close	KHROEZ, KHROES

---

collusion	KHRAOUGS
inclusion	EUPB/KLAOUGS

 Step 9: Short Forms

Colorado	KOL/RA/TKOE [KRO*/KRO*]	exhort	KPORT [KPHORT]
coal	KOEL	hinge	HEUPB/-PBLG [HEUPBG]
col- (prefix)	KOL, KHR-	I think	EU/THEU [EUPBG]
-col (suffix)	KOL	in respect	TPH-RPT
		Inc.	EUPB/*BG [EUPB/KR-FPLT]
combination	KPWEU/TPHAEUGS [KPWEUPBGS]	incorporate	EUPB/KORPT
impinges	EUPL/PEUPB/-PBLGS [EUPL/PEUPBG/-S]	incorporated	EUPB/KORPT/-D
		incorporations	EUPB/KORPGS/-S
		ink	EUPB/-BG [*EUPBG]
comment	KPHEPBT	inning	EUPB/-G
comet	KOPLT		
		concern	KOPB/SERPB [K-RPB]
communication	KPHAOUPB/KAEUGS	kern	KERPB
commune	KPHAOUPB		
communicate	KPHAOUPB/KAEUT	conclusion	KOPB/KHRAOUGS
		conclude	KOPB/KHRAOUD
compact	KOPL/PABGT		
exact	KPABGT	concussion	KOPB/KUGS
		cushion	KUGS
compel	KOPL/PEL		
excel	KPEL	conductor	KUBGT/TOR
expel	EBGS/PEL	con	KOPB
		conduct	KUBGT
compile	KOPL/PAOEUL	conduct or	KUBGT/OR
exile	KPAOEUL	Congress	KO*PBG
		congress	KOPBG
		Connecticut	KOPB/TPHET/KUT [K*T/K*T]
comport	KOPL/PORT	conned	KOPB/-D
chord	KHORD	conning	KOPB/-G
coarse	KOERS [KAORS]	cons	KOPB/-S
cor- (prefix)	KR-, KOR	consequence	KOPBS/KWEPBS
-cor (suffix)	KOR	consequent	KOPBS/KWEPBT
cord	KORD		
core	KOER	conform	KOPB/TPORPL
cored	KOER/-D	quorum	KWORPL
cores	KOER/-S		
corespondent	KO/SPOPBT [KO/RE/SPOPBD/EPBT]	constitution	KOPBS/TAOUGS [TAOUGS]
corn	KORPB	substitution	SUB/STAOUGS [STUGS]
corner	KORPB/ER		
coroner	KOR/TPHER [KOERPB]	consummation	KOPBS/PHAEUGS
Corp.	KO*RP	consumption	KOPB/SUPLGS [KOPB/SUFRPGS]
corporate	KORPT		
corporation	KORPGS		
corporations	KORPGS/-S	contain	KOPB/TAEUPB
corps	KOERP [KOERPZ]	cane	KAEUPB
corpse	KORPS [KOERPS]		
correspond	KOR/SPOPBD		
corresponded	KOR/SPOPBD/-D	contraction	KR*BGS
correspondence	KOR/SPOPBD/EPBS	contracts	KR-TS
correspondent	KOR/SPOPBT [KOR/SPOPBD/EPBT]	croaks	KROEBG/-S
corresponds	KOR/SPOPBDZ	cross examination	KR-BGS
course	KOURS	CROSS-EXAMINATION	KR-BGS/KR-BGS
court	KOURT		
Court	KO*URT		

cross-examine	KROEBGS

---

contradict	KOPB/TRA/TKEUBGT
	[KR*BGT]
contradiction	KOPB/TRA/TK*EUBGS
	[KR*GS]
contribution	KREUBGS
crick	KREUBG
cricks	KREUBG/-S

---

convenient	SRAOEPBT
convene	KOPB/SRAOEPB
convenience	SRAOEPBS
conveniently	SRAOEPBT/HREU
queen	KWAOEPB
queens	KWAOEPB/-S
seventeen	S*EFPB/TAOEPB
17	17
venal	SRAOEPBL
venial	SRAOEPB/KWRAL
Venn	SREPB

---

convince	KOPB/SREUPBS
quince	KWEUPBS

-corrode	KROED
crowed	KROE/-D

---

could be	KOUB [KOULD/PW-]
cob	KOB

---

could go	KOULD/TKPWO
cog	KOG

---

could he have	KOULD/HE/SR-
cove	KO*EF

---

could know	KOULD/TPHOE
coon	KAOPB

---

could the	KOULD/T-
cot	KOT
could it	KOULD/EUT

---

could you mean	KOULD/KWROU/PHAOEPB
Qume	KAOUPL

---

could you tell	KOULD/KWROU/TEL
cute	KAOUT

---

cower	KOU/ER [KO*UR]
coeur (medical)	KOUR

---

crafty	KRAF/TEU
craft	KRAFT

---

daily	TKAEU/HREU
dale	TKAEUL
Dale	TKA*EUL
deal	TKAOEL
detail	TKE/TAEUL

---

decision	TKE/SEUGS
crest	KR*ES
decrease	TKE/KRAOES
decrees	TKE/KRAOE/-S
sedition	SE/TKEUGS

---

deposition	TKEP/SEUGS [TKEPGS]
depo	TKEP/POE
depot	TKE/POE

---

description	TKE/SKREUPGS
	[TKREUPGS]
describe	TKE/SKRAOEUB
	[TKRAOEUB]

---

desirous	TKE/SAOEUR/OUS
desires	TKE/SAOEUR/-S

---

detain	TKE/TAEUPB
Dane	TKAEUPB

---

detective	TK-BGT
deduct	TKE/TKUBGT
deduction	TKE/TK*UBGS
deducts	TKE/TKUBGT/-S
defect	TKE/TPEBGT [TKEFBGT]
detect	TKE/TEBGT
duck	TKUBG
ducks	TKUBG/-S
duct	TKUBGT
ducts	TKUBGT/-S

---

did go	TKEUD/TKPWO
agree	AEU/TKPWRAOE
agreed	AEU/TKPWRAOE/-D
	[AEU/TKPWRAOED]
agrees	AEU/TKPWRAOE/-S
	[AEU/TKPWRAOES]
degree	TKE/TKPWRAOE
degrees	TKE/TKPWRAOE/-S
° (degree symbol wp cmd)	TK-RG
diagnose	TKAOEUG
	[TKAOEUG/TPHOES]
dying	TKAOEU/-G
grease	TKPWRAES
Greece	TKPWRAOES
	[TKPWRAO*ES]
greed	TKPWRAOED

---

did he	TKEUD/HE	death	TKE*T
de- *(prefix)*	TKE	debit	TKEBT
		debt	TKET

---

did he do	TKEUD/HE/TKO	did he want	TKEUD/HE/WAPBT
dead	TKED	department	TK-PT
deed	TKAOED	depth	TK*EPT

---

did he ever	TKEUD/HE/-FR	did not	TKEUD/TPHOT
defer	TKEFR	didn't	TK-PBT
di- *(prefix)*	TKEU		
did I	TKEUD/EU		
did I ever	TKEUD/EU/-FR	did you	TKEUD/KWROU
did I feel	TKEUFL	dew	TKAO*U
did I have the	TKEUF/T-	do	TKO
did I have	TKEUF	do you have	TKAOUF
die	TKAOEU	do you	TKO/KWROU
differ	TKEUFR	doe	TKOE
difference	TKEUFRPBS	dough	TKOU
different	TKEUFRPBT	due	TKAOU
difficult	TKEUFLT		
difficulty	TKEUFLT/TEU		
dill	TKEUL	did you believe	TKEUD/UBL
ditty	TKEUT/TEU	double	TKUBL
do I	TKO/EU	do you believe	TKAOUBL
-dy *(suffix)*	TKEU		
dye	TKAO*EU		
		did you do	TKEUD/KWROU/TKO
		dud	TKUD

---

did he have	TKEUD/HE/SR-	did you go	TKEUD/KWROU/TKPWO
deaf	TKEF	do you go	TKO/KWROU/TKPWO
defend	TKEFD [TKE/TPEPBD]	dug	TKUG
defendant	TK-FT		
definite	TKEF/TPHEUT [TKEFPBT]		
		did you know	TKEUD/KWROU/TPHOE
definitely	TKEF/TPHEUT/HREU [TKEFPBT/HREU]	do you know	TKO/KWROU/TPHOE [TKAO*UPB]
deft	TKEFT	does not	TKUZ/TPHOT
delve	TKEL/*F	doesn't	TKUPBT
develop	TKWOP	Don	TKO*PB
devil	TK*EFL	don	TKOPB
did he feel	TKEFL	don't	TKOEPBT
		done	TKOEPB
		down	TKOUPB
did he know	TKEUD/HE/TPHOE	dun	TKUPB
den	TKEPB	dune	TKAOUPB
denies	TKE/TPH*EU/-S		
dens	TKEPB/-S		
dense	TKEPBS	did you live	TKEUD/KWROU/HR*EUF
deny	TKE/TPH*EU	do you live	TKO/KWROU/HR*EUF
dictionary define *(twp cmd)*	TK-PB	dowel	TKOUL
-edness *(suffix)*	TK*PBS [TK-PBS] [/-D/*PBS]	dual	TKAOUL
		duel	TKAO*UL
		dull	TKUL
did he say	TKEUD/HE/SAEU [TKEBZ]	duly	TKAOU/HREU
December	TKES		

---

did he tell	TKEUD/HE/TEL

did you mean	TKEUD/KWROU/PHAOEPB	eastern	AOES/TERPB [AO*ERPB]
do you mean	TKO/KWROU/PHAOEPB [TKAOUPL]	ebb	EB
		urine	KWRAOURPB
dumb	TKUPL	urn	URPB
		Your Honor	KWROURPB

---

did you recall	TKEUD/KWROU/RAUL [TKURL]	economic	KPHEUBG
do you recall	TKO/KWROU/RAUL [TKAO*URL]	comic	KOPL/EUBG
dural	TKAOURL		

---

did you remember	TKURPL	efficiency	TPEURBT/SEU
do you remember	TKAOURPL	efficient	TPEURBT
do your	TKO/KWROUR	efficiently	TPEURBT/HREU
dour	TKOUR	official	TPEURBL
dower	TKOU/ER [TKO*UR]	fishes	TPEURB/-S

---

did you say	TKEUD/KWROU/SAEU [TKUBZ]	either	E/THER [AOERT]
did you see	TKEUD/KWROU/SAOE	earth	*ERT
deuce	TKAOUS	et cetera	ET/SET/RA
do you say	TKO/KWROU/SAEU	etc.	ETS
do you see	TKO/KWROU/SAOE	ether	AO*ET/ER
does	TKUZ		
does (plural noun)	TKOE/-S		
dose	TKOES	election	E/HR*EBGS [HR*EBGS]
dozen	TKUZ/-PB	electric	HREBG/TREUBG
dues	TKAOU/-S	electricity	HREBG/TREUS/TEU
dust	TK*US	elects	E/HREBGT/-S [HREBGT/-S]
		lex	HREBGS

---

did you think	TKEUD/KWROU/THEU	eleven	HR*EFPB
do you think	TKO/KWROU/THEU [TKAOUPBG]	leaven	HR*EF/-PB
dung	TKUPBG		
dunk	TKUPB/-BG [TK*UPBG]	emergency	PH-RPBLG
dunning	TKUPB/-G	emerge	E/PHERPBLG
		manage	PHAPBG

---

disputer	TKEUS/PAOUT/ER	managed	PHAPBG/-D
sputter	SPUT/ER	manager	PH-G
		managers	PH-GS
		manages	PHAPBG/-S
distinction	TKEUS/TEUPBGS	managing	PHAPBG/-G
zings	S*EUPBG/-S	mange	PHAEUPB/-PBLG [PHAEUPBG]
		manning	PHAPB/-G
do have	TKO/SR-	mansion	PHAPBGS
doff	TKOF	meeting	PHAOET/-G
		Meg	PH*EG
		mega- (prefix)	PHEG
doctor	TKOBG/TOR [TKR-]	megs	PHEG/-S
Doctor	TKO*BG/TOR [TKR*]	merge	PHERPBLG
doc	TKO*BG	mg	PH*G
dock	TKOBG		
Dr.	TKR-FPLT		

---

		employ	EPL/PHROEU
		ploy	PHROEU

---

eastbound	AO*ES/PWOUPBD [*EB]	enclosed	EPB/KHROEZ/-D
Earl	*ERL	clod	KHROD
early	*ER/HREU [ERL/HREU]	clog	KHROG
earn	ERPB	enclosing	EPB/KHROEZ/-G
easterly	AO*ES/ER/HREU [AO*ERL]		

© 1993, 2001 *StenEd*®

engineer	EPBG/TPHAOER	suppose	SU/POEZ [SPOEZ]
engine	EPB/SKWREUPB	supposition	SUP/SEUGS [SUP/POGS]
engine near	EPB/SKWREUPB/TPHAOER		
jeer	SKWRAOER	express	EBGS/PRESZ
		expression	EBGS/PREGS
enthusiasm	SPWAOUZ/KWRAFPL	suppress	SU/PRESZ [SPRESZ]
enthusiast	SPWAOUZ/KWRA*S	suppression	SU/PREGS [SPREGS]
enthusiastic	SPWAOUZ/KWRA*S/EUBG		
		extant	EBGS/TAPBT
envelope (n)	EPB/SRE/HROEP	scant	SKAPBT
envelop (v)	EPB/SREL/OP		
informal	TPH-FL	extol	EBGS/TOEL
		stole	STOEL
equality	E/KWAULT		
quality	KWAULT	extreme	EBGS/TRAOEPL
		stream	STRAOEPL
equip	E/KWEUP		
quip	KWEUP	extrude	EBGS/TRAOUD
		screwed	SKRAOU/-D
establish	PWHREURB		
establishing	PWHREURB/-G	exude	KPAOUD
establishment	PWHREURB/-PLT	skewed	SKAOU/-D
	[PWHREUPLT]		
stab	STAB	family	TPAPL/HREU
stabbing	STAB/-G	familiar	TPA/PHEUL/KWRAR
stack	STABG		[TPHRAR]
		familiarly	TPA/PHEUL/KWRAR/HREU
evaluation	E/SRAL/KWRAEUGS [*EFLGS]		[TPHRAR/HREU]
valuation	SRAL/KWRAEUGS		
		father	TPAUR [TPA*T/ER]
even	EFPB	fair	TPAEUR
en- (prefix)	EPB	fare	TPAER
-en (suffix)	/-PB	fatter	TPAT/ER
		fear	TPAOER
exam	KPAPL		
scam	SKAPL	fibula	TPEUB/HRA
		fib	TPEUB
expand	EBGS/PAPBD		
spanned	SPAPB/-D	fifteen	TPEUF/TAOEPB
		15	15
expend	EBGS/PEPBD	fen	TPEPB
expense	EBGS/PEPBS		
spend	SPEPBD	fifty-eight	TPEUFT/AEUGT
spends	SPEPBDZ	58	58
suspend	SUS/PEPBD	fate	TPAEUT
suspense	SUS/PEPBS		
		fifty-nine	TPEUFT/TPHAOEUPB
export	EBGS/PORT	59	59
spore	SPOER [SPOR]	fin	TPEUPB
sport	SPORT	fine	TPAOEUPB
support	SU/PORT [SPO*RT]		
		fifty-three	TPEUFT/THRAOE
expose	EBGS/POEZ	53	5/3
expos	EBGS/POE/-S	fee	TPAOE
Expos	*EBGS/POE/-S		
exposition	EBGS/POGS		

fighting	TPAOEUGT/-G	freight	TPRAEUGT [TPRAEUT]
fight	TPAOEUGT		

		forty-three	TPOURT/THRAOE
finance	TP-PBS	43	4/3
finances	TP-PBS/-S	free	TPRAOE

		forward	TPWARD [TPOR/WARD]
first	TP*EURS	for ward	TP-R/WARD
firs	TPEUR/-S	ford	TPORD
		Ford	TPO*RD

flowing	TPHROE/-G		
flog	TPHROG	fraction	TPRA*BGS
		fractious	TPRABG/-RBS

focus	TPOE/KUS	gallon	TKPWAL/HROPB
folks	TPOEBG/-S		[TKPWHROPB]
fox	TPOBGS	gal	TKPWAL

followed	TPOL/HROE/-D	garage	TKPWRAPBLG
flowed	TPHROE/-D	grand jury	TKPWR-PBLG
foaled	TPOEL/-D	Grand Jury	TKPWR*PBLG
fold	TPOELD [TPOLD]		

folly	TPOL/HREU	general	SKWREPB
foal	TPOEL	General	SKWR*EPB
		join (wp cmd)	SKWR-PB

for her	TP-R/HER	gentleman	SKWRE/PHAPB
fog	TPOG	gent	SKWREPBT
for it	TP-R/EUT	gentlemen	SKWRE/PHEPB
for the	TP-R/T- [TP-RT]	G-man	TKPW-RBGS/PHAPB
for	TP-R	G-men	TKPW-RBGS/PHEPB
for your	TP-R/KWROUR	gem	SKWREPL
for- *(prefix)*	TPOR		
fore	TPOER/SP-S	golly	TKPWOL/HREU
fore- *(prefix)*	TPOER	goal	TKPWOEL
forge	TPORPBLG	goalie	TKPWOEL/HRAOE
fort	TPORT		
forth	TPO*RT	governor	TKPWO*FR/TPHOR
forty-four	TPOURT/TPOUR	golf	TKPWOL/-F [TKPWOF]
44	4/4	govern or	TKPWO*FRPB/OR
four	TPOUR	govern	TKPWO*FRPB
4	4	government	TKPWO*FT
fourth	TPO*URT		
from it	TPR-/EUT	had	HAD
from the	TPR-T	dollar(s)	TKHRAR(/-S) [TKHRARS]
fright	TPRAOEUGT	-ed *(suffix)*	/-D
frit *(medical)*	TPREUT		
if our	TP-/OUR	had a	HAD/A
inform	TPH-F	ha	HA
information	TPH-FGS	hah	HA*
informing	TPH-FG		

for the reason	TP-RT/R-PB	had he	HAD/HE
foreign	TPOERPB [TPORPB]	's	AOES
		a cyst	A/S*EUS
		a sis	A/SEUS

forty-eight	TPOURT/AEUGT		
48	48		
fray	TPRAEU		

© 1993, 2001 *StenEd*®

assist	AEU/S*EUS
e- *(prefix)*	E
ease	AOEZ
east	AO*ES
Ed	*ED
educate	EPBLG/KAEUT [EGT]
education	EPBLG/KAEUGS [EGS]
he had	HE/HAD
he	HE
he is	HES
he would	HE/WOULD
he'd	HE/AOED [HAO*ED]
he's	HE/AOES [HAO*ES]
head	HED
heap	HAOEP
heed	HAOED
held	HELD
help	HEL/-P [H*EP]
helped	HEL/-PD [H*EP/-D]
helps	HEL/-PS [H*EP/-S]
hcp	HEP
hesitate	HEZ/TAEUT

---

had he ever	HAD/HE/-FR
heifer	HEFR

---

had not	HAD/TPHOT
hadn't	H-PBT
- *(hyphen)*	H-F

---

had you	HAD/KWROU
hew	HAO*U
hue	HAOU
Hugh	HAOUG
huh	HU
who	WHO

---

had you been	HAD/KWROU/PW-PB
hub	HUB

---

happy	HAP/PEU
happen	HAP [HAP/-PB]
happen I	HAP/EU [HAP/-PB/EU]
happy I	HAP/PEU/EU

---

hardy	HAR/TKEU
heard	HAERD
herd	HERD

---

have gone	SR-/TKPWOPB
having	SR-G

---

have I had	SR-/EU/HAD
individual	SREUPBLG
village	SREUL/APBLG

---

have not	SR-/TPHOT
haven't	SR-PBT

Hawaii	HA/WAOEU [H*EU/H*EU]
hay	HAEU
hey	HA*EU

---

hazard	HAZ/ARD
has	HAZ

---

he can	HE/K-
heck	HEBG

---

here is	HAOER/S-
hears	HAER/-S
hearse	HERS
her self	HER/SEL/-F
heres	HAOER/-S
here's	HAOER/AOES [HAO*ERS]
hers	HER/-S
herself	H*ERS

---

himself	H*EUPLS
hymns	H*EUPL/-S

---

honey	HOPB/TPHAOE
hone	HOEPB

---

honor	HOPB/TPHOR
honest	HOPB/*ES [HO*PBS]
hons	HOPB/-S

---

how was	HOUFS
how fast	HOU/TPA*S [HOUFZ]

---

how would	HOU/WOULD
how old	HOU/OELD [HOULD]
howled	HOUL/-D

I am	EU/APL
I'm	EU/AOEPL [AO*EUPL]
im- *(prefix)*	EUPL
immaterial	EUPL/TERL [EUPLT]

I can	EU/K-
-ic *(suffix)*	EUBG
incompetent	EUPB/KOFRP/TEPBT [EUBGT]

I couldn't care	EU/KOULD/-PBT/KAEUR [EUBGD/-PBT/KAEUR]
yuck	KWRUBG

I didn't have	KWREUF
eight-five	AEUBGT/TPAO*EUF
85	8/5

I don't know	KWROPB		if he could	TPEBGD
beyond	KWROPBD			
I don't see	EU/TKOPBT/SAOE			
- *(hyphen)*	H-F		if he had	TP-/HE/HAD
o- *(prefix)*	O		fed	TPED
-o *(suffix)*	(c)OE		Federal	TPRA*L [TP*ED/RAL]
oh	O*E		federal	TPRAL [TPED/RAL]
oh,	O*ERBGS			
on	OPB			
owe	KWROE		if he will	TP-/HE/HR-
			fell	TPEL
I recollect	EU/REBGT			
irk	EURBG		if I can	TPEUBG
			fifty-six	TPEUFT/SEUBGS
			56	56
I shall	EU/SHAL		fiscal	TPEUS/KAL
-ish *(suffix)*	EURB		fix	TPEUBGS
issue	EURB/SHAOU		fizz	TPEUZ
shoo	SHAO		physical	TPEUZ/KAL [TP-L]
should	SHOULD		physician	TPEU/SEUGS [TP-GS]
I understand	EU/UPBS [EUPBDZ]		if I go	TP-/EU/TKPWO
expect	KP-PT		fig	TPEUG
in	TPH-		figs	TPEUG/-S
in- *(prefix)*	EUPB		figure	TPEUG/KWRUR
inch	EUPB/-FP [EUFRPBLG]		figures	TPEUG/KWRUR/-S
inched	EUPB/-FPD		fission	TPEUGS
	[EUFRPBLG/-D]			
independence	EUPB/TKPEPBD/EPBS		if I remember	TP-/EURPL [TP*EURPL]
	[EUPB/TKPEPBS]		fir	TPEUR
independent	EUPB/TKPEPBD/EPBT		firm	TPEURPL
	[EUPB/TKPEPBT]			
Indiana	EUPBD/KWRA/TPHA		if I will	TP-/EU/HR-
	[*EUPB/*EUPB]		fill	TPEUL
inn	*EUPB		Phil	TP*EUL
inns	*EUPB/-S			
ins	TPH-S [TPH-/-S]			
inspect	TPH-PT		if the	TP-T
instance	EUPB/STAPBS		fit	TPEUT
instant	EUPB/STAPBT		fits	TPEUT/-S
respect	R-PT		if it	TP-/EUT
spec	SP*EBG		if it is	TP-/T-S
speck	SPEBG			
			if you	TP-/KWROU
I will	EU/HR-		few	TPU
aisle	AO*EUL			
I'll	EU/AOEL [*EUL]			
il- *(prefix)*	EUL		if you are	TP-/UR
ill	EUL		fur	TPUR
Illinois	EUL/TPHOEU		furnish	TPURPB/EURB
	[*EUL/*EUL]		furniture	TPURPB/KHUR
isle	AOEUL		if you remember	TPURPL
oil	OEUL		if your	TP-/KWROUR
if he can	TPEBG		if you can	TP-/UBG
affect	AFBGT [AEU/TPEBGT]		fuck	TPUBG
affected	AFBGT/-D			
	[AEU/TPEBGT/-D]			
effect	EFBGT [E/TPEBGT]			
effected	EFBGT/-D [E/TPEBGT/-D]			

 StenEd®

if you know	TP-/KWROUPB [TP*UPB]
faction	TPA*BGS
factious	TPABG/-RBS
fax	TPABGS
fifty-one	TPEUFT/WUPB
51	5/1
fun	TPUPB

if you recall	TP-/KWROU/RAUL [TP*URL]
furl	TPURL

if you understand	TP-/KWROU/UPBS
fund	TPUPBD
funds	TPUPBDZ

if you will	TP-/KWROU/HR- [TP*UL]
full	TPUL

imagine	PHAPBLG
imagination	PHAPBLG/TPHAEUGS
Madge	PHA*PBLG
mag	PHAG
magazine	PHAG/SAO*EPB
mare	PHAEUR
marry	PHAR/REU
mart	PHART
Mary	PHA*EUR/REU
	[PHA*R/REU]
mat	PHAT
math	PHA*T
mats	PHAT/-S
matter	PHAT/ER
May or	PHA*EU/OR
may or	PHAEU/OR
mayor	PHAEU/KWROR
merry	PHER/REU

immediate	PHAOED
immediately	PHAOED/HREU
med	PHED
medical	PHED/KAL
medicine	PHED/SEUPB
medley	PHED/HRAOE
Mel	PH*EL
mel (medical)	PHEL

important	PORPBT
importance	PORPBS
poor	PAOR
pore	POER
porn	PORPB
posterior	POS/TAOER/KWROR
pour	POUR
power	POU/ER [PO*UR]

-in connection with	TPH-/K*EBGS/W-
inaction	EUPB/A*BGS
incomes	TPH-BGS

in effect	TPH-/EFBGT
	[TPH-/E/TPEBGT]
in fact	TPH-FT
infect	EUPB/TPEBGT
infection	EUPB/TP*EBGS
infectious	EUPB/TPEBG/-RBS
infects	EUPB/TPEBGT/-S
invite	EUPB/SRAOEUT

in it	TPH-/EUT
in its	TPH-/EUTS
in the	TPH-T
knit	TPH*EUT
knits	TPH*EUT/-S
nit	TPHEUT
nits	TPHEUT/-S

in order	TPHORD
nod	TPHOD

in other words	TPHORDZ
nerds	TPHERDZ

in you	TPH-/KWROU
gnu	TPH*U
into	SPWAO
int(o)- (prefix)	SPW(O) [EUPB/T(O)]
knew	TPHAOU
new	TPHU
nu	TPHAO*U

increase	EUPB/KRAOES
income	TPH-BG

indict	EUPB/TKAOEUT
	[TKAO*EUT]
diet	TKAOEUT
indite	EUPB/TKAO*EUT

influence	EUPB/TPHRAOUPBS
flew	TPHRAOU
flu	TPHRU
flue	TPHRAO*U

injure	SKWREUR
injury	SKWRAOUR
Jr.	SKWR-R
junior	SKWRAOUPB/KWROR
juror	SKWRAOR
jury	SKWRUR

inquire	EUPB/KWAOEUR
choir	KWOEUR

© 1993, 2001 *StenEd*®

inquiry	EUPB/KWEU/REU	sed *(medical)*	SED
query	KWAOER/REU [KWER/REU]	see	SAOE
quire	KWAOEUR	seed	SAOED
		seer	SAOE/ER
		seers	SAOE/ER/-S
interest	SPWR*ES	sees	SAOE/-S
ent- *(prefix)*	SPW- [EPBT]	seize	SAOEZ
enter	SPWR- [EPBT/ER]	sere	SAOER
enter- *(prefix)*	SPWER	serious	SAOER/KWROUS [SAOERS]
		serous	SAOER/OUS

investigate	TPH*FS/TKPWAEUT	is many	S-/PH-
	[TPH*FGT]	system	S-PL
haves	SR-S		
haves or	SR-S/OR	is not	S-/TPHOT
invest	TPH*FS	isn't	S-PBT
investigation	TPH*FS/TKPWAEUGS	snot	STPHOT
	[TPH*FGS]		
investigator	TPH*FS/TKPWAEU/TOR	is on the	S-/OPBT
	[TPH*FRGT]	sot	SOT
investigate or	TPH*FS/TKPWAEUT/ OR		
vessel	SRES/SEL [SRESZ/EL]	is our	S-/OUR
vest	SR*ES	sour	SOUR

invoice	EUPB/SROEUS	it had	T-D
invoiced	EUPB/SROEUS/-D	Tuesday	TAOUZ
invoices	EUPB/SROEUS/-S		
voice	SROEUS	it is	T-S
void	SROEUD	it's	EUT/AOES [T*S]
voix *(medical)*	SROEU	its	EUTS
		itself	*EUTS
		teas	TAE/-S
irrelevant	EUR/REL/SRAPBT [EURLT]	tease	TAOEZ
ir- *(prefix)*	EUR	tees	TAOE/-S

is he	S-/HE	it will	T-L
cease	SAOES	their	THAEUR
cede	SAED	theirs	THAEURS
cirrus	SEUR/RUS	there are	THR-R
creed	KRAOED	there is	THR-S
safe	SAEUF	there	THR-
safe or	SAEUF/OR	there's	THR-/AOES [THR*S]
safer	SAEUFR	they are	THAEU/R- [THER]
said	SAEUD	they're	THAEU/AO*ER [THA*EUR]
salve	SA*F	threes	THRAOE/-S
satisfactory	SATS/TPABG/TREU		
	[STPOEUR]	it will be	EUT/HR-B [T-L/PW-]
satisfied	SATS/TPEU/-D	thereby	THR-B
	[STPAOEU/-D]	there by	THR-/PWEU
satisfies	SATS/TPEU/-S		
	[STPAOEU/-S]	January	SKWRAPB
satisfy	SATS/TPEU [STPAOEU]	Jan	SKWRA*PB
satisfying	SATS/TPEU/-G		
	[STPAOEU/-G]	lady	HRAEU/TKEU
save	SA*EUF	lade	HRA*ED
save or	SA*EUF/OR		
saver	SA*EUFR		
saving	SA*EUF/-G		
savor	SAEU/SROR		
sea	SAE		
sear	SAER		
sears	SAER/-S		
seas	SAE/-S		

laid	HRAEUD
lead	HRAED, HRAOED
led	HRED

----

laity	HRAEU/TEU
late	HRAEUT
lay it	HRAEU/EUT

----

lawsuit	HRAUT
laws	HRAU/-S
lieutenant	HRAOUPBT
loot	HRAOT
lute	HRAOUT

----

layman	HRAEU/PHAPB
lam	HRAPL
lamb	HRA*PL
lame	HRAEUPL

----

layer	HRAEU/ER
lair	HRAEUR

----

lazy	HRAEU/S*EU
lace	HRAEUS
lacy	HRAEU/SEU
lase	HRAEZ
laze	HRAEUZ

----

left	HREFT
less	HRESZ
-less	HRES
lest	HR*ES

----

length	HR*EPBT
lent	HREPBT

----

legislation	HREGS
legislate	HREGT
legs	HREG/-S
letting	HRET/-G

----

license	HRAOEUS/EPBS [HRAOEUPBS]
left hand	HREFT/HAPBD
left-hand	HREFT/H-F/HAPBD [HR*PBD]
lice	HRAOEUS
lie	HRAOEU
lies	HRAOEU/-S
listen	HR-PB
listened	HR-PBD
listens	HR-PBS
-ly (suffix)	HREU
lye	HRAO*EU

lyes	HRAO*EU/-S
will I	HR-/EU

----

lobby	HROB/PWEU
lobe	HROEB

----

locally	HROE/KHREU
lowly	HROE/HREU
local	HROE/KAL
locale	HROE/KAEL
low-cal	HROE/H-F/KAL

----

lock the	HROBG/T-
locate	HROE/KAEUT
lock it	HROBG/EUT
locket	HROBGT

----

look	HRAOBG
loo	HRAO

----

lotion	HROEGS
logs	HROG/-S

----

lower	HROE/ER
lore	HROER

----

luscious	HRURBS
lushes	HRURB/-S

----

machine	PHA/SHAOEPB
& (ampersand)	PH-PBD
machined	PHA/SHAOEPB/-D
machines	PHA/SHAOEPB/-S
Maryland	PHAEUR/HRAPBD [PH*D/PH*D]
M.D.	PH*D [PH-FPLT/TK*FPLT]
mice	PHAOEUS
min	PHEUPB
mince	PHEUPBS
minimum	PHEUPB/PHUPL
Minnesota	PH-PB [PH*PB/PH*PB]
mint	PHEUPBT
mints	PHEUPBT/-S
- (minus sign)	PH-PBS
minute	PHEUPB/UT [PH*EUPB] [PHAOEU/TPHAOUT]
minutes	PHEUPB/UT/-S [PH*EUPBS]
mis- (prefix)	PHEUS
miscellaneous	PHEUS/HRAEUPB/KWROUS
miss	PHEUSZ
Miss	PH-S
Mississippi	PHEUS/SEUP/PAOE [PH*S/PH*S]
Missouri	PHEU/SAO*U/RAOE [PHO*/PHO*]
mist	PH*EUS

MO	PH-RBGS/O*RBGS	members of the jury	PHEPBLG
M.O.	PH-FPLT/O*FPLT	Members of the Jury	PH*EPBLG
moan	PHOEPB	message	PHESZ/APBLG
Moe	PHO*E		
Monday	PHOPBD		
money order	PHUPB/ORD/ER	Michigan	PHEURB/TKPWAPB
money	PHUPB		[PH*EU/PH*EU]
mono- (prefix)	PHOPB	Mitch	PH*EUFP
month	PHO*PBT		
mouse	PHOUS		
mow	PHOE [PHOU]	might have	PHAOEUGT/SR-
Ms.	PH-Z		[PHAOEUF]
myself	PHAO*EUS	miff	PHEUF
		miffed	PHEUF/-D
		might have had	PHAOEUGT/SR-D
major	PHAEU/SKWROR		[PHAOEUFD]
marriage	PHAEURPBLG		
Marge	PHARPBLG	miles per hour	PHEURP
		miles an hour	PHARP
		mirror	PHEUR/ROR
March	PHA*R [PHA*R/-FP]	mister	PH*EUS/ER
mar	PHAR	moor	PHAOR
march	PHAR/-FP [PHA*RPBLG]	moot	PHAOT
		mor- (prefix)	PHOR
		more	PH-R
martial	PHART/-RBL	mote	PHOET
Marshall	PHA*R/-RBL	mother	PHOER [PHO*T/ER]
Martian	PHARGS	moths	PHO*T/-S
marshal	PHAR/-RBL	motor	PHOE/TOR
		Mott (medical)	PHOT
		Motter (medical)	PHOT/ER
Massachusetts	PHASZ/KHAOU/SETS	mower	PHOE/ER
	[PHA*/PHA*]		[PHOU/ER][PHO*UR]
ma	PHA	Mr.	PHR- [PHR-FPLT]
Mae	PHA*E	myrrh	PHEUR
make	PHAEUBG		
mass	PHASZ		
mast	PHA*S	million dollar(s)	PH-LD(Z)
may	PHAEU	mild	PHAOEULD
May	PHA*EU	mill	PHEUL
		milled	PHEUL/-D
		million	PH-L
maximum	PHABGS/PHUPL		
max	PHABGS		
Max	PHA*BGS	more or less	PH-R/OR/HRESZ [PHORLS]
		morals	PHORL/-S
		mother-in-law	PHOERPBL
may be	PHAEU/PW-		
maybe	PHAEUB		
		more than	PH-R/THAPB [PH-RPB]
		morn	PHORPB
may not	PHAEUPBT	mourn	PHOURPB
maintain	PHAEUPB/TAEUPB		
maintenance	PHAEUPBT/TPHAPBS		
		motion denied	PHOEGS/TKE/TPH*EU/-D
		mod	PHOD
measure	PHERB/SHUR [PH-RB]		
mesh	PHERB		
		mountain	PHOUPB/TAEUPB
		mount	PHOUPBT
mechanic	PH-BG	Mount	PHO*UPBT
mechanics	PH-BGS	Mt.	PH-T
Mexican	PHEBGS/KAPB		

 StenEd® **Step 9: Short Forms**

muscle	PHUS/-L	ninety-one	TPHAOEUPBT/WUPB
muffle	PHUFL	91	9/1
mull	PHUL	no one	TPHO/WUPB
mussel	PHUSZ/EL	non- *(prefix)*	TPHOPB
must sell	PH*US/SEL	none	TPHUPB
		nun	TPHU*PB

---

must have	PH*US/SR-	ninety-seven	TPHAOEUPBT/S*EFPB
muff	PHUF	97	9/7
must	PH*US	Nevada	TPHE/SRA/TKA
			[TPH*F/TPH*F]

---

my knowledge	PHEU/TPHOPBLG	ninety-six	TPHAOEUPBT/SEUBGS
Midge	PH*EUPBLG	96	9/6
midge *(medical)*	PHEUPBLG	nick	TPHEUBG
mitt	PHEUT	nicks	TPHEUBG/-S
myth	PH*EUT	nix	TPHEUBGS

---

national	TPHAGS/TPHAL	ninety-three	TPHAOEUPBT/THRAOE
	[TPHARBL]	93	9/3
gnarl	TPHARL	knee	TPHAOE
gnat	TPHAT	kneed	TPHAOE/-D
-nal *(suffix)*	TPHAL	need	TPHAOED
natch	TPHAFP		
natural	TPHAFP/RAL		

---

necessary	TPHES	no, sir	TPHORS
-ens *(suffix)*	/-PBS	-ening *(suffix)*	/-PBG
necessities	TPHES/TEU/-S	knob	TPHOB
-ness *(suffix)*	*PBS	know	TPHOE
nest	TPH*ES	knows	TPHOE/-S
		New Mexico	TPH-PL [TPH*PL/TPH*PL]
		no body	TPHO/PWOD/TKEU

---

negotiate	TPHE/TPWOE/SHAEUT	no	TPHO
	[TKPWOERBT]	No.	TPHOFPLT
negotiation	TPHE/TPWOE/SHAEUGS	nob	TPHO*B
	[TKPWOERBGS]	nobody	TPHOEB
gauche	TKPWOERB	noes	TPHO/-S
		Norse	TPHOERS
		northbound	TPHO*RT/PWOUPBD
			[TPH*B]

---

neither	TPHAO*ET/ER [TPHAOERT]	nose	TPHOEZ
	[TPHAO*EUT/ER]	nosey	TPHOE/S*EU
nether	TPH*ET/ER	notes	TPHOET/-S
nets	TPHET/-S	notice	TPHOETS [TPHOE/TEUS]
		nub	TPHUB
		numb	TPHUPL
		number	TPHUPL/PWER

---

ninety-eight	TPHAOEUPBT/AEUGT		[TPHURPL][TPHUPL/ER]
98	9/8	# *(number/pound sign)*	TPH-B
nate(s)	TPHAEUT(/-S)		
nay	TPHAEU		
nee	TPHA*EU		
neigh	TPHAEUG		

---

		normal	TPHOR/PHAL
		norm	TPHORPL

---

ninety-nine	TPHAOEUPBT/TPHAOEUPB	notary public	TPHOET/REU/
9	9		PUB/HREUBG
99	9/9		[TPH*P]
anyone	TPHEUPB	*new page (wp cmd)*	TPH-P
any one	TPHEU/WUPB		
nine	TPHAOEUPB		

---

notoriety	TPHOET/RAOEU/TEU	outside	O*UT/SAOEUD [OUDZ]
note right	TPHOET/RAOEUGT	-ous (suffix)	OUS
		oust	O*US

---

of course	OFBG	over the	O*EFR/T-
divorce	TKWORS [TKEU/SRORS]	overt	O*EFRT

---

off and on	AUF/APBD/OPB	overrule	O*FRL [O*FR/RAOUL]
	[AUF/SKP-/OPB][AUF/SKPOPB]	overall	O*FR/AUL
fawn	TPAUPB	overly	O*EFR/HREU

---

often	AUFPB	package	PABG/APBLG
oven	O*FPB	page	PAEUPBLG
		passage	PASZ/APBLG

---

on his	OPB/HEUZ	packet	PABG/ET
oz	OZ	pact	PABGT

---

on the grounds	OPBT/TKPWROUPBDZ	parade	PRAEUD
	[OEGDZ]	prayed	PRAEU/-D
ocean	OEGS	preyed	PRA*EU/-D

---

on the part of the	OEPT/OFT	particular	PHRAR
openings	OEP/-GS	particular letter	PHRAR/HRET/ER
operate	OERPT [OP/RAEUT]	peculiar	PE/KAOUL/KWRAR
operation	OERPGS [OP/RAEUGS]	tic	T*EUBG
opt	OPT	tick	TEUBG
option	OPGS	tickler	TEUBG/HRER

---

on your	OPB/KWROUR	pedestrian	PE/TKES/TRAPB [P*ED]
hour	HOUR	ped	PED
hours	HOUR/-S		
our	OUR		
ours	OURS		
ourself	O*URS		
ourselves	O*URS/-S		

---

opinion	P-PB	Pennsylvania	PEPBS/SRAEUPB/KWRA
pain	PAEUPB		[PA*/PA*]
pane	PAEPB	pa	PA
pin	PEUPB	pay	PAEU
pinion	PEUPB/KWROPB	pea	PAE
		pee	PAOE
		pen	PEPB

---

organization	ORGS	perfect	PER/TPEBGT [PEFRT]
organize	ORG	per	PER
organizes	ORG/-S		

---

other	O*ER	¶ (paragraph)	P-F
oar	AOR	paragraph	PRAF
or	OR		
or- (prefix)	O*R		
-or (suffix)	/(c)OR		
or gone	OR/TKPWOPB		
ore	OER		
Oregon	O*R/TKPWOPB [O*R/O*R]		

---

		peril	PER/REUL [P*ERL]
		pearl	PERL
		purl	PURL

---

		permanent	PERPL/TPHEPBT
		perm	PERPL

---

		petition	PE/TEUGS

 StenEd®

peat	PAET	prop	PROP
pet	PET	proper	PROP/ER
Pete	PAO*ET	propose	PRO/POEZ
pigs	PEUG/-S	pros	PROE/-S
		prose	PROEZ

pickup	PEUBG/*UP [P*UP]	product	PRUBGT
pick up	PEUBG/UP	prod	PROD
pip	PEUP	produce	PRO/TKAOUS [PRAOUS]
pup	PUP	produced	PRO/TKAOUS/-D
			[PRAOUS/-D]
picture	PEUBG/KHUR	proud	PROUD
percent	PER/SEPBT	prow	PROU
%	P-BGT	prowled	PROUL/-D
picket	PEUBGT [PEUBG/ET]		

platform	PHRAT/TPORPL	professor	PRO/TPES/SOR
plasm	PHRAFPL		[PROFS/SOR]
		prof	PROF
police	PHREUS	profess or	PRO/TPESZ/OR
plea	PHRAOE		[PROFS/OR]
pleas	PHRAOE/-S	proffer	PROFR
please	PHRAOEZ	proof	PRAOF
ply	PHRAOEU	prove	PRAO*UF
replies	RE/PHREU/-S		
reply	RE/PHREU	program	PRAPL
		pram	PRA*PL
popular	POP/KWRU/HRAR	promise	PROPLS
	[PO*P/HRAR]	prom	PROPL
poplar	POP/HRAR	proms	PROPL/-S

postpone	PO*S/POEPB	prudence	PRAOUD/EPBS [PRAOUPBS]
preponderance	P-P	prudes	PRAOUDZ
proposal	PRO/POE/SAL	prunes	PRAOUPB/-S

president	P-T [PREZ/TKEPBT]	public	PUB/HREUBG
precedent	PRES/TKEPBT	pub	PUB
President	P*T [PR*EZ/TKEPBT]	publication	PUBL/KAEUGS
press	PRESZ	publish	PUB/HREURB
prez	PREZ	pucks	PUBG/-S

principal	PREUPBS/PAL	purchase	PUR/KHAS
appraisal	AEU/PRAEU/SA*L	purr	PUR
prince	PREUPBS		
principally	PREUPBS/PHREU	quarterly	KWART/ER/HREU
principals	PREUPBS/PAL/-S	quarrel	KWARL
principle	PREUPBS/P-L		
principles	PREUPBS/P-LS	radical	RAD/KAL
		rad	RAD

probable	PROBL	rainy	RAEU/TPH*EU
probably	PROEBL	rain	RAEUPB
probe	PROEB	reign	RA*EUPB
problem	PROB	rein	RAEPB

proceed	PRO/SAOED [PRAOED]	rally	RAL/HREU
pro	PROE	real	RAEL
pro- *(prefix)*	PRO		
proceeds	PRO/SAOEDZ [PRAOEDZ]		

realize	RAEL/AOEUZ [RAELZ]
real eyes	RAEL/KWRAOEU/-S
reel	RAOEL
reels	RAOEL/-S

---

rather	RA*T/ER
repair	RE/PAEUR
rare	RAEUR

---

ready	RED/TKEU
read	RAED
red	RED
redirect examination	R-D
REDIRECT EXAMINATION	R-D/R-D
reed	RAOED

---

recent	RE/KREPBT
ren (medical)	REPB
resent	RE/SEPBT

---

refresh	RE/TPRERB
fresh	TPRERB

---

refusal	RE/TPAOU/SA*L
revel	R*EFL

---

remittance	REPLT/TAPBS
remit	REPLT
remittence	REPLT/EPBS

---

regulations	REG/HRAEUGS/-S
regs	R*EG/-S
regular	REG/HRAR [REG]
regulation	REG/HRAEUGS

---

represent	REPT
rep	REP
representation	REPGS
representative	REPT/T*EUF
republic	RE/PUB/HREUBG
republican	RE/PUBL/KAPB
Republican	R*E/PUBL/KAPB

---

resume	RE/SAOUPL [REZ/PHAEU]
rheum (medical)	RAOUPL
room	RAOPL

---

roughly	RUF/HREU
ruffle	RUFL

Saturday	SATD [SARD]
sat	SAT
seat	SAOET

---

seethe	SAO*ET
siege	SAOEPBLG

---

senior	SAOEPB/KWROR
Sr.	S-R

---

service	S-FS
serviced	S-FS/-D
save (wp cmd)	S*F
save document (wp cmd)	S*FD

---

seventy	SEFT [S*EFT]
70	7/0
vent	SREPBT

---

seventy-nine	S*EFT/TPHAOEUPB
79	79
vine	SRAOEUPB

---

she can	SHEBG
chic	SHAEBG [SHAO*EBG]
chick	KHEUBG
Schick (medical)	SHEUBG
shake	SHAEUBG
sheik	SHAOEBG
which I can	KH-/EU/K- [KH*EUBG]

---

she had	SHE/HAD
she would	SHELD
she'd	SHE/AOED [SHAO*ED]
shed	SHED
shield	SHAOELD

---

she have	SHE/SR-
chef	SHEF
chefs	SHEF/-S
which he was	KHEFS [KH-/HEFS]

---

she will	SHE/HR-
Scheele (medical)	SHAOEL
she'll	SHE/AOEL [SHAO*EL]
shell	SHEL

---

should you	SHOULD/KWROU
shoe	SHAOU
show	SHOE
somehow	SPHOU

---

shouldn't	SHOULD/-PBT [SHO*PBT]
should not	SHOULD/TPHOT
shunt	SHUPBT

© 1993, 2001 *StenEd*®

significance	SEUG/KAPBS
cig *(slang)*	SEUG
cigs *(slang)*	SEUG/-S
significant	SEUG/KAPBT
signify	SEUG/TPEU
situate	SEUFP/WAEUT [SEUFPT]
situated	SEUFP/WAEUT/-D [SEUFPT/-D]
situation	SEUFP/WAEUGS [SEUFPGS]
suede	SWAEUD
suite	SWAET
swayed	SWAEU/-D
sweat	SWET
sweet	SWAOET
-sy *(suffix)*	SEU

---

sixty-five	SEUBGT/TPAO*EUF
65	6/5
skiff	SKEUF

---

sixty-four	SEUBGT/TPOUR
64	6/4
scour	SKOUR

---

so he should	SOERBD
associate	SOERBT
associated	SOERBT/-D

---

so I will	SO/EU/HR-
so I would	SO/EU/WOULD
so ill	SO/EUL
soil	SOEUL
soil had	SOEUL/HAD
soiled	SOEUL/-D
solely	SOEL/HREU

---

so many	SO/PH-
some	SOPL
some- *(prefix)*	SPH-, S- *(varies)*
-some *(suffix)*	SOPL, -S/OPL *(varies)*
-some *(medical suffix)*	SOEPL
sum	SUPL

---

socially	SOERBL/HREU
social	SOERBL

---

somebody	SPH-/PWOD/TKEU [SPH-B]
some body	SOPL/PWOD/TKEU
sob	SOB

---

sorority	SO/ROR/TEU
so report	SO/RORT

---

sorry	SOR/REU
soar	SAOR
sore	SOER

South Carolina	SO*UT/KAR/HRAOEU/TPHA [S*BG/S*BG]
s.c. *(medical)*	S*BG

---

specification	SPEF/KAEUGS [SPEFBGS]
specific	SPEFBG
specifics	SPEFBG/-S

---

stand	STAPBD
Stan	STA*PB
stance	STAPBS
standard	STAPBD/ARD
stands	STAPBDZ

---

story	STOR/REU [STOEUR]
store	STOER [STOR]

---

student	STAOUPBT
stewed	STAOU/-D
stunt	STUPBT

---

subpoena	S-P
sup	SUP

---

subject	SUPBLGT
sub	SUB

---

substitute	STUT
institute	STAOUT

---

sufficient	SUF
sufficiency	SUF/SEU

---

suggestion	SUG/SKWREGS [SUGS]
suggest	SUGT
suggests	SUGT/-S

Sunday	SUPBD
son	SOPB
sun	SUPB
sundae	SUPB/TKAE
sunned	SUPB/-D

---

supplies	SPHRAOEU/-S
splice	SPHRAOEUS

---

sustain	SUS/TAEUPB
stain	STAEUPB

---

systolic	SEUS/TOL/EUBG
stoic	STOEUBG

---

take place	TAEUBG/PHRAEUS
tapes	TAEUP/-S

---

tally	TAL/HREU
tail	TAEUL
tale	TAEL
teal	TAOEL

---

tarry	TAR/REU
tear	TAER

---

television	TEL/SREUGS [T*FGS]
tuition	TWEUGS
twigs	TWEUG/-S

---

territory	TER/TOEUR
teart *(medical)*	TERT

Texas	TEBG/SAS [T*BGS/T*BGS]
Tex	TEBGS
text	T*EBGS

---

than	THAPB
-en *(suffix)*	/-PB
then	THEPB

---

than the	THAPB/T-
not	TPHOT
-n't *(suffix)*	-PBT

---

thank you	THA*UPBG
that you	THA/KWROU [THA*U]
thaw	THAU
that you had	THA/KWROU/HAD [THAUD]
thawed	THAU/-D

---

that had	THA/HAD [THAD]
thank	THA*PBG
thanked	THA*PBG/-D
thanks	THA*PBG/-S [THA*PBGS]
that is	THAS
that it	THA/EUT
that	THA
that the	THAT

---

that I	THA/EU
it	EUT
the	T-
they	THAEU

---

that is all	THAUL
that you will	THA/KWROU/HR-

---

that you tell	THA/KWROU/TEL
thought	THAUT

---

there have	THR-F
thereof	THROF
there of	THR-/OF

---

therefore	THR-FR
therefor	THR*FR
there for	THR-/TP-R
therefrom	THR-FRPL
there from	THR-/TPR-

---

they have	THAEU/SR- [THEF]
that I have	THAEUF
they've	THAEU/AO*EF [THA*EUF][THAEU/AOEF]

---

think	THEU
-ening *(suffix)*	/-PBG
thing	THEUPBG
thinning	THEUPB/-G

---

thirty-nine	THEURT/TPHAOEUPB
39	39
therein	THREUPB
there in	THR-/TPH-

---

title	TAOEUT/-L
tile	TAOEUL

---

to her	TO/HER
tore	TOER

---

to him	TO/HEUPL
to many	TO/PH-
Tom	TOPL [TO*PL]
tomb	TAOUPL
tome	TOEPL
tomorrow	TORPL
too many	TAOPL

---

to know	TO/TPHOE
ton	TOPB

---

to the	TO/T- [TO*T]
to it	TO/EUT
tot	TOT

---

to us	TO/US
-tous *(suffix)*	TOUS

---

to you	TO/KWROU
to this	TO/TH-
toe	TOE

StenEd®   **Step 9: Short Forms**

together	TOGT		very much	SR-R/PHUFP [SR-FP]
tow	TOU		vetch	SREFP
towing	TOU/-G			

			vicious	SREURBS
to your	TO/KWROUR		vision	SREUGS
tour	TAOUR [TOUR]			
tours	TAOUR/-S [TOUR/-S]			
tower	TOU/ER [TO*UR]		volunteer	SROL/TAOER
towers	TOU/ER/-S [TO*UR/-S]		voluntary	SROL/TAEUR
truly yours *(comp closing)*	TRAOU/HREU/KWROURS			

			wagon	WAG/TKPWOPB
today	TOD		wag	WAG
to day	TO/SP-S/TKAEU			
to do	TO/TKO [TAOD]			
toad	TOED		waiting	WAEUT/-G
Todd	TO*D		wait	WAEUT
			weight	WAEUGT

took	TAOBG			
too	TAO		Washington	WARBG/TOPB [WA*/WA*]
two	TWO		wash	WARB
to	TO			
2	2			

			we are	WER [WE/R-]
trolley	TROL/HRAOE		ware	WAEUR
troll	TROEL [TROL]		water	WAT/ER

			we were	WERP
twenty-nine	TWEPBT/TPHAOEUPB		we're	WE/AO*ER [WAO*ER]
29	29		wear	WAER
twin	TWEUPB		Weir *(medical)*	WAOER
twine	TWAOEUPB		were	W-R
			when it	WHEPB/EUT

unconscious	UPB/KOPB/-RBS		when the	WHEPB/T- [WH-T]
	[UPB/KORBS]		where	WR-
unction	UPBGS		which it	KH-/EUT
			which the	KH-T
			whit	WHEUT
unity	KWRAOUPB/TEU		wit	WEUT
unit	KWRAOUPBT		with it	W-/EUT
			with the	W-T
			with	W-
up the	UP/T-		witness	W-PBS
you want	UPT		witnesses	W-PBS/-S
			wits	WEUT/-S

upon the grounds	POPB/T-/TKPWROUPBDZ		we can	WEBG
pes	PES		wacky	WABG/KEU
pest	P*ES		weak	WAEBG
pose	POEZ		web	WEB
possess	PO/SESZ		webbing	WEB/-G
possession	PO/SEGS		week	WAOEBG
potion	POEGS		westbound	W*ES/PWOUPBD [W*B]

us	US		we had	WE/HAD
use	KWRAOUZ [KWRAOUS]		we did	WE/TKEUD
			we would	WE/WOULD
			we'd	WE/AOED [WAO*ED]
vehicles	SRAOEBG/-S		wed	WED
vex	SREBGS		Wednesday	WEPBZ

weds	WEDZ	whiffs	WHEUF/-S
weed	WAOED		
weld	WELD	where did you live	WR-/TKEUD/KWROU/
wield	WAOELD		HR*EUF
		where I have	WREUF
we have gone	WEF/TKPWOPB	where did you reside	WR-/TKEUD/KWROU/
we have	WEF [WE/SR-]		RE/SAO*EUD
we've	WE/AO*EF	where I had	WREUD
	[WE/AOEF][WAOEF][W*EF]		
weave	WAO*EF	where have	WR-F
weaving	WAO*EF/-G	whereof	WROF
we recall	WERL	where he can	WR-/HE/K- [WR*EBG]
westerly	W*ERL [W*ES/ER/HREU]	measure	PHERB/SHUR [PH-RB]
		member	PHEB
we want	WE/WAPBT	memo	PHEPL/PHOE
wept	WEPT	memorandum	PHEPL/RAPBD/UPL
		memory	PHEPL/REU
we will	WE/HR-	re- (prefix)	RE
wail	WAEUL	reck	REBG
we'll	WE/AOEL [WAO*EL]	recognize	REBG/TPHAOEUZ
weal	WAOEL	recollect	REBGT
well	WEL	recollection	R*EBGS
whale	WHAEUL	recommend	REPLD
what he will	WHA/HE/HR- [WHA*EL]	recommendation	REPLD/TKAEUGS
what I will	WHA/EU/HR- [WHA*EUL]		[REPLGS]
wheal	WHAEL	recommends	REPLDZ
wheel	WHAOEL	recto- (medical prefix)	REBGT [REBG/TO]
		rem	REPL
what I	WHA/EU [WHA*EU]	REM	R*EPL
way	WAEU		[R-RBGS/*ERBGS/PH*RBGS]
weigh	WAEUG	remember	REB
whey	WHAEU	remembering	REB/-G
		remembrance	REB/RAPBS
what the	WHAT	replace (wp cmd)	R-PLS
what	WHA	wreck	WREBG
what it	WHA/EUT		
		where I	WR-/EU [WR*EU]
when I	WHEPB/EU [WH*EU]	write	WRAOEUT [WREU]
why	WHAOEU	wry	WRAOEU
		right	RAOEUGT
when I am	WHEPB/EU/APL	rite	RAOEUT
	[WH*EUPL]		
whim	WHEUPL	where the	WR-T
with him	W-/HEUPL	where it	WR-/EUT
women	WEUPL		
		whether the	WHR-T
when I go	WHEPB/EU/TKPWO	whether it	WHR-/EUT
	[WH*EUG]		
Whig	WHEUG	which had	KH-D
wig	WEUG	charged	KHARPBLG/-D
		charges	KHARPBLG/-S
when I have	WHEPB/EUF [WH*EUF]	which is	KH-S
when I was	WHEPB/EUFS [WHEUFS]		
which I have	KHEUF	which he can	KH-/HE/K-
whiff	WHEUF	check	KHEBG

cheque	KHEBG/-BG
Czech	KH*EBG

which he is	KHES
chess	KHESZ
chest	KH*ES

which I will	KH-/EU/HR- [KH*EUL]
child	KHAOEULD
chill	KHEUL
chilled	KHEUL/-D
which I would	KH-/EULD [KHEULD]
which will	KH-L

which you	KHU
chew	KHAOU

which you can	KH-/UBG
chuck	KHUBG
Chuck	KH*UBG

which you mean	KH-/KWROU/PHAOEPB
chum	KHUPL

which you think	KH-/KWROU/THEU [KHUPBG]
chunk	KH*UPBG [KHUPB/-BG]

who can	WHOBG
hoc	HO*BG
hock	HOBG
hook	HAOBG

who is	WHO/S- [WHOS]
high school	HAOEU/SKAOL [HAOL]
hoose (medical)	HAOS
hop	HOP
hospital	HOPT
who's	WHO/AOES [WHO*S]
whose	WHOZ

who will	WHO/HR- [WHOL]
hole	HOEL
holey	HOE/HRAOE
holly	HOL/HREU
holy	HOE/HREU
who'll	WHO/AOEL [WHO*L]
whole	WHOEL

whoever	WHOFR
hover	HO*FR

will be	HR-B
lb.	HR*B
pounce	POUPBS
pound	POUPBD
pounds	POUPBDZ

will do	HR-/TKO
willed	HR-D

will go	HR-/TKPWO [HR*G]
willing	HR-G

will I be	HR-/EU/PW-
lib	HREUB

will I have	HR-/EUF
lift	HREUFT
list	HR*EUS
live	HR*EUF [HRAO*EUF]

will you be	HR-/KWROU/PW-
lubb (medical)	HRUB

will you go	HR-/KWROU/TKPWO
lug	HRUG

with an	W-/APB
with a	W-/A
wan	WAPB

within	W-PB
win	WEUPB

worry	WOR/REU
wore	WOER

would believe	WOUBL
wobble	WOBL
would you believe	WOULD/UBL

would have	WOUF
woof	WAOF
would you have	WOULD/UF

would he	WOULD/HE
woe	WOE

would he have	WOULD/HE/SR-
wove	WO*EF

would you	WOULD/KWROU
woo	WAO
would	WOULD
wow	WOU

would you be	WOULD/KWROU/PW-
would be	WOUB

would you mean	WOULD/KWROU/PHAOEPB	understand	UPBS
woman	WOPL	understood	UPBD
womb	WAOUPL	United States	KWRAOEUTS
would mean	WOULD/PHAOEPB		

----

would you tell	WOULD/KWROU/TEL	you will	KWROU/HR-
without	WOUT	you'll	KWROU/AOEL [KWRO*UL]
		yule	KWRAOUL

----

would you understand	WOULD/KWROU/UPBS	yourself	KWRO*URS
would understand	WOULD/UPBS	yours	KWROURS [KWROUR/-S]
wound	WAOUPBD	yourselves	KWRO*URS/-S
			[KWRO*URSZ]

----

wouldn't   WOULD/-PBT [WO*PBT]
want   WAPBT
won't   WOEPBT
wont   WOPBT
would not   WOULD/TPHOT

----

yes or no   KWRE/OR/TPHO
    [KWRORPB]
yearn   KWRERPB

----

yes, sir   KWRES
-ier (suffix)   KWRER
yes   KWRE

----

you are   KWROU/R- [UR]
eighty-four   AEUBGT/TPOUR
84   8/4
-ure (suffix)   KWRUR
yore   KWROER
you don't remember   KWROU/TKOEPBT/REB
you're   KWROU/AO*ER
    [KWRO*UR]
your   KWROUR

----

you don't know   KWROU/TKOEPBT/TPHOE
un- (prefix)   UPB
you know   KWRO*UPB
    [KWROU/TPHOE]
-down (suffix)   TKO*UPB [KWROUPB]
down   TKOUPB

----

you go   KWROU/TKPWO
ugh   UG

----

you shall   URB
usual   URBL
usually   URBL/HREU

----

you understand   KWROU/UPBS
inner   EUPB/ER
nor   TPH-R
nor- (prefix)   TPHOR
under   URPBD
under- (prefix)   UPBDZ

Step 9: Short Forms

STEP 9—EXERCISES
SHORT FORMS

PART 1
PHRASES—GOOD & BAD

The following exercises show many phrases that are frequently used by court reporters. If the outline used for a phrase is not the same as the outline used for any other word or phrase or common word part, it is safe to use it. However, if the phrase outline conflicts, either write out the separate words of the phrase or assign the phrase a non-conflicting outline.

Traditional phrases are underlined. You do not have to use phrases—even non-conflicting ones.

PART 1A
Ex. RT-94 (Tape 6/B @ 125 wpm) & RT-94 (Tape 6/B @ 180 wpm)

Can you tell how a people lived just by the trash they left behind? Do you know what the shape and material of tools indicate about a culture? Did you ever have to face hostile head-hunters and convince them you were friendly? All of these skills and dangers form part of the life of an anthropologist.

An anthropologist is the scientist who is involved in the study of past human existence—the physical and cultural history and varying ways of life. Anthropologists need a number of skills to do their work. Depending on the particular interests, an anthropologist may be trained in anatomy and languages as well as cultural studies. They are often accomplished explorers too since, to do their job, they have to go to the remote regions of the earth searching for the remains of lost cities or the primitive peoples of the world.

As part of their work, they will often be exposed to conditions of life which are difficult. In many villages there is no doctor at all, so illness could be a great danger, and the anthropologists must learn to treat themselves for most diseases and wounds. It is also often necessary for them to eat and drink exotic things which can cause difficulties to the digestive system. A requirement, then, is a cast-iron stomach.

I can remember talking with an anthropologist who spent several years in the Andes with a tribe of Indians. She had some frightening experiences. She got sick and the Indians could do nothing for her. She was lucky to recover. Another time an Indian came to her and threatened to kill her because he had dreamed she was a witch. At the end of her stay, she was glad to return to America.

PART 1B
Ex. RT-95 (Tape 6/B @ 125 wpm) &
RT-95 (Tape 6/B @ 180 wpm)

"Did I ever tell you about my days at sea?" said the old man. "I spent 15 years of my life on the sea. I did the cooking for a fishing crew. In those days, the ships all had sails, not engines like those they have today. When we went hunting shark, we would be at sea for months trying to find where they were.

"Did you ever harpoon a shark?" I asked.

"No, sir," said the old man. "We had a harpooner to do that. He was a strong man. He had the job of going out in a small boat to throw his harpoon as hard as he could into the shark. Then a long rope would play out, and the aim was to let the shark run until he was too tired to fight. If all went right, the shark would tire and could be killed by the others.

"Have you ever seen a white shark?"

"No, sir. There has never been such an animal that I had heard of."

"None that you had heard of," I added.

"I have something here to show you," he said, reaching for the white object on the desk.

"This is a shark's tooth which, as you can see, has been decorated. They say an old captain did it."

"Can you identify the picture on it?" I asked.

"I shall be glad to. It is a picture of a ship which can still be seen at the docks. If I have time, I will take you down to see it."

"Could you really do that? I would love to see it. Did you live and work on a ship like that?"

"Not quite as big, but that is the same kind. We will go down this afternoon, all right?"

"Thank you," I replied, "and I am looking forward to your tour."

PART 1C
Ex. RT-96 (Tape 6/B @ 125 wpm) &
RT-96 (Tape 6/B @ 180 wpm)

Are you having troubles with insect pests? Do you have ant nests all about you? If you can't go into your kitchen without spotting a mouse, we can help you.

We have a carefully trained crew of pest control experts. We want to help you. If you will just call us, we will come to your home. We will show you we do have the latest equipment so as to quickly rid you of any pests around your home. You are under no obligation. Just call, and I shall send an expert over right away to clean up your problem, as you will see.

PART 1D
Ex. RT-97 (Tape 6/B @ 125 wpm) &
RT-97 (Tape 6/B @ 180 wpm)

I was fascinated watching the daredevil as he prepared for his jump. From where I sat, I could see what were long streamers coming from his motorcycle. If he had any fear, I couldn't see it.

"Will he really jump?" I thought. "Did he really think he could survive?" As I had finished this thought, his motorcycle took off. "Will I have the courage to watch?" I wondered.

PART 2
BRIEFS—GOOD & BAD

PART 2A
FOR—FORE—FOUR—
INFORM—INFORMATION
Ex. RT-98 (Tape 6/B @ 125 wpm) & RT-98 (Tape 6/B @ 180 wpm)

For more than four years, the city has been waging a battle against traffic accidents. In the forefront of this campaign has been the young Director of Traffic Safety, Jim Marshall. As part of this program, he has attempted to set up a program to inform the public regarding safe driving and safe pedestrian conduct.

In recent days, a new project has come to the fore. This is an information program using TV spot advertising for the purpose of informing the public about safety practices. So far, the spots are being shown four times a day. Two of the four times are in so-called prime time.

One of the spots featured for the last week is designed to inform the public about safety inspection procedures and includes tips on having all four brakes checked and on the proper care for steering and suspension systems. Also included is information having to do with lights and tires.

A second spot recently featured information in driving under foreboding weather conditions, such as heavy rain or snow. There was much useful information about skids and the use of two or four snow tires or chains. There were also suggestions for driving under conditions of limited visibility.

Much of this current campaign is based on the concept of "forewarned is forearmed." That is, the emphasis is on informing the public about defensive driving—what to do to forestall an accident happening. Heretofore such safety programs have often opted for an emphasis on emergency measures only or on anti-speed campaigns. The new emphasis is on information for the average driver about how to avoid emergency situations whether on a four-lane highway or on a one-lane dirt path in the country.

All indications are that accident rates for the city are declining and have been doing so for the four years of the information campaign.

Note: Non-conflicting phrases may be written as a phrase or written out (e.g., for the = F-RT or F-R/T-).

The teacher was attempting to find out what the students might <u>know</u> about the current subject in biology. When he first asked them about the functions of the <u>nose</u>, <u>no</u> one raised a hand to answer.

Finally, he pointed to a student and said, "What do you <u>know</u> about the role of the <u>nose</u> in breathing?"

"I don't <u>know</u>, sir," replied the boy.

"Who <u>knows</u>"?

"I <u>know</u>," said a quavering voice. "The <u>nose</u> is the principal breathing organ for most creatures."

"What about insects?"

"Oh, <u>no, sir</u>. Insects have <u>no</u> <u>nose</u>."

"What does the <u>nose</u> have to do with perception?"

"Well," said a girl, "I <u>know</u> that people can smell different odors with the <u>nose</u> and that the <u>nose</u> has a good deal to do with tastes."

"It does?" said the teacher. "How? Who <u>knows</u>?"

A boy spoke up: "When I have a cold, I <u>know</u> that food doesn't taste the same. I guess, when you can't smell with your <u>nose</u>, it makes it hard to tell different flavors."

"There's <u>no</u> doubt about that," said another girl. "<u>No</u> matter how much I try, I can't tell the difference between chocolate and vanilla when my <u>nose</u> is stopped up."

"So," continued the teacher, "<u>no</u> one can taste very well when his <u>nose</u> is clogged. Does anyone <u>know</u> why <u>no</u> person can taste very well when this happens to the <u>nose</u>?"

"<u>No, sir</u>," said everyone. "We don't <u>know</u>, but we would like to <u>know</u> more about the <u>nose</u>."

PART 3
BRIEFS & PHRASES

Ex. RT-100, #1-130 (Tape 6/B @ 125 wpm), #131-250 (Tape 7/A @ 125 wpm)
Ex. RT-100, #1-150 (Tape 7/A @ 180 wpm), #151-250 (Tape 7/B @ 180 wpm)

The following sentences contain potentially conflicting briefs and phrases. Your translation will tell you which conflicts you should work on.

1. The house was built of native stone, and over the years has proved its durability and the ability to even withstand a major hurricane.

2. Ben Marshall, having been questioned about his absence from the benefit, claimed that a bee sting had caused him to be absent.

3. Hoping to learn a bit about the new computer by the end of the week, he prepared to bite the bullet and said, "I don't know much about it, but how many bytes does this thing have?"

4. We have to ride the bus every morning, but it is no fun to see the many cigarette butts strewn all about us.

5. She asked about you, but the last time we heard from her, she said not to butt in her business, but it is now time to forgive and forget.

6. How many comments have you gotten about your new burr haircut?

7. It is an absolute fact that he not only refused to salute the lieutenant, he actually called her a slut.

8. If you choose to abuse cigarettes and booze, you will hear not applause, but boos, from your loved ones.

9. There was some dissent as to whether or not the accident had caused his descent into madness.

10. Some thought it was all an act, and the copy of a recent letter showed his real ability to cope with it all.

11. Many cues about his demeanor prompted the detective to accuse him of the crime.

12. It is not an act if they are not speaking. There is an active tiff going on between them.

13. In addition to bones and pottery, the archeological digs unearthed a few gold coins.

14. Before the lengthy adjudication was over, everyone in the courtroom had drunk jugs of water from the cooler in the hallway.

15. After we administer the oath to this witness, he would like to add Mr. Ford's name to the list, and later add more names.

16. I must have an advance in pay in order to have a chance to buy either that van or any of the other vans I want.

17. Today, men's ties may dramatize anything from fishes to cartoons, and they will sell even if you don't advertise.

18. The use of cocaine is a vice which holds many in its grip like a vise, and often no amount of advice can lessen its vis, or power. Experts will advise that it vies for the title of most addictive drug with its infamous counterpart, viz., heroin.

19. It is not advisable to leave until the fog has cleared and the runway is visible.

20. The advisability of buying glasses is questionable when your visibility is tested by the person selling them.

21. I am afraid that my nerves are frayed after seeing my long lost relative in a frayed, wrinkled suit, unemployed and homeless.

22. After the captain returned from the bar on the avenue, he told us to stow his luggage aft, and we scurried after it.

23. Al, a leatherworker from Alabama, is very handy with an awl, and you will be happy with all of the goods we bought from him.

24. He will tell you of the allegation that he drank two quarts of ale in a dark alley, is now ailing severely, that he feels like hell; and I will tell you it's true because I was his ally.

25. She also wrote a letter to alert them of the danger.

26. Will always sends a letter to the attorney who handles his will if the title should change on his real property.

27. The old, bald ambulance driver balanced his medical instruments in his lap, calm even as the boy's mother bawled loudly, knowing the lad's life hung in the balance after being hit hard by the ball.

28. Another doctor made the imputation that amputation of the patient's leg was unnecessary.

29. We don't need to analyze why the annals of the medical society need to be published on an annual basis.

30. The students were anxious to examine the ancient writings.

31. An aide to the president prepared to address the group regarding a dress code, and I had to rush to his aid, adding that it was not yet final.

32. Only a few will allow that, and I am not one of them.

33. At the age of 82, his eyes are cold as ice, his voice will hiss at you like an evil viper, and he will readily acknowledge that he loves to womanize and is still a stubborn old ass.

 Step 9: Short Forms

34. We aim to please our customers, and I am sure you will agree.

35. We are able to hire you, and I believe you are very suitable for the position.

36. My head is beginning to ache, and I can swear that it has ached every day this week.

37. The announcer said, and I recollect, that you should stay in port unless your boat is the size of an aircraft carrier.

38. You will ace the test, and I say that all that practice will pay off.

39. The answer was and is still the same.

40. She still has hope and she is rising from the ashes like the phoenix, ready to change her life; and she will succeed, I am sure.

41. It appears that an ant stung the ape when he ate the pear.

42. In April, my antisocial aunt began to anticipate the appearance of the airplane, and she would peer out the window for long periods of time. Nothing could prepare her for the anticlimax when it did not appear, paring down her chances of marriage and causing her to jump off the pier.

43. The card game commenced in the anteroom, and the pair of aces I held made me happy to ante up.

44. And you believe that a whisper could be audible above the roar of that automobile?

45. It is the beginning of fall, and you feel awful when you see and smell the offal left after the hogs have been butchered.

46. The august chairperson of the committee gave the orders, and you go in August, I believe.

47. And you have identified him as the very dark-eyed man you see every day. If I asked you to identify him with his glasses off, would you certify that it is true, no ifs, ands, or buts about it?

48. And you recall an aural sensation before the onset of the migraine?

49. She is apt to get a part in the play; and when she does, she will want to live apart from her husband and get a new apartment.

50. He appreciates her work and will show his appreciation with the presentation of a precious stone set in gold.

51. A couple of the older residents of the region aren't permitted to drive, the reason being that they can't remember to drive on the right-hand side of the road and recently crashed into someone's residence.

52. We came here today to hear Debbie Harry, the girl with blond hair, sing an aria in the anterior area of the building, which will be loud enough to split your ear.

53. As I understand it, he was sent to the office after the scent of singed hair wafted from the sink in the science room.

54. After a second try, the secretary succeeded in having the section about sex harassment included.

55. Despite his assurance that the insurance is crucial to our financial well-being, we still are not sure and will check his credentials.

56. His mental and vital signs are good, and even at 7 feet tall, he is not at all abnormal.

57. At the present time, the President will address Congress.

58. Before we continue, let me have the attention of the man from Tennessee whose ten relatives have created such a tension in the courtroom that I am forced to set a continuance of the case at 10 tomorrow morning.

59. Bring me that exhibit before I sentence you to a night in the brig.

60. The bun has begun to go stale, and it's gotten too far gone to be any good for man or beast.

61. The cat got his hind legs caught behind the wicker chair.

62. It came as a great blow to him that his grades in reading could be low enough to place him below grade level.

63. Bert proved beyond a reasonable doubt that the birth took the better part of a night and occurred in the yard.

64. Before they could begin to build the skyscraper, Bill gave them a bill for a billion dollars, which included the bill of sale and the bill of lading.

65. The nurse applied a balm to the wound he suffered when a bomb tore apart the bottom of his foot.

66. After a large lunch, the portly counsel rose to offer the burden of proof in the case, and instead gave a loud burp, provoking the judge to bop his head with the gavel.

67. The rose bush was not on her path, but she made time to stop and smell the old-fashioned roses.

68. We are canning tomatoes now, and we canned beans earlier, but before we can go, Mom said we can do one thing—clean up the mess.

69. Can you do this new child custody case?

70. Could you on occasion give an indication to Kate that I have an objection to the cost of a cow and an ox for the company party which I have okayed for October 3 at 3 o'clock in Chicago?

71. Can you recall if she had a permanent curl at the time?

 Step 9: Short Forms

72. Can you remember when the witch put a curse on the mangy cur? Had it occurred then or did it occur later?

73. Can you say that it is proper to cuss a customer who has been rude to you?

74. Can you tell us how you got the cuts on your face?

75. And on which charge is he being held?

76. At the close of the year, I will throw out my old clothes and lose some weight.

77. After the inclusion of some new evidence, it was obvious that they were acting in collusion.

78. Efforts to communicate with members of the commune were in vain, and all communication with the outside world ceased.

79. The compact car was an exact replica of one made some years earlier.

80. I know that you can excel at anything, but you compel me to expel you for a week for this incident.

81. In his self-imposed exile, he began to compile a new reference book.

82. The core of the argument hinges on correspondence from the coroner to the corespondent in this case, and in respect to the course of action I must take, I exhort the corporation to comport itself well.

83. In conclusion, we can only conclude that the concussion would have been worse if the helmet did not serve to cushion the impact.

84. Despite having a strong constitution, he asked if the substitution of milk for coffee would be possible.

85. Consumption of a gourmet dinner and fine wines followed the consummation of the long-awaited business deal.

86. Counsel stated, "Before the witness croaks, let me cross-examine him about the mob contracts."

87. It is not a contradiction to say that the cricks in my neck were caused by my contribution to the log-splitting.

88. A meeting of the queens from seventeen countries will convene next month, and you are requested to come at your convenience.

89. Before the corn could be fed to the birds, the squirrels had stripped it of all but the cob.

90. He must have slipped a cog if he thought he could go with them.

91. The coon could know that the goldfish in my Japanese garden are tasty treats.

92. The doctor placed a cot on the boy's finger and said, "Could this injury have occurred on the playground or could it have been when he got home from school?'

93. Could you tell me where you bought that cute outfit?

94. The daily reports will reveal a great deal of detail about the company's operations.

95. After making her final decision, the ruler placed her crest on the decrees which were designed to bring about a decrease in sedition against the government.

96. Let's clarify the description of the suspect you made earlier. Would you describe again what he was wearing?

97. The doctor said, "I did go to Greece last week, and I agreed to diagnose your patient. I found that he is dying with a fever of very high degrees, a direct result of a greed for food with too much grease."

98. It was definitely hard as the devil to develop a case against the deaf defendant.

99. Did he know how dense it was to deny that he had spent the night in that den of iniquity where there is so much wickedness?

100. Did he say that the house would be ready by December?

101. Did he tell you that he hoped to resolve that large debt following the death of his wife by collecting on the insurance debit policy?

102. Did he want the students from the geology department to measure the depth of the water table?

103. Do you have enough dough to pay the bills that are due, or did you think you didn't have to pay them at all?

104. The doe and her fawns grazed peacefully in the morning dew.

105. Do you believe now or did you believe at that time that the policy paid double indemnity?

106. Did you do the design for the missile that turned out to be such a dud?

107. Did you go by the place they have dug a holding pond on your way to work?

108. Do you know what Don Harris, who lives down the beach by the large dune and doesn't have a job, has done now?

109. Do you live now, or did you live at the time, in that old, dull, brown house built with dowels?

110. After their disagreement regarding dual ownership of the property, the two men duly consented to resolve their problem with an old-fashioned duel.

111. Do you mean or did you mean at the time to call your boss dumb?

112. Doctor, when you performed the brain surgery, do you recall the condition of the dural matter?

 Step 9: Short Forms

113. Do you remember the dour expression on the widow's face when she was told the amount of the dower?

114. Do you now think or did you think at the time that dunning you for a load of cow dung could be so expensive?

115. Do you have the good manners to doff your hat when you meet the countess?

116. Dr. Davis was the only doctor on duty when the boat crashed into the dock.

117. Earl took the eastbound train early Saturday morning before the tide began to ebb. He hoped to find a better job where he did not have to carry out patients' urine in the smelly urn.

118. The official statement was that fishes such as swordfish, shark, and tuna may not be efficiently processed in an efficiency apartment.

119. The lex, or law, of this area states that an election must be held to select the manager of the electric plant even though not everyone here elects to have electricity.

120. I saw the managers emerge from the emergency meeting at the governor's mansion. It would cost megabucks to merge the companies.

121. Is this a ploy to gain favor, or do you really mean to employ his worthless son?

122. The city slickers began to jeer as the engineer guided the engine near the ramp loaded with pigs and chickens.

123. The high quality of United States citizenship derives from the equality of its citizens.

124. He is always quick to quip that his gym is well-equipped.

125. The district attorney will be establishing that after stabbing the victim, the defendant stole a stack of green bills.

126. When we heard about the valuation of the island's currency, we made a new evaluation of our vacation plans.

127. I am in suspense waiting to see the expense report that itemizes how much she spends on entertainment.

128. Do you support the position that people who play a professional sport should be allowed to export goods with their name on them?

129. The judge could not suppress his expression of surprise upon learning of the suppression of such important evidence.

130. I fear that my father has grown fatter from eating such rich fare, but he is still in fair health.

131. They attempted to treat the recently adopted child familiarly, but soon realized that until he was familiar with his new family, he could only exhibit shyness and uncertainty.

132. The fate of the 59 boat people grew grim as their number was reduced to 58 following a malfunction of the boat's fin, and they also had to contemplate a possible fine when they arrived.

133. The hungry fox set his focus on the pork loin the jovial folks had just put on the spit.

134. We followed the path along the creek that flowed down the mountain.

135. For your information, this is the fourth time that he has returned in a fright from the fort after looking for it in the fog.

136. The gal who cleans our office is mixing up a gallon of bleach with water.

137. The governor needs to decide to either govern or play golf and let someone else run the government.

138. Ed said that had he received his education back east, he would have saved himself a heap of trouble, because he developed a cyst on his head, and if he had taken heed of the help they offered and did not hesitate, he'd be hep to the problem and solve it with ease.

139. Had he ever seen a heifer of such size?

140. When the layoffs did not happen, I became so happy I forgot to pay my mortgage; but if that should happen again, I will try not to be so happy.

141. They have gone home after having done all their work.

142. He can tell them to go to heck now, but it was a lot different then.

143. He howled when asked, "How could you determine how old she is?"

144. I can see where being manic depressive could cause you to be ruled incompetent.

145. I recollect that if you irk this judge even slightly, you will be held in contempt.

146. I will tell you that I am too ill to walk down the aisle next week in Illinois, and that I would rather be using suntan oil on an isle in the Pacific.

147. If he will take the stand now, he can tell us how he fell down the stairs that night.

148. If I can fix the problem in my fiscal situation, I will be able to afford a physical from my wealthy physician.

149. If I go to the beach, do you think I give a fig about how my figure looks in a bathing suit?

150. If I remember correctly, their firm sells fir trees at Christmas.

151. If you are sure you want to furnish your living room with furniture covered with fur, that's fine with me; but if you remember the last time you redecorated, your spouse sent it all back.

 Step 9: Short Forms

152. If you understand the expense involved, and if you will wait quite some time, the account will then be full of funds.

153. I imagine that when the mayor asked Mary if she would marry him, she said, "It doesn't matter, I may or I may not." But she probably did some quick math and felt very merry.

154. The microbiology teacher stated, "In fact, there are many organisms which can infect the body, and in effect, they are too numerous to count."

155. When you got your new safari outfit, I knew that you had it in you to join the hunt into South Africa and capture a gnu for the zoo.

156. When he was a junior in college, Jim Thomas, Jr., received his first jury summons and subsequently was chosen to serve as a juror in a personal injury case.

157. The coast guard investigator took off his wet vest and threw it into the vessel, ready to investigate or just detain them.

158. In a shaky voice, she told them that the deal was void because they had never been invoiced.

159. Is he satisfied that the salve he developed for the treatment of serious inflammation of the serous membranes is safe?

160. The pirate said that his creed was to never cease to seize an opportunity to loot and pillage on the high seas.

161. It will be there by Tuesday, thereby eliminating the problem it had earlier.

162. They are so happy that it will soon be time to pick up the triplets who will be theirs, that they're preparing to buy threes of everything from bassinets to buggies.

163. The lieutenant advised that the only loot taken in the crime was an antique minstrel's lute, and that they could instigate a lawsuit to recover it.

164. The legislator found that the long process of passing legislation was letting his legs fall asleep.

165. The policeman listened as I told him a few lies about driving down the left-hand side of the road with my left hand because I had to scratch the lice on my head with my right hand, and he took away my license.

166. The only low-cal drink available in this locale is the lowly iced tea with saccharine from the local hangout.

167. After you locate the locket, you should take care to lock it away securely so you don't lose it again.

168. I sent a money order last Monday to Missouri for a machine that will mince food in minutes with a minimum of trouble.

169. The marshal of the town, whose name was Don Marshall, had to institute martial law after the invasion of the Martian space travelers.

170. We may be able to make it to Massachusetts in May to hear the priest perform the mass.

171. The maintenance man at the apartment complex may not be able to maintain his sanity when the students arrive.

172. I might have had reason to be miffed if you were any later.

173. It is a moot point—I do not want to hear anything more about how many miles an hour my mother was going when she drove the mower into the moat.

174. I was more than surprised that the morals of my mother-in-law began to decline and she chose to mourn my father-in-law for only one cold morn.

175. When the cloudiness slackens and the sky darkens, the little bird finds it necessary to leave the nest and search for the necessities of life for her babies.

176. The ambassador found it too gauche to negotiate with an undersecretary and halted negotiation of the treaty.

177. It was not an option on the part of the defendant to operate the openings of the dam, and I opt to postpone the proceedings until he recovers from his operation.

178. It is my opinion that the pain in the patient's side is a result of being punctured with the pin of the rack and pinion mechanism and not the broken pane of glass.

179. Organizers of the parade prayed that the pickpocket who preyed on large crowds would stay at home.

180. After he had tick fever, he developed a peculiar tic on one side of his face and was determined to stay out of those particular woods.

181. If you hand the ink pen to me, I will pay for the sugar pea seeds that your pa picked up in Pennsylvania.

182. Pete brought a petition before the court asking if the pigs he bought from the pet store could be kept in a pen lined with peat moss in his back yard.

183. The police department issued a series of pleas asking if the kidnapper would please release the woman, but they have yet to receive any replies.

184. The elementary school principal, who is a real prince of a man, asked all the parents to make an appraisal of the principles they are instilling in their children, because the education of their children is principally their job.

185. You are probably aware that a probe into the source of the problem showed that the chances that it would recur are probable.

186. The professor would like to proffer the proof at this time that he did in fact

profess or affirm his allegiance to the university.

187. He made the solemn promise that they would attend the junior and senior proms if they were forced to miss the sophomore prom.

188. A heavy rain began to pour from the sky, and the footman had to rein in the horses of the royal carriage during the parade marking a decade of the queen's reign.

189. The lady in the red dress is ready to submit to redirect examination, and the oath was read to her.

190. She can say that she is offended to be called a cute chick, which I can believe, but when you wear such chic clothes as a leather miniskirt and shimmy and shake in the local bar, what can you expect?

191. At times she would tell us about how she'd found the Viking shield she had under some old tools in the shed.

192. Should you show the new salesgirl somehow to display the shoe?

193. Shouldn't you advise the intern that the shunt should not, under any conditions, be moved?

194. Sweat dripped from his brow, and he swayed back and forth as he sat in the hotel suite, smoking a few cigs, eating some sweets, and pondering the signifi-

cance of the situation involving the suede leather coat.

195. She failed to associate his nasty appearance with the fact that he had associated with the dregs of society, so he should easily deceive her again.

196. A parasite in the soil had made the dog so ill that he had soiled the carpet, so I will treat it solely for that reason.

197. To some extent, the teacher found it irksome that so many of the biology students knew something about a chromosome and a ribosome, but had trouble with the sum of a simple equation.

198. I could hear somebody in the crowd begin to sob when he told the girl that she sure had some body.

199. I am sorry to hear how sore you are after you chose to soar through the air on a bungee cord.

200. The nuclear sub was the subject of much debate between the countries.

201. She worked as a substitute teacher at the vocational training institute.

202. As the sun shone brightly last Sunday afternoon, my son had a hot fudge sundae and sunned himself on the beach before the weekend was over.

203. We will just have to splice the rope together and make do until the new supplies arrive.

204. The blackberries will sustain us until we return to the cottage, but they will stain your white dress.

205. These tapes will reveal what actually did take place.

206. If there are more than enough boards to widen the deck, then let's build a planter with the remainder.

207. Thank you, I see that you thawed out the chicken that you had frozen last week and that you have started to thaw the beef.

208. The first time that I asked, they told me they did not know anything about it.

209. I do think that since his hair is thinning on top and lately he has been darkening it, that it could be a midlife crisis kind of thing.

210. Tom had started to read the weighty tome about the Egyptian tomb too many times. It may have been interesting to many, but to him it was a bore, and he would try again tomorrow.

211. For the test tomorrow, we are required to know how many pounds are in one ton.

212. The young mother told her tot to be good to the kitty and not to do anything else to it.

213. The mechanic said he will bring this to you when we tow in the car together.

214. Send a postcard to your family of the ancient tower you will see on your vacation tour.

215. The toad said to the tadpole, "Today I have many things to do, and first I must take you to day care."

216. The boys took too long to walk their two friends home.

217. My twin wound up 29 balls of twine.

218. Unity is a desirable state of mind to have in a military unit.

219. You want the coconuts, so you must climb up the tree.

220. The hallucinogenic potion was not found in his possession, and I move to drop the charges upon the grounds that even though he is a pest, he does not really pose a problem to society.

221. The vehicles tearing out of the high school parking lot vex the principal's patience.

222. The psychic had a disturbing vision of the vicious crime.

223. After I endured a two-hour wait in the doctor's waiting room, the nurse revealed my weight in a loud voice.

224. I will wash all of our laundry before we leave for Washington.

225. When it comes down to it, this witness and all the other witnesses concerned

© 1993, 2001 *StenEd*®

with the case were asked to keep their wits about them, but they really do not care a whit about it, to wit, some are asleep at the moment.

226. We can put that wacky purple webbing on the lawn chairs next week.

227. We had planned to wed last Wednesday, and we did ask the handyman to weed the flower garden and weld the arch, but he said we would regret it and it will be a long time till he weds.

228. We have gone to the reservation where we've seen the Indians weaving colorful blankets, and now we have developed a great desire to learn to weave fabrics using their techniques.

229. We recall that you stated you were traveling in a westerly direction.

230. We want you to know that he wept like a baby when he confessed.

231. What he will tell you, and what I will tell you also, is that the blue whale received a slight wheal from the impact of the boat's wheel and we'll wait to see how long it is before he is well.

232. What I came all the way to the cheese-making region of France to learn is how to separate the whey from the milk and weigh each kind correctly.

233. When I ask you why you did it, I expect an answer.

234. When I am with him, I am ready to go anywhere at the slightest whim, and many other women have felt the same.

235. When I was cooking dinner last night, which I have done too many nights this week, I caught a whiff of my neighbor's steak grilling; and I thought, "When I have sautéed the onions and garlic, he'll get a few whiffs of this, too."

236. After he was in the wreck, the senior member of the committee made the recommendation in a memorandum that since he can barely recognize anyone or remember anything, he recommends any measure where he can regain his memory.

237. The bank teller wore a wry smile as I asked her the right place where I needed to write my endorsement—an initiation rite for new accounts.

238. The newly-arrived Czech immigrant received his first check, which he can use for renting a new apartment.

239. After the chess game which he is so intensely involved with is over, he will be glad to get a few things off his chest.

240. The punch which I will serve at the party for my child is perfectly chilled, and here is some dip which I would like for you to chill.

241. You may wear ragged, holey clothes when the whole church and some others who will help will gather holly for the holy service.

242. Whoever thought that when the helicopter began to hover above us that it would clip the power line?

243. If he is not willing to go, I will go.

244. If I live through this exercise, will I have the strength left to lift weights and get everything done on my list?

245. Would you mean that the presence of a saline solution in the womb of the woman would mean that she had an abortion?

246. I would believe, but would you believe that the wobble in that wheel was there all along?

247. If you are 84 years old, and you don't remember your phone number, but quite a bit about days of yore, then you are ready to retire.

248. You don't know how ingrained the theory you know is until you try to unlearn it.

249. You understand that under the laws of the United States, you must undertake to uphold the highest qualities of the inner person.

250. You will find that the effort you'll expend learning realtime writing will result in many benefits both to yourselves as a group and to yourself as an individual, and success will be yours!

STEP 10
SPECIAL CONSIDERATIONS

Congratulations! You probably thought you'd never get through the first nine steps.

This final step contains the finishing touches for realtime writing. The following topics will be discussed:

- Capitalization;
- Compound Words;
- Homographs;
- Spelling Alphabets; and
- Text Entry Commands.

ACTION STEP

Work on one category at a time. When possible, principles have been given that can be used consistently.

The suggestions given for capitalization, compound words, homographs, and the spelling alphabets should be useful to you. The text entry commands are optional.

DICTIONARY MAINTENANCE

Capitalization

If your CAT system can handle the "force initial cap" and "force all caps" commands, enter them in your translation dictionary. Also enter any asterisked outlines that you plan to incorporate (e.g., PW*EUL for Bill).

Compound Words

It is suggested that you add the suffixes that will be useful to you (e.g., HRAO*EUBG for -like, WAO*EUZ for -wise). The "join" (SKWR-PB) and "space" (SP-S) commands are also very useful and most CAT systems can now handle them.

Homographs

It is recommended that you add the alternative pronunciations to your translation dictionary (e.g., KHROES and KHROEZ for close, RE/SAOUPL and REZ/PHAEU for resume) so you can write by sound and get the correct translation.

Spelling Alphabets

Once you become familiar with the spelling alphabets, you will want to add them to your translation dictionary. The *capital* letters (with and without periods) are particularly useful. You'll never be stumped when they throw a new acronym at you. Just write what you hear.

Stenoscription Commands

Many of these are applicable only for certain software systems (e.g., movement commands). They are listed here for those of you who use a CAT or stenoscription system that has many or all of these capabilities. Some you will not be able to enter into your dictionary. However, if you have a need for certain symbols (e.g., &, #, %), they may be added to your translation dictionary.

Detailed information on the five categories follows.

CAPITALIZATION

Most CAT and all stenoscription systems will accept a "force initial cap" command. Some will also accept a "force all caps" command. StenEd recommends K-P for initial cap and K-PS for all caps. The K-PS generally works as a toggle command; that is, write K-PS to <u>start</u> all caps and K-PS to <u>stop</u> all caps. (Note: If a word is always capitalized, no special designation is required; e.g., America.)

| Pat | K-P/PAT | WHEREFORE | K-PS/WR-FR/K-PS |
| Avenue | K-P/A*F | NOW COMES | K-PS/TPHOU/KOPL/-S/K-PS |

INITIAL CAPS
(WORDS WHICH OCCUR WITH & WITHOUT)

You may use an asterisk for the capitalized version of many words that often occur both with and without an initial capital. Add an asterisk to the first stroke. (Note: If an asterisk is already a part of the word or would cause a conflict; e.g., PA*T = path, A*F = avenue, use the K-P command.)

administration	AD/PHEUPB/STRAEUGS [AD/PH*RGS]	Administration	A*D/PHEUPB/STRAEUGS [A*D/PH*RGS]
bill	PWEUL	Bill	PW*EUL
bob	PWOB	Bob	PWO*B
china	KHAOEU/TPHA	China	KHAO*EU/TPHA
city	STEU	City	ST*EU
congress	KOPBG	Congress	KO*PBG
congressman	KOPBG/PHAPB [KPHAPB]	Congressman	KO*PBG/PHAPB [KPHA*PB]
congresswoman	KOPBG/WOPL [KWOPL]	Congresswoman	KO*PBG/WOPL [KWO*PL]
county	KOUPB/TEU	County	KO*UPB/TEU
court	KOURT	Court	KO*URT
courthouse	KOURT/HOUS [KROUS]	Courthouse	KO*URT/HOUS [KRO*US]
dad	TKAD	Dad	TKA*D
doctor	TKR-	Doctor	TKR*
federal	TPED/RAL [TPRAL]	Federal	TP*ED/RAL [TPRA*L]
ford	TPORD	Ford	TPO*RD
frank	TPRAPB/-BG	Frank	TPRA*PB/-BG
god	TKPWOD	God	TKPWO*D
gym	SKWREUPL	Jim	SKWR*EUPL
honorable	HOPB/RABL	Honorable	HO*PB/RABL
house	HOUS	House	HO*US
jack	SKWRABG	Jack	SKWRA*BG
January	SKWRAPB	Jan	SKWRA*PB
john	SKWROPB	John	SKWRO*PB
jury	SKWRUR	Jury	SKWR*UR
march	PHAR/-FP [PHA*RPBLG]	March	PHA*R (mar = PHAR)
mark	PHARBG	Mark	PHA*RBG
may	PHAEU	May	PHA*EU
medicaid	PHED/KAEUD	Medicaid	PH*ED/KAEUD
medicare	PHED/KAEUR	Medicare	PH*ED/KAEUR
mike	PHAOEUBG	Mike	PHAO*EUBG
mom	PHOPL	Mom	PHO*PL
navy	TPHAEU/SREU	Navy	TPHA*EU/SREU
president	P-T	President	P*T
senate	STPHAT	Senate	STPHA*T
senator	STPHAT/TOR [STPHART]	Senator	STPHA*T/TOR [STPHA*RT]
state	STAEUT	State	STA*EUT
street	STRAOET	Street	STRAO*ET
sue	SAOU	Sue	SAO*U
turkey	TUR/KAOE	Turkey	T*UR/KAOE
vice president	SR-PT	Vice President	SR*PT

© 1993, 2001 *StenEd*®

COMPOUND WORDS

To solve those persistent word boundary problems that don't fall into any easy category and are not frequent enough to learn a separate outline to distinguish the word form from the word part form, you can often add an asterisk to the second element of the compound word when you want it to attach to the first (e.g., backup = PWABG/*UP, back up = PWABG/UP). This system works on all CAT systems.

You should add these word ending strokes as suffixes to your personal CAT dictionary. It is more efficient to add suffix entries than to add all the individual compound words. If you add the outline *UP to translate as the suffix "up," the stroke *UP will attach "up" to any previous word. Thus, words such as "backup," "coverup," "holdup," "hookup," "lineup," etc., will not have to be entered as separate words.

This concept is also useful when people "make up" words. The suffixes "like" and "wise," for example, are liable to be tacked onto almost anything. "Grammarwise," it's incorrect. But it's done in spoken English frequently.

The Join Stroke (SKWR-PB)

On most CAT systems, you can force two words to join together by adding a "join command" to your translation dictionary. How you add this stroke depends on your CAT system. You want a "delete space" that acts as a prefix/suffix but translates as nothing. (See the appendix for instructions on adding this stroke to "some" CAT systems.)

Using the "join" stroke (we recommend the outline "SKWR-PB"), you would write the two-word "black bird" as PWHRABG/PWEURD and the compound "blackbird" as PWHRABG/SKWR-PB/PWEURD.

The Space Stroke (SP-S)

On most CAT systems, you can also separate components of a compound word by using a stroke that designates a space. How you add this stroke depends on your CAT system. You want the stroke to translate as a single space. You cannot add this stroke as a normal entry because you would then get a space before and/or after the space (i.e., you would end up with two or three spaces instead of one because when you add a word, it translates with a space before and/or after). (See the appendix for instructions on adding this stroke to "some" CAT systems.)

Using the "space" stroke (we recommend the outline "SP-S"), you could write the two words "black bird" as PWHRABG/SP-S/PWEURD and the compound "blackbird" as PWHRABG/PWEURD.

You will probably decide to use the asterisked suffix for the most common compound words (e.g., backup = PWABG/*UP) rather than opting for an extra "join" or "space" stroke. But for uncommon compound word parts, the "join" and "space" features are very useful.

Hyphenated Words

Including the hyphen in a hyphenated word will distinguish it from the two-word form. (E.g., front-wheel drive = TPROPBT/H-F/WHAOEL/TKRAO*EUF, bent front wheel = PWEPBT/TPROPBT/WHAOEL.)

Words that are *always* compound and *always* use hyphens can be entered in the CAT dictionary with a hyphen (e.g., good-bye), thus the hyphen need not be stroked.

COMPOUND WORDS

Many examples of compound words follow. They are listed alphabetically within their "ending word" group. (For additional examples, see StenEd's *Volume I: Theory* or the *Professional Dictionary*.)

Generally, only one outline has been given. Additional optional outlines, when available, can be found in the *Professional Dictionary*.

ACHE

backache	PWABG/A*EUBG	back ache	PWABG/AEUBG
bellyache	PWEL/HREU/A*EUBG	belly ache	PWEL/HREU/AEUBG
earache	AOER/A*EUBG	ear ache	AOER/AEUBG
headache	HED/A*EUBG [HAEUBG]	head ache	HED/AEUBG
heartache	HART/A*EUBG	heart ache	HART/AEUBG
toothache	TAO*T/A*EUBG	tooth ache	TAO*T/AEUBG

AWAY = A*EU/WAEU

breakaway	PWRAEBG/A*EU/WAEU	break away	PWRAEBG/AEU/WAEU
getaway	TKPWET/A*EU/WAEU	get away	TKPWET/AEU/WAEU
hideaway	HAOEUD/A*EU/WAEU	hide away	HAOEUD/AEU/WAEU
runaway	RUPB/A*EU/WAEU	run away	RUPB/AEU/WAEU

BACK = PWA*BG

comeback	KOPL/PWA*BG	come back	KOPL/PWABG
cutback	KUT/PWA*BG	cut back	KUT/PWABG
halfback	HAF/PWA*BG	half back	HAF/PWABG
kickback	KEUBG/PWA*BG	kick back	KEUBG/PWABG
playback	PHRAEU/PWA*BG	play back	PHRAEU/PWABG
setback	SET/PWA*BG	set back	SET/PWABG

DOWN = TKO*UPB OR KWROUPB

breakdown	PWRAEBG/TKO*UPB	break down	PWRAEBG/TKOUPB
countdown	KOUPBT/TKO*UPB	count down	KOUPBT/TKOUPB
letdown	HRET/TKO*UPB	let down	HRET/TKOUPB
markdown	PHARBG/TKO*UPB	mark down	PHARBG/TKOUPB
showdown	SHOE/TKO*UPB	show down	SHOE/TKOUPB
shutdown	SHUT/TKO*UPB	shut down	SHUT/TKOUPB

LIKE = HRAO*EUBG

businesslike	PWEUZ/HRAO*EUBG	business like	PWEUZ/HRAOEUBG
catlike	KAT/HRAO*EUBG	cat like	KAT/HRAOEUBG
childlike	KHAOEULD/HRAO*EUBG	child like	KHAOEULD/HRAOEUBG
lifelike	HRAOEUF/HRAO*EUBG	life like	HRAOEUF/HRAOEUBG
manlike	PHAPB/HRAO*EUBG	man like	PHAPB/HRAOEUBG
warlike	WAR/HRAO*EUBG	war like	WAR/HRAOEUBG

OFF = A*UF OR KWRAUF

kickoff	KEUBG/A*UF	kick off	KEUBG/AUF
layoff	HRAEU/A*UF	lay off	HRAEU/AUF
payoff	PAEU/A*UF	pay off	PAEU/AUF
runoff	RUPB/A*UF	run off	RUPB/AUF
takeoff	TAEUBG/A*UF	take off	TAEUBG/AUF
turnoff	TURPB/A*UF	turn off	TURPB/AUF

OUT = O*UT OR KWROUT

blackout	PWHRABG/O*UT	black out	PWHRABG/OUT
checkout	KHEBG/O*UT	check out	KHEBG/OUT
dropout	TKROP/O*UT	drop out	TKROP/OUT
printout	PREUPBT/O*UT	print out	PREUPBT/OUT
workout	WORBG/O*UT	work out	WORBG/OUT

© 1993, 2001 *StenEd*® **Step 10—Special Considerations**

UP = *UP OR KWRUP

backup	PWABG/*UP	back up	PWABG/UP
checkup	KHEBG/*UP	check up	KHEBG/UP
holdup	HOELD/*UP	hold up	HOELD/UP
lineup	HRAOEUPB/*UP	line up	HRAOEUPB/UP
makeup	PHAEUBG/*UP	make up	PHAEUBG/UP
pickup	PEUBG/*UP	pick up	PEUBG/UP
setup	SET/*UP	set up	SET/UP

WARD = WA*RD

backward	PWABG/WA*RD	back ward	PWABG/WARD
eastward	AO*ES/WA*RD	east ward	AO*ES/WARD
frontward	TPROPBT/WA*RD	front ward	TPROPBT/WARD
rearward	RAOER/WA*RD	rear ward	RAOER/WARD
southward	SO*UT/WA*RD	south ward	SO*UT/WARD
toward	TO/WA*RD [TWARD]	to ward	TO/WARD

WAY = WA*EU

anyway	TPHEU/WA*EU	any way	TPHEU/WAEU
driveway	TKRAO*EUF/WA*EU	drive way	TKRAO*EUF/WAEU
fairway	TPAEUR/WA*EU	fair way	TPAEUR/WAEU
pathway	PA*T/WA*EU	path way	PA*T/WAEU
runway	RUPB/WA*EU	run way	RUPB/WAEU
walkway	WAUBG/WA*EU	walk way	WAUBG/WAEU

WISE = WAO*EUZ

businesswise	PWEUZ/WAO*EUZ	business wise	PWEUZ/WAOEUZ
likewise	HRAOEUBG/WAO*EUZ	like wise	HRAOEUBG/WAOEUZ
moneywise	PHUPB/WAOEUZ	money wise	PHUPB/WAOEUZ
otherwise	O*ER/WAO*EUZ	other wise	O*ER/WAOEUZ
saleswise	SAELS/WAOEUZ	sales wise	SAEL/-S/WAOEUZ

WORK = WO*RBG

guesswork	TKPWESZ/WO*RBG	guess work	TKPWESZ/WORBG
homework	HOEPL/WO*RBG	home work	HOEPL/WORBG
housework	HOUS/WO*RBG	house work	HOUS/WORBG
piecework	PAOES/WO*RBG	piece work	PAOES/WORBG
teamwork	TAEPL/WO*RBG	team work	TAEPL/WORBG

OVER = OFR OR KWRO*EFR

The prefix "over-" is written O*FR; the suffix form is written OFR.

holdover	HOELD/OFR	hold over	HOELD/OEFR [HOELD/O*EFR]
leftover	HREFT/OFR	left over	HREFT/OEFR [HREFT/O*EFR]
moreover	PHOR/OFR [PHROFR]	more over	PH-R/OEFR [PH-R/O*EFR]
runover	RUPB/OFR	run over	RUPB/OEFR [RUPB/O*EFR]
takeover	TAEUBG/OFR	take over	TAEUBG/OEFR [TAEUBG/O*EFR]
turnover	TURPB/OFR	turn over	TURPB/OEFR [TURPB/O*EFR]

MISC

The following group of compounds can be distinguished by using the asterisk in the compound form or by using the SP-S stroke in the two-word form. StenEd uses the asterisk for the more common compound word elements and the SP-S stroke for the less common. Following are our recommendations, but do whatever method is easiest for you to remember.

Use Asterisk for One-Word Form

runabout	RUPB/A*BT	run about	RUPB/ABT
runaround	RUPB/A*RPBD	run around	RUPB/ARPBD

---

blackball	PWHRABG/PWAL [PWHRABL]	black ball	PWHRABG/SP-S/PWAL
heartbeat	HART/PWAET	heart beat	HART/SP-S/PWAET
blackbird	PWHRABG/PWEURD	black bird	PWHRABG/SP-S/PWEURD
heartbreak	HART/PWRAEBG	heart break	HART/SP-S/PWRAEBG
standby	STAPBD/PWEU	stand by	STAPBD/SP-S/PWEU
hairdo	HAEUR/TKO	hair do	HAEUR/SP-S/TKO
rainfall	RAEUPB/TPAUL [RAEUFL]	rain fall	RAEUPB/SP-S/TPAUL
heartfelt	HART/TPELT	heart felt	HART/SP-S/TPELT
downright	TKOUPB/RAOEUGT	down right	TKOUPB/SP-S/RAOEUGT
sunrise	SUPB/RAOEUZ	sun rise	SUPB/SP-S/RAOEUZ
darkroom	TKARBG/RAOPL	dark room	TKARBG/SP-S/RAOPL
sunset	SUPB/SET	sun set	SUPB/SP-S/SET
handshake	HAPBD/SHAEUBG	hand shake	HAPBD/SP-S/SHAEUBG
sunshine	SUPB/SHAOEUPB	sun shine	SUPB/SP-S/SHAOEUPB
standstill	STAPBD/STEUL	stand still	STAPBD/SP-S/STEUL
shortstop	SHORT/STOP	short stop	SHORT/SP-S/STOP
onto	OPB/TO	on to	OPB/SP-S/TO
keyword	KAOE/WORD	key word	KAOE/SP-S/WORD

Another group of compounds is handled as follows. Most of these can be solved by using brief forms, though, in most cases, an asterisk in the second word would also work if that is your preference.

anybody	TPHEUB	any body	TPHEU/PWOD/TKEU
anymore	TPHEUPL	any more	TPHEU/PH-R
anyone	TPHEUPB	any one	TPHEU/WUPB
anything	TPHEUG	any thing	TPHEU/THEUPBG
anyway	TPHEU/WA*EU	any way	TPHEU/WAEU
anywhere	TPHEUR	any where	TPHEU/WR-
everybody	EFRB	every body	EFR/PWOD/TKEU
everyday	EFRD	every day	EFR/TKAEU
everyone	EFRPB	every one	EFR/WUPB
everything	EFRG	every thing	EFR/THEUPBG
hereabouts	HAOERBTS	here about	HAOER/ABT
hereafter	HAOER/AFR	here after	HAOER/AF
hereby	HAOERB	here by	HAOER/PWEU
herein	HAOERPB	here in	HAOER/TPH-
hereof	HAOER/O*F	here of	HAOER/OF
hereto	HAOERT	here to	HAOER/TO
hereunder	HAOERPBD	here under	HAOER/URPBD
herewith	HAOER/W*EUT	here with	HAOER/W-
however	HOUFR	how ever	HOU/-FR
inasmuch	EUPB/S-FP	in as much	TPH-/AZ/PHUFP [TPH-/S-FP]
maybe	PHAEUB	may be	PHAEU/PW-
moreover	PHROFR	more over	PH-R/OEFR
nobody	TPHOEB	no body	TPHO/PWOD/TKEU
somebody	SPH-B	some body	SOPL/PWOD/TKEU
someday	STKAEU	some day	SOPL/TKAEU
someplace	SPHRAEUS	some place	SOPL/PHRAEUS
something	SPH-G [STHEUPBG]	some thing	SOPL/THEUPBG
sometime	STAOEUPL	some time	SOPL/TAOEUPL
someway	SPH-/WAEU (not SWAEU)	some way	SOPL/WAEU
thereabout	THR-BT	there about	THR-/ABT
thereafter	THRAF	there after	THR-/AF
thereat	THRAT	there at	THR-/AT
thereby	THR-B	there by	THR-/PWEU
therefor	THR*FR	there for	THR-/TP-R
therefrom	THR-FRPL	there from	THR-/TPR-
therein	THR-PB	there in	THR-/TPH-
thereof	THROF	there of	THR-/OF
thereon	THROPB	there on	THR-/OPB
thereto	THR-T	there to	THR-/TO
thereunder	THR-PBD [THR-RPBD]	there under	THR-/URPBD
thereupon	THRUP	there upon	THR-/POPB
wherein	WR-PB	where in	WR-/TPH-
whereon	WROPB	where on	WR-/OPB

© 1993, 2001 *StenEd*® **Step 10—Special Considerations**

WORDS WITH HYPHENS

To insure the proper translation, include the hyphen in the outline for the compound form that uses the hyphen. If a two-word sequence only occurs with the hyphen (not as a single compound or as two separate words), you need not include the hyphen. Optional outlines are not given.

Preferred usage often changes. What is hyphenated currently may lose the hyphen in the future. Dictionaries don't always agree on usage. We have used *One Word, Two Words, Hyphenated?* by Mary Louise Gilman as the final authority.

stand-alone	STAPBD/H-F/AEU/HRO*EPB	put-on	PUT/H-F/OPB
standalone	STAPBD/A*EU/HRO*EPB	put on	PUT/OPB
stand alone	STAPBD/AEU/HRO*EPB		
		right-on	RAOEUGT/H-F/OPB
run-down	RUPB/H-F/TKOUPB	right on	RAOEUGT/OPB
rundown	RUPB/TKO*UPB		
run down	RUPB/TKOUPB	run-on	RUPB/H-F/OPB
		run on	RUPB/OPB
know-how	TPHOE/H-F/HOU		
know how	TPHOE/HOU	sign-on	SAOEUPB/H-F/OPB
		sign on	SAOEUPB/OPB
built-in	PWEULT/H-F/TPH-		
built in	PWEULT/TPH-	fade-out	TPAEUD/H-F/OUT
		fade out	TPAEUD/OUT
drive-in	TKRAO*EUF/H-F/TPH-		
drive in	TKRAO*EUF/TPH-	real-time	RAEL/H-F/TAOEUPL
		realtime	RAEL/TAO*EUPL
live-in	HR*EUF/H-F/TPH-	real time	RAEL/TAOEUPL
live in	HR*EUF/TPH-		
		build-up	PWEULD/H-F/UP
run-in	RUPB/H-F/TPH-	buildup	PWEULD/*UP
run in	RUPB/TPH-	build up	PWEULD/UP
stand-in	STAPBD/H-F/TPH-	cover-up	KO*FR/H-F/UP
stand in	STAPBD/TPH-	coverup	KO*FR/*UP
		cover up	KO*FR/UP
trade-in	TRAEUD/H-F/TPH-		
trade in	TRAEUD/TPH-	grown-up	TKPWROUPB/H-F/UP
		grown up	TKPWROUPB/UP
show-off	SHOE/H-F/AUF		
show off	SHOE/AUF	mock-up	PHOBG/H-F/UP
		mockup	PHOBG/*UP
sign-off	SAOEUPB/H-F/AUF	mock up	PHOBG/UP
sign off	SAOEUPB/AUF		
		start-up	START/H-F/UP
spin-off	SPEUPB/H-F/AUF	start up	START/UP
spin off	SPEUPB/AUF		
		stuck-up	STUBG/H-F/UP
carry-on	KAEUR/REU/H-F/OPB	stuck up	STUBG/UP
carryon	KAEUR/REU/O*PB		
carry on	KAEUR/REU/OPB	screw-up	SKRAOU/H-F/UP
		screwup	SKRAOU/*UP
come-on	KOPL/H-F/OPB	screw up	SKRAOU/UP
come on	KOPL/OPB		
		walk-up	WAUBG/H-F/UP
head-on	HED/H-F/OPB	walkup	WAUBG/*UP
head on	HED/OPB	walk up	WAUBG/UP

IF THE COMPOUND WORD IS NEVER (OR RARELY) USED AS A TWO-WORD SE-QUENCE, do not use the asterisk. For example, you may hear "in <u>business women</u> are . . ." and "<u>businesswomen</u> are . . ." However, it is unlikely that you would hear "business woman" spoken sequentially as two separate words. **If you do, use the SP-S stroke to separate the words.**

It is always possible that one of these "safe" compounds would be spoken sequentially as two separate words, but it is unlikely enough for inclusion in this list.

Following are examples of compound words that do not require the asterisk (or the "join" stroke, if that is the option you have decided to use). Note: For compound words in which the first word is a plural noun, you may save a stroke by adding -S to the first stroke (e.g., saleswoman = SAELS/WOPL, rather than SAEL/-S/WOPL).

daylight	TKAEU/HRAOEUGT [TKAEULGT]	pocketbook	POBGT/PWAOBG
flashlight	TPHRARB/HRAOEUGT [TPHR-LT]	scrapbook	SKRAP/PWAOBG
gaslight	TKPWAS/HRAOEUGT	textbook	T*EBGS/PWAOBG
headlight	HED/HRAOEUGT [H-LT]	yearbook	KWRAOER/PWAOBG
highlight	HAOEU/HRAOEUGT		
limelight	HRAOEUPL/HRAOEUGT	homemaker	HOEPL/PHAEUBG/ER
spotlight	SPOT/HRAOEUGT [SP-LT]	lawmaker	HRAU/PHAEUBG/ER
stoplight	STOP/HRAOEUGT [ST-LT]	pacemaker	PAEUS/PHAEUBG/ER
sunlight	SUPB/HRAOEUGT [SULGT]	peacemaker	PAES/PHAEUBG/ER
taillight	TAEUL/HRAOEUGT [T*LT]	troublemaker	TRUBL/PHAEUBG/ER
bathhouse	PWA*T/HOUS	businesswoman	PWEUZ/WOPL
birdhouse	PWEURD/HOUS	chairwoman	KHAEUR/WOPL
boardinghouse	PWAORD/-G/HOUS	councilwoman	KOUPB/SEUL/WOPL [KOUPBS/WOPL]
clubhouse	KHRUB/HOUS	policewoman	PHREUS/WOPL [PHRAPL]
courthouse	KOURT/HOUS [KROUS]	saleswoman	SAELS/WOPL [SWOPL]
farmhouse	TPARPL/HOUS	spokeswoman	SPOEBGS/WOPL
outhouse	O*UT/HOUS		
penthouse	PEPBT/HOUS	strawberry	STRAU/PWER/REU
storehouse	STOER/HOUS	scoreboard	SKOER/PWAORD
townhouse	TOUPB/HOUS	lifeboat	HRAOEUF/PWOET
warehouse	WAEUR/HOUS	harebrained	HA*ER/PWRAEUPB/-D
			[HAEUR/PWRAEUPBD]
barroom	PWAR/RAOPL	coldhearted	KOELD/HART/-D
bathroom	PWA*T/RAOPL [PWA*RPL]	stockholder	STOBG/HOELD/ER
bedroom	PWED/RAOPL [PW*ERPL]	bookkeeper	PWAOBG/KAOEP/ER
classroom	KHRASZ/RAOPL [KHRAOPL]	safekeeping	SAEUF/KAOEP/-G
courtroom	KOURT/RAOPL [KRAOPL]	peacemaking	PAES/PHAEUBG/-G
lunchroom	HRUPB/-FP/RAOPL	teammate	TAEPL/PHAEUT
	[HRUFRPBLG/RAOPL]	hairpiece	HAEUR/PAOES
mushroom	PHURB/RAOPL	fireproof	TPAOEUR/PRAOF
restroom	R*ES/RAOPL [R*ERPL]	workshop	WORBG/SHOP
storeroom	STOER/RAOPL	milestone	PHAOEUL/STOEPB
washroom	WARB/RAOPL	drugstore	TKRUG/STOER
		cocktail	KOBG/TAEUL
bankbook	PWA*PBG/PWAOBG	uptight	UP/TAOEUGT
checkbook	KHEBG/PWAOBG	caseworker	KAEUS/WORBG/ER
handbook	HAPBD/PWAOBG	bookworm	PWAOBG/WORPL
logbook	HROG/PWAOBG	typewriter	TAOEUP/WREU/ER
notebook	TPHOET/PWAOBG		[TAOEUP/WREUR]
passbook	PASZ/PWAOBG	handwriting	HAPBD/WREU/-G
			[HAPBD/WREUG]

 Step 10—Special Considerations

HOMOGRAPHS

Homographs are words that have the same spelling but differ in pronunciation. Because it is more natural to write words phonetically, homographs often have different outlines for their different uses when the sound varies. In reality, all outlines for the word(s) will translate correctly (e.g., whether you write PWAEUSZ or PWASZ for "He sang bass," the word will translate "bass").

Homographs with different vowel sounds (e.g., short vs. long) generally have separate outlines. Many homographs whose only difference is the syllable accented may share the same outline. For example, the word "record" is generally stroked RORD, but may also be written RE/KORD or REBG/ORD, depending on pronunciation. All three outlines will translate as "record."

Following is a list of selected homographs. When appropriate, accent marks are given to show the pronunciation. Practice sentences will illustrate the usage of these words.

a buse´ (-s sound)	AEU/PWAOUS	live (long i)	HRAO*EUF
a buse´ (-z sound)	AEU/PWAOUZ	live (short i)	HR*EUF
bass (long a)	PWAEUSZ	min´ ute (noun)	PHEUPB/UT
bass (short a)	PWASZ	mi nute´ (adj)	PHAOEU/TPHAOUT
bow (long o)	PWOE	mis use´ (-s sound)	PHEUS/KWRAOUS
bow (ow sound)	PWOU	mis use´ (-z sound)	PHEUS/KWRAOUZ
can (verb, aux)	K-	ob´ ject (noun)	OBT
can (verb or noun)	K- [KAPB]	ob ject´ (verb)	OBT
close (-s sound)	KHROES	per´ fect (adj)	PER/TPEBGT [PEFRT]
close (-z sound)	KHROEZ	per fect´ (verb)	PER/TPEBGT [PEFRT]
com´ pact (adj)	KOPL/PABGT	Pol´ ish (long o)	POEL/EURB
com pact´ (verb)	KOPL/PABGT	pol´ ish (short o)	POL/EURB
con´ duct (noun)	KUBGT	ref´ use (noun)	REF/KWRAOUS
con duct´ (verb)	KUBGT	re fuse´ (verb)	RE/TPAOUZ
con´ test (noun)	KOPB/T*ES	re sume´ (verb)	RE/SAOUPL
con test´ (verb)	KOPB/T*ES	res´ (u) me (noun)	REZ/PHAEU
con´ trast (noun)	KOPB/TRA*S	sub´ ject (noun)	SUPBLGT
con trast´ (verb)	KOPB/TRA*S	sub ject´ (verb)	SUPBLGT
dove (long o)	TKO*EF	tear (long a)	TAEUR
dove (short o)	TKO*F	tear (long e)	TAER
en´ trance (noun)	SPWRAPBS	use (-s sound)	KWRAOUS
en trance´ (verb)	SPWRAPBS	use (-z sound)	KWRAOUZ
house (-s sound)	HOUS	will (noun)	HR- [WEUL]
house (-z sound)	HOUZ	will (verb, aux)	HR-
in´ crease (noun)	EUPB/KRAOES	wind (noun)	WEUPBD
in crease´ (verb)	EUPB/KRAOES	wind (verb)	WAOEUPBD
lead (long e)	HRAOED	wound (noun)	WAOUPBD
lead (short e)	HRAED	wound (verb)	WOUPBD

SPELLING ALPHABETS
for Acronyms, Initials
& Spelling Words Out

Acronyms are extremely common in court work and in everyday English. They are created when the initials of a series of words or word parts are combined to form a single word or combination of letters. Some acronyms may occur with or without periods (e.g., USA or U.S.A.).

StenEd has four alphabets that allow you to write any acronym or initial or to spell a word out in a consistent, conflict-free manner.

- Lower case letters without periods;
- Upper case letters without periods;
- Lower case letters with periods; and
- Upper case letters with periods.

There are two variations with each alphabet: the letter standing alone and the letter attached. Use the letter "standing alone" for the first letter in the acronym; use the letter "attached to left" for all subsequent letters in the acronym. (Some CAT systems allow you to use only the standalone alphabet with subsequent letters attaching until another word is written.)

Following are the alphabets to use when no period is required.

TO APPEAR WITHOUT A PERIOD

Lower Case	Standing Alone	Attached to Left	Upper Case	Standing Alone	Attached to Left
a	A*	A*BGZ	A	ARBGS	A*RBGS
b	PW*	PW*BGZ	B	PW-RBGS	PW*RBGS
c	KR*	KR*BGZ	C	KR-RBGS	KR*RBGS
d	TK*	TK*BGZ	D	TK-RBGS	TK*RBGS
e	*E	*EBGZ	E	ERBGS	*ERBGS
f	TP*	TP*BGZ	F	TP-RBGS	TP*RBGS
g	TKPW*	TKPW*BGZ	G	TKPW-RBGS	TKPW*RBGS
h	H*	H*BGZ	H	H-RBGS	H*RBGS
i	*EU	*EUBGZ	I	EURBGS	*EURBGS
j	SKWR*	SKWR*BGZ	J	SKWR-RBGS	SKWR*RBGS
k	K*	K*BGZ	K	K-RBGS	K*RBGS
l	HR*	HR*BGZ	L	HR-RBGS	HR*RBGS
m	PH*	PH*BGZ	M	PH-RBGS	PH*RBGS
n	TPH*	TPH*BGZ	N	TPH-RBGS	TPH*RBGS
o	O*	O*BGZ	O	ORBGS	O*RBGS
p	P*	P*BGZ	P	P-RBGS	P*RBGS
q	KW*	KW*BGZ	Q	KW-RBGS	KW*RBGS
r	R*	R*BGZ	R	R-RBGS	R*RBGS
s	S*	S*BGZ	S	S-RBGS	S*RBGS
t	T*	T*BGZ	T	T-RBGS	T*RBGS
u	*U	*UBGZ	U	URBGS	*URBGS
v	SR*	SR*BGZ	V	SR-RBGS	SR*RBGS
w	W*	W*BGZ	W	W-RBGS	W*RBGS
x	KP*	KP*BGZ	X	KP-RBGS	KP*RBGS
y	KWR*	KWR*BGZ	Y	KWR-RBGS	KWR*RBGS
z	STK*	STK*BGZ	Z	STK-RBGS	STK*RBGS

© 1993, 2001 *StenEd*®

Some examples for using the non-period alphabets follow. (Optional briefs are not listed.)

wpm	W*/P*BGZ/PH*BGZ	USA	URBGS/S*RBGS/A*RBGS
mph	PH*/P*BGZ/H*BGZ	RPR	R-RBGS/P*RBGS/R*RBGS
prn	P*/R*BGZ/TPH*BGZ	VCR	SR-RBGS/KR*RBGS/R*RBGS

Note: In some stenoscription systems, you may need to press the space command (SP-S) before spelling out using lower-case letters. With these systems, letters with an asterisk (A*, PW*, KR*, etc.) automatically stick together.

The lower case without period dictionary is also useful for spelling out words, letter-by-letter, for on-line dictionary entries and in the transcript itself.

If periods are required, use the following alphabets.

TO APPEAR WITH A PERIOD

Lower Case	Standing Alone	Attached to Left	Upper Case	Standing Alone	Attached to Left
a.	A*PD	A*PLD	A.	AFPLT	A*FPLT
b.	PW*PD	PW*PLD	B.	PW-FPLT	PW*FPLT
c.	KR*PD	KR*PLD	C.	KR-FPLT	KR*FPLT
d.	TK*PD	TK*PLD	D.	TK-FPLT	TK*FPLT
e.	*EPD	*EPLD	E.	EFPLT	*EFPLT
f.	TP*PD	TP*PLD	F.	TP-FPLT	TP*FPLT
g.	TKPW*PD	TKPW*PLD	G.	TKPW-FPLT	TKPW*FPLT
h.	H*PD	H*PLD	H.	H-FPLT	H*FPLT
i.	*EUPD	*EUPLD	I.	EUFPLT	*EUFPLT
j.	SKWR*PD	SKWR*PLD	J.	SKWR-FPLT	SKWR*FPLT
k.	K*PD	K*PLD	K.	K-FPLT	K*FPLT
l.	HR*PD	HR*PLD	L.	HR-FPLT	HR*FPLT
m.	PH*PD	PH*PLD	M.	PH-FPLT	PH*FPLT
n.	TPH*PD	TPH*PLD	N.	TPH-FPLT	TPH*FPLT
o.	O*PD	O*PLD	O.	OFPLT	O*FPLT
p.	P*PD	P*PLD	P.	P-FPLT	P*FPLT
q.	KW*PD	KW*PLD	Q.	KW-FPLT	KW*FPLT
r.	R*PD	R*PLD	R.	R-FPLT	R*FPLT
s.	S*PD	S*PLD	S.	S-FPLT	S*FPLT
t.	T*PD	T*PLD	T.	T-FPLT	T*FPLT
u.	*UPD	*UPLD	U.	UFPLT	*UFPLT
v.	SR*PD	SR*PLD	V.	SR-FPLT	SR*FPLT
w.	W*PD	W*PLD	W.	W-FPLT	W*FPLT
x.	KP*PD	KP*PLD	X.	KP-FPLT	KP*FPLT
y.	KWR*PD	KWR*PLD	Y.	KWR-FPLT	KWR*FPLT
z.	STK*PD	STK*PLD	Z.	STK-FPLT	STK*FPLT

Hint: To help remember the lower case with period alphabet, think of -PD (A*PD) as period, -PLD (A*PLD) as period and to the left.

Some examples for using the alphabets with periods follow. (Optional briefs are generally not listed.)

f.o.b.	TP*PD/O*PLD/PW*PLD	C.P.A.	KR-FPLT/P*FPLT/A*FPLT
i.o.u.	EU*PD/O*PLD/*UPLD	N.Y.C.	TPH-FPLT/KWR*FPLT/KR*FPLT
p.r.n.	P*PD/R*PLD/TPH*PLD [P*RPB]	O.D.	O-FPLT/TK*FPLT

Many acronyms may occur with or without periods. The trend seems to be less periods. Use whatever format is appropriate for your situation.

CPA	KR-RBGS/P*RBGS/A*RBGS	C.P.A.	KR-FPLT/P*FPLT/A*FPLT
FBI	TP-RBGS/PW*RBGS/*EURBGS	F.B.I.	TP-FPLT/PW*FPLT/*EUFPLT
USA	U-RBGS/S*RBGS/A*RBGS	U.S.A.	U-FPLT/S*FPLT/A*FPLT

The upper-case alphabet with periods is used for initials. Traditionally, two or more initials written together have included a space. Modern usage often omits the space. Use whatever is appropriate for your situation.

C. D. Scott	KR-FPLT/TK-FPLT/SKO*T	or	KR-FPLT/TK*FPLT/SKO*T
R. T. Wright	R-FPLT/T-FPLT/WRAOEUGT	or	R-FPLT/T*FPLT/WRAOEUGT
Alex B. Carter	AL/EBGS/PW-FPLT/KART/ER		

By combining the alphabets, you can write acronyms that contain both upper and lower case.

| Btu | PW-RBGS/T*BGZ/*UBGZ [PW-RBGS/T*U] | Ph.D. | P-RBGS/H*PLD/TK*FPLT [PAEUFPD] |
| Hz | H-RBGS/STK*BGZ | Rx | R-RBGS/KP*BGZ [R*BGS] |

Acronyms that are pronounced as a word may be written as individual letters or as the sounded word (as long as no conflict is created).

	Written as Letters	as a Word
AWOL	A-RBGS/W*RBGS/O*RBGS/HR*RBGS	AEU/WOL
ASCII	A-RBGS/S*RBGS/KR*RBGS/*EURBGS/*EURBGS	AS/KAOE
NASA	TPH-RBGS/A*RBGS/S*RBGS/A*RBGS	TPHAS/SA

Similarly, some of you have probably adopted briefs for some commonly used acronyms. This is fine as long as the brief causes no conflict.

Acronyms that are also words may be written as words (with proper capitalization requirements) or as individual letters.

	Written as Letters	as a Word
CARE	KR-RBGS/A*RBGS/R*RBGS/*ERBGS	K-PS/KAEUR/K-PS
NOW	TPH-RBGS/O*RBGS/W*RBGS	K-PS/TPHOU/K-PS
SAT	S-RBGS/A*RBGS/T*RBGS [SA*T] [S-RBGS/A*T]	K-PS/SAT/K-PS

The alphabets can be used in conjunction with other symbols.

AT&T	A-RBGS/T*RBGS/PH*PBD/T-RBGS	
Q&A	KW-RBGS/PH*PBD/ARBGS	(Q & A = KW-RBGS/PH-PBD/ARBGS)
d/b/a	TK*/SHR-RB/PW*/SHR-RB/A*	
n/a	TPH*/SHR-RB/A*	
d.t.'s	TK*PD/T*PLD/AOES [TKE/TAOEZ]	
EPA's	ERBGS/P*RBGS/A*RBGS/AOES	

Note: Because the the <u>s</u>lash (SHR-RB) and <u>a</u>mpersa<u>nd</u> (PH*PBD) should be prefix/suffix entries in your translation dictionary, use of the "attach to left" letters is optional.

STITCHING

Most CAT systems allow you to use "banks" when spelling out a proper name for the record. This is accomplished by stroking the identifying stitching bank recommended by your particular CAT system, then spelling the name. If the actual letter is on the keyboard, use it . If the letter does not occur on the keyboard, use a character combination to form it. Generally you will stroke the bank twice to end this spelling mode.

Thus, if you want the translation to be "M-A-R-T-I-N," you would write:

[CAT-SPECIFIC IDENTIFIER] /PH/A/R-/T-/EU/TPH-/[CAT-SPECIFIC IDENTIFIER/CAT-SPECIFIC IDENTIFIER]

If your CAT system does not have a stitching mode, you will have to create a stitching alphabet. Use the letters a through z on the initial side of the keyboard in combination with a non-conflicting letter combination on the right (e.g., ATSDZ, PW-TSDZ, KR-TSDZ, etc.). For other suggestions, see StenEd's *Volume I: Theory*.

STENOSCRIPTION COMMANDS
PUNCTUATION AND SYMBOLS

The more standard punctuation marks have already been covered in *Step 7: Punctuation*. Many of the more specialized punctuation and symbols are useful in realtime writing. They are repeated here for your convenience. Adopt any that will be useful to you.

Punctuation/Symbol	Sample Use	Outline
Ampersand (space before and after)	Q & A	PH-PBD
Ampersand (prefix/suffix)	Q&A	PH*PBD
Apostrophe (suffix)	writers'	AOE
Apostrophe + s (suffix)	writer's	AOES
Apostrophe Used for Omitted Years (prefix)	'97	AO*E
Asterisk (space before and after)	use * to	STR-BG
Asterisk (suffix)	Note 1* is	STR*BG
At Symbol (space before and after)	shirts @ $5	T-T
At Symbol (prefix/suffix)	jcr@aol	T*T
Backslash (prefix/suffix)	c:\wp51	PWHR-RB
Bracket, Opening (prefix)	[start	PWR-BG
Bracket, Closing (stop)(suffix)	stop]	PWR-BGS
Bullet	•	PWHRET
Cent(s) Symbol (suffix)	2¢	S-TS
Colon (suffix, one space following)	follows:	-FRPLT
Colon (suffix, two spaces following, cap next)	follows:	KHR-PB
Colon in Time (prefix/suffix)	5:30	KHR*PB
Comma (suffix)	stop,	-RBGS
Comma Used with Numbers (prefix/suffix)	1,000	-RBGZ
Comma + End Quotes (suffix)	,"	KW-RBGTS
Dash (prefix/suffix)	one—not two	TK-RB
Decimal Point (prefix/suffix)	2.1	P*PBT
Decimal Point (prefix)	.01	P-PBT
Degree Symbol (suffix)	32°	TK-RG
Division Symbol (space before and after)	4 ÷ 2	TKW-D
Dollar Sign (prefix)	$5	TKHR-R
Ellipsis (suffix, periods connected)	but...	HR-PS
Ellipsis (suffix, periods separated)	but. . .	HR-PZ
Equal Sign (space before and after)	a = b	KW-L
Equal Sign (prefix/suffix, used with List Files)	a=b	KW*L
Exclamation Point (suffix, two spaces, cap next)	stop!	STKPWHR-FPLT
Greater Than (space before and after)	2 > 1	TKPWR*PB
Hyphen (prefix/suffix)	ex-teacher	H-F
Hyphen (space before and after)	2 - 1	H-FS
Hyphen (suffix)	2- and	H*F
Less Than (space before and after)	1 < 2	HR*PB
Minus Sign (space before and after)	2 - 1	PH-PBS
Minus sign (prefix)	and -2	PH*PBS
Multiplication Symbol (times)(space before and after)	2 x 2	T-PLZ
Number Symbol (pound sign)(prefix)	#1	TPH-B
One-Half Symbol (suffix)	5$1/2$	HAFS
One-Quarter Symbol (suffix)	5$1/4$	KWARS
Parenthesis, Opening (prefix)	(start	STPH-FPLT
Parenthesis, Closing (suffix)	stop)	STPH-FPLD
Percent (suffix)	99%	P-BGT
Period (suffix, two spaces, cap next)	stop.	-FPLT
Period + End Quote (suffix, two spaces, cap next)	stop."	KW-FPLTS
Plus Sign (space before and after)	2 + 2	P-LS
Plus Sign (suffix)	2+	P*LS
Question Mark (suffix, two spaces, cap next)	stop?	STPH-
Quotation Mark, Beginning (prefix)	"start	KW-T
Quotation Mark, Ending (stop)(suffix)	stop"	KW-TS
Quotation Mark, Single, Beginning (prefix)	'start	SKW-T
Quotation Mark, Single, Ending (stop)(suffix)	stop'	SKW-TS
Semicolon (suffix)	stop;	-FRBGS
Slash (prefix/suffix)	1/2	SHR-RB
Tilde (no space before and after)	~	T*LD
Times (space before and after)	2 x 2	T-PLZ

The following commands are used in text entry applications. Stenoscription not only provides realtime translation features, but realtime editing capabilities as well—and all from the stenotype keyboard. You may or may not have a need for them at this time; however, they are included in this realtime text for the following two reasons. (Note: Not all commands are applicable to all stenoscription/CAT systems.)

1. Many reporting firms and freelancers are considering accepting text stenoscription jobs as an adjunct to their court reporting assignments.

2. Text entry software is becoming more popular for use in medical transcription and other steno-scription applications. In addition, some CAT companies are including various text entry features in their realtime CAT systems.

COMMANDS USED IN WORD PROCESSING

Alt [Alt] key	T-LT
Bold on/off (toggles)	PW*LD
Bold word at cursor	PW*LDZ
Cap (capitalize first character next word)	K-P
Cap (capitalize first character previous word)	K*P
Cap (cap first character each highlighted word)	K-FP
Cap/all caps/uncap highlighted word (toggle the case)	KR-P
Caps Lock on/off (cap all letters in word; repeat to cancel)	K-PS
Center Line	STPH-RL
Control [Ctrl] key	KR-RL
Dictionaries, access on line	TK*BGTS
Display Steno Notes	STPH*TS
Enter [Enter] key	SPW-R
Escape [Esc] key	SK-P
Exit, Save &	S-BGS
Exit, Quit & (don't save)	KW-BGS
Find (Text)	TP*PBD
Find Again (Repeat)	R*PT
Find Next Untranslate	TP*UPBT
Find Outline	TPO*UT
Find Stroke	TPO*EBG
Global, open window to create auxiliary	TKPWHR*BGS
Global, open window to create job	TKPWHR*PBLG
Global, open window to create main	TKPWHR*PL
Globals, access online	TKPWHR*BLS
Italics on/off (toggles)	THR-BGS
Italicize word at cursor	THR-BGSZ
Join current word to next word stroked	SKWR-PB
Join two previous words	SKWR*PB
New Line (flush left, no cap)	TPH*L
New Page (hard page)	TPH-P
Paragraph (period, new line, indent, cap next)	P-F
Paragraph (period, new line, flush left, cap next)	P*F
Print Menu, display	PR-PL
Quit & Exit (don't save changes)	KW-BGS
Retrieve	TR*F
Save & Exit	S-BGS
Save & Resume	S*F
Save & Resume (Word)	S*FD

 Step 10—Special Considerations

Save & Resume (WordPerfect) -- S*FPD
Shift [Shift] key ---SH-FT
Spacebar (forces a space before next word translates)------------ SP-S
Spacebar (used with numbers/letters in some systems)---------- SP-Z
Spell Check/Speller ---SP-L
Stitch Current Entry --ST-FP
Stitch Previous Entry ---ST*FP
Tab (cap next)---T*B
Tab (no cap next)---T-B
Underline on/off (toggles) ---TPH-RL
Underline Previous Word --TPH-RLD
Underline Word at cursor ---TPH-RLZ
Undo last function --AO*PS
Undo last stroke--* (asterisk key)

MOVEMENT COMMANDS
(Most require initial STKPWHR- plus direction)

Beginning of Document/Text ------------------------ STKPWHR-BD
Beginning of Text/Document ----------------------- STKPWHR-BT
Beginning of Line /Right Screen -------------------- STKPWHR-BL
End of Document/Text -------------------------------- STKPWHRED
End of Text/Document -------------------------------- STKPWHRET
End of Line/Right Screen ---------------------------- STKPWHREL
Left by Character (←) ------------------------------- STKPWHR-L
Left by Word ([Ctrl]←) ----------------------------- STKPWHR-LD
Left Screen/Beginning of Line ---------------------- STKPWHR-LS
Right by Character (→) ----------------------------- STKPWHR-R
Right by Word ([Ctrl]→) ---------------------------- STKPWHR-RD
Right Screen/End of Line --------------------------- STKPWHR-RS
Up by Line (↑) ------------------------------------- STKPWHRU
Up by Page [PgUp] --------------------------------- STKPWHRUP
Up by Screen -------------------------------------- STKPWHRUS
Down by Line (↓) ---------------------------------- STKPWHR-D
Down by Page [PgDn] ------------------------------ STKPWHR-PD
Down by Screen ------------------------------------ STKPWHR-DZ
Go To (page number) ------------------------------- TKPW-T

DELETE COMMANDS
(Most require initial DL- (TKHR-) plus direction)

Backspace (delete previous character or space)- PW-S
Delete character at cursor [Delete] ---------------- TKHR-
Delete Stroke Just Written -------------------------- * (asterisk key)
Delete Word to Left (previous word) -------------- TKHR-LD
Delete Word to Right (current word) -------------- TKHR-RD
Delete Remainder of Line from Cursor ----------- TKHR-RL
Delete Line -- TKHR-L
Delete Remainder of Page from Cursor ----------- TKHR-RP

The exercises that follow give **practice material for the techniques covered in this step that are, or could be, applicable to reporting and captioning**. Practice those exercises which are applicable to your situation(s).

Exercises on the categories covered in this step follow:

- Capitalization
- Compound Words
- Homographs
- Spelling Alphabets
- Text Entry Commands

 Step 10—Special Considerations

STEP 10—EXERCISES
SPECIAL CONSIDERATIONS

CAPITALIZATION
Ex. RT-101 (Tape 7/B @ 125 wpm) & RT-101 (Tape 7/B @ 180 wpm)

1. Is <u>Jim</u> still working out at the <u>gym</u>?

2. To fix the flat, <u>Jack</u> had to <u>jack</u> up the car.

3. The <u>Court</u> will recall the <u>jury</u> after recess.

4. Was <u>Jan</u> born on <u>January</u> 21, 1977 or 1978?

5. My <u>dad</u> said <u>Mom</u> was called for <u>jury</u> duty.

6. Has <u>Bill</u> paid the <u>March</u> electricity <u>bill</u> yet?

7. Do you think <u>Dad</u> will be better by <u>March</u>, <u>Doctor</u>?

8. Will you call that witness this afternoon, <u>Counsel</u>?

9. The <u>doctor</u> thinks <u>Mae</u> <u>may</u> be entirely cured by <u>May</u>.

10. The <u>House</u> and <u>Senate</u> will reconvene in early October.

11. They <u>forded</u> the stream in their trusty 1988 <u>Ford</u> Bronco.

12. My <u>house</u> is on the corner of 3rd <u>Avenue</u> and 22nd <u>Street</u>.

13. The senior <u>senator</u> from Florida is <u>Senator</u> <u>Bob</u> Graham.

14. The <u>Honorable</u> <u>Jim</u> Hayes will be presiding in <u>court</u> today.

15. Is that <u>Defendant's</u> or <u>Government's</u> <u>Exhibit</u> 1 you have in your hand?

16. She has been a <u>congresswoman</u> longer than <u>Congresswoman</u> Schroeder.

17. Every weekend, <u>Mike</u> takes the <u>mike</u> and acts as the <u>MC</u> at the local club.

18. I urge you to write to your <u>congressman</u> about this horrible <u>state</u> of affairs.

19. Environmentalists hope that <u>Vice President</u> <u>Gore</u> will make a difference.

20. How long has <u>Jan</u> been an environmental engineer for the <u>State</u> of Florida?

21. Have you seen the beautiful <u>china</u> <u>Mark</u> and <u>Sue</u> bought on their visit to <u>China</u>?

22. Was ex-<u>President</u> <u>Ford</u> pleased with the 1992 <u>presidential</u> election results?

23. Some <u>governors</u> opposed the ruling, but <u>Governor</u> <u>Ray</u> <u>Scott</u> was in favor of it.

24. The Putnam <u>County</u> <u>Courthouse</u> is, as you would expect, located in the <u>county</u> seat.

25. You can <u>mark</u> my words, that type of behavior will irreparably <u>mar</u> your reputation.

26. Most members of the Clinton <u>Administration</u> are concerned about the <u>federal</u> deficit.

27. The <u>Court</u> ruled that, since the <u>march</u> was peaceful, the complaint would be dismissed.

28. <u>NOW COMES</u> Plaintiffs <u>May</u> and <u>John</u> Hudson, by and through their attorney, <u>Bob</u> S. Heflin.

29. Tomorrow, <u>Pat</u> and <u>Frank</u> are going to the <u>courthouse</u> to see if they can <u>sue</u> the <u>city</u> for negligence.

30. The brochure distributed by the <u>League</u> of <u>Women</u> <u>Voters</u> gave information on the candidates running for <u>president</u>, <u>vice president</u>, and <u>congress</u>.

COMPOUND WORDS
PART 1
Ex. RT-102 (Tape 7/B @ 125 wpm) & RT-102 (Tape 7/B @ 180 wpm)

1. My backache is gone, but my head aches now.

2. The cutback at work has forced me to cut back on my entertaining.

3. I hope my car doesn't break down again, or I might have a nervous breakdown.

4. Did you see the show down the road, "Showdown at Sunset Corral"?

5. She should act more businesslike if she expects a business like hers to succeed.

6. He was able to finish his work and kick off his shoes just in time to watch the opening kickoff.

7. This show is such a turnoff that I'm going to turn off the TV.

8. He said he would print out a printout of the transcript during lunch.

9. If you carry out the trash, I'll run down to the corner and pick up some carryout Chinese food.

10. I back up my files every day. In fact, I make a backup of some files twice a day.

11. He wanted to borrow my pickup truck to pick up some lumber.

12. As he walked toward the exit, the attendant asked him to proceed to Ward B.

13. She couldn't find any way to come up with the down payment anyway.

14. His daydreaming caused him to drive way past the driveway.

15. We decided to get away and spend some time at our quaint little mountain getaway.

16. The runaway had run away from home two times before.

17. He was sure he was right, but other wise people felt otherwise.

18. Were you at home working on your homework last night?

19. Because she missed her exit, she had to turn around on the turnaround.

20. The rainfall was so soothing that I closed my book and just listened to the rain fall.

21. He was downright rude when she politely asked him to put it down right there.

22. Once I finish this apple turnover, I'm going to turn over a new leaf and stop eating desserts.

23. Once she completed Step 5 in her real-time textbook, she felt ready to begin doing realtime at work.

24. He would have been able to start up his new company earlier if the start-up costs had not been so high.

25. If he had had his head on straight, he probably wouldn't have been involved in that head-on collision.

26. These built-in bookcases were built in 1989.

27. You might not have as much computer know-how as she, but you know how to write these sentences correctly.

28. Only a show-off like her would show off her expensive jewelry at the charity ball for the homeless.

 Step 10—Special Considerations

COMPOUND WORDS
PART 2
Ex. RT-103 (Tape 7/B @ 125 wpm) & RT-103 (Tape 7/B @ 180 wpm)

George Smith sat down to await the arrival of his brother, Harold, who had been away studying in Paris. He had been gone for five years or thereabout. However, he had kept in touch with George through letters and was thereupon informed of all the happenings in Cedar Creek, his hometown.

As a blackbird sang in a tree outside the living room window, George saw Harold get out of a taxi and walk toward the door. He was a handsome man, and George would never forget the winsome smile that lighted his brother's face as he opened the door and stepped inside. Even though the house was in a run-down state, it was home to Harold and thereby looked wonderful. Whereas the house had hereto seemed gray and dingy to George, he now saw it as a shiny castle through Harold's eyes. He was filled with a wonder similar to that which spacemen must feel during liftoff on a moon flight.

To Harold, each familiar object in the house was a source of amazement. Therein lived all of his childhood memories. As he moved from room to room, touching this ashtray, picking up that book, he relived many pleasant moments from the past.

Resting his hand on the hardwood banister, he remembered how he and George used to slide merrily down its gleaming, if scratched, surface, feeling very brave and adventurous.

His football helmet, carelessly tossed years earlier on top of a battered suitcase in the corner of his bedroom, reminded him of the day of team tryouts when he was overjoyed to win a position on the third string team. Likewise, a deflated basketball and a splintered baseball bat brought to mind other athletic triumphs.

Moreover, a small wooden horse in a cupboard recalled the time when the plant where his father worked had experienced a massive layoff, and the boys' father, out of work, had earned extra money by selling handmade figurines which he carved at home throughout the time he was unemployed. For many years thereafter, he had carved figures in his spare time to sell at Christmas. Children especially loved them.

Looking out across the backyard, Harold spied his lonesome, dilapidated tree house high in the old elm tree. It had been his favorite boyhood haunt, and he had spent many warm summertime days lazily dreaming of future success and glory. He was sure one day he would be the first person from his neighborhood to become President of the United States.

Strolling into the greenhouse, Harold noted that the setup of plants had not changed in any way whatsoever. Whichever way he turned, he was surrounded by the scent of his favorite flowers and foliage. Whenever he had smelled the fragrance of roses while abroad, he was thereby reminded of home. He could still see his grandfather working in the greenhouse, watering and spraying his prize-winning blossoms. Whoever would have thought that the scent of flowers could make one so nostalgic?

Seeing his home through his brother's eyes, George was therefore able to appreciate that which he had grown accustomed to over the long years of residence. It seems that only by being away in unfamiliar surroundings can one truly relish the pleasure of coming home.

HOMOGRAPHS

Ex. RT-104 (Tape 7/B @ 125 wpm) & RT-104 (Tape 7/B @ 180 wpm)

abuse
1. The prisoner was told not to <u>abuse</u> the privilege of being allowed to see his wife.
2. The man's <u>abuse</u> of the dog frightened the boy, and he called the police.

bass
3. The large <u>bass</u> on John's line fought to escape.
4. Mr. Smith sings <u>bass</u> in the barbershop quartet.

bow
5. The archer's <u>bow</u> was broken during the contest, but luckily he had another.
6. We were told to <u>bow</u> in the presence of the king and queen.

can
7. Grandmother filled the <u>can</u> with homemade cookies which soon disappeared.
8. In the summer, we <u>can</u> <u>can</u> vegetables from the garden.

close
9. The race was <u>close</u>, but my candidate won.
10. If you <u>close</u> all the windows, it will feel too <u>close</u> in here.

conduct
11. His <u>conduct</u> was deplorable.
12. He must learn to <u>conduct</u> himself in a more mannerly fashion.

dove
13. The <u>dove</u> soaring high above the clouds was a sign of peace.
14. The Indian <u>dove</u> gracefully off the high cliff into the sparkling water below.

lead
15. Harry was given the <u>lead</u> in the class play, but he refused to participate.
16. She was asked to <u>lead</u> the way to the campground, but she got lost.
17. Would you like some pencil <u>lead</u>?

live
18. Ruth and Marilyn, my two best friends, <u>live</u> in my neighborhood.
19. The gun contained <u>live</u> ammunition and went off accidentally.

minute
20. Not more than a <u>minute</u> had passed, but to the girl it seemed like hours.
21. The <u>minute</u> speck of dust in his eye caused him great pain.

misuse
22. The new toy had been damaged by the boy's <u>misuse</u> of it.
23. If you <u>misuse</u> the book, it will be ruined.

perfect
24. If I can <u>perfect</u> this last detail, the entire job will be <u>perfect</u>.

polish
25. He spoke <u>Polish</u> fluently because of the many years he had spent in Poland.
26. The maid was told to <u>polish</u> the table until it shone.

refuse
27. The <u>refuse</u> was taken away by the trash collector.
28. If you <u>refuse</u> the invitation, you will not be invited again.

resume
29. He submitted his <u>resume</u> along with his job application.
30. He will <u>resume</u> his talk as soon as the audience becomes quiet.

use
31. What's the <u>use</u> of buying it if you won't <u>use</u> it?
32. She <u>used</u> to <u>use</u> that day-care center, but she doesn't <u>use</u> it any more.

will
33. The man's <u>will</u> left all his money to his wife and children.
34. I <u>will</u> go to the hospital if the doctor feels it is necessary.

wind
35. The <u>wind</u> blew the tree down, and it fell on the house.
36. <u>Wind</u> the yarn into a ball, or it will become tangled.

wound
37. The <u>wound</u> he received in battle was serious and required surgery.
38. Joe <u>wound</u> the rope around the tree, preventing the horse from escaping.

 Step 10—Special Considerations

SPELLING ALPHABETS

Ex. RT-105 (Tape 8/A @ 125 wpm) & RT-105 (Tape 8/A @ 180 wpm)

Some acronyms in the following sentences can be written with or without periods. Use whatever format is appropriate for your situation. Similarly, plurals and other inflected forms of acronyms may be formed by adding the inflected ending with or without an apostrophe (e.g., VIPs or VIP's). Use whichever usage is standard for your situation.

1. She passed her 180 <u>wpm</u> take with ease, but she stumbled on the 200 <u>wpm</u> Jury Charge.

2. Fortunately, he was only traveling at 30 <u>mph</u> at the time of impact.

3. If you don't learn your <u>abc's</u>, you'll never amount to anything.

4. In addition to being a member of <u>NCRA</u> and <u>FCRA</u>, she has passed the <u>CSR</u>, <u>RPR</u>, and <u>CM</u> exams.

5. The headquarters for both the <u>CIA</u> and the <u>FBI</u> are located in or near Washington, <u>D.C.</u>, the capital of the <u>USA</u>.

6. I'll write you an <u>i.o.u.</u> for the <u>c.o.d.</u> package you picked up for me this morning.

7. The package was shipped <u>f.o.b.</u> <u>N.Y.C.</u>

8. If the <u>I.R.S.</u> audits us, our <u>C.P.A.</u> assures us there will be no problem.

9. We were quite saddened when we learned that the daughter of a friend of ours had <u>OD'ed</u> on <u>LSD</u>.

10. Claiming to be blessed with <u>ESP</u>, the <u>M.D.</u> insisted that I would be better by tomorrow.

11. The <u>MO's</u> of both crimes were almost identical.

12. The plane's <u>ETA</u> is 5:50 p.m. <u>EST</u>.

13. I had never seen so many <u>VIP's</u> at one time.

14. The headquarters of most governmental agencies such as the <u>DOD</u>, Department of Defense; the <u>DOE</u>, Department of Energy; the <u>DOJ</u>, Department of Justice; <u>DOT</u>, Department of Transportation; the <u>EPA</u>, Environmental Protection Agency; the <u>FCC</u>, Federal Communications Commission; the <u>FTC</u>, Federal Trade Commission; the <u>HHS</u>, Health and Human Services; the <u>ICC</u>, Interstate Commerce Commission; and <u>OMB</u>, the Office of Management and Budget are located within the city limits of Washington, <u>D.C.</u>

15. Before moving west and joining the <u>LAPD</u>, he was an officer with the <u>NYPD</u> for nine years.

16. Though he insisted he was not <u>AWOL</u>, he could not find his pass.

17. Now that I have an <u>IBM</u> compatible, it's easy to make <u>ASCII</u> files for my clients.

18. One of the accident victims was <u>DOA</u>, but the other one, who was later identified as Mr. <u>D. S.</u> Roberts, was barely injured.

19. <u>R. S.</u> Scott, with the aid of <u>J. M.</u> Williams and <u>R. E.</u> Davis, will give the presentation.

20. According to the program, <u>M. S.</u> Carter, <u>P. J.</u> Simpson, and William <u>O.</u> Morris will be on the panel.

21. <u>J. D.</u> Anton will receive his <u>Ph.D.</u> from <u>FSU</u> later this month.

22. Ms. <u>R. T.</u> Simmons will be giving the realtime demonstration.

STENOSCRIPTION COMMANDS

Ex. RT-106 (Tape 8/A @ 100 wpm) & RT-106 (Tape 8/A @ 160 wpm)

The sentences that follow give practice material for those text entry outlines that could conceivably be useful in reporting and captioning. If you have no use for a particular symbol, just skip that sentence.

1. The Q&A on the AT&T case was grueling.

2. In the 1980's, it was reported that 2,242,602 government employees had the authority to classify documents as secret.

3. The costs are as follows: 1 candy bar @ 40¢ each or 3 for $1; a small bag of popcorn @ 75¢, a large bag @ $1.25; and a small soda @ 80¢, a jumbo soda for $1.50.

4. The asterisk (*) has historically been an underused key on the stenotype machine.

5. To change directories, type cd\ at the C prompt. (E.g., to change to the directory that is named "steno," type cd\steno [C: cd\steno] and hit ENTER.)

6. The average change in a woman's standard of living in the year after a divorce has been reported to be -73%.

7. At 1:30 a.m. last night, her temperature was 101.2° F.

8. $20 \div 5 = 4$, $4 \times 4 = 16$. $20 > 16$, therefore, $4 \times 4 < 20 \div 5$.

9. Did you get the last sentence right? I got it!

10. Item #4 clarifies that by stating, "a notary public and/or an officer of the court."

11. The cost of the Vietnam War in 1983 dollars was $430.2 billion; cost of the American Civil War was $36.9 billion.

12. Only .01% of all life forms known to have ever existed exist today.

13. The number of pounds of hazardous waste generated per capita in the United States in 1950: 4.6; in 1987: 2,600.

14. In the late 1980's, Japanese teenagers spent 59 hours per week in class or studying; Soviet teenagers, 51.5 hours; American teenagers, 38 hours.

15. In court work, a dash (—) often appears at the end of an incomplete thought or sentence; in literary work, an ellipsis (. . .) may be used to show incompleteness.

16. He's so good in sales that he has been known to convince some people that $2 + 2 = 5$ or that $2 - 2 = 1$.

17. In the last 3.5 million years, the heat of the sun has increased 25%.

18. The temperature got down to -5° C last night.

19. My 12- and 14-year-old daughters are beginning to want more freedom.

20. In the late 1980's, one-third of the U.S. landmass was owned by the federal government.

21. The longest recorded flight by a chicken is 302' 8".

22. The percentage change, between 1965 and 1987, in the number of young married couples without children was +82.

23. "Unless the economy begins to improve," she commented, "the 'have-nots' will begin to outnumber the 'haves.'"

24. The portion of American households that were made up of a single person in 1955: 1/10; 1987: 1/4.

APPENDIX

BEYOND WORDS

CLEAN WRITING

As mentioned in the introduction to this text, the three most important elements for realtime writing are summarized as following the three C's.

1. **Clean**

2. **Consistent**

3. **Conflict Free**

Steps 1 through 10 have presented consistent, conflict-free techniques for avoiding all conflicts. The third ingredient, clean notes, consists of eliminating shadows and drops as much as humanly possible.

SHADOWS & DROPS

The most common result of shadowing or of dropping a letter is creating a word that the computer can't translate. The biggest danger of shadowing, however, is creating a mistranslation. For example, if you shadow an -L in "cut" (KUT), you are creating—and the computer will translate—the word "cult" (KULT).

Word list and narrative practice is given for the letters (and letter sequences) most often shadowed. If you have additional shadows or drops, it is suggested that you make up your own list of the type(s) of word you are most likely to misstroke.

The following word lists include the letter sequences which most often cause shadows. The letters most often shadowed are underlined in the subheading.

-ND ENDINGS
-PBD_Z_ & -PB_L_D
Ex. RT-107 (Tape 8/A @60 wpm) & RT-107 (Tape 8/A @75 wpm)

band	reprimand	comprehend	pretend	find	pound
bland	sand	condescend	recommend	inclined	round
brand	stand	contend	reprehend	kind	sound
command	strand	defend	send	mind	surround
contraband	withstand	depend	spend	refined	wound
countermand		descend	suspend	wind	
demand	amend	distend	tend		abscond
disband	append	dividend	trend	bound	beyond
expand	apprehend	end	transcend	compound	blond
gland	ascend	expend	unbend	confound	bond
grand	attend	friend		expound	diamond
hand	bend	lend	behind	found	pond
land	blend	mend	bind	ground	respond
manned	commend	offend	blind	mound	

-NT ENDINGS
-PBT<u>S</u> & -PB<u>LT</u>
Ex. RT-108 (Tape 8/A @60 wpm) & RT-108 (Tape 8/A @75 wpm)

ant
aunt
chant
enchant
grant
pant
plant
scant
slant
supplant
transplant

accent
augment
belligerent
benevolent
bent
cement
cent
comment
compliment
condiment
confident
confluent
consent
consequent
content

continent
corpulent
dent
detriment
different
diffident
diligent
dissent
dissident
document
element
eloquent
embodiment
eminent
establishment
event
evident
excellent
experiment
extent
ferment
fraudulent
frequent
imminent
impenitent
impertinent
implement

impotent
improvident
impudent
incident
increment
indent
indigent
indolent
innocent
insolent
instrument
intelligent
irreverent
invent
lament
lenient
negligent
meant
occident
opulent
orient
parliament
portent
precedent
predicament
prevalent
prevent

provident
regiment
rent
resent
resident
reticent
reverent
rudiment
scent
sediment
sentiment
spent
subservient
succulent
supplement
temperament
tenement
tent
torment
truculent
turbulent
vehement
vent
violent
virulent
went

flint
glint
hint
imprint
lint
mint
peppermint
print
splint
sprint
squint
stint
tint

account
amount
count
discount
dismount
fount
miscount
mount
paramount
surmount
tantamount

(vowel) + F or V
-F<u>L</u> & -F<u>R</u>
Ex. RT-109 (Tape 8/A @60 wpm) & RT-109 (Tape 8/A @75 wpm)

accumulative
accusative
active
administrative
affirmative
alternative
appreciative
captive
combative
commemorative
communicative
comparative
conceive
consecutive
conservative
correlative
cursive
declarative

decorative
definitive
diminutive
engrave
executive
expletive
figurative
forgive
formative
fugitive
furtive
give
glove
have
imaginative
imperative
indicative
informative

inquisitive
insensitive
leave
live
lucrative
massive
motive
narrative
native
negative
of
operative
passive
pensive
prerogative
primitive
prohibitive
provocative

punitive
quantitative
regenerative
relieve
remunerative
restive
sedative
sensitive
sieve
speculative
stove
substantive
talkative
tentative
transitive

(vowel) + T
-<u>L</u>T & -T<u>D</u>
Ex. RT-110 (Tape 8/A @60 wpm) & RT-110 (Tape 8/A @75 wpm)

at	bait	abet	fit	height	knot
bat	calculate	bet	flit	ignite	lot
brat	circulate	cadet	kit	invite	not
cat	concentrate	debt	knit	kite	patriot
chat	date	duet	misfit	night	plot
combat	debate	forget	omit	plight	pot
cravat	elate	fret	quit	quite	rot
fat	fate	get	remit	smite	shot
flat	hate	inset	sit	tight	slot
gnat	indicate	jet	skit	white	trot
hat	inmate	let	slit		yacht
mat	irate	met	spit	allot	
pat	irritate	net	split	apricot	butt
rat	litigate	pet	wit	blot	cut
sat	locate	sweat		boycott	halibut
scat	mandate	threat	bite	camelot	hut
slat	migrate	wet	blight	clot	jut
vat	narrate	yet	contrite	cot	nut
	ornate		daylight	dot	peanut
abdicate	plate	admit	delight	got	rut
advocate	stipulate	befit	excite	hot	shut
agitate		bit	expedite	idiot	slut
ate		chit	fight	jot	

(vowel) + S
-S<u>Z</u> & -<u>G</u>S & -<u>L</u>S
Ex. RT-111 (Tape 8/A @60 wpm) & RT-111 (Tape 8/A @75 wpm)

advertise	eulogize	revise	copyist	optimist
advise	exercise	rise	cyst	pacifist
agonize	fanaticize	sacrifice	dentist	pathologist
analyze	fertilize	scrutinize	desist	persist
apologize	formalize	size	dogmatist	pessimist
appetize	guise	socialize	dramatist	physicist
arise	humanize	specialize	egotist	protagonist
authorize	hypnotize	summarize	enlist	psychologist
baptize	idealize	supervise	evangelist	purist
capitalize	idolize	surmise	extremist	rationalist
capsize	improvise	surprise	fatalist	realist
characterize	incise	sympathize	federalist	resist
chastise	jeopardize	tranquilize	fist	scientist
civilize	journalize	vocalize	florist	socialist
colonize	legalize	wise	humorist	soloist
compromise	localize		hypnotist	specialist
criticize	magnetize	antagonist	idealist	stylist
crystallize	materialize	apologist	journalist	terrorist
decentralize	memorize	artist	jurist	theorist
demobilize	modernize	bigamist	linguist	twist
despise	moralize	biologist	list	unionist
disguise	naturalize	capitalist	mist	vocalist
dramatize	paralyze	chemist	motorist	wrist
economize	penalize	colonist	nationalist	
emphasize	polarize	columnist	naturalist	
enterprise	prize	conformist	novelist	
epitomize	realize	consist	oculist	

(vowel) + D

-TD

Ex. RT-112 (Tape 8/A @60 wpm) & RT-112 (Tape 8/A @75 wpm)

bad	dread	grade	pad	shade
bed	dud	greed	paid	shed
bled	dude	head	plead	skid
bleed	fad	heed	pled	slid
blood	fade	hid	premed	slide
broad	feed	hide	prod	sped
cloud	feud	hood	proud	speed
cod	flood	kid	putrid	spread
code	fluid	lid	rabid	squad
crud	food	loud	raid	stood
crude	fraud	mad	rid	tweed
dad	glad	mod	ride	void
dead	good	mood	sad	wed
deed	grad	mud	seed	weed

SPW- & SW-

STPW & SKW-

Ex. RT-113 (Tape 8/A @60 wpm) & RT-113 (Tape 8/A @75 wpm)

entail	entomb	integrate	intern	sweep
entangle	entrain	integrity	internal	sweet
enter	entrance	intellectual	interpret	swell
enterprise	entrap	intelligent	intricate	swept
entertain	entreat	intemperate	intrigue	swerve
enthrall	entrench	intend	swagger	swift
enthrone	entropy	intense	swallow	swill
enthuse	entrust	intensify	swam	swim
enthusiasm	entry	intensive	swank	swindle
entice	intact	intent	swap	swipe
entire	intake	intercede	swarm	switch
entirely	intangible	interchange	swat	swollen
entitle	integer	interconnect	swear	swore
entity	integral	interfere	sweaty	sworn

SP-

STP

Ex. RT-114 (Tape 8/B @60 wpm) & RT-114 (Tape 8/B @75 wpm)

space	speak	sphinx	splendid	spot
spacious	spear	spice	splint	spotless
Spain	special	spicy	splinter	sprain
span	specialist	spider	split	spread
spank	specific	spigot	splotchy	spree
spar	speck	spin	spoil	spring
spare	spectator	spine	spoke	sprinkle
spark	speculate	spire	spoken	sprite
sparkle	sped	spirit	sponge	sprout
sparse	speech	spit	sponsor	spruce
spasm	speed	spite	spoof	spun
spastic	spell	spiteful	spoon	spunk
spat	spend	splash	sporadic	sputter
spatula	sphere	splatter	sport	spy

Appendix

T + (vowel)
Ex. RT-115 (Tape 8/B @60) & RT-115 (Tape 8/B @75)

(Shown with words which could result if first word is shadowed)

T-	TP-	TK-	ST-
tab	fab	dab	stab
table	fable		stable
tail	fail	Dale	stale
take	fake		stake
tame	fame	dame	
tan	fan	Dan	Stan
tear	fare	dare	stare
team		deem	steam
tear	fear	dear	steer
tend	fend		extend
tense	fence	dense	
tent		dent	extent
tick		Dick	stick
tie	fie	die	sty
tile	file	dial	style
till	fill	dill	still
tin	fin	din	
tire	fire	dire	
toe	foe	doe	stow
told	fold		stoled
toll	foal	dole	stole
tone	phone		stone
tool	fool		stool
tore	fore	door	store
town	found	down	
trade	frayed		strayed
train		drain	strain
trait	freight		strait
tried	fried	dried	stride
try	fry	dry	

H + (vowel)
Ex. RT-116 (Tape 8/B @60) & RT-116 (Tape 8/B @75)

(Shown with words which could result if first word is shadowed)

H-	HR-	PH-
hack	lack	mack
had	lad	mad
hag	lag	mag
hair	lair	mare
ham	lam(b)	ma'am
hand	land	manned
hard	lard	marred
hark	lark	mark
hash	lash	mash
hatch	latch	match
hate	late	mate
here	leer	mere
hedge	ledge	
height	light	might
hen	Len	men
hill	Lil	mill
hint	lint	mint
hip	lip	
hire	liar	mire
hiss	list	miss
hock	lock	mock
hog	log	
horn	lorn	morn
host	lost	most
hot	lot	
house	louse	mouse
hug	lug	mug
hump	lump	mump
hunch	lunch	munch
hush	lush	mush

NOTE: Most of these groups of words are potential conflicts because of shadows only (e.g., hate/late/mate). Others will only conflict if you shadow <u>and</u> you don't write certain types of words definitively (e.g., hiss/list/miss).

-L SHADOW

Each week a thousand men and women are killed in auto accidents in this country. Despite recent design changes to prevent unsafe cars, there has not been the hoped-for great reduction in the death rate.

One of the problems is the lack of interest shown by the public in using the safety devices found in most cars. There are just too many motorists who don't wear lap and shoulder belts. They say they don't find them comfortable or forget to use them. Statistics have shown that death is much less likely and injuries much less severe in an accident where the people wore such restraints.

This is not to say that safety devices can eliminate accidents and death. It is only a starting point. More important yet is to get the negligent and unsafe driver off the streets. This calls for a hard look at our laws and law enforcement.

There are many people driving who are incompetent and who drive under the influence of sedatives and alcohol. Laws are needed which, when passed, will allow police officers to get convictions allowing them to confiscate such people's permits and license plates to prevent them from killing either themselves or others on the highway.

The rise in the death rate has become serious enough that such a course is perhaps the only means by which the current highway violence may be ended.

Worldwide television is now a fact of life. As yet, the extent of its use has not been that great, but this will not be the case in the not-too-distant future. As more ground stations are set up to transmit signals across space to satellites, there will be a rise in international broadcasting.

Soon a man on the farmlands of Kansas may be able to watch shows from Great Britain. A New Yorker may be able to see a romance in Mandarin. Students may be able to hear a lecture live from France.

There are some problems which remain to be solved, of course. Some countries are upset that their people may see shows which are a threat to their society. This is true in those lands where personal liberty is least emphasized and where dogmatists fear the light of new concepts. It may be that such countries will never participate.

There is also some criticism about the possible use of around-the-world television as a start towards world government. This has aroused some ardent nationalists.

Despite these opponents, we can soon expect some form of television relayed from the expanse of space to become a frequent part of our lives.

-S SHADOW

Ex. RT-119 (Tape 8/B @125) &
RT-119 (Tape 8/B @180)

It was late and the night sky was sparkling with millions of tiny points of light as the little craft took off from the airport. Its red and yellow wing lights winked on and off as the pilot pushed to gain altitude above the trees. To most eyes, this would seem like any other flight, but this was a very urgent one. The pilot was being sent on a vital mission to save a life.

A little infant in a distant town had been stricken by violent illness which threatened permanent disability or death. The child was waging a valiant struggle, but only a shot of a new serum could save her. It was the task of the pilot to fly this life-saving substance to her.

As the aircraft continued to lift itself skyward, many thoughts raced through the pilot's mind. He thought of how important this flight was to the parents of the little infant and how much it meant to the people of that distant town to have him volunteer to attempt to reach the infant in time.

As the hours raced past, the pilot's hope grew. He felt he would make it on time and that permanent harm could be prevented. It was with a great sigh of relief and delight that he looked down on the dim lights of the small landing strip on the ridge and the bright red light of the ambulance that would take the precious fluid to the innocent infant.

-Z SHADOW

Ex. RT-120 (Tape 8/B @125) &
RT-120 (Tape 8/B @180)

The wind came over the rise, blowing a steady stream of sand toward the little cluster of tents huddled near the oasis. The oasis was the only place of refuge in this land of desolation and decay. Several generations of hot wind from the east and an even hotter sun had baked the surrounding ground for miles around. It was to this oasis that the caravans came on their long treks across the desert toward the far cities of the trade routes.

There was a little pond in the center of the oasis from which the camels could drink and where the traders could seek respite from the blinding sun and wind. The oasis seemed to almost be suspended in time. It had been there as long as the traders could remember, offering a kind and welcome haven for travelers across the mounds of sand.

Now a band of men sat around a slowly fading fire, watching their camels munch the tender ends of some grasses which grew around the edge of the little pond. These men had journeyed a great distance and had still farther to go. To them this little strand of green and blue was a heaven-sent gift which made their whole journey possible and which would enable them to trade for the fine spices, diamonds, and gold which waited at the end of the trip.

-R SHADOW

PART 1
Ex. RT-121 (Tape 8/B @125) &
RT-121 (Tape 8/B @180)

The government often sets off speculation about motives when some of its staff members speak and act without sufficient thought. There are some who are not believers in the honesty of professional bureaucrats anyway, and they see such conduct as proving the point.

An example of this was given the other day when a minor official got his figures mixed up when giving the profit picture in some sector of the economy. Because of his error, the stock market briefly dropped five points. When it came out that some friend of the man's boss had made a quick profit because of this, there was a swift reaction about unlawful acts involving the government. In this case, as the evidence proved, there was no offense though all involved were on the receiving end of a rather graphic reprimand.

There have been, of course, cases of proven misconduct in office. We have ourselves seen a few such cases in recent times. But it may be going too far to say, if we catch a few men reaching into the till, that everyone is.

Most politicians are honest enough, possibly more so than much of the public gives them credit for. Perhaps the critics of the government ought to be a little more reasonable.

PART 2
Ex. RT-122 (Tape 8/B @125 wpm) &
RT-122 (Tape 8/B @180 wpm)

Athletes tend to be aggressive people with a positive self-image which enables them to catch a ball a little better, to reach a little higher, or to drive themselves a little harder. Unfortunately, some athletes have been given the label of being dumb. It is felt that strong men and women often lack cognitive skills.

This image is not true. Many athletes have been intelligent and articulate professional people when they pursued careers off the playing field. They have proven to be more than just gorillas striving to develop abdominal muscles by lifting 500 pounds.

Being an athlete calls for the development of the mind as well. One must incessantly learn new techniques. One must condition the mind to endure excessive pain and rough action in the swift events of a contest.

Athletes must be believers in themselves and in their skills. This calls for as much investment of time and concentration as in the classroom. Athletes learn to be sharp enough to outthink their rivals, and all their instinctive abilities are involved. Matching wits in a game is often as much a challenge as resolving a math problem.

These cognitive skills are carried on in life. There is evidence for this given by the many ex-athletes who are active in many sophisticated fields.

 Appendix

-P SHADOW

Ex. RT-123 (Tape 8/B @125) &
RT-123 (Tape 8/B @180)

It was just one of those little states, remote from most of the civilized world, where life has been unchanged for 500 years or more. Most of the people lived by cultivating the land or by pursuing simple cottage industry. Here one could see fields where men drive oxen rather than a tractor and where primitive pottery is still used for cooking and storing.

It is to this land that the diminutive doctor had come to strive to curb the disease and unsanitary conditions which were rife across the country. He had set up his tiny clinic under a grove of trees at the edge of the great rain forest. At first, there was mistrust and even hate from the disparate local clans who feared the hypodermics and surgeon's knives of the white doctor.

It was only when a great epidemic of plague hit the tiny land that the natives turned to the medical man. In the face of this threat they suddenly became eager to commit their lives to him. With great sacrifice and sensitive care, he was able to save many of the natives from death in the face of this nightmarish disease. He also taught them how to avert future plagues by an active concern for sanitation and cleanliness. He also helped to set up a program to eradicate the plague-carrying rat population through a massive campaign of extermination.

Now, after many years of fighting disease, the doctor will leave to return home. He will now leave behind an active hospital and a corps of native doctors and nurses who will operate it. Even after he leaves, his spirit will still continue to drive the vitally needed medical program.

P- SHADOW

Ex. RT-124 (Tape 8/B @125) &
RT-124 (Tape 8/B @180)

There are many fables about the Knights of the Round Table—those men of might who fought hard for truth and justice in the Middle Ages. It is easy to imagine such a knight, to see him perched high on a tall steed, with lance at the ready for the fray. Everyone has seen films showing a knight at the lists or great fairs, proving his skills and training against another in fencing and jousting, hoping to win fame and make his mark as a hero or win the hand of some fair damsel.

In reality, the age of knighthood was one of great fear and hate. Many knights were brutal men who thought nothing of hacking a foe from head to toe with some vicious weapon for the mere pleasure of killing and maiming. Other knights would try to attack a helpless castle or town in order to loot and rape. Helpless peasants tilling the fields would be hit or have their houses burned down for no reason by these men-at-arms.

The deeds of knights became so harsh that the church felt the need to try to tame these men by tending them toward other trades and other goals. But even the church had little luck in discouraging the mass terror and slaughter of these armored thugs.

-G SHADOW

Ex. RT-125 (Tape 8/B @125) & RT-125 (Tape 8/B @180)

Because of his ability, he was given a great amount of responsibility in the firm. It was unusual at his age, since such duties usually went to older employees. He has exhibited his skill and his amiability, despite moments when he wondered if he was finally in over his head.

His success has been more than respectable and has enabled him to live in a fine home and to be able to do most of the things, such as charity work, that he has always desired. This has caused him to be much happier than he ever thought.

R- SHADOW

Ex. RT-126 (Tape 8/B @125) & RT-126 (Tape 8/B @180)

A wholly new chapter was written in the history of behavior research when a team of psychologists finished a project on the common housefly. They discovered some things not known before, particularly about the high birth rate among flies.

The director, whose name is becoming famous, has already started to push for an even more thorough project if someone can be found to donate the funds. Once the money is at hand, he expects to have some results which he feels will be astounding. These results may lead to a rethinking of some basic ideas about behavior.

S- SHADOW

Ex. RT-127 (Tape 8/B @125) & RT-127 (Tape 8/B @180)

It is difficult to believe they will actually complete the job this week. Just think, it was only 11 months ago that they broke ground for the project.

From the beginning, it seemed an impossible goal had been set. There seemed little chance to finish such a job in so short a time. Now it looks like they did it, and they can tell everyone about their success and the beautiful building they have put up there.

K- SHADOW

Ex. RT-128 (Tape 8/B @125) & RT-128 (Tape 8/B @180)

It was a simple case of fraud. The man had taken advantage of an old lady to get her savings that she had worked for. He had proceeded to throw the money away on cheap liquor and shapely women. The loss was between $4- and $5,000.

When the old lady realized what had happened, she had a consultation with her lawyer, who told her to have the man arrested. The trial went quickly, and to the man's consternation, he was sentenced to a term of several years, and all his threats wouldn't get him out.

SPECIAL DICTIONARY ENTRIES

Dictionary entries that require special formatting (e.g., prefixes, suffixes, punctuation, etc.) need to include a special command to effect this formatting when you enter them into your CAT dictionary. Some of these commands have been covered in the Dictionary Maintenance sections of Steps 1 through 10. They are summarized here.

Unfortunately, all CAT systems do not use the same command for a particular function. For example, most CAT systems use the tilde (~) as a "delete space" when entering prefixes and suffixes. Some use the caret (^), however, while others may use yet a different symbol.

You should refer to your CAT system documentation to see how to enter formatted items such as a prefix, suffix, prefix/suffix, cap next word, force two spaces, etc. If anything you add (using the instructions given in your CAT system instruction manual) does not translate the way you expect, call your CAT company representative. (Your CAT company, not StenEd, can help you out.) The "Space," "Join," and "Cap" commands, in particular, are done in unique ways.

Following is a summary of the various types of dictionary entries. This is a simplified listing. It covers the basic aspects of formatting, but, again, because of the way different CAT translation programs are written, there are exceptions. It is strongly recommended that you refer to your CAT documentation and/or CAT company rep when you have questions.

StenEd outlines are given for these items. It is recommended that you use the StenEd outlines unless they conflict with other entries in your CAT dictionary.

WORD ENTRIES

ENTER IN DICTIONARY

ENGLISH	OUTLINE	TRANSLATION	COMMENTS

NORMAL ENTRY (SPACE BEFORE AND AFTER)

word	WORD	word	a normal word entry
pro	PROE	pro	a normal word entry
less	HRESZ	less	a normal word entry

PREFIX ENTRY (ATTACHES TO THE NEXT STROKE)

pro~	PRO	pro...	a prefix entry
a~	AEU	a...	a prefix entry
in~	EUPB	in...	a prefix entry

SUFFIX ENTRY (ATTACHES TO THE PREVIOUS STROKE)

~less	HRES	...less	a suffix entry
~ed	-D	...ed	a suffix entry (past tense inflected ending)
~ment	-PLT	...ment	a suffix entry

Note: ... denotes that a root word or word part will be attached before or after the entry when translated.

PUNCTUATION & SYMBOL ENTRIES

ENTER IN DICTIONARY

ENGLISH	OUTLINE	TRANSLATION	COMMENTS

NORMAL ENTRY (SPACE BEFORE AND AFTER)

&	PH-PBD	&	Ampersand with spaces
-	H-FS	-	Hyphen/Minus sign with spaces
—	TK-RB	—	Dash

PREFIX ENTRY (ATTACHES TO THE NEXT STROKE)

#~	TPH-B	#...	Pound/Number sign
-~	PH*PBS	-...	Minus sign (e.g., -3)
.~	P-PBT	....	Point/Decimal (e.g., .5)

SUFFIX ENTRY (ATTACHES TO THE PREVIOUS STROKE)

~%	P-BGT	...%	Percent sign
~'	AOE	...'	Apostrophe
~-	H*FS	...-	Hyphen as suffix (e.g., 3- and . . .)

PREFIX/SUFFIX ENTRY (ATTACHES TO THE PREVIOUS *AND* NEXT STROKES)

~&~	PH*PBD	...&...	Ampersand, no spaces
~:~	KHR*PB	...:...	Colon in time (e.g., 1:30 p.m.)
~-~	H-F	...-...	Hyphen, no spaces

MULTIPLE SPACES AFTER *AND* CAP NEXT WORD

Note: Different CAT systems format the following differently. These examples are shown for illustrative purposes only.

^Q	STKPWHR-	Q ...	Question bank, tab, cap next word
^A	-FRPBLGTS	A ...	Answer bank, tab, cap next word
^.	-FPLT	. ...	Period, two spaces, cap next word
^?	STPH-	? ...	Interrog, two spaces, cap next word

CAUTION!

Sometimes, because of intelligence programmed into the CAT system, the formatting symbol you would logically expect to use will not work.

If something does not translate the way you expect it to, consult your CAT manual or company rep. The intent of this section is to help you, not confuse you, honestly. But there are so many variations in adding formatted dictionary entries that consistent, logical instructions that will work with <u>all</u> CAT/stenoscription systems are not always possible.

 Appendix

CAPITALIZATION

Capitalization will automatically occur after specially formatted items such as Q (question bank), A (answer bank), . (period), and ? (interrog). In addition, some words are always capitalized (e.g., American, Jones, Texas). Capitalized versions of other words can be included in your CAT dictionary with an asterisk (see Step 10) and thus require no additional stroke.

The cap commands (StenEd uses K-P and K-PS) can be used any time you want a word capitalized that would not otherwise be capitalized using standard CAT technology. We recommend "K-P" for "initial cap" and "K-PS" for "all caps" because they are easy to remember and easy to write. If they conflict with something else you write, choose alternate outlines.

CAPITALIZE NEXT LETTER

All CAT systems have a way to capitalize an entry. Look in your CAT documentation for the symbol(s). Use the symbol(s) as a dictionary entry and use K-P (or other non-conflicting outline) for the stroke.

English	Outline	Comments
symbol(s) for your CAT system	K-P	The next word is capped. There is no English translation.

CAPITALIZE ALL LETTERS

CAT systems generally do not allow for capping all letters. Stenoscription systems generally do. If your translation system can handle such a command and the directions for entering this command cannot be found in your system documentation, ask your CAT rep for instructions.

symbol(s) for your system	K-PS	Every letter is capped until you hit K-PS again. There is no English translation.

JOIN & SPACE COMMANDS

There strokes are used as a "catch-all" for those word boundary problems which occur infrequently and have no other "obvious," easy-to-remember solution. (See page 203 for a discussion of these two commands.)

StenEd uses the outline "J-N" for "join," and "SP-S" for "space." We recommend these outlines because they are easy to remember and easy to write. If they conflict with something else you write, choose alternate outlines.

JOIN COMMAND

If your CAT system has a separate "delete space" command such as tilde (~), caret (^), or other symbol, include this symbol as a separate dictionary entry, with J-N (SKWR-PB) (or other non-conflicting outline) as the steno.

symbol(s) for your system	SKWR-PB	Joins two words or strokes together. There is no English translation.

SPACE COMMAND

Not all CAT systems provide for this capability. If you aren't sure, ask your CAT rep. If you can, include the space symbol as a separate dictionary entry, with SP-S (or other non-conflicting outline) as the steno.

symbol(s) for your system	SP-S	Separates two words or strokes. There is no English translation.

NUMBERS
WRITING NUMBERS AS SPOKEN

We expect that most CAT companies will incorporate the StenEd "Numbers Over 100 Option" described on page 141. With this method, numbers can be written as spoken and translate correctly with a finite number of dictionary entries.

This number logic will not work by adding dictionary entries alone; i.e., a software modification must be made to the CAT system itself. If your CAT company has added this number logic to their system, contact them for the update release number and what entries, if any, you will have to make to your dictionary. *(If your CAT company has not added the the StenEd number logic, encourage them to do so.)*

Some sample dictionary entries that you will make follow. These are only examples and will vary among CAT systems. Depending upon how your CAT company writes the number logic, you may or may not have to add some individual numbers to your CAT dictionary.

ENTER IN DICTIONARY

ENGLISH	OUTLINE	COMMENTS
^$	TKHR-R	Dollar sign
~,~	-RBGZ	Number comma
^¢	S-TS	Cent symbol
^_hundred	HURBGS	Hundred field
^_thousand	THOURBGS	Thousand field
^_million	PHEURBGS	Million field
^_billion	PWEURBGS	Billion field
^_trillion	TREURBGS	Trillion field

CAT technology is becoming more sophisticated. As writers become more experienced in realtime applications, they will want their translation system to do more than CAT systems of the past have done. They will expect more refined features from their CAT/captioning/stenoscription systems. Encourage your CAT vendor to respond.

THE *StenEd*® THEORY
A BRIEF HISTORY

What is StenEd?

Stenotype Educational Products, Inc. (StenEd) was founded in 1979 by Beverly Loeblein Ritter for the purpose of writing/publishing conflict-free stenotype textbooks that would take full advantage of past, present, and future CAT technology.

StenEd's main texts include realtime theory; vocabulary/usage; realtime steno dictionaries; dictation/ speedbuilding for Q&A, jury charge, and literary; reporter reference; stenoscription; and medical. StenEd products also include audio cassettes and computer tutorials that correspond to many of the textbooks. StenEd is not a CAT company; instead, we provide the educational materials that teach writers how to be most efficient with all CAT and stenoscription systems. StenEd does provide CAT dictionaries (main and medical) which can be very effectively used by all writers trained in the StenEd theory.

Beverly L. Ritter has been working with CAT and writing conflict-free educational materials for over 25 years. She has been President of StenEd since 1979. Previous to founding StenEd, she was Director of Education and later Vice President of Stentran Systems (1973-1979), one of the earliest CAT companies. She began her working career as an English teacher in Montgomery County, Maryland (1965-1973). She received her B.A. from the University of Maryland in 1965.

The StenEd Theory . . .

What has evolved into the StenEd theory was originally developed in 1973 to provide a sound, conflict-free foundation for reporters to be able to use CAT most efficiently. Today, StenEd is being recognized nationally as, by far, the best theory for realtime—indeed for all—CAT applications.

As you might expect, in the 1970's (and in much of the 80's) most people thought it was overkill to try to be conflict free. Many people believed that it was impossible. In addition, many believed that to try to teach a beginning student to write in a conflict-free manner would impede their progress and they would never reach reporter speeds. Both of these beliefs have been proven false, and conflict-free, realtime writing is becoming the norm for the profession.

Today, throughout the English-speaking world, StenEd is taught in more schools than any other theory.

StenEd's main customers have traditionally been schools. However, we have been asked by experienced reporters, especially those giving realtime seminars, and schools teaching StenEd who get transfer students from non-StenEd schools to summarize the StenEd theory in a text to be used by experienced reporters as a guide to writing realtime. Thus, the creation of *10 Steps to Realtime Writing*.

Appendix   © 1993, 2001 *StenEd*®   **237**

INDEX

ad, potential conflict(s), 152
-ad, 111
ad/add, 52, 53
add(s), potential conflict(s), 152
add/ad, 52, 53
add more, potential conflict(s), 151
add Mr., potential conflict(s), 151
addition, potential conflict(s), 151
addition/edition, 53
address, potential conflict(s), 152
a dress, potential conflict(s), 152
ade/ades/aid/aide/aides/aids/AIDS, 46, 53
ades/aid/aide/aides/aids/AIDS/ade, 46, 53
adherence/adherents, 53
adieu/ado, 53
adjudication, potential conflict(s), 151
administer, potential conflict(s), 151
Administration, administration, 200
ado/adieu, 53
adolescence/adolescents, 53
ads, potential conflict(s), 152
advance, potential conflict(s), 151
advertise, potential conflict(s), 152
advice, potential conflict(s), 152
advice/advise, 52, 53
advisability, potential conflict(s), 152
advisable, potential conflict(s), 152
advise, potential conflict(s), 152
advise/advice, 52, 53
adviser/advisor, 53
aesthetic/esthetic, 53
affect, potential conflict(s), 166
affected, potential conflict(s), 166
affluence/effluence, 53
affluent/effluent, 53
afraid, potential conflict(s), 152
a frayed, potential conflict(s), 152
aft, potential conflict(s), 152
aft/after-/after, 87
after, 16; potential conflict(s), 152
after/after-, 19, 22, 83
after/after-/aft, 87
after-, 90; potential conflict(s), 152
after-/after, 19, 22, 83
after-/after/aft, 87
after it, potential conflict(s), 152
aftermath, 87
aftermath/after math, 83
after the, potential conflict(s), 152
age, potential conflict(s), 153
-age, 111
agree(s), potential conflict(s), 160
agreed, potential conflict(s), 160
ahead, 87
aid, potential conflict(s), 152
aid/aide/aides/aids/AIDS/ade/ades, 46, 53
aide, potential conflict(s), 152
aide/aides/aids/AIDS/ade/ades/aid, 46, 53
ail, potential conflict(s), 152
ail/ale, 53
ail/ale/eel, 47
ailing, potential conflict(s), 152
aim, potential conflict(s), 153
aimlessly, 107
ain't, 128
air, potential conflict(s), 154
air/-ier/ere/-er/er-/err, 104
air/ere/err/heir/hare/hair/here/hear/ear, 47
air/heir/hair/hare/hear/here/ear/ere/err/er-/-er, 53
aircraft, potential conflict(s), 153
airplane, potential conflict(s), 153
airy/eerie/Erie, 53
aisle, potential conflict(s), 166
aisle/I'll/isle, 48
aisle/I'll/isle/I will/ill, 53
-aj, potential conflict(s), 153
-ak, 111
al-, 90; potential conflict(s), 152

al-/Al, 87
al-/Al/all, 83
al-/Al/all/-al/awl, 49
al-/Al/all/-al/awl/awe, 18, 21
Al, potential conflict(s), 152
Al/al-, 87
Al/al-/all, 83
Al/al-/all/awl/-al, 49
Al/al-/all/awl/-al/awe, 18, 21
Al/al-/all/awl/-al/awe/ow/owl, 53
Al/awe/-al/all/awl, 101
Al buy/alibi, 83
-al, 108, 111, 239; potential conflict(s), 152
-al/-el/-il/-ol/-le soundalikes, 51
-al/Al/all/awl/al-, 49
-al/Al/all/awl/al-/awe, 18, 21
-al/Al/all/awl/awe, 101
Alabama, potential conflict(s), 152
ale, potential conflict(s), 152
ale/ail, 53
ale/eel/ail, 47
alert, potential conflict(s), 152
a letter, potential conflict(s), 152
Alex B., 210
alias, 87
alibi, 87
alibi/Al buy, 83
alimentary/elementary, 53
all caps, 199, 200; potential conflict(s), 158
all, 16; potential conflict(s), 152
all/Al/al-, 83
all/Al/awl/al-/-al, 49
all/Al/awl/al-/awe/-al, 18, 21
all/Al/awl/awe/-al, 101
allay/alley/ally, 52
allegation, potential conflict(s), 152
alley, potential conflict(s), 152
alley/ally/allay, 52
allowed/aloud/a loud, 53
allude/elude, 54
allusion/elusion/illusion, 54
allusive/elusive/illusive, 54
ally, potential conflict(s), 152
ally/allay/alley, 52
-ally, 107, 108, 111
along/a long, 83, 148
aloud/a loud/allowed, 53
alphabet, Step 1, 5-14; 148
alphabet, lower case letters with periods, 208, 209
alphabet, lower case letters without periods, 208
alphabet, upper case letters with periods, 208, 209
alphabet, upper case letters without periods, 208
alphabets, spelling, 208-210; 219
also, 16, 238; potential conflict(s), 152
also/always/wills, 19, 22
alt, 212
altar/alter, 49, 54
always, 16, 238; potential conflict(s), 152
always/wills/also, 19, 22
am, 16; potential conflict(s), 152
am/apple, 54
am/him/many exercise, 35
am/him/many/hymn, 18, 21
a.m., 138; potential conflict(s), 152
ambitious, 109
ambitiously, 109
ambitiousness, 109
ambulance, potential conflict(s), 152
amend/emend, 54
ampersand (&), 129, 210, 211, 234; potential conflict(s), 169
ample, 108
amputation, potential conflict(s), 152
an, 16, 18; potential conflict(s), 153
an/-an, 105
an/and/a, 18, 20; exercise, 26
-an, 111

-an/an, 105
anal, potential conflict(s), 152
analyze, potential conflict(s), 152
-ance, 111
-ance/answer, 105
ancient, potential conflict(s), 152
and, 16; potential conflict(s), 153
and/a/an, 18, 20; exercise, 26
and he had, potential conflict(s), 152
and he will, potential conflict(s), 152
and I, potential conflict(s), 152
and I am, potential conflict(s), 153
and I believe, potential conflict(s), 153
and I can, potential conflict(s), 153
and I could, potential conflict(s), 153
and I had, potential conflict(s), 152
and I recollect, potential conflict(s), 153
and is, potential conflict(s), 153
and I say, potential conflict(s), 153
and I will, potential conflict(s), 152
and I would, potential conflict(s), 152
and she, potential conflict(s), 153
and she is, potential conflict(s), 153
and the, potential conflict(s), 153
and you believe, potential conflict(s), 153
and you feel, potential conflict(s), 153
and you go, potential conflict(s), 153
and you have, potential conflict(s), 153
and you recall, potential conflict(s), 154
and you remember, potential conflict(s), 154
and you will, potential conflict(s), 152
annals, potential conflict(s), 152
announce, potential conflict(s), 154
annual, potential conflict(s), 152
another, 16
answer, potential conflict(s), 153
answer/-ance, 105
answer bank, 234, 235
ant, potential conflict(s), 153
ant/-ant, 105
ant/aunt, 49, 54, 148
-ant, 111
-ant/ant, 105
ante, potential conflict(s), 153
ante/ante-/anti/anti-, 87
ante/ante-/anti/anti-/auntie, 54
ante-, 90;, potential conflict(s), 153
ante-/ante/anti-/anti, 87
ante-/ante/anti/anti-/auntie, 54
antedate, 87
anterior, potential conflict(s), 154
anti, potential conflict(s), 153
anti/anti-/ante/ante-, 87
anti/anti-/ante/ante-/auntie, 54
anti-, 90, 239; potential conflict(s), 153
anti-/anti/ante-/ante, 87
anti-/anti/ante/ante-/auntie, 54
anticipate, potential conflict(s), 153
antisocial, 87
anxious, potential conflict(s), 152
any, 16, 19
any/-ny, 107
anybody, any body, 204; potential conflict(s), 154
anybody else, potential conflict(s), 154
anymore, any more, 204
anyone, any one, 204; potential conflict(s), 171
anything, any thing, 204
anyway, any way, 203, 204
anywhere, any where, 204
a parent, potential conflict(s), 154
apart, potential conflict(s), 154
apartment, potential conflict(s), 154
a part, potential conflict(s), 154
ape, potential conflict(s), 153
a peal, a peel, potential conflict(s), 154
a point, potential conflict(s), 154
apostrophe ('), 127, 128, 129, 138, 211, 234
apostrophe s ('s), 128
apparent, potential conflict(s), 154

chick, potential conflict(s), 174
chick/chic/sheik, 56
child, potential conflict(s), 179
childishness, 110
childlike, child like, 202
children's, 128
Chile/chilly/chili, 52, 56
chill, potential conflict(s), 179
chilled, potential conflict(s), 179
chilly/chili/Chile, 52, 56
china, China, 200
choir, potential conflict(s), 167
choir/quire, 56
choose/chews, 49, 56
choral/coral/corral, 50, 56
chord, potential conflict(s), 159
chord/cord, 50
chord/cord/cored, 56
chow/ciao, 56
chronical/chronicle, 56
chuck, Chuck, potential conflict(s), 179
chum, potential conflict(s), 179
chunk, potential conflict(s), 179
chute/shoot, 56
-chy, 107, 111
-cial (shal sound), 109, 111, potential
    conflict(s), 156
-cially, 109, 111
ciao/chow, 56
cig (slang), potential conflict(s), 175
cigs (slang), potential conflict(s), 175
-cious, 109, 111
-ciously, 109
-ciousness, 109, 111
cirrus, potential conflict(s), 168
cirrus/serious/serous, 56
cite/site/sight, 51, 56
cite/site/sight/kite, 50
city, City, 200
civil, 6, 108
-cket, 111
classroom, 206
clause/claws, 56
-cle, 108, 111
clean writing, appendix, 223-232
clear screen, stenoscription command,
    213
clear screen and start new document,
    stenoscription command, 213
clef/cleft, 56
click, 86
click/clique, 52, 56
climactic/climatic, 56
climb/clime, 56
clippings, 38
clique/click, 52, 56
clock, potential conflict(s), 158
clod, potential conflict(s), 162
clog, potential conflict(s), 162
close, 207; potential conflict(s), 158
close/clothes, 56
closing parenthesis ( )), 127, 129, 149,
    211
closing quotes ("), 127, 129, 149, 211
clothes, potential conflict(s), 158
clothes/close, 56
clubbing/cluck, 40
clubhouse, 206
cluck/clubbing, 40
Clyde/collide, 56
co-, 90; potential conflict(s), 158
co-/could, 83
co-/could/company, 87
co-/could/company/cow, 19, 22
Co., potential conflict(s), 158
coal, potential conflict(s), 159
coarse, potential conflict(s), 159
coarse/course, 49
coarse/course/cores, 56
coast, potential conflict(s), 158
coat/cot, 6, 148
coated/coded, 56
cob, potential conflict(s), 160
cocktail, 206

cod, potential conflict(s), 158
c.o.d., potential conflict(s), 158
C.O.D., potential conflict(s), 158
code/co-ed, 56
coded/coated, 56
co-ed/code, 56
coeur (medical), potential conflict(s), 160
coexist, 87
coexist/could exist, 83
coffer/cougher, 56
cog, potential conflict(s), 160
coif/quaff, 56
col-, 86, 90; potential conflict(s), 159
-col, potential conflict(s), 159
colander, potential conflict(s), 157
coldhearted, 206
colic, 86
coll-, 86, 90
coll-/comm-/corr-, exercise, 93
colleague/klieg, 56
collect, 86
collide/Clyde, 56
collusion, potential conflict(s), 158
colon (:), 127, 129, 130, 138, 149, 211
colon in time (:), 129, 211, 234
colonel/kernel, 50, 57
Colorado, potential conflict(s), 159
comb-, 90
combination, potential conflict(s), 159
come, 16; potential conflict(s), 158
comeback, come back, 202
comet, potential conflict(s), 159
comic, potential conflict(s), 162
comm-, 86, 90
comm-/corr-/coll-, exercise, 93
comma (,), 127, 129, 130, 211
comma and quotation mark (,"), 129,
    211
comma used with numbers (,), 129, 139,
    140, 211, 236
comment, potential conflict(s), 159
common, 86
commune, potential conflict(s), 159
communicate, potential conflict(s), 159
communication, potential conflict(s),
    159
comp-, 86, 90
compact, 86, 207; potential conflict(s),
    159
companies, potential conflict(s), 158
company, potential conflict(s), 158
company/co-/could, 87
company/co-/could/cow, 19, 22
compare, 86
compel, potential conflict(s), 159
compile, potential conflict(s), 159
compile/exile, 84
complacence/complaisance, 57
complacent/complaisant, 57
complainant/complaint, 57
complement/compliment, 57
comport, potential conflict(s), 159
compound words, 199, 201-206;
    exercises, 216-217
con, 86, 90; potential conflict(s), 159
concern, potential conflict(s), 159
concern/kern, 57
conclude, potential conflict(s), 159
conclusion, potential conflict(s), 159
concur/conquer, 57
concussion, potential conflict(s), 159
conditions, potential conflict(s), 158
conduct, 207; potential conflict(s), 159
conductor, conduct or, potential
    conflict(s), 159
confess, potential conflict(s), 157
confirmation/conformation, 57
conflict, 86
conform, potential conflict(s), 159
conformation/confirmation, 57
congestion, 109
congress, Congress, 200; potential
    conflict(s), 159

congressman, Congressman, 200
congresswoman, Congresswoman, 200
Connecticut, potential conflict(s), 159
conned, potential conflict(s), 159
conning, potential conflict(s), 159
conquer/concur, 51, 57
cons, potential conflict(s), 159
conscious, 109
consciously, 109
consciousness, 109
consequence, potential conflict(s), 159
consequent, potential conflict(s), 159
consonance/consonants, 57
consonant sound soundalikes, 50-52
consonants, 5; exercises, 8-9
consonants, final, exercise, 119
consonants/consonance, 56
constitution, potential conflict(s), 159
consul/council/counsel, 57
consummation, potential conflict(s), 159
consumption, potential conflict(s), 159
contain, potential conflict(s), 159
contest, 207
continence/continents/countenance, 57
continuance, potential conflict(s), 156
continue, potential conflict(s), 156
continue answer, potential conflict(s),
    156
continuing, potential conflict(s), 156
contraction, potential conflict(s), 159
contractions, 128; exercise, 132, 133
contracts, potential conflict(s), 159
contradict, potential conflict(s), 160
contradiction, potential conflict(s), 160
contrast, 207
contribution, potential conflict(s), 160
control, stenoscription command, 212
convene, potential conflict(s), 160
convenience, potential conflict(s), 160
convenient, potential conflict(s), 160
conveniently, potential conflict(s), 160
convention, 109
convince, potential conflict(s), 160
convulsion, 109
coo, potential conflict(s), 158
coo/coop/co-op/coup/coupe/cue/queue, 49,
    57
coon, potential conflict(s), 160
coop/co-op/coup/coupe/cue/queue/coo, 49,
    57
cope, potential conflict(s), 151
copy, 107; potential conflict(s), 151
cor-, potential conflict(s), 159
-cor, potential conflict(s), 159
coral/corral/choral, 50, 56
cord, potential conflict(s), 159
cord/chord, 50, 84
cord/chord/cored, 56
cordially yours, potential conflict(s), 158
core(s), potential conflict(s), 159
core/corps/corpse, 57
cored, potential conflict(s), 159
cored/chord/cord, 56
cores/coarse/course, 56
corespondent, potential conflict(s), 159
corespondents/correspondence/
    correspondents, 57
corn, potential conflict(s), 159
corner, potential conflict(s), 159
corner/coroner, 57
coroner, potential conflict(s), 159
coroner/corner, 57
Corp., potential conflict(s), 159
corporal/corporeal, 57
corporate, potential conflict(s), 159
corporation(s), potential conflict(s), 159
corporeal/corporal, 57
corps, potential conflict(s), 159
corps/corpse, 52
corps/corpse/core, 57
corpse, potential conflict(s), 159
corpse/corps, 52
corpse/corps/core, 57
corr-, 86 90

---

he can, potential conflict(s), 165
he'd, 128;, potential conflict(s), 165
he'd/head/heed/he had, 60
he'd/head/heed/Ed/he would/held, 149
he had, potential conflict(s), 165
he had/head/heed/he'd, 60
he is, potential conflict(s), 165
he'll, 47, 128; potential conflict(s), 152
he'll/heal/heel/hail/hale, 47
he'll/heal/heel/he will/hell, 60
he's, 128; potential conflict(s), 165
he will, potential conflict(s), 152
he will/hell/heal/heel/he'll, 60
he would, potential conflict(s), 165
head, potential conflict(s), 165
head/heed/he'd/he had, 60
headache, head ache, 202
headlight, 206
head on, head-on, 205
heal, potential conflict(s), 152
heal/heel, 46
heal/heel/he'll/hail/hale, 47
heal/heel/he'll/he will/hell, 60
healthy, 107
heap, potential conflict(s), 165
hear, potential conflict(s), 155
hear/here, 46
hear/here/hair/hare, 47
hear/here/hair/hare/heir/ear/ere/err/air,
    47
hear/here/hair/hare/heir/ear/ere/err/air/
    er-/-er, 53
hear/here/her, 18, 21; exercise, 33
heard, potential conflict(s), 165
heard/herd, 49, 60
hearings, 38
hears, potential conflict(s), 165
hearse, potential conflict(s), 165
hearse/hers, 40, 60
heartache, heart ache, 202
heartbeat, heart beat, 204
heart break, heartbreak, 204
heartfelt, heart felt, 204
hearty/hardy, 60
heck, potential conflict(s), 165
heed, potential conflict(s), 165
heed/he'd/he had/head, 60
heel, potential conflict(s), 152
heel/heal, 46
heel/heal/he'll/hail/hale, 47
heel/heal/he'll/he will/hell, 60
heifer, potential conflict(s), 165
heir, potential conflict(s), 155
heir/hair/hare/here/hear/ear/ere/err/air,
    47
heir/hair/hare/here/hear/ear/ere/err/air/
    er-/-er, 53
held, potential conflict(s), 165
hell, potential conflict(s), 152
hell/heal/heel/he'll/he will, 60
help menu (F3), stenoscription
    command, 212
help, 106; potential conflict(s), 165
helped, potential conflict(s), 165
helps, 38; potential conflict(s), 165
hence/hens/Hen's, 60
hep, potential conflict(s), 165
her, 16
her/here/hear, 18, 21; exercise, 33
herb/Herb, 60
herd, potential conflict(s), 165
herd/heard, 49, 60
here, potential conflict(s), 155
here/hear, 46
here/hear/hair/hare, 47
here/hear/hair/hare/heir/ear/air/ere/err,
    47
here/hear/hair/hare/heir/ear/ere/err/er-/-
    er/air, 53
here/hear/her, exercise, 33
here about, 204
hereabouts, 204
hereafter, here after, 204
hereby, here by, 204

herein, here in, 204
here is, potential conflict(s), 165
hereof, here of, 204
heres, potential conflict(s), 165
here's, 128; potential conflict(s), 165
hereto, here to, 204
hereunder, here under, 204
herewith, here with, 204
heroin/heroine, 52, 60
hers, potential conflict(s), 165
hers/hearse, 40, 60
herself, her self, potential conflict(s),
    165
hertz/Hertz/hurts, 60
hesitate, potential conflict(s), 165
hetero, 89
hetero-, 89, 90
heterosexual, 89
hew, potential conflict(s), 165
hew/hue/huge/Hugh, 60
hey, potential conflict(s), 165
hey/hay, 46, 60
hi/high/hie, 48, 60
hide/Hyde, 60
hideaway, hide away, 202
hie/hi/high, 48, 60
higher/hire, 51, 60, 148
high frequency words, Step 2, 15-36;
    148; alphabetized, 16; exercises, 20-
    36; potential conflicts, 17, 18, 19
highlight, 206
high per/hyper-/hyper, 88
high school, potential conflict(s), 179
him, 16; potential conflict(s), 152
him/am/many, exercise, 35
him/am/many/hymn, 18, 21
him/hymn, 60
himself, potential conflict(s), 165
hind, potential conflict(s), 157
hinge, potential conflict(s), 160
hippie/hippy, 60
hire/higher, 51, 60, 148
his, 16, 18; potential conflict(s), 153
his/hiss, 60
his/hiss/-s/is/as/as-/ass, 18, 20
his/is/as, 37, 148; exercise, 28
his/is/as/-s, 101
hiss, potential conflict(s), 153
hiss/his, 60
hiss/his/-s/is/as/as-/ass, 18, 20
historian, 106
ho/hoe, 60
hoar/hoer/whore, 60
hoard/horde, 49
hoard/horde/whored, 60
hoarse/horse, 49
hoarse/horse/whores, 60
hoc, potential conflict(s), 179
hoc/hock/hawk, 60
hock, potential conflict(s), 179
hock/hawk/hoc, 60
hoe/ho, 60
hoer/whore/hoar, 60
hoes/hose, 61
hold/holed, 40, 61
holdover, hold over, 203
holdup, hold up, 203
hole, potential conflict(s), 179
hole/whole, 50, 61
holed/hold, 40, 61
holey, potential conflict(s), 179
holey/holy, 105
holey/holy/holly/wholly, 52, 61
holly, potential conflict(s), 179
holly/holy/wholly/holey, 52, 61
holy, potential conflict(s), 179
holy/holey, 105
holy/wholly, 50
holy/wholly/holey/holly, 52, 61
home, stenoscription command, 213
homemaker, 206
homework, home work, 203
homo, 89
homo-, 89, 90

homogenic, 89
homographs, 199, 207; exercise, 218
homonyms, 45 (also see soundalikes)
homophones, 45 (also see soundalikes)
hone, potential conflict(s), 165
honest, potential conflict(s), 165
honey, potential conflict(s), 165
honor, potential conflict(s), 165
honorable, Honorable, 200
hons, potential conflict(s), 165
hook, potential conflict(s), 179
hoose (medical), potential conflict(s),
    179
hop, potential conflict(s), 179
hope, 39
hoped, 39
hopefully, 107
hoping, 39
horde/hoard, 49
horde/hoard/whored, 60
horse/hoarse, 60
horse/hoarse/whores, 61
hose/hoes, 60
hospital, potential conflict(s), 179
hostel/hostile, 61
hour(s), potential conflict(s), 172
hour/our, 19, 22, 61
house, 200, 207
House, 200
housework, house work, 203
hover, potential conflict(s), 179
however, how ever, 204
how fast, potential conflict(s), 165
howled, potential conflict(s), 165
how old, potential conflict(s), 165
how was, potential conflict(s), 165
how would, potential conflict(s), 165
hub, potential conflict(s), 165
hue, potential conflict(s), 165
hue/huge/Hugh/hew, 60
huge/Hugh/hew/hue, 60
Hugh, potential conflict(s), 165
Hugh/hew/hue/huge, 60
huh, potential conflict(s), 165
humerus/humorous, 52, 61
hundred, 140, 141
hundred, number field, 236
hundred million, 141
hundred thousand, 141
hurts/hertz/Hertz, 60
hustle, 108
Hyde/hide, 60
hydro, 89
hydro-, 89, 90
hydropower, 89
hymn, potential conflict(s), 152
hymn/him, 60
hymn/him/am/many, 18, 21
hymns, potential conflict(s), 165
hyper-, 90, 239
hyper-/hyper/high per, 88
hypertension, 88
hyphen (-), 127, 129, 130, 211, 234, 239;
    potential conflicts, 165, 166
hyphens,words with, 205
hypo, 89
hypo-, 89, 90, 239
hypothetical, 89
Hz, 210

i (long), 6, 11, 14; exercise, 11
i (long) soundalikes, 46, 48; exercise, 73
i (short), 5, 6
i, spelling alphabet, 208
i., spelling alphabet, 209
i-, 90, 239; potential conflict(s), 153
i-/I, 83, 87
i-/I/aye/eye, 54
i-/I/aye/eye/-y, 18, 21
-i (e sound), 105, 111
-i (i sound), 111
I, 16, 17, 105; potential conflict(s), 153
I, spelling alphabet, 208
I., spelling alphabet, 209

I/eye, exercise, 31
I/eye/-y, 101
I/i-, 83, 87
I/i-/eye/aye, 54
I/i-/eye/aye/-y, 18, 21
I am, potential conflict(s), 165
-ial, 239
-ibility, 111
-ible, 111
-ibly, 111
-ic, 104; potential conflict(s), 165
I can, potential conflict(s), 165
ice, potential conflict(s), 153
icon, 87
I couldn't care, potential conflict(s), 165
id, potential conflict(s), 154
-id, 111
I'd, 128; potential conflict(s), 154
I'd/eyed, 60
ideal/I deal, 83
identified, potential conflict(s), 154
identifies, potential conflict(s), 154
identify, potential conflict(s), 154
I did, potential conflict(s), 154
I didn't have, potential conflict(s), 165
idle/idol/idyll, 51, 61
I don't know, potential conflict(s), 166
I don't see, potential conflict(s), 166
idyll/idle/idol, 51, 61
-ie, 105, 111
-ier, 111; potential conflict(s), 180
-ier/ere/-er/er-/err/air, 104
-iest, 104, 111
if, 16, 18; potential conflict(s), 154
if/-if, 105
if/have/of, 148
if/have/of/very, exercise, 25
if/have/of/very/off, 18, 20
-if, 111
-if/if, 105
if he can, potential conflict(s), 166
if he could, potential conflict(s), 166
if he had, potential conflict(s), 166
if he will, potential conflict(s), 166
if I, potential conflict(s), 154
if I can, potential conflict(s), 166
if I go, potential conflict(s), 166
if I remember, potential conflict(s), 166
if I should/fished, 37
if it, potential conflict(s), 166
if it is, potential conflict(s), 166
if I will, potential conflict(s), 166
if our, potential conflict(s), 164
ifs, potential conflict(s), 154
if the, potential conflict(s), 166
if you, potential conflict(s), 166
if you are, potential conflict(s), 166
if you can, potential conflict(s), 166
if you know, potential conflict(s), 167
if your, potential conflict(s), 166
if you recall, potential conflict(s), 167
if you remember, potential conflict(s), 166
if you understand, potential conflict(s), 167
if you will, potential conflict(s), 167
I had, potential conflict(s), 154
I have, potential conflict(s), 154
I have had, potential conflict(s), 154
-ik, 111
il-, 90; potential conflict(s), 166
il-/ill/I'll, 88
-il, 108, 111
-il/ill, 105
-il/-ol/-le/-al/-el soundalikes, 51
ill, potential conflict(s), 166
ill/-il, 105
ill/I'll, 128
ill/I'll/aisle/isle/I will, 53
ill/I'll/il-, 88
I'll, 128; potential conflict(s), 166
I'll/ill, 128
I'll/ill/il-, 88
I'll/isle/aisle, 48

I'll/isle/aisle/I will/ill, 53
illegal, 88
illicit/elicit, 58
Illinois, potential conflict(s), 166
illusion/allusion/elusion, 54
illusive/allusive/elusive, 54
-ily, 107, 111
im-, 90; potential conflict(s), 165
im-/I'm, 88
I'm, 128; potential conflict(s), 165
I'm/im-, 88
imagination, potential conflict(s), 167
imagine, potential conflict(s), 167
immanent/imminent, 61
immaterial, potential conflict(s), 165
immediate, potential conflict(s), 167
immediately, potential conflict(s), 167
imminent/immanent, 61
impart, 87
impartial, 109
impartially, 109
impatience/inpatients, 61
impatient, 88
impinges, potential conflict(s), 160
importance, potential conflict(s), 167
important, potential conflict(s), 167
imputation, potential conflict(s), 152
in, 4, 16; potential conflict(s), 166
in/in-, 83, 85
in/in-/inn, 18, 20, 61, 88
in/-in, 105
in-, 90, 233; potential conflict(s), 166
in-/en-, exercise, 97
in-/in, 83, 85; exercise, 98
in-/in/inn, 18, 20, 61, 88
-in, 111
-in/in, 105
-in/-on/-en, exercise, 116
inaction, potential conflict(s), 167
inactive, 88
inactive/in active, 84
inasmuch, in as much, 204
Inc., potential conflict(s), 160
Inc./ink, 61
inch, potential conflict(s), 166
inched, potential conflict(s), 166
incidence/incidents, 61
incite/insight/in sight, 50, 61
inclusion, potential conflict(s), 160
income(s), potential conflict(s), 167
incompetent, potential conflict(s), 165
incomplete, 85
in connection with, potential conflict(s), 167
incorporate, potential conflict(s), 160
incorporated, potential conflict(s), 160
incorporations, potential conflict(s), 160
increase, 207; potential conflict(s), 167
indeed, 85
independence, potential conflict(s), 166
independence/independents, 61
independent, potential conflict(s), 166
Indiana, potential conflict(s), 166
indicate, potential conflict(s), 160
indication, potential conflict(s), 160
indict, potential conflict(s), 167
indict/indite, 61
indifferent, 85
indifferent/in different, 83
indigence/indigents, 61
indite, potential conflict(s), 167
indite/indict, 61
individual, potential conflict(s), 165
in effect, potential conflict(s), 167
inequity/iniquity, 61
in fact, potential conflict(s), 167
infect(s), potential conflict(s), 167
infection, potential conflict(s), 167
infectious, potential conflict(s), 167
inflected endings, Step 3, 37-44; 148;
    exercises, 40, 41, 42-43, 43-44, 115
influence, 85; potential conflict(s), 167
inform, potential conflict(s), 164
inform/information/for/fore/four,

exercise, 183
informal, potential conflict(s), 163
information, potential conflict(s), 164
information/for/fore/four/inform,
    exercise, 183
informing, potential conflict(s), 164
-ing, 37, 38, 39, 111; exercise, 40, 41, 42-
    43, 43-44; potential conflict(s), 156
-ingly, 107, 111
ingress, 85
-ings, 38, 111
iniquity/inequity, 61
in it, potential conflict(s), 167
initial cap, 199, 200
initial consonants, exercise, 95
initials, 210
in its, potential conflict(s), 167
injure, potential conflict(s), 167
injury, potential conflict(s), 167
ink, potential conflict(s), 160
ink/Inc., 61
inn(s), potential conflict(s), 166
inn/in-/in, 18, 20, 61, 88
inner, potential conflict(s), 180
inning, potential conflict(s), 160
innocence/innocents, 61
in order, potential conflict(s), 167
in other words, potential conflict(s), 167
inpatients/impatience, 61
inquire, potential conflict(s), 167
inquiry, potential conflict(s), 168
in respect, potential conflict(s), 160
ins, potential conflict(s), 166
insert/typeover, stenscription
    command, 212
insight/in sight/incite, 50, 61
inspect, potential conflict(s), 166
instance, potential conflict(s), 166
instance/instants, 61
instant, potential conflict(s), 166
instants/instance, 61
institute, potential conflict(s), 175
insurance, potential conflict(s), 156
insure, potential conflict(s), 156
insure/ensure, 58
int-, 86, 90
int-/enter-/inter-/enter/inter/ent-,
    exercise, 99
int(o)-, potential conflict(s), 167
intend, 86
intense/intents, 61
inter/inter-/enter/enter-/ent-/int-,
    exercise, 99
inter/inter-/enter/enter-/into, 88
inter-, 90
interchange, 88
interest, potential conflict(s), 168
interrog (?), 127, 129, 130, 211, 234,
    235; potential conflict(s), 155
in the, potential conflict(s), 167
into, 16, 19, 238; potential conflict(s),
    167
into/inter-/inter/enter-/enter, 88
intra-, 86, 90
intrastate, 86
intro, 89
intro-, 86, 89, 90
introduce, 86
introvert, 89
inversions, 6, 13; exercise, 13
inverted -er/-or conflicts, 17
invest, potential conflict(s), 168
investigate, potential conflict(s), 168
investigation, potential conflict(s), 168
investigator, potential conflict(s), 168
investigate or, potential conflict(s), 168
invite, potential conflict(s), 167
invoice(s), potential conflict(s), 168
invoiced, potential conflict(s), 168
in you, potential conflict(s), 167
i.o.u., 209
-ious, 239
ir-, 90; potential conflict(s), 168
I recollect, potential conflict(s), 166

irk, potential conflict(s), 166
irrelevant, potential conflict(s), 168
-ish, 109, 111; potential conflict(s), 166
is he, potential conflict(s), 168
-ishment, 109, 111
-ishness, 109, 110, 111
is, 16, 17; potential conflict(s), 153
is/as/his, 37, 148; exercise, 28
is/as/his/-s, 101
is/as/his/-s/as-/ass/hiss, 18, 20
-is, 111
I shall, potential conflict(s), 166
is in, potential conflict(s), 155
is it, potential conflict(s), 155
isle, potential conflict(s), 166
isle/aisle/I'll, 48
isle/aisle/I'll/I will/ill, 53
islet/eyelet, 58
-ism, 111
is many, potential conflict(s), 168
is much, potential conflict(s), 155
is not, potential conflict(s), 168
isn't, 128; potential conflict(s), 168
isolate, 87
is on the, potential conflict(s), 168
is our, potential conflict(s), 168
is such, potential conflict(s), 155
issue, potential conflict(s), 166
-ist, 104, 111
is the, potential conflict(s), 155
-istic, 111
it, 16, 18; potential conflict(s), 176
it/-it, 105
it/at/the, 148
it/at/the/they, 18, 20
it/the exercise, 23
-it, 111
-it/it, 105
itchy, 107
it'd, 128
it had, potential conflict(s), 168
I think, potential conflict(s), 160
it is, potential conflict(s), 168
it is/its/it's, 128
it is/its/it's/itself, 61
-itis, 106, 111
it'll, 128
its, 16; potential conflict(s), 168
its/it's/it is, 128
its/it's/it is/itself, 19, 21, 61
it's, 128; potential conflict(s), 168
it's/it is/its, 128
it's/it is/its/itself, 19, 21, 61
itself, potential conflict(s), 168
itself/it's/its/its, 19, 21, 61
it will, potential conflict(s), 168
it will be, potential conflict(s), 168
-ity, 107, 111
I understand, potential conflict(s), 166
-ive, 101, 111; potential conflict(s), 154
I've, 128; potential conflict(s), 154
-iveness, 110, 111
I was, potential conflict(s), 154
I will, potential conflict(s), 166
I will/ill/aisle/I'll/isle, 53
-ize, 111; potential conflict(s), 153
-ize/-s/-ss/-s sound/-z sound, 102
-izer, 111

j, spelling alphabet, 208
j., spelling alphabet, 209
j-, initial consonant, 5
-j, final consonant, 5
-j, potential conflict(s), 153
J, spelling alphabet, 208
J., spelling alphabet, 209
jack, Jack, 200
jack/Jack, 61
jam/jamb, 61
Jan, 200; potential conflict(s), 168
Jan/January, 61
January, 138, 200; potential conflict(s), 168
Jean/gene(s)/jeans/Gene, 60

jeans/genes, 46
jeans/genes/Gene/Jean, 60
jeer, potential conflict(s), 163
jell/gel, 59
jest/just/gist, 59
jewel/joule, 61
jibe/gibe, 59
Jim, 200
Jim/gym, 60
jinx, 106
jobless, 105
john/John, 61
john, John, 200
join command, 130 199, 201, 212, 235; potential conflict(s), 164
joule/jewel, 61
Jr., potential conflict(s), 167
juggler/jugular, 61
jugs, potential conflict(s), 151
jugular/juggler, 61
July, 138
June, 138
junior, potential conflict(s), 167
juror, potential conflict(s), 167
jury, 200; potential conflict(s), 167
Jury, 200
just, 16
just/gist/jest, 59
justice, 16

k, spelling alphabet, 208
k., spelling alphabet, 209
k-, initial consonant, 5
-k, final consonant, 5
-k, potential conflict(s), 157
K, spelling alphabet, 208
K., spelling alphabet, 209
K- shadow, avoiding, exercise 232
Kate, potential conflict(s), 159
Kay, potential conflict(s), 159
keg, potential conflict(s), 157
kern, potential conflict(s), 159
kern/concern, 57
kernel/colonel, 50, 57
key, potential conflict(s), 159
key/quay, 47, 61
keyword, key word, 204
kg, potential conflict(s), 157
kickback, kick back, 202
kickoff, kick off, 202
kill/kiln, 61, 106
killings, 38
kiln/kill, 61, 106
kit, potential conflict(s), 157
kite/site/sight/cite, 50
-kle, 108, 111
klieg/colleague, 56
knave/nave, 61
knead/need, 46
knead/need/kneed, 61
knee, potential conflict(s), 171
kneed, potential conflict(s), 171
kneed/need/knead, 61
knew, 16; potential conflict(s), 167
knew/new, 19, 21
knew/new/nu/gnu, 60
knight/night, 50, 61
knit(s), potential conflict(s), 167
knit/nit, 61
knob, potential conflict(s), 171
knob/nob/nobody/no body, 61
knot/not, 18, 21
knot/not/naught, 61
know, 16; potential conflict(s), 171
know-how, know how, 205
know/no, 18, 21, 61
know/no/knows/no, sir/nose, exercise, 184
knowledge, potential conflict(s), 153
known, 16
known/non-/none/nun, 49
knows, potential conflict(s), 171
knows/nose/noes, 61
knows/nose/no, sir/no/know, exercise,

184
KUB (medical), potential conflict(s), 157
-ky, 107, 111

l, spelling alphabet, 208
l., spelling alphabet, 209
l-, initial consonant, 5
-l, final consonant, 5
-l, potential conflict(s), 152
-l soundalikes, exercise, 79
-l(e), 108; exercise, 124
-l/-ly exercise, 123; potential conflicts, 123
L, spelling alphabet, 208
L., spelling alphabet, 209
-L shadow, avoiding, exercise 228
lace, potential conflict(s), 169
lacks/lax, 61
lacy, potential conflict(s), 169
lade, potential conflict(s), 168
lade/lead/led/laid, 47, 61
lady, potential conflict(s), 168
laid, 38; potential conflict(s), 169
laid/lade/lead/led, 47, 61
lain/lane, 46
lain/lane/lean/lien, 47
lain/lane/lean/lien/Lane, 61
lair, potential conflict(s), 169
lair/layer, 51, 62
laity, potential conflict(s), 169
lam, potential conflict(s), 169
lam/lamb, 62, 106
lam/lapel, 108
lamb, potential conflict(s), 169
lamb/lam, 62, 106
lame, potential conflict(s), 169
lane/lain, 46
lane/lain/lean/lien, 47
lane/lain/lean/lien/Lane, 60
lapel/lam, 108
laps/lapse, 40, 62
lase, potential conflict(s), 169
late, potential conflict(s), 169
lawful, 105
lawmaker, 206
laws, potential conflict(s), 169
lawsuit, potential conflict(s), 169
lax/lacks, 61
lay it, potential conflict(s), 169
lay/lei, 62
layer, potential conflict(s), 169
layer/lair, 51, 62
layman, potential conflict(s), 169
layoff, lay off, 202
lays/laze, 62
laze, potential conflict(s), 169
laze/lays, 62
lazy, potential conflict(s), 169
lb., potential conflict(s), 179
-lb, 106, 111
-lch, 106, 111
-le/-al/-el/-il/-ol soundalikes, 51
lea/lee/Lee; 62
leach/leech, 62
lead, 207; potential conflict(s), 169
lead/led/laid/lade, 47, 61
leader/liter, 62
leak/leek, 62
lean/lien/lain/lane, 47
lean/lien/lain/lane/Lane, 61
leased/least, 62
leaven, potential conflict(s), 162
leaven/eleven, 59
led, potential conflict(s), 169
led/laid/lade/lead, 47, 61
ledge end/legend, 62
lee/Lee/lea, 62
leech/leach, 62
leek/leak, 62
left, potential conflicts, 169
left arrow (left by character), stenoscription command, 213
left by word, stenoscription command, 213

left hand, left-hand, potential conflict(s), 169
leftover, left over, 203
left screen, stenoscription command, 213
legend/ledge end, 62
legible, 108
legislate, potential conflict(s), 169
legislation, potential conflict(s), 169
legs, potential conflict(s), 169
lei/lay, 62
lends/lens, 62
length, potential conflict(s), 169
lens/lends, 62
lent, potential conflict(s), 169
less, 233; potential conflic5(s), 169
less/-less, 105
-less, 4, 111, 233; potential conflict(s)
lessen/lesson/less on, 62
lesser/lessor/less sore, 62
-lessly, 107, 111
-lessness, 110, 111
lesson, 105
lesson/less on, 148
lesson/less on/lessen, 62
lessor/less sore/lesser, 62
less than (<), 129, 211
lest, potential conflict(s), 169
let us/lettuce/lets/let's, 62
let's, 128
let's/let us/lettuce/lets, 62
letdown, let down, 202
lets/let's/let us/lettuce, 62
letter, potential conflict(s), 152
letting, potential conflict(s), 169
lettuce/lets/let's/let us, 62
levee/levy, 52, 62
lex, potential conflict(s), 162
-lf, 106, 111
-lge, 106, 111
liable/libel, 51, 62, 102
liar/lier/lyre, 62
lib, potential conflict(s), 179
libel/liable, 51, 62, 102
lice, potential conflict(s), 169
license, potential conflict(s), 169
lichen/liken, 62
licker/liqueur/liquor, 51, 62
lie, potential conflict(s), 169
lie/lye, 48, 62
lien/lain/lane/lean, 47
lien/lain/lane/lean/Lane, 61
lier/lyre/liar, 62
lies, potential conflict(s), 169
lieu/loo/Lou, 62
lieutenant, potential conflict(s), 169
lifeboat, 206
lifelike, life like, 202
lift, potential conflict(s), 179
light/lite, 51, 62
lightening/lightning, 62
like, 16, 19
-like, 111, 199, 202
liken/lichen, 62
likewise, like wise, 203
lime/Lyme, 62
limelight, 206
line/lion, 62
lineup, line up, 203
links/lynx, 62
lion/line, 62
liqueur/liquor/licker, 51, 62
list, potential conflict(s), 179
listen(s), potential conflict(s), 169
listened, potential conflict(s), 169
list files, stenoscription command, 212
lite/light, 51, 62
liter/leader, 62
literary, 104, 107
little, 16
live, 207; potential conflict(s), 179
live-in, live in, 205
-lk, 106, 112
-lm, 106, 112

-ln, 106, 112
lo/low, 62
load/lode, 48
load/lode/lowed, 62
loan/lone, 48, 62
loath/loathe, 62
lobby, potential conflict(s), 169
lobe, potential conflict(s), 169
local, potential conflict(s), 169
local/locale/low-cal, 51, 62
locale, potential conflict(s), 169
locale/low-cal/local, 51, 62
locally, potential conflict(s), 169
locate, potential conflict(s), 169
locket, potential conflict(s), 169
lock it, potential conflict(s), 169
lock the, potential conflict(s), 169
lode/load, 48
lode/load/lowed, 62
logbook, 206
-logical, 110, 112
-logically, 110, 112
-logist, 110, 112
logs, potential conflict(s), 169
-logy, 110, 112
loil/loyal, 62
loiterer, 104
lone/loan, 48, 62
long a soundalikes, exercise, 71
long a/long e soundalikes, exercise, 73
long e soundalikes, exercise, 72
long e/long a soundalikes, exercise, 73
long i soundalikes, exercise, 73
long o soundalikes, exercise, 74
long o/long u soundalikes, exercise, 74
long u soundalikes, exercise, 74
long u/long o soundalikes, exercise, 74
long vowels, 6; exercises, 9-14
loo, potential conflict(s), 169
loo/Lou/lieu, 62
look, potential conflict(s), 169
loot, potential conflict(s), 169
loot/lute, 62
lore, potential conflict(s), 169
lore/lower, 51
lore/lower/lure, 48, 62
lotion, potential conflict(s), 169
Lou/lieu/loo, 62
loud, 7
low/lo, 62
low-cal, potential conflict(s), 169
low-cal/local/locale, 51, 62
lowed/load/lode, 62
lower case letters with periods, alphabet, 208-210
lower case letters without periods, alphabet, 208-210
lower, potential conflict(s), 169
lower/lore, 51
lower/lore/lure, 48, 62
lowly, potential conflict(s), 169
loyal, 108
loyal/loil, 62
-lp, 106, 112
-ls, potential conflict(s), 152
-lsion, 109, 112
lubb (medical), potential conflict(s), 179
luck I/lucky, 102
lucky, 107
lucky/luck I, 102
lug, potential conflict(s), 179
lumbar/lumber, 62
lunchroom, 206
lung/lunge, 106
lure/lower/lore, 48, 62
luscious, potential conflict(s), 169
lushes, potential conflict(s), 169
lute, potential conflict(s), 169
lute/loot, 62
-lve, 106, 112
-ly, 107, 112' potential conflict(s), 169
-ly/-l, potential conflicts, 123; exercise, 123
lye(s), potential conflict(s), 169

lye/lie, 48, 62
Lyme/lime, 62
lynx/links, 62
lyre/liar/lier, 62

m, spelling alphabet, 208
m., spelling alphabet, 209
m-, initial consonant, 5
-m, final consonant, 5
M, spelling alphabet, 208
M., spelling alphabet, 209
ma, potential conflict(s), 170
ma/maw, 62
mace/maize/maze, 52, 62
machine(s), potential conflict(s), 169
machined, potential conflict(s), 169
Macintosh/mackintosh, 62
madam/madame, 62
made, 16
made/maid, 19, 22, 46, 62
Madge, potential conflict(s), 167
Mae, potential conflict(s), 170
Mae/may/May, 19, 22, 62
mag, potential conflict(s), 167
magazine, potential conflict(s), 167
maid/made, 19, 22, 46, 62
mail/male, 46, 62
mail/male/meal, 47
maim/maple, 62
main, potential conflict(s), 152
main/mane, 46
main/mane/Maine/mean/mien/mesne, 47, 62
Maine, potential conflict(s), 152
Maine/mane/mean/mien/mesne/main, 47, 62
maintain, potential conflict(s), 170
maintenance, potential conflict(s), 170
maize/maze/mace, 52, 62
major, potential conflict(s), 170
majority, 107
make, 16; potential conflict(s), 170
makeup, make up, 203
male/mail, 46, 62
male/mail/meal, 47
mall/maul, 49
mall/maul/moll/mole, 62
man, 16, 19
manage(s), potential conflict(s), 162
managed, potential conflict(s), 162
manager(s), potential conflict(s), 162
managing, potential conflict(s), 162
mandate/man date, 62
mane, potential conflict(s), 152
mane/main, 46
mane/main/mean/mien/mesne/Maine, 47, 62
mange, potential conflict(s), 162
manlike, man like, 202
manner/manor/manure/man or/man nor, 62
manning, potential conflict(s), 162
manor/manure/man or/man nor/manner, 62
mansion, potential conflict(s), 162
mantel/mantle/man tell, 51, 62
manure/man or/man nor/manner/manor, 62
many, 16, 19;potential conflict(s), 152
many/am/him exercise, 35
many/am/him/hymn, 18, 21
maple/maim, 62
mar, 200; potential conflict(s), 170
mar/march/March, 63
marc/mark/Mark/mashing, 63
march, 200; potential conflict(s), 170
march/March/mar, 63
March, 138, 200; potential conflict(s), 170
March/mar/march, 63
mare, potential conflict(s), 167
mare/mayor, 51
mare/mayor/may or, 63, 148
Marge, potential conflict(s), 170

-s, avoiding shadows, exercise 225
-s/-er/-or, exercise, 118
-s/-ss, exercise, 114
-s/-ss/-s sound/-z sound/-ize, 102
-s/-st exercise, 120
-s/-z soundalikes, 52; exercises, 81; 114
-s/as/his/is, 101
-s/as/his/is/as-/ass/hiss, 18, 20
-s/inverted -er conflicts, 117
S, spelling alphabet, 208
S., spelling alphabet, 209
S- shadow, avoiding, exercise 232
-S shadow, avoiding, exercise 229
sac/sack, 67
sacks/sax, 40
sacks/sax/sacs, 67
safe, 4, potential conflict(s) 168
safe/save, 5, 101, 148
safekeeping, 206
safer, potential conflict(s), 168
safer/save your/saver/savior/savor, 67
safe or, potential conflict(s), 168
said, 16, 38; potential conflict(s), 168
said/sed, 19, 21, 67
sail/sale, 46, 67
sail/sale/seal, 47
saint, potential conflict(s), 155
salary, 104, 107
sale/sail, 46, 67
sale/sail/seal, 47
saleswise, sales wise, 203
saleswoman, 206
salt/sought, 67
salute, potential conflict(s), 151
salve, potential conflict(s), 168
sands/sans, 67
sane/seine, 67
sane/seine/seen/scene, 47
sans/sands, 67
sat, potential conflict(s), 174
sat/SAT, 67
SAT, 210
SAT/sat, 67
satisfactory, potential conflict(s), 168
satisfied, potential conflict(s), 168
satisfies, potential conflict(s), 168
satisfy, potential conflict(s), 168
satisfying, potential conflict(s), 168
Saturday, 138, 238; potential conflict(s),
    174
save, 4; potential conflict(s), 168
save/safe, 5, 101, 148
save, stenoscription command, 212;
    potential conflict(s), 174
save and exit, stenoscription command;
    potential conflict(s), 155
save document, stenoscription
    command, 212; potential conflict(s),
    174
saver, potential conflict(s), 168
saver/savior/safer/save your, 67
save oar(s)/save ore/save other/savor/
    save or, 101
save or, potential conflict(s), 168
save or/save oar(s)/save ore/save other/
    savor, 101
save your/saver/savior/savor/safer, 67
saving, potential conflict(s), 168
savior/savor/safer/save your/saver, 67
savor, potential conflict(s), 168
savor/safer/save your/saver/savior, 67
savor/save or/save oar(s)/save ore/save
    other, 101
saw, 7
sax/sacks, 40
sax/sacs/sacks, 67
s.c. (medical), potential conflict(s), 175
scam, potential conflict(s), 163
scant, potential conflict(s), 163
scarce/scares, 40, 67
scene, potential conflict(s), 155
scene/seen, 46, 67
scene/seen/sane/seine, 47
scent, potential conflict(s), 155

scent/cent/sent, 50, 56
scents/sense/cents, 56
Scheele (medical), potential conflict(s),
    174
Schick (medical), potential conflict(s),
    174
science, potential conflict(s), 155
-scle, 108, 112
scoreboard, 206
Scott, 210
scour, potential conflict(s), 175
scram/scrapple, 67
scrapbook, 206
scrapple/scram, 67
screen, potential conflict(s), 155
screen, stenoscription command, 212
screwed, potential conflict(s), 163
screwup, screw-up, screw up, 205
scribble, 108
scrip/script, 67
scuff, potential conflict(s), 156
se-, 90
se-/see/sea, 88
sea(s), potential conflict(s), 168
sea/see, 46, 67
sea/see/se-, 88
seal/ceil, 56
seal/sail/sale, 47
seal/sealing/ceiling, 50
sealing/ceiling, 56
sealing/ceiling/seal, 50
seam/seem, 46, 67
seamen/see men/semen, 67
sear(s), potential conflict(s), 168
sear/sere/seer, 51, 67
search, 106
search -> (forward), stenoscription
    command, 212
search <- (backward), stenoscription
    command, 212
season(s), potential conflict(s), 155
seat, potential conflict(s), 174
seated/seeded, 67
sec, potential conflict(s), 155
second, 137; potential conflict(s), 155
secretarial, 106
secretaries, potential conflict(s), 155
secretary, potential conflict(s), 155
sect, potential conflict(s), 155
section, potential conflict(s), 155
sects/sex, 67
secure, 88; potential conflict(s), 156
sed (medical), potential conflict(s), 168
sed/said, 19, 21, 67
sedition, potential conflict(s), 160
see, 16; potential conflict(s), 168
see/sea, 46, 67
see/sea/se-, 88
seed, potential conflict(s), 168
seed/cede, 46, 56
seed/cede/creed, 50
seeded/seated, 67
seem/seam, 46, 67
see men/semen/seamen, 67
seen, potential conflict(s), 155
seen/scene, 46, 67
seen/scene/sane/seine, 47
seer(s), potential conflict(s), 168
seer/sear/sere, 51, 67
sees, potential conflict(s), 168
sees/seize/cease, 56
seethe, potential conflict(s), 174
seine/sane, 67
seine/sane/seen/scene, 47
seize, potential conflict(s), 168
seize/cease/crease, 50
seize/cease/sees, 56
self, potential conflict(s), 151
self/self-, 88
self/-self, 105
self-, 90; potential conflict(s), 151
self-/self, 88
-self, 112; potential conflict(s), 151
-self/self, 105

self-discipline, 88
sell/cell, 6, 50, 56, 84
seller/cellar, 50, 56
semen/seamen/see men, 67
semi/semi-, 88
semi-, 90, 239
semi-/semi, 88
semicircle, 88
semicolon (;), 127, 129, 211
seminal/Seminole, 67
senate, Senate, 200
senator, Senator, 200
senior, potential conflict(s), 174
sense/cents/scents, 56
senses/census, 56
sensor/censer/censor, 56
sensor/censer/censor/censure, 50
sent, potential conflict(s), 155
sent/scent/cent, 50, 56
Seoul/sol/sole/soul, 67
September, 138; potential conflict(s),
    151
sere, potential conflict(s), 168
sere/seer/sear, 51, 67
serf/surf, 67
serge/surge, 67
serial/cereal, 50, 56
serious, potential conflict(s), 168
serious/serous/cirrus, 56
serous, potential conflict(s), 168
serous/cirrus/serious, 56
serve, 106
server, 104
service, potential conflict(s), 174
serviced, potential conflict(s), 174
-ses (e sound), 112
session/cession, 50, 56
setback, set back, 202
settler/settlor, 67
setup, set up, 203
seven, 136; potential conflict(s), 151
seventeen, 136; potential conflict(s), 160
seventeenth, 137
seventh, 137
seventieth, 137
seventy, 136, 238; potential conflict(s),
    174
seventy-eight, 136
seventy-eighth, 137
seventy-nine, potential conflict(s), 174
sever, potential conflict(s), 151
sever/zephyr, 67
Sever (medical), potential conflict(s),
    151
severe, potential conflict(s), 151
sew/so/sow, 19, 21
sew/so/sow (ou sound)/sow (long o), 67
sewer/soar/sore/suer, 51
sewer/soar/sore/suer/sour, 67
sewn/sown/zone, 67
sex, potential conflict(s), 155
sex/sects, 67
-sh, 106, 112
shadows, 223
shake, potential conflict(s), 174
shake/chic/sheik/, 47
shall, potential conflict(s), 156
she, 16, 18
shear/sheer, 46, 67
she can, potential conflict(s), 174
shed, potential conflict(s), 174
shed/she'd, 128
she'd, 128; potential conflict(s), 174
she'd/shed, 128
sheer/shear, 46, 67
she had, potential conflict(s), 174
she have, potential conflict(s), 174
sheik, potential conflict(s), 174
sheik/chic/chick, 56
sheik/chic/shake, 47
shell, potential conflict(s), 174
shell, stenoscription command, 212
she'll, 128; potential conflict(s), 174
sheriff, potential conflict(s), 151

-ssion, 109, 112
-ssional, 109, 112
-ssionally, 109, 112
-st, 104, 106, 112, 239; exercise, 120; potential conflict(s), 155
-st, ordinal numbers, 137
-st/-s exercise, 120
St., potential conflict(s), 155
stab, potential conflict(s), 163
stabbing, potential conflict(s), 163
stabbing/stack, 37, 40, 148
stack, potential conflict(s), 163
stack/stabbing, 37, 40, 148
staff/staph, 68
staid/stayed, 40, 68
stain, potential conflict(s), 175
stair/stare, 46, 68
stair/stare/steer, 47
stake/steak, 46, 68
stale/steal/steel, 47
stamp, 104, 106
Stan, potential conflict(s), 175
stance, potential conflict(s), 175
stand(s), potential conflict(s), 175
standalone, stand-alone, stand alone, 205
standard, potential conflict(s), 175
standby, stand by, 204
stand-in, stand in, 205
standstill, stand still, 204
staph/staff, 68
stare/stair, 46, 68
stare/stair/steer, 47
stark/stashing, 40
start-up, start up, 205
stashing/stark, 40
state, State, 200
stationary/stationery, 52, 68
statistical, 108
statistically, 107 108
stayed/staid, 40, 68
steak/stake, 46, 68
steal/steel, 46, 68
steal/steel/stale, 47
steam/steeple, 68
-sted, 104, 112
steel/steal, 46, 68
steel/steal/stale, 47
steeple/steam, 68
steer/stair/stare, 47
-sten, 104, 112
StenEd, a brief history, 237
stenoscription commands, 199; exercise, 220
stenoscription word processing commands, 212-213
stenograph, 110
stenographer, 110
stenographic, 110
stenography, 110
Stenotype Educational Products, Inc., a brief history, 237
-ster, 104, 112
stereo, 89
stereo-, 89, 90
stereotype, 89
sterile, 105
stewed, potential conflict(s), 175
-stic, 104, 112
-stical, 108, 112
-stically, 107, 108, 112
stile/style, 68
-sting, 104, 112
-stion, 109, 112
stitching, 210
-stle, 108, 112
stockholder, 206
stoic, potential conflict(s), 175
stole, potential conflict(s), 163
stoplight, 206
store, potential conflict(s), 175
storehouse, 206
storeroom, 206
story, potential conflict(s), 175

straight/strait, 51, 68
strategy, 107
strawberry, 206
stream, potential conflict(s), 163
street, Street, 200; potential conflict(s), 155
-sts, 104, 112
stuck-up, stuck up, 205
student, potential conflict(s), 175
study, 107
stung/stunning, 40
stunt, potential conflict(s), 175
style/stile, 68
sub, potential conflict(s), 175
sub/sub-, 88
sub-, 90
subbing/suck, 40
subject, 207; potential conflict(s), 175
subpoena, potential conflict(s), 175
substitute, potential conflict(s), 175
substitution, potential conflict(s), 159
succeed, potential conflict(s), 156
succeeded, potential conflict(s), 156
success(es), potential conflict(s), 156
succor/sucker, 68
such, 16, 19
suck(s), potential conflict(s), 156
suck/subbing, 40
sucked, potential conflict(s), 156
sucker/succor, 68
suction, potential conflict(s), 156
sue, 200
sue/Sue, 68
Sue, 200
suede, potential conflict(s), 175
suede/swayed, 40, 68
suer/sewer/soar/sore, 51
suer/sewer/soar/sore/sour, 67
sufficiency, potential conflict(s), 175
sufficient, potential conflict(s), 175
suffixes,Step 6, 101-126; 148; adding to dictionary, 233; alphabet, 101
suffixes, inflected endings, 101, 104; exercise, 115
suffixes, summary, 111-112
suggest(s), potential conflict(s), 175
suggestion, potential conflict(s), 175
suit/soot, 49, 68
suite, potential conflict(s), 175
suite/sweet, 46, 68
sum, potential conflict(s), 175
sum/some/some-, 19, 22
sum/some/-some, 102
summarize/summerize, 68
summary/summery, 52, 68
sun, potential conflict(s), 175
sun/son, 49, 68
sundae, potential conflict(s), 175
sundae/Sunday, 68
Sunday, 138, 238; potential conflict(s), 175
Sunday/sundae, 68
sung/sunning, 40
sunlight, 206
sunned, potential conflict(s), 175
sunning/sung, 40
sunrise, sun rise, 204
sunset, sun set, 204
sunshine, sun shine, 204
sup, potential conflict(s), 175
super/super-, 88
super-, 90, 239
super-/super, 88
superman, 88
supplies, potential conflict(s), 175
support, potential conflict(s), 163
suppose, potential conflict(s), 163
supposition, potential conflict(s), 163
suppress, potential conflict(s), 163
suppression, potential conflict(s), 163
sure, potential conflict(s), 156
sure/shore, 48, 67
surf, 106

surf/serf, 67
surge/serge, 67
surgically, 108
suspend, potential conflict(s), 163
suspense, potential conflict(s), 163
sustain, potential conflict(s), 175
sw- & spw-, avoiding shadows, exercise 226
swayed, potential conflict(s), 175
swayed/suede, 40, 68
sweat, potential conflict(s), 175
sweet, potential conflict(s), 175
sweet/suite, 46, 68
swell(s), potential conflict(s), 155
switch, stenoscription command, 212
sword/soared, 68
-sy, 107, 112; potential conflict(s), 175
symbol entries, dictionary, 234
symbol/cymbal, 57
symbols and punctuation, 211
symbols, 211
symmetry/cemetery, 56
sync/zinc/sink, 68
syntax/sin tax, 68
system, potential conflict(s), 168
systolic, potential conflict(s), 175

t, spelling alphabet, 208
t., spelling alphabet, 209
t-, initial consonant, 5
t-, avoiding shadows, exercise 227
-t, final consonant, 5
-t, avoiding shadows, exercise 225
-t/-ght, 102
-t(e)/-ght soundalikes, 51
-t/-th exercise, 121
-t/-ty exercise, 123; potential conflicts, 123
T spelling alphabet, 208
T., spelling alphabet, 209
tab, stenoscription command, 213
tack/tact/tacked, 68
tacks/tax, 40, 68
tact/tacked/tack, 68
tail, potential conflict(s), 176
tail/tale, 46, 68
tail/tale/teal, 47
taillight, 206
take, potential conflict(s), 156
take place, potential conflict(s), 176
takeoff, take off, 202
takeover, take over, 203
-tal, potential conflict(s), 156
tale, potential conflict(s), 176
tale/tail, 46, 68
tale/tail/teal, 47
talk, 106
tall, potential conflict(s), 156
tally, potential conflict(s), 176
tapes, potential conflict(s), 176
tarry, potential conflict(s), 176
tat, potential conflict(s), 156
taught/taut, 51, 68
tax, 39
tax/tacks, 40, 68
taxes, 39
taxi, 105
-tch, 112
tea, potential conflict(s), 156
tea/tee, 46, 68
teal, potential conflict(s), 176
teal/tail/tale, 47
team/teem, 46, 68
teammate, 206
teamwork, team work, 203
tear, 207; potential conflict(s), 176
tear/tier, 47, 68
teart (medical), potential conflict(s), 176
teas, potential conflict(s), 168
teas/tease/tees, 68
tease, potential conflict(s), 168
tease/tees/teas, 68
tee, potential conflict(s), 156
tee/tea, 46, 68

© 1993, 2001 *StenEd*®

teem/team, 46, 68
tees, potential conflict(s), 168
tees/teas/tease, 68
television, potential conflict(s), 176
ten, 136; potential conflict(s), 156
ten dollars, 139
ten is/tens/tense, 37
Tennessee, potential conflict(s), 156
tens/tense, 37, 40
tens/tense/ten is, 37
tens/tense/tents, 68
tense/tens, 37, 40
tense/tens/ten is, 37
tense/tens/tents, 68
tenser/tensor, 68
tensor/tenser, 68
tenth, 137
tents/tens/tense, 68
tern/turn, 68
territory, potential conflict(s), 176
test, 104
tested, 104
testee/testy, 68
testimony, 3
testing, 104
tests, 104
testy/testee, 68
Tex, potential conflict(s), 176
Texas, potential conflict(s), 176
text, 109; potential conflict(s), 176
textbook, 206
-th, 106, 112
-th, ordinal numbers, 137
-th/-t exercise, 121
than, 16; potential conflict(s), 176
than the, potential conflict(s), 176
than/then, 19, 21; exercise, 36
thank(s), potential conflict(s), 176
thanked, potential conflict(s), 176
thank you, potential conflict(s), 176
that, 16; potential conflict(s), 176
that/that the, 18, 20
that had, potential conflict(s), 176
that I, potential conflict(s), 176
that I have, potential conflict(s), 176
that is, potential conflict(s), 176
that is all, potential conflict(s), 176
that it, potential conflict(s), 176
that'll, 128
that's, 128
that the, potential conflict(s), 176
that the/that, 18, 20
that you, potential conflict(s), 176
that you had, potential conflict(s), 176
that you tell, potential conflict(s), 176
that you will, potential conflict(s), 176
thaw, potential conflict(s), 176
thawed, potential conflict(s), 176
the, 16, 17; potential conflict(s), 176
the/it exercise, 23
the/it/at, 148
the/it/at/they, 18, 20
the/they exercise, 24
the president, the President, potential
  conflict(s), 156
theater/theatre, 68
their, 16, 18; potential conflict(s), 168
their/there/there is/there are/they are
  exercise, 34
their/there/they're, 128
their/there/they're/they are, 18, 21, 68
theirs, potential conflict(s), 168
theirs/there's, 68
them, 16, 19
then, 16, 19; potential conflict(s), 176
then/than, 19, 21; exercise, 36
there, 16; potential conflict(s), 168
there/their/they are/there is/there are
  exercise, 34
there/their/they're, 128
there/their/they're/they are, 18, 21, 68
thereabout, there about, 204
thereafter, there after, 204
there are, potential conflict(s), 168

there are/they are/their/there/there is
  exercise, 34
thereat, there at, 204
thereby, there by, 204; potential
  conflict(s), 168
therefor, there for, 204; potential
  conflict(s), 176
therefor/therefore/there for, 68
there for/therefor/therefore, 68
therefore, potential conflict(s), 176
therefore/there for/therefor, 68
therefrom, 204; potential conflict(s), 176
there from, 204; potential conflict(s),
  176
there have, potential conflict(s), 176
therein, there in, 204; potential
  conflict(s), 176
there is, potential conflict(s), 168
there is/there are/they are/their/there
  exercise, 34
there'll, 128
thereof, there of, 204; potential
  conflict(s), 176
thereon, there on, 204
there's, there's, potential conflict(s), 168
there's/theirs, 68
thereto, there to, 204
thereunder, there under, 204
thereupon, there upon, 204
thesaurus, stenoscription command, 212
these, 16, 19
they, 16, 18; potential conflict(s), 176
they/the exercise, 24
they/the/it/at, 18, 20
they are, 17; potential conflict(s), 168
they are/their/there/there is/there are
  exercise, 34
they are/they're, 128
they are/they're/there/their, 18, 21, 68
they'd, 128
they have, potential conflict(s), 176
they'll, 128
they're, 128; potential conflict(s), 168
they're/their/there, 128
they're/their/there/they are, 18, 21, 68
they're/they are, 128
they've, 128; potential conflict(s), 176
thing, 16; potential conflict(s), 176
thing/thinning, 40
think, 16, 107; potential conflict(s), 176
thinning, potential conflict(s), 176
thinning/thing, 40
third, 137, 149
thirteen, 136
thirteenth, 137
thirtieth, 137
thirty, 136
thirty-nine, potential conflict(s), 176
thirty-second, 137
thirty-two, 136
this, 16, 17, 18
thought, potential conflict(s), 176
thousand, 140, 141
thousand, number field, 236
three, 135, 136
threes, potential conflict(s), 168
threw, 16
threw/through, 19, 22, 68
throe(s)/throw(s), 48, 68
throne/thrown, 48, 68
through, 16
through/threw, 19, 22, 68
throw(s)/throe(s), 48, 68
thrown/throne, 48, 68
Thursday, 138
-thy, 107, 112
thyme/time, 19, 22, 48, 68
-tial, 109, 112; potential conflict(s), 156
-tially, 109, 112
tic, potential conflict(s), 172
tic/tick, 69
tick, potential conflict(s), 172
tick/tic, 69
tickler, potential conflict(s), 172

tidal/title, 69
tide/tied, 40, 69, 148
tied/tide, 40, 69, 148
-tient, 106, 112
tier/tear, 68
ties, potential conflict(s), 152
tiff, potential conflict(s), 151
tile, potential conflict(s), 176
timber/timbre, 69
time, 16
time/thyme, 19, 22, 48, 68
times & dates, 138; exercise, 144
times symbol (x), 129, 211
tin, potential conflict(s), 156
ting, potential conflict(s), 156
-tion, 109, 112, 239
-tional, 109, 112
-tionally, 109, 112
-tious, 109, 112
-tiously, 109, 112
-tiousness, 109, 112
tit, potential conflict(s), 156
title, potential conflict(s), 176
title/tidal, 69
-tive, 112
-tize, potential conflict(s), 152
-tle, 108, 112
to, 16; potential conflict(s), 177
to/too/two, 18, 20, 69; exercise, 27
toad, potential conflict(s), 177
toad/toed, 40
toad/toed/towed, 69
toaster, 104
today, to day, potential conflict(s), 177
Todd, potential conflict(s), 177
to do, potential conflict(s), 177
toe, potential conflict(s), 176
toe/tow, 48, 69
toed/toad, 40
toed/toad/towed, 69
together, potential conflict(s), 177
to her, potential conflict(s), 176
to him, potential conflict(s), 176
toil, 7
to it, potential conflict(s), 176
to know, potential conflict(s), 176
told/tolled, 40, 69
Tom, potential conflict(s), 176
to many, potential conflict(s), 176
tomb, potential conflict(s), 176
tome, potential conflict(s), 176
tomorrow, potential conflict(s), 176
ton, potential conflict(s), 176
ton/tun, 69
too, 16, 19; potential conflict(s), 177
too/two/to, 18, 20, 69; exercise, 27
took, potential conflict(s), 177
too many, potential conflict(s), 176
toot, potential conflict(s), 156
tooter/tutor, 69
toothache, tooth ache, 202
tore, potential conflict(s), 176
tort/torte, 69
tortious/tortuous, 69
tot, potential conflict(s), 176
to the, potential conflict(s), 176
to this, potential conflict(s), 176
tour(s), potential conflict(s), 177
-tous, potential conflict(s), 176
to us, potential conflict(s), 176
tow, potential conflict(s), 177
tow/toe, 48, 69
toward, to ward, 203
towed/toad/toed, 69
tower(s), potential conflict(s), 177
towing, potential conflict(s), 177
townhouse, 206
toy, 7
to you, potential conflict(s), 176
to your, potential conflict(s), 177
trace/trays, 40, 69
track/tract/tracked, 69
trade-in, trade in, 205
trait, potential conflict(s), 156

trance/trans/trans-, 69, 88
trans-, 90
trans-/trance/trans, 69, 88
transact, 88
transience/transients, 69
tray/trey, 69
trays/trace, 40, 69
treat, potential conflict(s), 156
trey/tray, 69
tri-, 90
tri-/try, 88
tricolor, 88
trillion, 140, 141
trillion, number field, 236
trim/triple, 69, 108
troll, potential conflict(s), 177
trolley, potential conflict(s), 177
troop/troupe, 49, 69
trooper/trouper, 69
trophy, 107
troublemaker, 206
troupe/troop, 49, 69
trouper/trooper, 69
truly yours (comp closing), potential
   conflict(s), 177
trussed/trust, 69
trustee/trusty, 52, 69, 102
try/tri-, 88
-tual, 110, 112
-tually, 110, 112
tucks/tux, 40, 6869
Tuesday, 138; potential conflict(s), 168
tuition, potential conflict(s), 176
tuition/twigs, 37
tun/ton, 69
turban/turbine, 69
-ture, 110, 112
turkey, Turkey, 200
turn/tern, 68
turnoff, turn off, 202
turnover, turn over, 203
tutor/tooter, 69
tutorial, 106
tux/tucks, 40, 69
twat, potential conflict(s), 156
twelfth, 137
twelve, 136
twentieth, 137
twenty, 136
twenty-first, 137
twenty-nine, potential conflict(s), 177
twenty-one, 136
twigs, potential conflict(s), 176
twigs/tuition, 37
twin, potential conflict(s), 177
twine, potential conflict(s), 177
twit, potential conflict(s), 156
two, 16, 136; potential conflict(s), 177
two/to/too, 18, 20, 69; exercise, 27
two sum(s), 102
-ty, 107, 112; potential conflict(s), 156
-ty/-t exercise, 123; potential conflicts,
   123
typeover/insert, stenoscription
   command, 212
typewriter, 206
typically, 107

u (long), 6, 11; exercise, 12; soundalikes,
   46, 48; exercise, 74
u (long) /o (long) soundalikes, exercise,
   74
u (short), 5, 6
u, spelling alphabet, 208
u., spelling alphabet, 209
u-, 90
u-/you, 87
-u, 105, 112
U, spelling alphabet, 208
U., spelling alphabet, 209
-uate, potential conflict(s), 153
ugh, potential conflict(s), 180
ultimate, 87
-um, 112

un-, 86, 90; potential conflict(s), 180
un-/under-/under, exercise, 100
unceded/unseated/unseeded, 69
unction, potential conflict(s), 177
undelete/cancel (F1), stenoscription
   command, 212
under, 16, 238; potential conflict(s), 180
under/under-, 88
under/under-/un-, exercise, 100
under-, 90; potential conflict(s), 180
under-/under, 88
under-/under/un-, exercise, 100
underline cancel, stenoscription
   command, 212
underline, stenoscription command, 212
understand, potential conflict(s), 180
understood, potential conflict(s), 180
underworld, 88
undo/undue, 69
undue/undo, 69
unit, potential conflict(s), 177
United States, potential conflict(s), 180
unity, potential conflict(s), 177
unjust, 86
unreal/unreel, 69
unseated/unseeded/unceded, 69
up, 16, 19
-up, 112, 201, 203
up arrow (up by line), stenoscription
   command, 213
up by page (page up), stenoscription
   command, 213
upon, 16
upon the grounds, potential conflict(s),
   177
upper case letters with
   periods.alphabet, 208-210
upper case letters without
   periods.alphabet, 208-210
up screen, stenoscription command, 213
up the, potential conflict(s), 177
uptight, 206
-ure , potential conflict(s), 180
-ure/-er/-or, exercise, 118
urine, 87; potential conflict(s), 162
urn, potential conflict(s), 162
urn/earn, 49, 58
us, 16; potential conflict(s), 177
us/-us, 105
-us, 109, 112
-us/us, 105
USA, 209
U.S.A., 209
use, 16, 47, 207; potential conflict(s),
   177
usual, potential conflict(s), 180
usually, potential conflict(s), 180
usurp, 87

v, spelling alphabet, 208
v., spelling alphabet, 209
v-, initial consonant, 5
-v(e), 5, 6, 8, 9, 112
-v, final consonant, 5
-v, avoiding shadows, exercise 224
-v(e)/-f, 5; exercise, 8-9; 101
V, spelling alphabet, 208
V., spelling alphabet, 209
vail/vale/veil/veal, 47, 69
vain/vane/vein, 46, 69
vale/veil/veal/vail, 47, 69
valuation, potential conflict(s), 163
van(s), potential conflict(s), 151
vane/vein/vain, 46, 69
variance/variants, 69
vary, potential conflict(s), 154
vary/very, 69
VCR, 209
veal/vail/vale/veil, 47, 69
vehicles, potential conflict(s), 177
veil/veal/vail/vale, 47, 69
vein/vain/vane, 46, 69
-vel, 112
-ven, 104, 112

venal, potential conflict(s), 160
venial, potential conflict(s), 160
Venn, potential conflict(s), 160
venous/Venus, 52, 69
vent, potential conflict(s), 174
Venus/venous, 52, 69
-ver, 112
-ver/-fer, 104
veracious/voracious, 69
verb, 106
-vern, 104, 112
verses/versus/vs., 69
version, 109
versus/vs./verses, 69
very, 16; potential conflict(s), 154
very/of/if/have exercise, 25
very/of/if/have/off, 18, 20
very/vary, 69
very much, potential conflict(s), 177
vessel, potential conflict(s), 168
vest, potential conflict(s), 168
vetch, potential conflict(s), 177
veterinarian, 106
vex, potential conflict(s), 177
vial/vile, 48, 69
vice, potential conflict(s), 152
vice/vise, 52, 69
vice president, Vice President, 200
vicious, potential conflict(s), 177
video, 89
video-, 89, 90
videotape, 89
vies, potential conflict(s), 152
vile/vial, 48, 69
village, potential conflict(s), 165
vindicative/vindictive, 69
vine, potential conflict(s), 174
vis, potential conflict(s), 152
vise, potential conflict(s), 152
vise/vice, 52, 69
visibility, potential conflict(s), 152
visible, potential conflict(s), 152
vision, potential conflict(s), 177
viz, potential conflict(s), 152
voice, potential conflict(s), 168
void, potential conflict(s), 168
voix (medical), potential conflict(s), 168
voluntary, potential conflict(s), 177
volunteer, potential conflict(s), 177
voracious/veracious, 69
vowels, 5, 6, 7, 9, 10, 11, 12, 13, 14;
   soundalikes, 46-49; soundalike
   exercises, 71-76
vowels, words beginning with, exercise,
   95
vowels,words ending in, exercise, 115
vs./verses/versus, 69
-vy, 107, 112

w, spelling alphabet, 208
w., spelling alphabet, 209
w-, initial consonant, 5
w-/wh-, 84
w-/wr-, 84
W, spelling alphabet, 208
W., spelling alphabet, 209
Wac/whack, 69
wacky, potential conflict(s), 177
Wacs/wax/whacks, 69
wade/weighed, 69
wag, potential conflict(s), 177
wagon, potential conflict(s), 177
wail, potential conflict(s), 178
wail/whale, 69
waist/waste, 46, 69
wait, potential conflict(s), 177
wait/weight, 51, 69
waiting, potential conflict(s), 177
waive/wave, 46, 69
waive/wave/weave, 47
waiver/waver, 69
walkup, walk-up, walk up, 205
walkway, walk way, 203
wan, potential conflict(s), 179

© 1993, 2001 *StenEd*®